UNIVERSITY OF CAMBRIDGE
DEPARTMENT OF APPLIED ECONOMICS

MONOGRAPHS

18

SECOND ABSTRACT OF
BRITISH HISTORICAL STATISTICS

UNIVERSITY OF CAMBRIDGE
DEPARTMENT OF APPLIED ECONOMICS

MONOGRAPHS

This series consists of investigations conducted by members of the Department's staff and others working in direct collaboration with the Department.

The Department of Applied Economics assumes no responsibility for the views expressed in the Monographs published under its auspices.

SECOND ABSTRACT
OF BRITISH
HISTORICAL STATISTICS

BY

B. R. MITCHELL

AND

H. G. JONES

CAMBRIDGE

AT THE UNIVERSITY PRESS

1971

Published by the Syndics of the Cambridge University Press
Bentley House, 200 Euston Road, London N.W.1
American Branch: 32 East 57th Street, New York, N.Y.10022

© Cambridge University Press 1971

Library of Congress Catalogue Card Number: 72–128502

ISBN: 0 521 08001 0

Printed in Great Britain
at the University Printing House, Cambridge
(Brooke Crutchley, University Printer)

CONTENTS

PREFACE

The inception of this volume owes a great deal to Professor W. B. Reddaway, who was at that time Director of the University of Cambridge Department of Applied Economics. When the time came to reprint the first *Abstract of British Historical Statistics*, which I produced at the Department with the collaboration of Miss Phyllis Deane in 1962, I hoped to take the opportunity to extend the series shown there, which mostly were taken only to 1938. It became apparent, however, that the resultant volume would be both very bulky and very expensive. Professor Reddaway then suggested that a separate volume of recent historical statistics would provide a reasonably convenient supplement to the original *Abstract*, and would make possible the inclusion of a number of new tables which began too late to make their inclusion worthwhile in a volume ending in 1938. The publishers accepted this, and, moreover, agreed that the new volume should include various tables, going back well before 1938, which had had to be left out in 1962.

This brief account of the origins of this book will serve to explain – and, I hope, excuse – its dual nature. It is primarily intended as a continuation of the *Abstract of British Historical Statistics*, and so far as possible series for 1938 onwards are linked to those given in that work; but it is also a supplement containing new series.

The general format of this volume closely follows that of its predecessor, although there have been a few rearrangements of chapters, and the introductory texts are generally much shorter owing to the normally greater adequacy of recent statistics. In addition, bibliographies of the kind that were formerly included have not been thought necessary for the period since 1938; so that it is only for topics which are newly included here that there is much bibliographic material, and this is given in the introductory texts.

The general principles which have guided us in compiling the tables which follow have been the same as those which governed the original *Abstract*, and we cannot define our objective better than by quoting the words used in the General Introduction to that book: 'to provide the user of historical statistics with informed access to a wide range of economic data without the labour of identifying sources or of transforming many annual sources into comparable time series'. Nor, perhaps, can we excuse our deficiencies more effectively than was done there, when it was said that 'since the snags of a statistical series often emerge only when it has been fully exploited for analytical purposes...it will be evident that our notes and comments are at best a tentative and incomplete critique'.

As in the earlier volume, we have preferred to use 'raw' data where possible, rather than 'processed' statistics, unless these latter are clearly superior, because, for instance, they take account of a variety of information which is too great or too scattered to contemplate publishing. This applied to many of the index number series which are shown here. But there is, of course, frequently a certain artificiality about this distinction between 'raw' and 'processed' data, especially in recent years. Much of the data which are published by government departments these days is, in fact, the result of elaborate calculations and computations, and its 'rawness' is more apparent than real.

The work of extracting the figures and compiling them into series which are, so far as possible, consistent and comparable has been shared more or less equally between Mr H. G. Jones and myself. In the process we have both incurred various obligations, and we should like to acknowledge them here. Apart from Professor Reddaway, to whom I have already referred, and the Department of Applied Economics, which has supported us throughout, our principal debts for advice are to Miss Phyllis Deane, who helped to plan the contents of this book; to Dr C. H. Feinstein, who was particularly helpful over the chapter on national income and expenditure; and to Mr A. R. Thatcher, Director of Statistics at the Department of Employment and Productivity, who gave valuable advice and assistance with the chapters on the labour force and on wages. Others who have provided us with material, for which we are grateful, have been the Board of Trade, the Central Statistical Office, the National Debt Office, and the Northern Ireland Ministry of Agriculture. In addition we are glad to acknowledge the courtesy of the following in permitting the publication of copyright or unpublished material:

> Dr C. H. Feinstein
> The British Iron and Steel Federation
> The British Road Federation
> The Cotton Board
> The Governor and Company of the Bank of England
> The International Tin Council
> Her Majesty's Stationery Office

and the editors of the following:

> *The Colliery Year Book and Coal Trades Directory*
> the Commonwealth Economic Committee's *Wool Intelligence*
> *The International Cotton Bulletin*
> *Journal of the Royal Statistical Society*

Finally we wish to record our thanks for the help given to us by various librarians, especially Miss Olga Hickson of the Department of Applied Economics, Mr Finkell of the Marshall Library, and Mr Vickery of the Official Publications Department of the Cambridge University Library.

B. R. MITCHELL

LIST OF ABBREVIATIONS

The following abbreviations are used throughout the volume:

  — = nil

  ... = not available

  - - = less than half of the smallest digit used in the table

Abstract = *Statistical Abstract of the United Kingdom,* or *Annual Abstract of Statistics*

J.R.S.S. = *Journal of the Royal Statistical Society*

  S.P. = *Sessional Paper* (followed by the date and volume number)

CHAPTER I

POPULATION AND VITAL STATISTICS

TABLES

With the exception of table 15, showing divorces, all the tables in this chapter follow on from those in the first *Abstract of British Historical Statistics* (1962), or at any rate are the nearest recent equivalent. There are, however, two special cases – tables 1 and 4. Table 1 shows the population at the decennial censuses, and the figures have been taken back to 1801, thus in large part repeating table 2 of the first volume. The reason for this is the publication in the 1961 Census *Report* of the figures of intercensal increase on a 'compound interest' basis – that is in terms of cumulative percentage change per year between censuses, instead of in the older form of decennial rates of increase. Since the annual cumulative figures of rate of increase seemed worth including, it followed that the statistics of population on which they were based should also be given. This makes it necessary to draw attention again to the possible defects of the censuses. Those of both 1801 and 1811 have been held to be deficient. Professor A. J. Taylor estimated the deficiency of the former at 5 per cent,[1] and Professor J. T. Krause reckoned this to be the lower limit, with 3 per cent

[1] A. J. Taylor, 'The Taking of the Census, 1801–1951', in the *British Medical Journal*, 7 April 1951.

deficiency in 1811 as a similarly modest estimate.[2] Whilst later censuses may have had their imperfections, these have generally been held to be negligible; though one must point out that the margins of error in the 10 per cent sample census of 1966 make its use dangerous except for broad aggregates or for purposes for which approximations are adequate. For this reason figures for 1966 have not been included here in those tables where smallish groups of the population are shown, since there is considerable doubt about comparability with earlier, complete censuses.

Table 4, like table 1, goes back into the nineteenth century; and in this case, also, the reason is the publication in the 1961 Census *Report* of a more detailed breakdown of earlier statistics – more detailed both through the use of five-year rather than ten-year age groups for the whole range from 15 to 84 years of age, and also through the separate indication of divorced persons. Again, as in table 1, some repetition from the first volume of *Historical Statistics* seemed worthwhile in order to have a complete table on the new basis.

None of the other tables drawn from Census *Reports* appear to call for any comment additional to those in the notes, except perhaps to recall that in table 7 the principle of selection of the towns shown was to include all with a population of 10,000 or more in 1801 or of 100,000 or more in 1961 (other than those in Greater London). Nor is there any need for explanation of any of the tables of vital statistics.

The last two tables give the rather inadequate summaries of external migration which have been collected for most of the last thirty years or so. Table 16 represents an endeavour to provide series which are roughly comparable with the older statistics which were given in the first *Historical Statistics*. The drawbacks of these were pointed out on page 4 of that book. Table 17 is rather more satisfactory, in that it is more complete; though the many changes in the scope of the statistics collected result in a good deal of internal inconsistency. Most of it, fortunately, is not of great significance.

[2] J. T. Krause, 'Changes in English Fertility and Mortality', in *E.H.R.* XI (August 1958)

Population and Vital Statistics 1. United Kingdom Population (by Sex) and Intercensal Increases – 1801–1966

NOTES

[1] SOURCES: *Reports* of the Censuses of 1961 and 1966 for England & Wales, Scotland, and Northern Ireland.
[2] The population of Islands in the British Seas has not been included.

[3] The figures of intercensal increase are given here as a percentage per year (i.e. compounded), whereas in the first *Abstract of British Historical Statistics* the percentage increase between censuses was shown.

A. England & Wales

	Total Population (000s)			Increase since Previous Census (000s)			Intercensal Increase (per cent per year)			Females per 1,000 Males
	Persons	Males	Females	Persons	Males	Females	Persons	Males	Females	
1801 Mar. 9/10	8,893	4,255	4,638	...	...	...	...	...	...	1,057 (a)
1811 May 26/27	10,164	4,874	5,291	1,272	619	653	1·32	1·34	1·30	1,054 (a)
1821 May 27/28	12,000	5,850	6,150	1,836	977	859	1·67	1·84	1·52	1,036 (a)
1831 May 29/30	13,897	6,771	7,126	1,897	921	976	1·48	1·47	1·48	1,040 (a)
1841 June 6/7	15,914	7,778	8,137	2,017	1,006	1,011	1·36	1·39	1·33	1,046
1851 Mar. 30/31	17,928	8,781	9,146	2,013	1,004	1,010	1·22	1·24	1·20	1,042
1861 Apr. 7/8	20,066	9,776	10,290	2,139	995	1,144	1·13	1·08	1·18	1,053
1871 Apr. 2/3	22,712	11,059	11,653	2,646	1,283	1,363	1·25	1·24	1·25	1,054
1881 Apr. 3/4	25,974	12,640	13,335	3,262	1,581	1,681	1·35	1·34	1·36	1,055
1891 Apr. 5/6 (b)	29,003	14,060	14,942	3,028	1,420	1,608	1·11	1·07	1·14	1,063
1901 Mar. 31/ Apr. 1	32,528	15,729	16,799	3,525	1,668	1,857	1·16	1·13	1·18	1,068
1911 Apr. 2/3	36,070	17,446	18,625	3,543	1,717	1,826	1·04	1·04	1·04	1,068
1921 June 19/20	37,887	18,075	19,811	1,816	630	1,187	0·48	0·35	0·61	1,096
1931 Apr. 26/27	39,952	19,133	20,819	2,066	1,058	1,008	0·54	0·58	0·50	1,088
(1939 mid-year estimate	*41,460*	*19,920*	*21,540*	*1,508*	*787*	*721*	*0·37*	*0·41*	*0·34*	*1,081)*
1951 Apr. 8/9	43,758	21,016	22,742	2,298 (c)	1,096 (c)	1,202 (c)	0·54 (c)	0·53 (c)	0·54 (c)	1,082
1961 Apr. 23/24	46,105	22,304	23,801	2,347	1,288	1,058	0·52	0·59	0·45	1,067
(1966 10% sample Apr. 24/25	47,136	22,841	24,294	1,031	537	494	...	...	...	1,064)

B. Scotland

	Persons	Males	Females	Persons	Males	Females	Persons	Males	Females	Females per 1,000 Males
1801	1,608	739	869	...	...	...	...	...	...	1,176
1811	1,806	826	980	197	87	110	1·14	1·10	1·18	1,185
1821	2,092	983	1,109	286	156	129	1·48	1·75	1·25	1,129
1831	2,364	1,114	1,250	273	132	141	1·23	1·27	1·20	1,122
1841	2,620	1,242	1,378	256	127	128	1·03	1·09	0·98	1,110
1851	2,889	1,375	1,513	269	134	135	1·00	1·05	0·96	1,100
1861	3,062	1,450	1,612	174	74	99	0·58	0·53	0·64	1,112
1871	3,360	1,603	1,757	298	153	144	0·93	1·01	0·86	1,096
1881	3,736	1,799	1,936	376	196	179	1·06	1·16	0·98	1,076
1891 (b)	4,026	1,943	2,083	290	143	147	0·75	0·77	0·73	1,072
1901	4,472	2,174	2,298	446	231	215	1·06	1·13	0·99	1,057
1911	4,761	2,309	2,452	289	135	154	0·63	0·60	0·65	1,062
1921	4,882	2,348	2,535	122	39	83	0·25	0·16	0·33	1,080
1931	4,843	2,326	2,517	−40	−22	−17	−0·08	−0·10	−0·07	1,083
(1939 mid-year	*5,007*	*2,412*	*2,594*	*164*	*87*	*77*	*0·41*	*0·45*	*0·37*	*1,076)*
1951	5,096	2,434	2,662	90 (c)	22 (c)	68 (c)	0·15 (c)	0·08 (c)	0·22 (c)	1,094
1961	5,179	2,483	2,697	83	48	35	0·16	0·20	0·13	1,086
(1966 10% sample	5,168	2,479	2,689	−11	−4	−8	...	...	...	1,085)

See p. 4 for footnotes.

C. Northern Ireland

	Total Population (000s)			Increase since Previous Census (000s)			Intercensal Increase (per cent per year)			Females per 1,000 Males
	Persons	Males	Females	Persons	Males	Females	Persons	Males	Females	
1821 (d)	1,380	665	715	...	...	...	...	...	...	1,075
1831 (d)	1,574	762	812	194	97	96	1·32	1·37	1·28	1,065
1841	1,649	800	849	75	37	38	0·47	0·49	0·45	1,062
1851	1,443	698	745	−206	−102	−105	−1·33	−1·35	−1·32	1,067
1861	1,396	668	729	−46	−30	−16	−0·33	−0·44	−0·22	1,091
1871	1,359	647	712	−37	−21	−17	−0·27	−0·32	−0·24	1,100
1881	1,305	621	684	−54	−26	−28	−0·40	−0·41	−0·40	1,102
1891	1,236	590	646	−69	−30	−38	−0·54	−0·51	−0·57	1,094
1901	1,237	590	647	1	- -	1	0·01	0·00	0·02	1,097
1911	1,251	603	648	14	13	1	0·11	0·22	0·02	1,075
1926 Apr. 18/19	1,257	608	648	6	6	- -	0·03	0·06	0·00	1,066
1937 Feb. 28/ Mar. 1	1,280	623	657	23	15	8	0·16	0·22	0·13	1,054
1951	1,371	668	703	91	45	47	0·49	0·50	0·49	1,053
1961	1,425	694	731	54	26	28	0·38	0·38	0·39	1,053
1966 Oct. 9/10	1,485	724	761	60	30	30	0·75	0·76	0·74	1,051

(a) In computing the proportion of females to males the following estimates of the numbers of men in the Army, Navy, and Merchant Service at home have been adopted:

1801	1811	1821	1831
131,818	145,137	87,740	78,968

(b) The figures for this year have been adjusted to counteract a tendency by certain enumerators to confuse males and females in the completion of a new type of enumeration book introduced at this census.
(c) The increases are reckoned from mid-1939.
(d) Excluding members of the Armed Forces stationed at home.

4

Population and Vital Statistics 2. Estimated Mid-Year Home Population (by Sex) – England & Wales, Scotland, Northern Ireland, and Republic of Ireland 1938–65

NOTES

[1] SOURCE: *Registrar General's Statistical Review of England & Wales.*

[2] The Republic of Ireland population for the period after 1921 was not given in the first *Abstract of British Historical Statistics*. The figures are as follows (in thousands):

	Persons	Males	Females		Persons	Males	Females
1922	3,022	1,529	1,493	1925	2,985	1,512	1,473
1923	3,014	1,526	1,488	1926	2,971	1,507	1,464
1924	3,005	1,521	1,484	1927	2,957	1,502	1,455

	Persons	Males	Females		Persons	Males	Females
1928	2,944	1,498	1,446	1933	2,962	1,512	1,450
1929	2,937	1,496	1,441	1934	2,971	1,518	1,453
1930	2,927	1,493	1,434	1935	2,971	1,520	1,451
1931	2,933	1,497	1,436	1936	2,967	1,520	1,447
1932	2,949	1,505	1,444	1937	2,948	1,510	1,438

[3] From 1952 figures for the Irish Republic relate to early April.

(in thousands)

	England & Wales Area: 37,342,463 acres			Scotland Area: 20,075,023 acres			Northern Ireland Area: 3,495,617 acres			Republic of Ireland Area: 17,367,247 acres		
	Persons	Males	Females	Persons	Males	Females	Persons	Males	Females	Persons	Males	Females
1938	41,215	19,792	21,423	4,993	2,405	2,588	1,286	625	661	2,937	1,505	1,432
1939	41,460	19,920	21,540	5,007	2,412	2,594	1,295	630	665	2,934	1,503	1,431
1940 (a)	41,862	20,216	21,646	5,065	2,454	2,611	1,299	634	665	2,958	1,515	1,443
1941 (a)	41,748	20,141	21,607	5,160	2,492	2,668	1,308	633	675	2,993	1,533	1,460
1942 (a)	41,897	20,180	21,717	5,174	2,508	2,666	1,329	648	681	2,963	1,499	1,464
1943 (a)	42,259	20,397	21,862	5,189	2,521	2,668	1,341	656	685	2,946	1,490	1,456
1944 (a)	42,449	20,473	21,976	5,210	2,534	2,676	1,357	665	692	2,944	1,487	1,457
1945 (a)	42,636	20,549	22,087	5,187	2,508	2,679	1,359	666	693	2,952	1,490	1,462
1946 (a)	42,700	20,611	22,089	5,167	2,509	2,658	1,350	662	688	2,957	1,496	1,461
1947 (a)	43,050	20,822	22,228	5,120	2,476	2,643	1,350	661	689	2,974	1,505	1,469
1948 (a)	43,502	21,091	22,411	5,150	2,496	2,654	1,362	667	695	2,985	1,512	1,473
1949 (a)	43,785	21,239	22,546	5,156	2,501	2,655	1,371	672	699	2,981	1,513	1,468
1950 (a)	44,020	21,357	22,663	5,168	2,506	2,662	1,377	674	703	2,969	1,510	1,459
1951	43,815	21,044	22,771	5,102	2,439	2,664	1,373	669	704	2,961	1,507	1,454
1952	43,955	21,110	22,845	5,101	2,437	2,664	1,375	670	705	2,953	1,501	1,452
1953	44,109	21,206	22,903	5,099	2,436	2,664	1,384	675	709	2,949	1,498	1,451
1954	44,274	21,288	22,986	5,104	2,437	2,667	1,387	676	711	2,941	1,493	1,448
1955	44,441	21,389	23,052	5,112	2,442	2,669	1,394	679	715	2,921	1,479	1,442
1956	44,667	21,517	23,150	5,120	2,447	2,673	1,397	681	716	2,898	1,463	1,435
1957	44,907	21,648	23,259	5,125	2,450	2,675	1,399	681	717	2,885	1,456	1,429
1958	45,109	21,744	23,365	5,141	2,461	2,680	1,402	684	719	2,853	1,439	1,414
1959	45,386	21,885	23,501	5,162	2,473	2,689	1,408	686	722	2,846	1,435	1,411
1960	45,775	22,097	23,678	5,177	2,483	2,694	1,420	692	728	2,832	1,427	1,405
1961	46,205	22,353	23,852	5,184	2,485	2,699	1,427	696	732	2,818	1,417	1,402
1962	46,709	22,660	24,049	5,197	2,495	2,702	1,435	700	736	2,824	1,419	1,405
1963	47,028	22,834	24,194	5,205	2,499	2,705	1,446	705	741	2,841	1,427	1,414
1964	47,401	23,044	24,358	5,206	2,500	2,707	1,458	711	747	2,849	1,431	1,418
1965	47,763	23,227	24,536	5,204	2,497	2,707	1,469	716	753	2,855	1,433	1,422

(a) These figures relate, so far as England & Wales, Scotland and Northern Ireland are concerned, to total population, i.e. to home population plus members of H.M. Forces overseas, less members of the Armed Forces of other countries temporarily in the United Kingdom. In 1951 figures of total population were as follows: England & Wales 44,008; Scotland 5,169. No figure of total population in 1951 was published for Northern Ireland in the source. The difference between home and total population is almost entirely represented by differences in the male population.

Population and Vital Statistics 3. Population by Sex and Age-Group (Quinary) – England & Wales, Scotland, Northern Ireland and Republic of Ireland, 1951–66

NOTES
[1] SOURCES: *Reports* of the Censuses of 1951, 1961, and 1966.
[2] Figures for England & Wales, and for Scotland for 1966 are based on a 10 per cent sample census. Details of the estimated margins of error can be found in the *Reports*.

A. England & Wales

(in thousands)

	1951			1961			1966		
	Persons	Males	Females	Persons	Males	Females	Persons	Males	Females
All Ages	43,757·8	21,015·6	22,742·2	46,104·5	22,303·8	23,800·7	47,135·5	22,840·6	24,294·9
0–4	3,717·8	1,903·7	1,814·1	3,597·0	1,846·1	1,750·9	4,013·7	2,059·1	1,954·6
5–9	3,161·9	1,616·4	1,545·5	3,262·3	1,670·6	1,591·7	3,572·8	1,835·8	1,737·0
10–14	2,811·9	1,428·6	1,383·3	3,725·2	1,907·3	1,817·9	3,254·3	1,663·1	1,591·2
15–19	2,704·5	1,335·3	1,369·2	3,200·7	1,622·0	1,578·7	3,681·8	1,870·5	1,811·4
20–24	2,927·4	1,427·2	1,500·2	2,878·3	1,434·4	1,443·9	3,142·8	1,574·3	1,568·5
25–29	3,279·9	1,625·2	1,654·1	2,846·2	1,446·0	1,400·2	2,844·0	1,443·1	1,400·9
30–34	3,078·5	1,513·9	1,564·6	2,984·3	1,501·6	1,482·7	2,795·5	1,410·3	1,385·2
35–39	3,323·2	1,632·5	1,690·7	3,241·9	1,616·2	1,625·7	2,947·5	1,477·0	1,470·5
40–44	3,365·2	1,657·9	1,707·3	3,036·6	1,493·8	1,542·8	3,181·4	1,574·5	1,606·9
45–49	3,172·2	1,556·4	1,615·8	3,228·8	1,583·8	1,645·0	2,973·2	1,454·7	1,518·5
50–54	2,824·8	1,317·9	1,506·9	3,221·1	1,575·4	1,645·7	3,117·2	1,520·2	1,597·0
55–59	2,423·0	1,089·3	1,333·7	2,927·8	1,407·8	1,519·9	3,049·0	1,468·6	1,580·4
60–64	2,142·8	938·8	1,204·0	2,458·1	1,096·3	1,361·8	2,706·6	1,260·4	1,446·2
65–69	1,829·4	780·6	1,048·8	1,978·8	818·9	1,159·9	2,155·9	912·0	1,244·0
70–74	1,427·8	591·2	836·6	1,541·7	599·6	942·1	1,600·7	618·7	982·0
75–79	923·7	374·5	549·2	1,068·9	389·1	679·8	1,114·3	395·2	719·0
80–84	446·0	164·8	281·2	605·1	204·6	400·5	637·2	205·1	432·1
85 and over	197·8	60·8	137·0	302·0	90·2	211·8	347·6	98·0	249·6

B. Scotland

	1951			1961			1966		
	Persons	Males	Females	Persons	Males	Females	Persons	Males	Females
All Ages	5,096·4	2,434·4	2,662·1	5,179·3	2,482·7	2,696·6	5,168·2	2,478·8	2,689·5
0–4	470·8	241·0	229·8	469·2	240·1	229·1	476·8	244·4	232·4
5–9	397·8	202·5	195·3	420·7	215·1	205·7	445·8	227·4	218·4
10–14	386·5	195·7	190·8	449·1	230·1	219·1	410·3	211·3	198·9
15–19	361·8	173·2	188·7	374·1	187·4	186·7	419·2	213·4	205·8
20–24	364·1	172·4	191·7	333·0	159·4	173·7	325·7	160·7	165·0
25–29	381·2	187·2	194·0	327·0	161·0	166·0	308·9	150·4	158·5
30–34	344·9	166·1	178·8	332·5	162·8	169·7	307·6	151·1	156·5
35–39	368·5	177·6	190·8	347·3	170·5	176·9	321·4	156·3	165·1
40–44	370·1	180·0	190·1	320·5	153·2	167·2	332·8	161·6	171·2
45–49	349·5	168·7	180·9	342·6	163·9	178·8	307·5	145·5	162·0
50–54	308·0	141·3	166·6	342·2	164·3	177·9	328·8	155·6	173·1
55–59	260·2	115·8	144·9	312·5	147·3	165·2	319·0	150·2	168·8
60–64	224·7	97·9	126·8	259·5	113·2	146·4	281·8	128·8	153·0
65–69	192·2	83·2	108·9	204·6	83·4	121·1	224·3	92·0	132·3
70–74	151·3	65·7	85·6	153·9	60·2	93·7	162·1	62·0	100·1
75–79	97·7	41·6	56·2	105·4	40·2	65·2	106·4	37·9	68·5
80–84	45·8	17·8	28·0	57·9	21·7	36·2	59·9	21·0	39·0
85 and over	19·8	6·4	13·4	27·2	9·0	18·2	30·1	9·3	20·8
not stated	1·1	0·5	0·6	—	—	—	—	—	—

C. Northern Ireland

(in thousands)

	1951			1961			1966		
	Persons	Males	Females	Persons	Males	Females	Persons	Males	Females
All Ages	1,370·9	667·8	703·1	1,425·0	694·2	730·8	1,484·8	723·9	760·9
0–4	137·8	70·6	67·2	146·5	75·4	71·2	160·5	83·0	77·5
5–9	129·2	66·1	63·1	132·4	68·1	64·3	146·3	75·1	71·2
10–14	111·7	56·9	54·8	133·2	68·1	65·0	132·0	67·7	64·3
15–19	108·5	55·4	53·1	120·2	60·3	60·0	125·7	63·5	62·2
20–24	100·9	48·7	52·2	93·8	46·9	46·9	106·4	52·4	54·0
25–29	99·5	47·9	51·6	85·2	41·6	43·6	87·8	43·4	44·3
30–34	91·2	44·7	46·6	86·5	41·6	44·9	83·8	41·1	42·7
35–39	94·1	45·5	48·6	90·9	43·9	47·0	84·8	40·9	43·9
40–44	89·1	43·0	46·0	85·1	41·6	43·4	88·2	42·7	45·5
45–49	80·8	38·8	42·0	87·0	42·1	44·9	83·6	40·9	42·7
50–54	76·3	36·1	40·3	82·0	39·6	42·5	83·4	40·2	43·2
55–59	62·2	28·9	33·3	72·5	34·4	38·2	77·5	37·0	40·5
60–64	54·5	24·4	30·1	65·7	29·4	36·3	68·6	31·3	37·3
65–69	47·4	21·6	25·8	52·2	23·0	29·2	58·2	25·3	32·9
70–74	40·5	18·3	22·2	40·1	17·0	23·1	43·1	18·1	25·1
75–79	27·2	12·4	14·8	27·0	11·3	15·7	28·8	11·5	17·3
80–84	13·7	6·0	7·3	16·2	6·7	9·4	16·4	6·3	10·1
85 and over	6·1	2·4	3·7	8·4	3·2	5·2	9·6	3·5	6·1

D. Republic of Ireland

	1951			1961			1966		
	Persons	Males	Females	Persons	Males	Females	Persons	Males	Females
All Ages	2,960·6	1,506·6	1,454·0	2,818·3	1,416·5	1,401·8	2,884·0	1,449·0	1,435·0
0–4	312·8	160·2	152·6	300·8	153·4	147·4	315·9	161·3	154·6
5–9	281·0	143·5	137·6	287·7	147·0	140·7	299·0	152·4	146·5
10–14	260·9	132·7	128·2	288·8	148·3	140·5	285·5	145·6	139·8
15–19	241·2	125·7	115·4	233·8	120·3	113·5	259·4	133·3	126·0
20–24	202·2	105·4	96·8	158·0	80·4	77·6	185·3	94·7	90·6
25–29	198·4	100·0	98·8	145·4	72·3	73·1	149·3	75·0	74·3
30–34	191·6	96·4	95·1	152·8	75·2	77·5	146·6	73·8	72·8
35–39	200·9	102·3	98·6	166·8	81·6	85·2	154·3	76·5	77·8
40–44	180·3	94·0	86·3	170·3	84·8	85·5	163·4	81·0	82·4
45–49	160·9	82·4	78·5	174·6	89·0	85·6	166·5	83·6	82·9
50–54	163·0	82·9	80·1	157·1	81·7	75·4	165·0	84·3	80·6
55–59	128·8	65·0	63·8	136·1	68·6	67·5	147·1	75·8	71·2
60–64	122·0	61·3	60·7	131·1	64·4	66·6	123·8	61·6	62·2
65–69	107·5	54·1	53·4	103·5	51·1	52·3	114·2	55·0	59·2
70–74	100·1	49·1	51·0	92·8	44·1	48·7	90·1	42·2	47·9
75–79	64·5	31·6	32·9	63·2	29·7	33·5	62·8	28·7	34·1
80–84	30·9	14·6	16·2	37·0	16·7	20·4	35·6	15·8	19·8
85 and over	13·3	5·5	7·8	18·5	7·7	10·8	20·3	8·1	12·2

7

Population and Vital Statistics 4. Proportions of Each Age-Group (by Sex) according to Marital Condition – England & Wales, and Scotland 1851–1961

NOTES

[1] SOURCE: *Reports* of the Census of 1961 for England & Wales, and for Scotland.
[2] The divorced were not separately enumerated before 1921.

[3] In Scotland, persons who failed to state their marital condition were excluded from the statistics from 1911 onwards.

A. England & Wales, Males

(per thousand of the appropriate sex in each age-group)

		1851	1861	1871	1881 (a)	1891 (a)	1901 (b)	1911	1921	1931	1951	1961
All Ages	S	625	612	613	619	620	608	592	550	518	438	437
	M	337	351	351	346	345	357	372	414	444	523	530
	W	38	37	36	34	35	35	35	36	38	35	30
	D								0	1	4	4
15 and over	S	411	388	384	392	406	411	403	365	356	265	256
	M	529	554	559	553	540	536	545	584	593	684	700
	W	60	58	57	55	54	53	52	50	50	46	39
	D								1	1	5	6
15–19	S	996	995	994	995	996	997	998	996	997	995	989
	M	4	5	5	5	4	3	2	4	3	5	11
	W	0	0	0	0	0	0	0	0	0	0	0
	D								0	0	0	0
20–24	S	797	775	767	777	806	826	857	822	861	762	690
	M	200	223	230	221	193	173	142	177	138	237	309
	W	3	2	3	2	2	1	1	1	1	0	0
	D								0	0	0	0
25–29	S	441	402	392	392	429	450	492	446	471	349	294
	M	547	587	596	598	563	544	503	548	525	646	702
	W	12	11	11	10	8	6	5	6	4	2	1
	D								1	0	3	3
30–34	S	259	226	230	229	244	254	272	231	218	190	175
	M	718	755	750	751	739	732	716	756	771	799	818
	W	23	20	21	20	17	14	12	12	9	4	2
	D								1	1	7	6
35–39	S	180	153	151	152	163	174	186	163	137	133	132
	M	785	817	818	818	809	802	794	818	847	851	856
	W	35	30	31	30	28	24	20	18	14	7	4
	D								1	2	9	8
40–44	S	142	130	122	123	128	140	148	137	113	109	107
	M	806	826	834	834	830	822	820	837	863	872	876
	W	52	44	44	43	42	38	32	25	22	11	7
	D								1	2	9	9
45–49	S	121	108	99	99	104	116	127	124	110	98	95
	M	810	831	842	842	835	826	824	837	855	878	882
	W	69	62	59	59	61	58	49	38	33	17	12
	D								1	2	7	10

See p. 14 for footnotes.

A. England & Wales, Males (*cont*).

(per thousand of the appropriate sex in each age-group)

		1851	1861	1871	1881 (*a*)	1891 (*a*)	1901 (*b*)	1911	1921	1931	1951	1961
50–54	S	107	102	96	94	96	104	114	115	107	86	89
	M	794	809	821	821	817	810	809	824	839	876	880
	W	98	88	83	85	87	86	77	60	53	31	22
	D								1	1	6	10
55–59	S	101	90	88	81	83	87	98	106	104	77	86
	M	771	789	799	806	798	790	789	802	814	867	870
	W	128	121	113	113	119	123	113	91	81	51	37
	D								1	1	5	8
60–64	S	95	91	91	84	86	90	100	100	100	79	79
	M	721	729	739	748	740	732	729	758	771	830	849
	W	184	179	170	168	174	178	171	141	128	87	65
	D								1	1	4	6
65–69	S	86	86	83	81	76	80	88	94	96	84	73
	M	666	668	679	685	688	668	665	688	708	771	812
	W	248	246	238	234	236	252	247	217	195	143	111
	D								1	1	3	4
70–74	S	84	81	80	76	73	75	80	86	85	85	76
	M	574	572	582	586	588	577	577	599	621	682	734
	W	342	347	338	338	339	348	343	314	293	231	187
	D								1	1	2	3
75–79	S	78	75	74	72	71	67	71	75	76	82	79
	M	489	474	477	484	487	476	475	501	507	568	624
	W	433	451	449	444	442	457	454	424	416	348	295
	D								0	1	1	2
80–84	S	66	71	67	66	66	63	64	67	63	74	77
	M	395	363	373	378	380	373	370	391	392	443	487
	W	538	566	560	556	554	564	565	542	544	482	435
	D								0	1	1	1
85 and over	S	76	74	62	63	63	62	61	70	56	65	73
	M	290	272	270	271	274	263	258	272	268	311	337
	W	634	654	668	666	663	675	681	657	676	623	589
	D								1	1	1	1

B. England & Wales, Females

		1851	1861	1871	1881 (*a*)	1891 (*a*)	1901 (*b*)	1911	1921	1931	1951	1961
All Ages	S	598	587	586	592	596	585	571	535	500	405	388
	M	330	339	339	333	329	340	356	383	413	488	498
	W	72	74	75	75	75	74	73	82	86	102	106
	D								0	1	6	7
15 and over	S	385	369	361	367	387	395	390	368	354	248	219
	M	504	519	522	516	499	496	506	520	534	616	636
	W	111	112	116	116	114	108	104	111	111	129	136
	D								1	1	7	9

See p. 14 for footnotes.

Population and Vital Statistics 4. *continued*

B. England & Wales, Females (*cont.*)

(per thousand of the appropriate sex in each age-group)

		1851	1861	1871	1881 (a)	1891 (a)	1901 (b)	1911	1921	1931	1951	1961
15–19	S	975	969	968	974	980	984	988	982	982	956	934
	M	25	30	32	25	19	15	12	18	18	44	66
	W	0	0	0	0	0	0	0	0	0	0	0
	D								0	0	0	0
20–24	S	687	664	652	665	701	726	757	726	742	518	420
	M	308	331	343	331	296	272	242	270	257	480	577
	W	5	5	5	4	3	2	1	3	1	1	1
	D								0	0	1	1
25–29	S	398	368	356	353	394	410	434	410	406	217	157
	M	584	613	624	630	593	579	558	568	587	770	835
	W	19	19	20	17	13	11	8	21	6	5	3
	D								1	1	8	6
30–34	S	249	232	224	221	245	257	270	260	249	146	109
	M	711	729	735	741	724	718	711	697	733	827	875
	W	40	39	41	38	31	25	19	42	16	14	6
	D								1	2	13	9
35–39	S	179	173	168	165	177	200	210	204	206	133	98
	M	758	765	766	770	765	752	752	740	755	831	875
	W	63	62	66	65	58	48	38	55	37	23	13
	D								1	2	13	14
40–44	S	145	142	141	140	149	168	180	179	181	142	97
	M	756	760	758	760	756	750	755	751	749	810	859
	W	100	97	100	100	95	82	66	69	67	35	27
	D								1	2	13	17
45–49	S	126	122	124	123	129	143	165	168	168	152	105
	M	739	744	740	734	728	726	729	739	733	780	828
	W	135	134	136	143	143	131	107	93	97	58	50
	D								1	2	11	17
50–54	S	119	116	117	115	118	129	150	159	159	150	122
	M	688	692	690	684	680	680	685	700	707	737	778
	W	193	192	193	201	202	191	165	140	132	104	84
	D								1	1	9	15
55–59	S	114	107	109	110	113	122	135	155	157	155	138
	M	639	643	637	627	616	612	624	638	656	668	706
	W	248	251	255	263	271	266	241	206	186	170	143
	D								1	1	6	13
60–64	S	116	111	109	107	107	111	128	151	155	156	144
	M	536	532	535	530	523	520	534	551	574	574	610
	W	347	357	356	363	370	369	338	297	270	265	237
	D								0	1	5	10
65–69	S	110	104	104	106	109	112	120	139	158	154	152
	M	448	449	441	433	425	417	424	441	461	477	493
	W	442	447	454	461	466	471	456	419	380	366	349
	D								0	1	3	6

See p. 14 for footnotes.

B. England & Wales, Females (*cont.*)

(per thousand of the appropriate sex in each age-group)

		1851	1861	1871	1881 (*a*)	1891 (*a*)	1901 (*b*)	1911	1921	1931	1951	1961
70–74	S	112	106	104	105	107	112	123	139	156	157	155
	M	337	336	327	319	314	300	307	325	342	368	367
	W	551	558	570	576	579	588	570	535	501	472	475
	D								0	0	2	4
75–79	S	109	103	97	100	104	110	120	133	149	162	155
	M	243	232	234	225	215	204	206	214	223	257	250
	W	648	665	670	675	681	686	674	653	627	579	592
	D								0	0	1	2
80–84	S	110	100	97	99	107	111	121	132	144	167	161
	M	150	142	147	141	130	121	118	131	128	154	152
	W	740	757	756	760	763	768	760	738	728	679	686
	D								0	0	1	1
85 and over	S	107	91	91	95	105	119	126	130	142	172	172
	M	81	77	74	69	64	59	55	67	61	77	71
	W	812	832	835	836	831	823	818	802	796	751	756
	D								0	0	0	1

C. Scotland, Males

		1851	1861	1871	1881 (*a*)	1891 (*a*)	1901 (*b*)	1911	1921	1931	1951	1961
All Ages	S	668	658	661	663	663	655	642	607	583	500	486
	M	298	309	306	304	304	312	322	355	376	458	478
	W	34	33	33	33	33	33	36	38	40	40	33
	D								0	1	2	3
15 and over	S	463	441	444	452	463	471	462	431	419	322	290
	M	482	505	502	495	485	478	485	514	524	621	661
	W	55	54	54	53	53	51	54	55	56	54	46
	D								1	1	3	4
15–19	S	996	996	997	997	998	997	998	995	996	996	988
	M	4	3	3	3	2	3	2	5	4	4	12
	W	0	0	0	0	0	0	0	0	0	0	0
	D								0	0	—	—
20–24	S	834	833	842	848	866	874	884	854	882	800	704
	M	163	165	156	150	132	125	115	145	117	199	295
	W	2	2	2	2	2	1	1	1	1	0	0
	D								0	0	0	0
25–29	S	513	477	487	493	536	550	582	538	564	418	308
	M	477	513	502	496	455	443	412	456	431	577	689
	W	10	10	11	11	9	7	6	6	5	3	1
	D								1	0	2	2
30–34	S	322	283	286	287	318	334	360	316	307	240	189
	M	656	698	693	692	663	649	625	668	681	749	806
	W	23	19	21	21	19	17	15	14	11	6	2
	D								1	1	5	4

See p. 14 for footnotes.

C. Scotland, Males (*cont.*)

(per thousand of the appropriate sex in each age-group)

		1851	1861	1871	1881 (*a*)	1891 (*a*)	1901 (*b*)	1911	1921	1931	1951	1961
35–39	S	226	199	195	197	214	232	252	233	201	172	153
	M	739	772	774	771	755	741	723	744	779	812	836
	W	34	30	31	32	32	27	25	22	19	10	5
	D								1	2	6	5
40–44	S	183	164	163	158	172	187	202	194	170	145	132
	M	765	793	791	797	783	771	759	772	800	835	852
	W	52	43	45	45	45	41	40	33	29	15	9
	D								1	2	5	6
45–49	S	152	138	134	130	137	152	169	176	165	135	124
	M	776	801	804	808	800	787	772	776	791	837	852
	W	71	61	62	62	63	61	59	47	43	24	17
	D								1	2	5	7
50–54	S	141	132	129	125	129	139	150	160	159	125	121
	M	766	781	786	791	785	771	766	766	776	829	844
	W	94	86	84	85	86	90	84	73	64	42	29
	D								1	1	4	6
55–59	S	121	126	120	112	113	120	130	147	154	116	121
	M	756	761	767	771	770	757	750	743	750	813	824
	W	123	113	113	116	117	123	120	109	96	68	49
	D								1	1	3	5
60–64	S	118	126	122	111	116	122	126	136	145	120	119
	M	713	716	720	727	720	705	700	706	709	768	791
	W	168	158	158	162	164	173	174	157	145	109	85
	D								1	1	3	4
65–69	S	101	113	119	109	106	107	117	122	136	131	112
	M	675	668	673	670	671	655	639	651	650	690	742
	W	224	219	208	221	223	238	244	226	213	177	143
	D								1	1	2	3
70–74	S	100	110	121	108	106	107	111	114	123	130	117
	M	603	600	594	588	588	573	560	561	574	594	654
	W	297	289	285	304	306	320	329	325	303	274	227
	D								1	1	1	2
75–79	S	87	98	110	108	106	103	102	97	109	119	124
	M	540	516	515	499	509	481	475	466	472	490	531
	W	373	386	375	393	385	417	423	436	418	389	343
	D								0	1	1	1
80–84	S	78	84	105	108	96	98	98	93	102	108	122
	M	445	445	437	407	423	395	373	364	355	379	406
	W	477	471	458	485	481	507	529	543	542	512	471
	D								—	0	1	1
85 and over	S	83	81	97	81	89	95	95	82	92	94	113
	M	358	338	311	317	304	280	266	263	252	251	272
	W	559	581	591	603	606	625	639	655	655	655	615
	D								0	1	0	0

See p. 14 for footnotes.

Population and Vital Statistics 4. *continued*

D. Scotland, Females

(per thousand of the appropriate sex in each age-group)

		1851	1861	1871	1881 (a)	1891 (a)	1901 (b)	1911	1921	1931	1951	1961
All Ages	S	637	630	629	629	631	623	615	586	565	475	447
	M	279	286	287	290	290	300	311	333	353	427	448
	W	84	84	84	82	79	76	74	80	81	94	99
	D								1	1	4	5
15 and over	S	455	443	432	430	442	445	440	424	415	316	270
	M	419	431	439	444	438	443	452	464	475	556	592
	W	126	127	129	126	119	112	108	111	109	122	131
	D								1	1	5	7
15–19	S	979	979	978	982	988	983	986	979	977	965	942
	M	21	21	22	18	12	16	14	21	23	35	58
	W	0	0	0	0	0	0	0	0	0	0	0
	D								0	0	0	0
20–24	S	748	741	738	735	764	764	782	754	771	602	482
	M	247	255	258	261	233	234	216	242	228	396	516
	W	5	4	4	3	2	2	2	4	1	1	1
	D								0	0	1	1
25–29	S	466	460	443	431	478	475	502	480	495	290	190
	M	512	520	537	553	511	515	491	501	498	698	803
	W	23	20	20	17	12	10	7	19	6	6	3
	D								1	1	6	4
30–34	S	316	311	301	288	312	318	333	322	324	190	144
	M	634	645	653	673	657	657	648	637	657	784	842
	W	49	44	45	39	31	25	20	40	17	17	8
	D								1	2	9	7
35–39	S	249	253	250	233	240	256	259	259	261	171	136
	M	673	672	677	699	703	695	701	685	697	793	835
	W	78	75	73	68	57	49	40	54	39	28	17
	D								1	2	9	12
40–44	S	223	220	219	206	206	219	223	226	232	186	131
	M	650	662	667	683	697	696	707	703	699	765	820
	W	127	117	114	111	97	84	70	70	68	41	36
	D								1	2	7	13
45–49	S	209	199	202	194	188	197	213	211	219	203	142
	M	624	642	640	650	668	671	675	691	683	720	783
	W	167	159	158	156	144	132	112	97	96	70	63
	D								1	2	7	12
50–54	S	207	204	199	193	185	186	203	203	211	203	167
	M	560	574	580	589	605	615	627	649	656	672	720
	W	234	222	221	217	210	199	170	147	131	119	103
	D								1	2	6	10
55–59	S	205	198	192	192	181	179	190	206	206	207	192
	M	499	516	528	526	548	550	567	581	606	601	632
	W	296	287	280	281	271	272	244	213	187	187	167
	D								1	1	5	8

See p. 14 for footnotes.

D. Scotland, Females (*cont.*)

(per thousand of the appropriate sex in each age-group)

		1851	1861	1871	1881 (a)	1891 (a)	1901 (b)	1911	1921	1931	1951	1961
60–64	S	211	212	203	196	192	183	188	203	207	211	203
	M	404	409	423	428	443	446	476	494	516	509	529
	W	386	379	374	376	366	371	336	302	275	276	261
	D								1	1	4	6
65–69	S	205	207	201	195	190	184	187	198	216	215	213
	M	336	335	349	349	361	356	369	388	410	420	418
	W	459	457	451	455	449	459	444	413	373	363	364
	D								1	1	2	5
70–74	S	211	214	209	205	200	197	196	200	218	219	220
	M	250	244	251	252	260	250	259	278	297	320	305
	W	539	542	540	543	540	554	544	522	484	459	472
	D								0	1	2	3
75–79	S	208	209	208	200	191	201	200	193	211	220	227
	M	176	175	174	178	187	167	167	173	186	212	205
	W	616	616	618	622	622	632	633	633	602	566	566
	D								0	0	1	2
80–84	S	217	210	214	208	212	204	210	195	212	223	233
	M	104	105	105	104	111	91	101	97	102	123	117
	W	679	685	681	688	677	706	689	708	686	653	648
	D								0	0	1	2
85 and over	S	191	186	194	194	203	207	212	188	202	225	235
	M	56	53	61	55	64	40	41	47	52	58	52
	W	753	761	745	751	733	753	747	765	745	716	712
	D								0	0	1	1

(*a*) The proportions for 1881 and 1891 have been estimated from data for 10-year age-groups between the ages of 25 and 64 and the age-group 65 and over, in the case of England & Wales.

(*b*) The proportions for 1901 have been estimated from data for 10-year age-groups between the ages of 25 and 84.

Population and Vital Statistics 5. Population of Conurbations 1931–66

NOTES
[1] SOURCE: Census *Reports*.

[2] All figures are adjusted to the present area of the conurbation, except as indicated in footnote (*a*).

(in thousands)

	Greater London	South-East Lancashire	West Midlands	West Yorkshire	Merseyside	Tyneside	Clydeside
1931	8,216	2,427	1,933	1,655	1,347	827	1,690
1951	8,348	2,423	2,237	1,693	1,382	836	1,758
1961	8,183 (*a*)	2,428	2,347	1,704	1,384	855	1,802
1966 (*b*)	7,671	2,404	2,374	1,708	1,338	832	1,766

(*a*) For the 1966 Census the area was changed from that of the old Greater London conurbation to that governed by the Greater London Council. The population of the latter in 1961 was 7,997,000.

(*b*) The 1966 census was based on a 10 per cent sample, and the margin of error involved should be borne in mind in making comparisons with earlier years.

Population and Vital Statistics 6. Population of the Counties of the British Isles – 1951–66

NOTES

[1] SOURCES: *Reports* of the Censuses of 1961 for England & Wales and for Scotland, of 1961 and 1966 for Northern Ireland, and for 1956, 1961, and 1966 for the Republic of Ireland.

[2] The population of Belfast county borough is not shown in the population of any of the counties of Northern Ireland, nor is that of Aberdeen City shown in the population of any of the counties of Scotland.

A. England

(in thousands)

	1951	1961
Bedfordshire	312	381
Berkshire	403	504
Buckinghamshire	386	488
Cambridgeshire (whole)	256	279
(Isle of Ely	89	89
Cheshire	1,259	1,369
Cornwall	345	342
Cumberland	285	294
Derbyshire	826	878
Devonshire	798	824
Dorsetshire	291	313
Durham	1,464	1,516
Essex	2,045	2,288
Gloucestershire	939	1,002
Hampshire (whole)	1,293	1,433
(Isle of Wight	96	96
Herefordshire	127	131
Hertfordshire	610	833
Huntingdonshire	69	80
Kent	1,564	1,702
Lancashire	5,118	5,129
Leicestershire	631	683
Lincolnshire (whole)	706	743
(Holland	102	103
(Kesteven	130	135
(Lindsey	474	505
London	3,348	3,200
Middlesex	2,269	2,235
Norfolk	548	561
Northamptonshire (whole)	424	473
(Soke of Peterborough	64	75
Northumberland	798	821
Nottinghamshire	841	903
Oxfordshire	276	309
Rutland	21	24
Shropshire	290	297
Somerset	551	599
Staffordshire	1,619	1,734
Suffolk (whole)	443	472
(Suffolk East	322	343
(Suffolk West	121	129
Surrey	1,603	1,731
Sussex (whole)	938	1,078
(Sussex East	615	666
(Sussex West	323	412
Warwickshire	1,862	2,025
Westmorland	67	67
Wiltshire	387	423
Worcestershire	525	570
Yorkshire (East Riding)	511	527
Yorkshire (North Riding)	525	554
Yorkshire (West Riding)	3,586	3,645

B. Wales

(in thousands)

	1951	1961
Anglesey	51	52
Brecknockshire	57	55
Caernarvonshire	124	122
Cardiganshire	53	54
Carmarthenshire	172	168
Denbighshire	171	174
Flintshire	145	150
Glamorganshire	1,203	1,230
Merionethshire	41	38
Monmouthshire	425	445
Montgomeryshire	46	44
Pembrokeshire	91	94
Radnorshire	20	18

C. Scotland

Aberdeenshire	145	136
Angusshire	275	278
Argyllshire	63	59
Ayrshire	321	343
Banffshire	50	46
Berwickshire	25	22
Buteshire	19	15
Caithness-shire	23	27
Clackmannanshire	38	41
Dumfriesshire	86	88
Dunbartonshire	164	185
East Lothianshire	52	53
Fifeshire	307	321
Inverness-shire	85	83
Kincardineshire	28	26
Kinross-shire	7	7
Kircudbrightshire	31	29
Lanarkshire	1,614	1,626
Midlothianshire	566	580
Morayshire	48	49
Nairnshire	9	8
Orkney	21	19
Peeblesshire	15	14
Perthshire	128	127
Renfrewshire	325	339
Ross & Cromarty	61	58
Roxburghshire	46	43
Selkirkshire	22	21
Shetland	19	18
Stirlingshire	188	195
Sutherlandshire	14	14
West Lothianshire	89	93
Wigtownshire	32	29

Population and Vital Statistics 6. *continued*

D. Northern Ireland

	(in thousands)			
	1951	1956	1961	1966
Antrim	231		274	314
Armagh	114		118	125
Down	241		267	287
Fermanagh	53		52	50
Londonderry	156		165	175
Tyrone	132		134	136

E. Irish Republic

	1951	1956	1961	1966
Carlow	34	34	33	34
Cavan	66	62	57	54
Clare	81	77	74	74
Cork	341	337	330	340
Donegal	132	122	114	109
Dublin	693	706	718	795
Galway	160	156	150	148
Kerry	127	122	116	113
Kildare	66	66	64	66
Kilkenny	65	64	62	60
Laoghis	48	47	45	45
Leitrim	41	37	33	31
Limerick	141	138	133	137
Longford	35	33	31	29
Louth	69	69	67	70
Mayo	142	133	123	116
Meath	66	67	65	67
Monaghan	55	52	47	46
Offaly	53	52	52	52
Roscommon	68	64	59	56
Sligo	61	57	54	51
Tipperary	133	129	124	123
Waterford	75	74	71	73
Westmeath	54	54	53	53
Wexford	90	87	83	83
Wicklow	63	60	58	60

NOTE

SOURCE: *Reports* of the Censuses of 1951 and 1961.

(in thousands)

	1931 (a)	1951 (a)	1951 (b)	1961
Aberdeen	170	183	183	185
Bath	69 (c)	79	79	81
Belfast (e)	438 (d)	444	444	416
Birkenhead	152	143	143	142
Birmingham	1,003	1,113	1,113	1,107
Blackburn	123	111	111	106
Blackpool	106	147	147	153
Bolton	177	167	167	161
Bournemouth	117	145	145	154
Bradford	299	292	292	296
Brighton	147	156	158	163
Bristol	404 (c)	443	443	437
Cambridge	70	82	82	96
Cardiff	227 (c)	244	244	257
Carlisle	57	68	68	71
Chester	46	48	57	59
Colchester	49	57	57	65
Coventry	178	258	258	306
Derby	143	141	141	132
Dudley	60	63	64	63
Dundee	177	177	177	183
Edinburgh	439	467	467	468
Exeter	68	76	76	80
Gateshead	125	115	115	103
Glasgow	1,093	1,090	1,090	1,055
Greenock	79	76	77	75
Halifax	98	98	98	96
Huddersfield	123	129	129	131
Hull	314	299	299	303
Ipswich	88	105	107	117
King's Lynn	24	26	26	28
Leeds	483	505	506	511
Leicester	258	285	285	273
Liverpool	856	789	791	746
Luton	70	110	110	132
Macclesfield	36	36	36	38
Manchester	766	703	703	662
Middlesbrough	139	147	147	157
Newcastle-upon-Tyne	286	292	292	270
Newport (Mon.)	98	106	106	108
Northampton	97	104	104	105
Norwich	... (c)	121	121	120
Nottingham	276	306	308	312
Oldham	... (c)	121	123	115
Oxford	81	99	99	106
Paisley	88	94	94	96
Plymouth	202 (c)	208	208	204
Portsmouth	252	234	234	215
Preston	120	119	121	113
Reading	97	114	114	120
St Helens	107	110	113	109

See p. 20 for footnotes.

Population and Vital Statistics 7. *continued*

	1931 (*a*)	1951 (*a*)	1951 (*b*)	1961
Salford	223	178	178	155
Sheffield	518	513	513	494
Shrewsbury	37	45	45	50
Southampton	176	178	190	205
Southend-on-Sea	130	152	152	165
South Shields	113 (*c*)	107	107	110
Stockport	126	142	142	143
Stoke-on-Trent	277	275	275	265
Sunderland	186 (*c*)	182	182	190
Swansea	165	161	161	167
Tynemouth	66	67	67	70
Wakefield	59 (*c*)	60	60	61
Wallasey	98	101	101	103
Walsall	103	115	115	118
Warrington	82	81	81	76
Wigan	85	85	85	79
Wolverhampton	139	163	163	151
Worcester	52	60	62	66
Yarmouth	57	51	51	53
York	94	105	105	104

(*a*) 1951 boundaries.
(*b*) 1961 boundaries.
(*c*) Owing to destruction of records during the war, it was not possible in these cases to make an exact computation of the 1931 population within the 1951 boundaries. The figures shown here are incomplete, and seriously defective ones have been omitted altogether.
(*d*) There was a full census of Northern Ireland in 1966, at which the Belfast population was 398 thousand.

Population and Vital Statistics 8. Births and Birth Rates – England & Wales, Scotland, and Northern Ireland 1938–65

NOTE
SOURCES: *Registrar General's Statistical Review for England & Wales*; *Annual Reports of the Registrar General for Scotland*; and *for Northern Ireland*.

A. England & Wales

	Number of Births (in thousands)				Births	
	Males	Females	Total	Legitimate	per 1,000 Population	per 1,000 Women Aged 15–44
1938	318	303	621	595	15·1	62·4
1939	316	299	614	588	14·8	61·3
1940	303	288	590	564	14·1	58·7
1941	297	282	579	548	13·9	57·9
1942	336	316	652	616	15·6	65·2
1943	353	332	684	640	16·2	68·6
1944	388	364	751	696	17·7	75·7
1945	350	330	680	617	15·9	68·8
1946	422	398	821	767	19·2	83·7
1947	454	427	881	834	20·5	90·6
1948	399	376	775	733	17·8	80·2
1949	376	354	731	694	16·7	76·0
1950	359	338	697	662	15·8	73·0
1951	349	329	678	645	15·5	71·6
1952	346	328	674	641	15·3	71·8
1953	352	332	684	651	15·5	73·5
1954	346	327	674	642	15·2	72·9
1955	344	324	668	637	15·0	72·8
1956	360	340	700	666	15·7	77·0
1957	372	351	723	688	16·1	70·0
1958	381	360	741	705	16·4	82·1
1959	386	363	749	711	16·5	83·0
1960	404	381	785	742	17·1	86·7
1961	418	394	811	763	17·6	89·1
1962	432	407	839	784	18·0	90·5
1963	438	416	854	795	18·2	90·9
1964	451	425	876	813	18·5	92·6
1965	443	420	863	797	18·1	91·2

B. Scotland

	Males	Females	Total	Legitimate	per 1,000 Population	per 1,000 Women Aged 15–44
1938	45·4	43·2	88·6	83·2	17·7	74·0
1939	44·7	42·2	86·9	81·7	17·4	72·1
1940	44·2	42·2	86·4	81·3	17·1	71·4
1941	46·1	43·6	89·7	83·8	17·5	73·5
1942	46·4	44·3	90·7	84·2	17·6	74·2
1943	48·5	46·2	94·7	87·5	18·4	78·7
1944	49·5	46·4	95·9	88·3	18·5	79·9
1945	44·8	42·2	86·9	89·4	16·9	73·1
1946	53·9	50·6	104·4	97·5	20·3	89·5
1947	58·0	55·1	113·1	106·8	22·3	97·1

B. Scotland (*cont.*)

	Number of Births (in thousands)				Births	
					per 1,000 Population	per 1,000 Women Aged 15–44
	Males	Females	Total	Legitimate		
1948	51·9	48·5	100·3	94·5	19·7	86·6
1949	49·2	46·5	95·7	90·5	18·8	83·4
1950	47·8	44·7	92·5	87·7	18·1	81·0
1951	46·7	43·9	90·6	86·0	17·8	79·5
1952	46·3	44·2	90·4	86·1	17·7	80·0
1953	46·9	44·1	90·9	86·7	17·8	81·3
1954	47·4	44·9	92·3	88·1	18·1	83·5
1955	47·5	45·0	92·5	88·5	18·1	84·4
1956	49·0	46·4	95·3	91·2	18·6	87·9
1957	50·4	47·6	98·0	94·0	19·1	91·3
1958	51·0	48·5	99·5	95·4	19·4	93·4
1959	51·1	48·1	99·3	95·2	19·2	93·6
1960	51·9	49·4	101·3	96·9	19·6	96·4
1961	52·0	49·2	101·2	96·6	19·5	96·9
1962	53·9	50·4	104·3	99·3	20·1	99·0
1963	52·7	50·0	102·7	97·4	19·7	97·1
1964	53·7	50·7	104·4	98·8	20·0	98·6
1965	52·0	48·6	100·7	94·8	19·3	96·3

C. Northern Ireland

	Males	Females	Total	Legitimate	per 1,000 Population	per 1,000 Women Aged 15–44
1938	13·2	12·5	25·7	24·6	20·0	85·2
1939	12·9	12·3	25·2	24·1	19·5	82·5
1940	13·2	12·2	25·4	24·2	19·5	83·2
1941	14·1	12·8	26·9	25·6	20·5	85·4
1942	15·3	14·4	29·6	28·2	22·3	93·5
1943	16·3	15·2	31·5	29·8	23·5	99·5
1944	15·8	15·1	30·9	29·2	22·8	96·7
1945	14·9	14·1	29·0	27·4	21·3	91·0
1946	15·5	14·7	30·1	28·8	22·3	95·8
1947	16·0	15·2	31·3	30·1	23·2	100·5
1948	15·3	14·3	29·5	28·5	21·7	94·5
1949	15·0	14·1	29·1	28·0	21·2	92·8
1950	14·9	13·9	28·8	27·8	21·0	91·8
1951	14·6	13·8	28·5	27·6	20·7	91·1
1952	14·8	13·9	28·8	27·8	20·9	98·3
1953	15·0	13·9	29·0	28·2	20·9	98·3
1954	14·8	14·0	28·8	28·0	20·8	98·2
1955	15·1	13·9	29·0	28·3	20·8	98·7
1956	15·1	14·4	29·5	28·7	21·1	101·7
1957	15·5	14·6	30·1	29·4	21·5	104·8
1958	15·7	14·6	30·3	29·6	21·6	105·9
1959	15·9	14·9	30·8	30·1	21·9	107·3
1960	16·6	15·4	32·0	31·2	22·5	110·8
1961	16·4	15·5	31·9	31·1	22·4	111·5
1962	16·8	15·8	32·6	31·8	22·7	112·7
1963	17·3	16·1	33·4	32·5	23·1	114·4
1964	17·6	16·7	34·3	33·3	23·6	116·5
1965	17·7	16·2	33·9	32·9	23·1	114·5

Population and Vital Statistics 9. Deaths (by Sex) – England & Wales, Scotland, and Northern Ireland 1938–65

NOTES

[1] SOURCES: *Registrar General's Statistical Review for England & Wales*; *Annual Report of the Registrar General for Scotland*; and *for Northern Ireland.*

[2] From 3 September 1939 to 31 December 1949, for males, and from 1 June 1941 to 31 December 1949, for females, the mortality rates are based upon civilian deaths only; but, as in other years, the number of deaths include those of non-civilians registered in this country.

(in thousands)

	England & Wales		Scotland		Northern Ireland	
	Males	Females	Males	Females	Males	Females
1938	247	232	31·8	31·1	8·7	8·9
1939	256	244	33·0	31·4	8·7	8·8
1940	303	278	37·6	35·1	9·6	9·4
1941	281	254	37·7	34·9	10·2	9·9
1942	251	229	33·8	31·1	9·1	8·4
1943	259	242	34·3	32·4	9·1	8·6
1944	258	234	33·3	31·3	8·6	8·4
1945	252	236	32·0	30·7	8·2	8·2
1946	252	240	32·7	31·9	8·4	8·3
1947	268	250	33·8	32·4	8·6	8·3
1948	243	227	30·8	30·1	7·7	7·4
1949	261	250	31·9	31·6	7·9	7·7
1950	261	249	32·2	31·8	8·0	7·8
1951	282	268	33·1	32·7	8·9	8·7
1952	258	240	31·4	30·1	7·7	7·1
1953	259	244	30·3	28·6	7·7	7·1
1954	260	242	31·5	29·9	7·7	7·4
1955	267	252	31·3	30·3	7·9	7·5
1956	268	253	31·7	30·1	7·6	7·2
1957	266	248	31·6	29·5	7·9	7·3
1958	271	256	31·8	30·3	7·9	7·2
1959	270	258	32·5	30·6	8·0	7·4
1960	269	257	31·7	30·1	7·9	7·4
1961	281	271	32·8	31·1	8·4	7·7
1962	285	272	32·7	30·5	7·9	7·3
1963	292	280	34·1	31·4	8·3	7·6
1964	275	260	31·8	29·3	8·0	7·3
1965	282	267	32·6	30·3	8·2	7·4

Population and Vital Statistics 10. Crude Death Rates and Infant Mortality – England & Wales, Scotland, and Northern Ireland 1938–65

NOTE
SOURCES: *Registrar General's Statistical Review for England & Wales*; *Annual Report of the Registrar General for Scotland*; and *for Northern Ireland.*

	Deaths per Thousand Persons			Deaths per Thousand Males			Deaths per Thousand Females			Deaths of Infants under One Year per Thousand Live Births		
	England & Wales	Scotland	N. Ireland	England & Wales	Scotland	N. Ireland	England & Wales	Scotland	N. Ireland	England & Wales	Scotland	N. Ireland
1938	11·6	12·6	13·7	12·5	13·2	14·0	10·8	12·0	13·5	53	70	75
1939	12·1	12·9	13·5	13·0	13·7	13·9	11·3	12·1	13·2	51	69	71
1940	14·4	14·9	14·6	16·1	16·6	15·2	12·9	13·4	14·1	57	78	86
1941	13·5	14·7	15·2	15·7	16·7	15·6	11·8	13·1	14·9	60	83	77
1942	12·3	13·3	13·3	14·4	15·2	14·0	10·7	11·8	12·7	51	69	76
1943	13·0	14·0	13·4	15·3	15·9	13·9	11·3	12·4	12·9	49	65	78
1944	12·7	13·6	12·8	15·3	15·7	13·2	10·8	12·0	12·4	45	65	67
1945	12·6	13·2	12·3	15·0	15·1	12·6	10·8	11·7	12·1	46	56	68
1946	12·0	13·1	12·5	13·4	14·1	13·0	10·9	12·1	12·1	43	54	54
1947	12·3	13·1	12·6	13·6	13·9	13·2	11·3	12·3	12·1	41	56	53
1948	11·0	12·0	11·2	11·9	12·7	11·7	10·1	11·4	10·7	34	45	46
1949	11·8	12·5	11·5	12·6	13·0	12·0	11·1	11·9	11·1	32	41	45
1950	11·6	12·5	11·6	12·3	13·1	12·1	11·0	12·0	11·1	30	39	41
1951	12·5	12·9	12·8	13·4	13·6	13·3	11·8	12·3	12·4	30	37	41
1952	11·3	12·1	10·8	12·2	12·9	11·4	10·5	11·3	10·1	28	35	39
1953	11·4	11·5	10·7	12·2	12·5	11·4	10·7	10·7	10·1	27	31	38
1954	11·3	12·0	10·9	12·2	12·9	11·5	10·5	11·2	10·4	25	31	33
1955	11·7	12·1	11·1	12·5	12·8	11·6	10·9	11·4	10·6	25	30	32
1956	11·7	12·1	10·6	12·5	12·9	11·2	10·9	11·3	10·1	24	29	29
1957	11·5	11·9	10·9	12·3	12·9	11·6	10·7	11·0	10·1	23	29	29
1958	11·7	12·1	10·8	12·4	12·9	11·6	11·0	11·3	10·0	23	28	28
1959	11·6	12·2	10·9	12·3	13·1	11·6	11·0	11·4	10·3	22	28	28
1960	11·5	11·9	10·8	12·2	12·8	11·4	10·9	11·2	10·2	22	26	27
1961	11·9	12·3	11·3	12·6	13·2	12·1	11·4	11·5	10·5	21	26	27
1962	11·9	12·2	10·6	12·6	13·1	11·3	11·3	11·3	9·9	22	27	27
1963	12·2	12·6	11·0	12·8	13·6	11·8	11·6	11·6	10·2	21	26	27
1964	11·3	11·7	10·5	11·9	12·7	11·3	10·7	10·8	9·8	20	24	26
1965	11·5	12·1	10·6	12·2	13·0	11·4	10·9	11·2	9·8	19	23	25

Population and Vital Statistics 11. Death Rates per 1,000 in Different Age-Groups – England & Wales 1938–65

NOTE

SOURCE: *The Registrar General's Statistical Review of England & Wales.*

A. Males

	0–1 (a)	1–4	5–9	10–14	15–19	20–24	25–34	35–44	45–54	55–64	65–74	75–84	85 and over
1938	60	4·9	1·9	1·3	2·0	2·7	2·8	4·6	10·2	23·1	53·7	130·1	263·6
1939 (b)	56	3·7	1·7	1·1	1·9	2·6	2·7	4·4	10·3	24·3	55·4	139·1	280·8
1940 (b)	64	5·2	2·1	1·5	2·8	4·8	4·1	5·8	12·5	28·3	61·3	151·8	303·2
1941 (b)	67	5·6	2·3	1·5	2·9	5·6	4·6	5·6	11·0	25·1	55·2	134·6	258·8
1942 (b)	57	3·7	1·7	1·2	2·1	4·8	3·9	4·7	9·6	22·4	51·2	120·7	232·9
1943 (b)	55	3·5	1·6	1·1	2·1	5·0	4·0	4·8	10·0	22·8	51·4	122·6	234·1
1944 (b)	50	3·1	1·6	1·2	2·0	4·8	4·3	4·8	9·6	22·7	50·6	116·5	212·0
1945 (b)	51	2·8	1·4	1·0	1·8	4·8	3·8	4·2	9·1	22·3	50·3	115·7	204·7
1946 (b)	48	2·3	1·0	0·9	1·5	2·7	2·2	3·6	8·9	22·3	49·7	117·4	232·3
1947 (b)	46	2·4	1·0	0·8	1·6	2·1	2·1	3·4	9·0	22·9	52·5	125·9	266·5
1948 (b)	38	1·9	0·9	0·6	1·3	1·5	1·9	3·2	8·2	21·6	49·0	108·6	210·2
1949 (b)	36	1·7	0·8	0·6	1·3	1·6	1·8	3·1	8·4	22·6	53·2	120·7	249·0
1950	34	1·4	0·8	0·6	1·0	1·4	1·7	2·9	8·3	22·5	53·3	122·5	250·4
1951	34	1·4	0·7	0·6	0·9	1·4	1·6	3·0	8·6	24·3	58·8	136·9	307·8
1952	31	1·3	0·6	0·5	0·9	1·3	1·4	2·8	7·9	22·2	53·1	122·1	265·1
1953	30	1·3	0·6	0·5	0·8	1·2	1·4	2·6	7·8	22·2	53·7	123·4	258·1
1954	29	1·1	0·5	0·4	0·8	1·1	1·3	2·7	7·7	21·9	53·3	123·0	249·6
1955	28	1·0	0·5	0·5	0·9	1·2	1·3	2·5	7·7	22·0	54·2	128·5	256·2
1956	27	1·0	0·5	0·4	0·8	1·1	1·2	2·5	7·5	22·1	54·2	127·5	256·2
1957	26	1·0	0·5	0·4	0·9	1·2	1·2	2·5	7·5	22·3	54·0	119·9	226·8
1958	25	1·0	0·5	0·4	0·8	1·1	1·2	2·4	7·4	21·9	54·3	124·6	242·6
1959	25	1·0	0·5	0·4	0·9	1·1	1·1	2·4	7·2	21·8	53·6	122·2	240·0
1960	25	1·0	0·5	0·4	0·9	1·2	1·1	2·4	7·2	21·4	52·5	119·6	232·1
1961	24	1·0	0·5	0·4	0·9	1·1	1·2	2·4	7·3	21·9	54·7	124·5	256·9
1962	24	0·9	0·4	0·4	0·9	1·1	1·1	2·4	7·3	22·1	55·3	125·2	261·1
1963	24	1·0	0·5	0·4	0·9	1·1	1·1	2·5	7·5	22·4	56·0	129·4	272·8
1964	22	0·9	0·5	0·4	1·0	1·1	1·1	2·5	7·3	21·3	52·0	115·8	234·0
1965	21	0·9	0·5	0·4	1·0	1·1	1·1	2·5	7·4	21·4	53·0	118·4	242·4

See p. 26 for footnotes.

B. Females

	0–1 (a)	1–4	5–9	10–14	15–19	20–24	25–34	35–44	45–54	55–64	65–74	75–84	85 and over
1938	46	4·3	1·8	1·1	1·7	2·3	2·5	3·6	7·0	15·5	38·8	98·1	228·9
1939	44	3·3	1·3	1·0	1·6	2·3	2·5	3·5	7·1	15·7	40·5	106·2	251·1
1940	49	4·5	1·8	1·3	2·3	2·9	2·9	4·1	8·0	17·7	45·0	116·4	267·5
1941 (c)	52	5·0	1·9	1·2	2·3	2·8	2·9	3·8	7·3	15·4	39·5	101·5	241·7
1942 (c)	44	3·2	1·3	0·9	1·7	2·4	2·4	3·2	6·4	13·9	35·4	91·0	209·2
1943 (c)	43	3·2	1·2	1·0	1·7	2·4	2·5	3·3	6·4	13·9	36·4	95·9	213·5
1944 (c)	40	2·6	1·2	0·9	1·6	2·4	2·4	3·1	6·2	13·4	34·6	89·7	188·8
1945 (c)	40	2·4	1·0	0·8	1·4	2·1	2·1	2·9	5·9	13·3	34·6	90·2	189·5
1946 (c)	37	1·9	0·8	0·7	1·2	1·8	2·0	2·8	5·8	13·3	34·6	92·4	206·2
1947 (c)	36	2·0	0·8	0·6	1·2	1·8	1·9	2·7	5·7	13·1	35·2	96·6	219·8
1948 (c)	30	1·6	0·6	0·6	1·1	1·6	1·8	2·5	5·3	12·2	32·1	84·5	183·5
1949 (c)	28	1·4	0·6	0·5	1·0	1·4	1·7	2·5	5·4	12·8	35·5	95·8	217·5
1950	26	1·3	0·5	0·4	0·8	1·1	1·5	2·3	5·3	12·6	34·7	96·6	216·9
1951	26	1·3	0·5	0·4	0·6	0·9	1·3	2·3	5·3	13·0	36·9	104·4	249·1
1952	24	1·0	0·4	0·3	0·5	0·8	1·1	2·1	4·9	11·9	32·3	89·6	212·3
1953	24	1·1	0·4	0·4	0·5	0·7	1·1	2·1	4·8	11·6	32·1	90·7	218·8
1954	22	0·8	0·3	0·3	0·5	0·6	1·0	2·1	4·8	11·4	31·6	87·4	209·7
1955	21	1·0	0·4	0·3	0·4	0·6	0·9	1·9	4·7	11·3	32·3	90·9	222·9
1956	20	0·8	0·3	0·3	0·4	0·5	0·9	1·9	4·5	11·2	31·8	90·1	222·7
1957	20	0·9	0·3	0·3	0·5	0·5	0·9	1·9	4·6	11·2	30·9	84·2	199·2
1958	20	0·8	0·3	0·2	0·4	0·5	0·8	1·8	4·5	10·9	30·9	87·5	215·6
1959	20	0·8	0·3	0·3	0·4	0·5	0·8	1·8	4·4	10·8	30·5	86·3	215·4
1960	19	0·8	0·3	0·3	0·4	0·4	0·7	1·7	4·4	10·6	29·5	84·4	210·4
1961	19	0·8	0·3	0·3	0·4	0·5	0·7	1·8	4·5	10·8	30·9	87·8	214·1
1962	19	0·8	0·3	0·3	0·4	0·5	0·8	1·8	4·4	10·8	30·2	86·9	213·8
1963	18	0·8	0·3	0·2	0·4	0·4	0·7	1·8	4·5	10·9	30·7	88·7	220·2
1964	17	0·7	0·3	0·3	0·4	0·5	0·7	1·8	4·4	10·3	28·2	78·8	190·3
1965	16	0·8	0·3	0·3	0·4	0·5	0·7	1·8	4·4	10·3	28·3	79·2	197·1

(a) Per 1,000 live births.
(b) Civilian mortality only from 3 September 1939 to 31 December 1949.

(c) Civilian mortality only from 1 June 1941 to 31 December 1949.

Population and Vital Statistics 12. Death Rates per 1,000 in Different Age-Groups – Scotland 1938–65

NOTE
SOURCE: *Annual Report of the Registrar General for Scotland.*

A. Males

	0–1	1–4	5–9	10–14	15–24	25–34	35–44	45–54	55–64	65–74	75–84	85 and over
1938	81·6	7·0	1·9	1·4	2·5	3·2	5·6	11·6	23·8	57·0	137·7	319·9
1939	82·1	4·8	1·9	1·4	2·5	3·2	5·6	12·0	25·2	59·5	146·1	356·2
1940 (a)	95·0	7·0	2·4	1·5	3·3	4·1	6·6	13·2	27·8	63·6	156·1	408·7
1941 (a)	100·5	6·5	2·5	1·7	3·7	4·9	6·8	13·3	26·6	58·4	146·3	299·0
1942 (a)	85·4	4·6	1·7	1·4	3·3	4·0	5·8	11·9	23·9	54·0	132·4	278·3
1943 (a)	79·1	4·4	1·9	1·4	3·5	4·4	6·3	11·6	23·9	53·8	131·0	300·7
1944 (a)	80·5	4·0	1·8	1·4	3·2	3·8	5·8	11·0	24·1	52·5	121·3	289·3
1945 (a)	65·0	3·5	1·5	1·2	2·9	4·1	5·6	10·8	23·7	51·6	118·2	284·9
1946 (a)	73·2	3·5	1·4	1·1	2·3	2·6	4·8	11·4	24·4	54·4	121·2	279·3
1947	66·7	3·2	1·4	0·9	2·1	2·6	4·4	11·1	25·0	55·1	135·0	295·0
1948	53·7	2·6	1·1	1·0	1·9	2·5	4·2	10·1	24·1	51·3	120·1	257·4
1949	47·9	2·2	1·1	0·8	1·8	2·3	4·1	10·2	25·1	55·2	128·0	272·5
1950	45·1	2·1	0·8	0·6	1·5	2·0	3·7	10·3	26·0	56·3	132·4	280·1
1951	43·5	1·8	0·9	0·5	1·3	2·1	3·6	10·4	26·4	59·0	140·0	298·4
1952	41·7	1·6	0·8	0·5	1·2	1·8	3·3	9·7	25·3	56·6	131·4	270·8
1953	36·6	1·5	0·8	0·6	1·2	1·8	3·5	9·1	24·9	55·6	122·6	242·4
1954	36·7	1·5	0·6	0·4	1·1	1·7	3·2	9·5	26·1	56·4	129·1	274·2
1955	34·9	1·4	0·6	0·5	1·0	1·6	3·3	9·5	25·2	57·2	127·5	280·5
1956	34·3	1·2	0·5	0·5	1·0	1·6	3·1	9·2	25·2	59·1	129·9	277·6
1957	34·8	1·3	0·7	0·5	1·0	1·5	3·1	9·5	25·6	57·8	123·6	269·8
1958	32·5	1·0	0·5	0·5	1·0	1·4	3·2	9·0	24·9	59·6	127·1	272·8
1959	33·4	1·3	0·5	0·5	0·9	1·4	3·1	9·2	25·5	60·1	131·7	274·8
1960	31·5	1·2	0·6	0·5	0·9	1·5	2·9	9·1	25·1	58·0	126·2	250·5
1961	30·6	1·2	0·6	0·4	1·0	1·4	3·2	9·1	26·1	59·4	131·5	275·8
1962	32·7	1·1	0·5	0·5	0·9	1·4	3·3	9·2	25·4	59·6	129·6	266·2
1963	29·6	1·2	0·6	0·5	0·9	1·4	3·3	9·6	26·8	62·6	137·1	279·2
1964	28·5	0·9	0·5	0·4	0·9	1·2	3·2	9·3	25·7	58·2	121·1	250·4
1965	26·1	1·0	0·6	0·5	1·0	1·3	3·1	9·2	25·7	68·1	126·3	267·4

See p. 28 for footnote.

B. Females

	0–1	1–4	5–9	10–14	15–24	25–34	35–44	45–54	55–64	65–74	75–84	85 and over
1938	65·7	6·2	1·9	1·3	2·5	3·0	4·4	8·3	18·2	45·2	108·6	261·0
1939	61·5	4·1	1·7	1·1	2·3	3·0	4·3	8·5	17·8	45·6	114·9	281·2
1940 (a)	68·3	6·4	2·1	1·3	2·7	3·3	4·6	8·5	19·7	48·6	122·3	317·3
1941 (a)	75·8	6·6	2·0	1·6	3·2	3·5	4·6	8·5	18·0	45·3	113·4	274·5
1942 (a)	65·2	4·1	1·4	1·2	3·0	3·3	4·0	7·2	16·5	40·3	100·7	246·7
1943 (a)	60·9	3·9	1·6	1·2	3·2	3·3	4·1	7·5	17·0	40·9	100·0	272·9
1944 (a)	60·8	3·2	1·4	1·1	2·9	3·1	3·7	7·1	15·7	38·9	97·3	256·3
1945 (a)	47·2	3·0	1·1	1·0	2·6	3·1	3·5	7·0	15·4	39·8	95·8	257·3
1946 (a)	56·5	2·8	1·1	0·9	2·4	3·3	3·4	6·8	15·8	40·7	98·1	271·0
1947	50·8	2·9	1·1	1·0	2·5	2·9	3·4	6·7	15·8	40·5	104·3	253·3
1948	38·7	2·0	0·9	0·9	2·4	2·7	3·3	6·6	15·0	38·5	98·2	218·4
1949	37·5	1·9	0·7	0·6	2·2	2·6	3·2	6·6	15·4	41·5	107·1	233·0
1950	34·9	1·6	0·6	0·4	1·6	2·3	3·1	6·4	15·8	41·4	109·6	244·6
1951	33·2	1·6	0·6	0·5	1·2	1·9	3·0	6·3	15·6	43·5	115·6	267·9
1952	32·5	1·4	0·5	0·4	1·0	1·6	2·7	6·1	14·6	40·3	102·6	234·1
1953	27·6	1·3	0·5	0·4	0·8	1·4	2·6	6·0	13·5	36·9	98·4	221·8
1954	28·0	1·1	0·4	0·4	0·7	1·3	2·6	6·2	14·4	37·5	103·0	233·9
1955	28·5	1·0	0·5	0·4	0·6	1·3	2·4	5·6	14·1	39·1	103·8	248·1
1956	25·4	1·0	0·4	0·3	0·5	1·1	2·2	5·5	13·8	38·1	103·2	249·7
1957	26·1	0·8	0·4	0·4	0·5	1·0	2·5	5·4	13·6	36·8	95·8	239·0
1958	25·4	0·9	0·3	0·3	0·5	1·1	2·4	5·5	13·6	37·0	100·1	238·5
1959	25·1	1·1	0·3	0·3	0·5	0·9	2·3	5·2	13·7	37·0	100·5	245·2
1960	24·4	0·9	0·5	0·3	0·5	0·9	2·2	5·2	12·9	36·2	97·3	228·1
1961	22·8	0·9	0·3	0·3	0·4	0·8	2·2	5·5	13·4	36·7	100·3	232·9
1962	22·8	1·0	0·4	0·3	0·4	0·9	2·2	5·3	13·2	35·0	97·0	223·3
1963	23·0	0·9	0·3	0·2	0·4	1·0	2·3	5·5	13·7	35·9	98·5	225·3
1964	22·0	0·9	0·3	0·3	0·4	0·8	2·0	5·5	12·7	33·9	86·0	204·4
1965	20·8	0·8	0·3	0·3	0·5	0·8	2·2	5·3	12·7	34·2	89·6	215·3

(a) Civilians only.

Population and Vital Statistics 13. Death Rates per 1,000 in Different Age-Groups – Northern Ireland 1950–2 to 1965–7

NOTES

[1] SOURCES: Census *Reports* for Northern Ireland, 1951, 1961, and 1966; and *Annual Reports of the Registrar General for Northern Ireland*.

[2] All figures are obtained by dividing the census population of each age-group into the average yearly number of deaths in the census years and the years on each side of that.

A. Males

	1950–2	1960–2	1965–7
0–4	10·8	6·6	5·5
5–9	0·8	0·6	0·5
10–14	0·6	0·4	0·4
15–19	0·9	0·8	0·8
20–24	1·6	1·0	1·1
25–34	1·9	1·2	1·1
35–44	3·6	2·5	2·8
45–54	9·0	7·6	7·5
55–64	21·9	22·2	21·7
65–74	53·1	50·9	51·2
75–84	118·3	118·4	113·7
85 and over	243·8	255·0	241·0

B. Females

	1950–2	1960–2	1965–7
0–4	8·6	5·2	4·8
5–9	0·5	0·3	0·3
10–14	0·6	0·2	0·2
15–19	0·7	0·5	0·4
20–24	1·1	0·6	0·4
25–34	1·8	0·8	0·8
35–44	2·9	1·9	1·9
45–54	6·4	5·0	4·6
55–64	15·7	11·8	11·1
65–74	41·2	34·9	31·3
75–84	107·8	96·3	85·1
85 and over	225·4	221·3	197·6

Population and Vital Statistics 14. Marriages and Marriage Rates – England & Wales, Scotland, and Northern Ireland 1938–65

NOTE

SOURCES: *The Registrar General's Statistical Review of England & Wales*; *Annual Report of the Registrar General for Scotland*; and *for Northern Ireland*.

	Thousands of Marriages			Rate per 1,000 of Population		
	England & Wales	Scotland	Northern Ireland	England & Wales	Scotland	Northern Ireland
1938	362	38·7	8·6	17·6	15·5	13·4
1939	440	46·2	9·2	21·2	18·5	14·2
1940	471	53·5	9·8	22·5	21·2	15·1
1941	389	47·6	12·0	18·6	18·6	18·3
1942	370	47·4	11·7	17·7	18·4	17·6
1943	296	38·2	10·2	14·0	14·8	15·1
1944	303	37·0	9·5	14·3	14·3	14·0
1945	398	48·6	10·5	18·7	18·9	15·4
1946	386	45·8	9·8	18·1	17·8	14·5
1947	401	44·4	9·5	18·6	17·5	14·1
1948	397	43·7	9·4	18·2	17·2	13·8
1949	375	41·7	9·2	17·1	16·4	13·4
1950	358	40·5	9·1	16·3	15·8	13·3
1951	361	41·4	9·4	16·5	16·2	13·7
1952	349	41·2	9·3	15·9	16·1	13·5
1953	345	40·9	9·4	15·6	16·0	13·6
1954	342	42·0	9·2	15·4	16·4	13·2
1955	358	43·2	9·5	16·1	16·9	13·7
1956	353	44·0	9·4	15·8	17·2	13·4
1957	347	42·7	9·4	15·4	16·7	13·4
1958	340	41·2	9·3	15·1	16·0	13·2
1959	340	40·4	9·6	15·0	15·7	13·7
1960	344	40·1	9·9	15·0	15·5	13·9
1961	347	40·6	9·9	15·0	15·7	13·8
1962	348	40·2	9·8	14·9	15·5	13·8
1963	351	39·7	10·2	14·9	15·2	14·0
1964	359	40·2	10·6	15·2	15·5	14·6
1965	371	40·5	10·5	15·5	15·6	14·2

Population and Vital Statistics 15. Divorces –
England & Wales 1858–1965, Scotland 1855–1965

NOTES

[1] SOURCES: England & Wales Decrees for Dissolution, 1858–1909 – Appendix III to *Report* of the Royal Commission on Divorce (*S.P.* 1912/13 xx); other figures for England & Wales – *Registrar General's Statistical Review of England & Wales*; Scottish figures – *Annual Reports of the Registrar General for Scotland* (especially that for 1920).

[2] The Registrar General does not give annual figures for England & Wales before 1906, but he does give the following quinquennial averages of divorces and nullity decrees:

1876–80	277·0	1896–1900	490·0
1881–5	335·6	1901–5	563·2
1886–90	353·4		
1891–5	371·8		

	England & Wales Decrees for Dissolution	England & Wales Divorce and Nullity Decrees	Scotland Divorce and Nullity Decrees		England & Wales Decrees for Dissolution	England & Wales Divorce and Nullity Decrees	Scotland Divorce and Nullity Decrees
1855	...	...	11	1895	478	...	117
1856	...	...	16	1896	486	...	133
1857	...	...	18	1897	583	...	142
1858	179	...	12	1898	436	...	135
1859	141	...	24	1899	525	...	176
1860	127	...	23	1900	494	...	144
1861	118	...	27	1901	601	...	158
1862	153	...	26	1902	608	...	204
1863	160	...	9	1903	614	...	194
1864	166	...	2	1904	634	...	182
1865	147	...	4	1905	623	...	167
1866	146	...	4	1906	650	546	173
1867	144	...	5	1907	598	644	200
1868	181	...	13	1908	672	638	189
1869	186	...	7	1909	685	694	192
1870	194	...	17	1910	...	581	223
1871	190	...	11	1911	...	580	234
1872	203	...	12	1912	...	587	249
1873	238	...	25	1913	...	577	250
1874	281	...	38	1914	...	856	347
1875	304	...	33	1915	...	680	242
1876	283	...	40	1916	...	990	267
1877	322	...	29	1917	...	703	297
1878	380	...	66	1918	...	1,111	485
1879	390	...	55	1919	...	1,657	820
1880	340	...	80	1920	...	3,090	776
1881	302	...	71	1921	...	3,522	500
1882	345	...	69	1922	...	2,588	382
1883	361	...	65	1923	...	2,667	363
1884	337	...	87	1924	...	2,286	438
1885	316	...	76	1925	...	2,605	451
1886	387	...	97	1926	...	2,622	425
1887	390	...	80	1927	...	3,190	474
1888	392	...	107	1928	...	4,018	504
1889	370	...	100	1929	...	3,396	519
1890	400	...	87	1930	...	3,563	469
1891	342	...	107	1931	...	3,764	569
1892	354	...	118	1932	...	3,894	488
1893	362	...	112	1933	...	4,042	510
1894	381	...	120	1934	...	4,287	468

	England & Wales Decrees for Dissolution	England & Wales Divorce and Nullity Decrees	Scotland Divorce and Nullity Decrees		England & Wales Decrees for Dissolution	England & Wales Divorce and Nullity Decrees	Scotland Divorce and Nullity Decrees
1935	...	4,069	498	1950		30,870	2,196
1936	...	4,057	642	1951		28,767	1,944
1937	...	4,886	649	1952		33,922	2,718
1938	...	6,250	788	1953		30,326	2,365
1939	...	7,955	884	1954		28,027	2,216
1940	...	7,755	780	1955		26,816	2,073
1941	...	6,368	762	1956		26,265	1,883
1942	...	7,618	1,017	1957		23,785	1,739
1943	...	10,012	1,312	1958		22,654	1,781
1944	...	12,312	1,731	1959		24,286	1,699
1945		15,634	2,223	1960		23,868	1,823
1946		29,829	2,924	1961		25,394	1,825
1947		60,254	2,513	1962		28,935	2,035
1948		43,698	2,047	1963		32,052	2,235
1949		34,856	2,438	1964		34,868	2,446
				1965		37,785	2,688

Population and Vital Statistics 16. Passenger Movement by Sea between the United Kingdom and Non-European Countries – 1938–65

NOTES

[1] SOURCE: *Board of Trade Journal*.

[2] The figures in this table differ from the similar series in the first *Abstract of British Historical Statistics* because of the exclusion in that work of passengers travelling indirectly via continental ports or ports in the Irish Republic, and of passengers on pleasure cruises. Incomplete figures which are directly comparable with those in *Historical Statistics* are as follows:

Passengers to U.K. Ports (thousands)				Passengers from U.K. Ports (thousands)			
1938	244	1946	116	1938	264	1946	214
1939–45	...	1947	182	1939–45	...	1947	245

Passengers to U.K. Ports (thousands)				Passengers from U.K. Ports (thousands)			
1948	231	1954	331	1948	308	1954	373
1949	253	1955	342	1949	318	1955	375
1950	269	1956	325	1950	333	1956	386
1951	271	1957	301	1951	370	1957	392
1952	296	1958	300	1952	390	1958	337
1953	302	1959	312	1953	369	1959	334

[3] The distinction between Commonwealth citizens and aliens cannot be made after 1962 owing to changes in the merchant shipping regulations.

(in thousands)

	Passengers by Sea to the U.K.			Passengers by Sea from the U.K.		
	Total	Commonwealth Citizens	Aliens	Total	Commonwealth Citizens	Aliens
1938	222	160	62	241	162	79
1939–46	...	...	...	...	...	...
1947	181	134	46	244	190	54
1948	230	172	58	307	245	63
1949	252	196	56	316	256	61
1950	262	200	62	325	258	68
1951	265	202	63	363	283	80
1952	290	209	81	383	301	82
1953	292	212	80	359	277	82
1954	316	233	83	359	277	82
1955	327	238	89	361	276	85
1956	318	229	89	380	293	87
1957	288	207	81	379	302	77
1958	290	210	80	326	351	75
1959	289	215	74	311	241	70
1960	303	227	76	290	225	65
	---(a)	---(a)	--(a)	---(a)	---(a)	--(a)
1961	289	223	66	280	220	60
	---(b)	--(b)			---(b)	--(b)
1962	276	200	76	287	216	71
1963	251	...	...	296	...	...
1964	245	...	...	284	...	...
1965	232	...	...	262	...	...

(a) With effect from 1961 countries in Africa and the Middle East which bordered on the Mediterranean Sea were classified as European.

(b) From 1 June 1962 South Africans were classified as aliens instead of Commonwealth citizens.

Population and Vital Statistics 17. Balance of Civilian Passenger Movement by
Sea and Air – United Kingdom 1936–65

NOTE
SOURCE: *Registrar General's Statistical Review of England & Wales.*

(in thousands)

	Non-European Countries		European Countries		
	Total	Citizens of the Commonwealth and Irish Republic (a)	Irish Republic	Others	All Countries
1936	+3·4	+9·8	+29·0	+37·6	+70·0
1937	−8·8	+4·0	+31·2	+33·7	+56·1
1938	−19·9	−2·7	+18·4	+31·3	+29·8
1939–45	...	...	...	...	...
1946	−98·0	−101·0	+3·5	+42·6 (b)	−141·7 (c)
1947	−63·0	−56·0	+16·0	+60·0 (b)	−28·0 (c)
1948	−77·9	−73·1	+21·2	+82·6 (b)	−8·9 (c)
	-----(d)	-----(d)		-----	
1949	−78·0	−68·1	+16·8	+38·9	−22·3
1950	−68·1	−57·9	+11·4	+30·0	−26·7
1951	−117·2	−97·0	+16·3	+10·7	−90·2
1952	−105·3	−92·8 (b)	+30·9	+23·6	−50·8
1953	−76·3	−65·8 (b)	+28·7	+22·7	−24·9
1954	−45·7	−43·6 (b)	+33·8	+30·4	+18·5
1955	−32·0	−37·7 (b)	+44·2	+64·4	+76·6
				-----(e)	
1956	−69·6	−62·9 (b)	+41·7	+83·2	+55·4
1957	−140·6	−95·6 (b)	+51·0	+51·4	−38·2
1958	−43·9	−41·3 (b)	+28·3	+63·8	+48·2
1959	−9·5	−28·7 (b)	+29·6	+51·4	+71·5
1960	+31·8	+2·5 (b)	+34·7	+55·5	+122·0
	——(f)	——(f)	——(f)	——(f)	——(f)
1961	+56·8	+3·7 (b)	+18·3	+94·9	+170·0
		-----(a, b)			
1962	+10·7	−16·2 (a, b)	+11·7	+55·5	+77·9

1963	−57·1	−54·0 (b)	+4·3	+37·7	−15·1
1964	−77·4	−54·1	+11·3	+41·9	−24·3
1965	−82·6	−42·9	+25·6	+43·2	−13·8

(*a*) Excluding South Africans from 1 June 1962.
(*b*) Excluding air passengers.
(*c*) This figure includes air movement which cannot be allocated to specific places.
(*d*) Excludes air passengers prior to 1949.
(*e*) From 1965 includes passenger movement to and from Ferryfield and Lydd airports.

(*f*) From 1961 day trips between the Isle of Man and the Irish Republic, and between England and continental Europe, are excluded; as are movements to and from the Channel Islands. Also from 1961 countries in Africa and the Middle East which bordered the Mediterranean Sea were classified as European.

CHAPTER II

LABOUR FORCE

TABLES

All the tables in this chapter are related to series given in the first *Abstract of British Historical Statistics* (1962), though various changes in classification have made comparability over time a good deal less than perfect. This applies with greatest force, perhaps, to table 1, and the lack of any attempt by the Census officials in 1961 to make comparisons with earlier years on the basis of the current classification of occupations is disappointing. Perfection of definition has proved inimical to long-period comparisons in the past; but with over a century of experience behind them, it is a pity that the Census officials should permit an almost complete break in comparability at this stage. Such comparison as they have provided – on the basis of a very small sample, recoded to the 1951 occupational classification, and for England and Wales only – is shown as Part A of table 1. In Part B the 1961 figures on the latest classificatory basis have to be shown on their own. The 1966 sample Census seems to be virtually worthless for many of the small categories involved.

The remaining tables in this chapter represent but a small selection of the historical statistics available on this subject, and the reader seeking more detail should go to the admirable volume prepared by the Department of Employment and Productivity *British Labour Statistics: Historical Abstract 1886–1968*. None of the series given here seems to call for particular comment beyond that given in the notes, though perhaps one should stress the very complete nature of the break in tables 2 and 4 occasioned by the coming of comprehensive national insurance in 1948.

Labour Force 1. Occupations at Censuses – Great Britain 1951–61

NOTES TO PART A

[1] SOURCE: Census *Report*, 1961 (General Volume).
[2] The new classification of occupations used in 1961 'introduced a number of changes in principle which make it impossible to make direct comparisons even between fairly large aggregates of occupation codes' between 1961 and earlier censuses. The figures shown here result from an attempt to make a comparison between 1951 and 1961 by recording a sub-sample of 100,000 out of the 10 per cent sample part of the 1961 data to the occupation code they would have had in 1951. The 1961 figures were not adjusted for sample bias.

A. Occupations in 1951 and 1961 in England & Wales

(in thousands)

	Males		Females	
	1951	1961	1951	1961
Agriculture, Horticulture, and Forestry	961·3	741·4	97·5	70·8
Fishing	15·2	10·8	—	—
Mining and Quarrying	589·7	469·6	1·3	0·2
Treatment of Non-Metalliferous Mining Products (other than coal)	81·2	76·6	46·4	40·2
Gas and Coke Manufacture, and Chemicals and Allied Trade	93·0	108·8	11·1	10·0
Metal Manufacture, Engineering, and Allied Trades	2,260·2	2,460·6	197·9	199·6
Textiles	197·6	144·6	359·1	245·4
Leather, Leather Goods, and Fur	116·9	83·6	64·9	65·2
Clothing, etc. (other than shoes)	124·2	96·8	437·2	364·4
Food, Drink, and Tobacco	148·9	134·8	83·9	65·6
Wood, Cane, and Cork	433·3	428·4	13·3	12·0
Paper and Printing	161·7	200·8	81·1	84·4
Other Manufactures	84·5	94·2	40·7	43·4
Building and Contracting	840·5	838·2	1·4	1·0
Painting and Decorating	298·6	283·0	10·4	9·2
Administrators, Managers (n.e.s.), and Directors	406·2	525·6	45·9	67·6
Transport and Communications	1,403·7	1,400·4	130·1	147·6
Commerce, Finance, and Insurance (excl. clerical staff)	1,227·5	1,462·4	757·8	910·6
Professional and Technical Occupations (excl. clerical staff)	714·2	1,108·0	523·1	674·6
Armed Forces	527·7	295·4	16·7	11·2
Civilian Defence Services	158·2	190·8	2·9	2·4
Entertainment and Sport	82·1	77·0	21·7	21·8
Personal Service	465·6	492·4	1,464·1	1,555·8
Clerks, Typists, etc.	861·7	956·2	1,270·5	1,725·4
Warehousemen, Storekeeper, Packers, and Bottlers	348·3	398·8	181·2	213·6
Stationary Engine Drivers, Crane Drivers, Tractor Drivers, etc.	225·9	226·0	2·0	1·8
Workers in Unskilled Occupations (not elsewhere specified)	1,118·9	1,193·6	378·4	437·0
Others	116·7	150·2	32·4	64·6

Labour Force 1. *continued*

NOTE TO PART B
SOURCE: Census *Reports*, 1961 (Occupation Volumes).

B. Occupations in Great Britain, 1961

(in thousands)

	Males		Females	
	England & Wales	Scotland	England & Wales	Scotland
Farming and Forestry	739·84	119·37	78·46	10·33
Fishing	14·31	9·42	—	0·02
Mining and Quarrying	457·55	69·16	0·35	0·09
Gas, Coke, and Chemical Manufacture	117·95	11·41	13·33	2·36
Glass and Ceramics	65·85	5·12	35·76	1·07
Furnaces, Forges, Foundries, and Rolling Mills	205·16	25·16	10·24	0·80
Electrical and Electronic Goods	433·31	45·12	54·57	1·38
Engineering and Allied Trades	2,157·06	224·03	252·66	19·56
Woodworking	392·69	52·90	10·53	0·77
Leatherworking	86·51	5·55	62·97	2·05
Textiles	146·70	21·38	252·37	45·32
Clothing	86·04	7·04	361·43	29·22
Food, Drink, and Tobacco	253·28	41·09	88·03	13·88
Paper and Printing	202·87	19·70	100·12	13·23
Other Manufactures	173·76	11·02	118·13	5·23
Construction	513·75	56·31	0·50	0·05
Painting and Decorating	294·38	28·04	11·92	1·51
Drivers of Stationary Engines, Cranes, etc.	280·12	30·44	2·79	0·17
Labourers (not elsewhere specified)	1,100·32	142·58	91·91	5·81
Transport and Communications	1,236·22	147·25	131·35	16·83
Warehousemen, Storekeepers, Packers, and Bottlers	478·25	45·58	274·93	26·60
Clerical Workers	1,045·38	91·74	1,795·97	176·97
Sales Workers	1,165·12	114·23	898·05	112·60
Service, Sport and Recreation	740·28	80·95	1,512·72	161·57
Administrators and Managers	562·63	40·06	38·53	1·89
Professional and Technical Workers and Artists	1,172·77	106·39	707·32	82·37
Armed Forces	295·56	20·85	11·52	0·89
Inadequate Description	231·42	11·50	128·93	3·89
TOTAL POPULATION AGED 15 AND OVER (a)	16,992·30	1,818·49	18,705·94	2,052·37
Total Economically Inactive	2,343·22	235·10	11,660·55	1,315·91

(a) These figures are the sums of the economically active and inactive, and because of sample bias are slightly larger than the recorded totals aged 15 and over.

Labour Force 2. Numbers of Insured Employees (by Industry) – United Kingdom 1938–65

NOTES
[1] SOURCES: *Ministry of Labour Gazette,* and information kindly supplied by the Department of Employment and Productivity from their forthcoming publication *British Labour Statistics: Historical Abstract, 1886–1968.*
[2] All figures include unemployed workers attached to particular industries, and the grand total also includes some unemployed workers not attached to particular industries.
[3] The figures were collected at the following times: 1938–47 – July; 1948 – end June; 1949–65 – June.

A. 1938–47

(in thousands)

	Males					Females				
	1938	1939 (a)	1945	1946	1947	1938	1939 (a)	1945	1946	1947
Agriculture and Forestry	540	533	512	562	574	47	50	143	109	96
Fishing	33	32	11	20	25	1	1	—	—	—
Mining and Quarrying	990	968	776	792	807	6	6	14	13	13
Non-Metalliferous Mining Products other than coal	61	61	40	57	65	3	3	8	7	7
Brick, Tile, Pipe, etc., Making	107	99	30	55	63	7	7	5	6	6
Pottery and Earthenware	36	34	15	23	28	46	45	24	32	36
Glass	43	42	28	37	43	11	11	17	17	15
Chemicals, etc.	185	194	233	218	228	73	77	196	129	113
Metal Manufacture	325	336	283	296	320	20	21	71	56	47
Engineering, Shipbuilding, Electrical Goods, Vehicles, etc.	1,977	2,064	2,373	2,253	2,441	402	419	1,109	712	649
Textiles	459	493	231	292	340	746	732	430	458	480
Leather and Leather Goods	48	48	28	36	44	30	31	22	25	27
Clothing	204	203	110	135	164	492	500	309	364	387
Food, Drink, and Tobacco	356	359	256	304	341	278	283	226	231	231
Woodworking, etc.	230	224	128	179	206	44	43	58	50	44
Paper, Printing, etc.	291	294	148	211	248	199	201	124	144	155
Building and Contracting	1,393	1,417	637	1,036	1,172	15	16	25	26	24
Other Manufactures	105	109	86	138	168	66	69	72	105	113
Gas, Water, and Electricity	215	214	142	191	218	12	12	27	22	19
Transport and Communications	875	863	764	910	978	42	43	190	142	112
Distributive Trades	1,422	1,394	635	827	951	908	924	850	873	862
Commerce, Banking, Finance, and Insurance	186	181	88	136	146	96	99	144	124	127
Miscellaneous Trades and Services	1,115	1,152	1,036	1,262	1,387	841	877	1,319	1,245	1,248
GRAND TOTAL (d)	11,358	11,428	8,602	10,647	11,100	4,385	4,424	5,398	4,925	4,820

See p. 42 for footnotes.

Labour Force 2. *continued*

B. 1948–58, Males

	1948	1949	1950	1951	1952	1953	1954	1955	1956	1957	1958
Agriculture and Forestry	689	682	676	645	600	590	585	576	548	537	523
Fishing	37	36	33	32	32	30	29	27	27	26	26
Mining and Quarrying	872	871	847	847	862	865	855	849	845	854	841
Bricks and Fireclay Goods	71	74	76	75	78	79	79	77	76	75	70
Pottery and Earthenware	34	35	37	36	36	34	34	34	34	31	31
Glass	50	52	53	55	53	50	52	55	56	58	58
Other Non-Metalliferous Mining Products	85	84	87	90	92	94	96	98	98	98	96
Chemicals, etc.	314	322	336	345	354	351	357	370	377	384	393
Metal Manufacture	475	480	485	488	495	490	489	503	514	517	511
Engineering, Ship-building, and Electrical Goods	1,465	1,473	1,475	1,490	1,547	1,558	1,583	1,639	1,682	1,706	1,731
Vehicles	828	844	864	884	931	952	995	1,035	1,058	1,038	1,055
Metal Goods not elsewhere specified	330	327	321	323	323	316	314	326	331	335	337
Precision Instruments, Jewellery, etc.	83	85	88	88	85	85	86	90	92	93	93
Textiles	412	429	456	461	420	433	443	432	423	428	414
Leather, Leather Goods, and Fur	51	49	49	48	43	44	43	43	40	40	39
Clothing	191	198	198	201	190	192	192	187	184	188	180
Food, Drink, and Tobacco	448	468	481	487	491	499	503	506	511	514	530
Manufactures of Wood and Cork	237	245	251	251	240	241	242	244	235	234	231
Paper and Printing	296	310	325	328	332	328	341	354	362	373	378
Other Manufacturing Industries	146	142	147	156	150	150	158	167	169	173	176
Building and Contracting	1,335	1,321	1,325	1,314	1,313	1,330	1,341	1,357	1,397	1,389	1,363
Gas, Water, and Electricity	302	311	329	333	343	343	343	346	345	347	345
Transport and Communications	1,563	1,553	1,559	1,517	1,527	1,502	1,486	1,473	1,478	1,480	1,474
Distributive Trades	1,096	1,124	1,135	1,132	1,135	1,143	1,165	1,183	1,203	1,235	1,247
Insurance, Banking, and Finance	268	281	277	273	274	273	278	282	282	290	294
Public Administration (b)	1,013	1,029	1,025	1,008	1,009	1,013	1,014	985	988	988	987
Professional Services	474	477	512	529	548	552	567	573	594	614	632
Miscellaneous Services	503	486	469	459	449	451	442	431	427	429	435
GRAND TOTAL (d)	13,778	13,828	13,937	13,906	13,966	14,001	14,123	14,224	14,389	14,487	14,512

See p. 42 for footnotes.

C. 1948–58, Females

	1948	1949	1950	1951	1952	1953	1954	1955	1956	1957	1958
Agriculture and Forestry	128	114	112	105	103	103	100	100	97	98	94
Fishing	1	1	1	1	1	1	1	1	1	- -	- -
Mining and Quarrying	16	17	18	18	19	20	20	21	21	28	24
Bricks and Fireclay Goods	7	7	8	8	9	9	9	9	9	8	8
Pottery and Earthenware	42	43	45	45	46	45	44	45	44	40	39
Glass	18	17	18	19	19	17	18	20	19	19	19
Other Non-Metalliferous Mining Products	12	12	12	13	13	13	13	14	14	14	13
Chemicals, etc.	133	136	139	141	142	142	147	151	154	154	151
Metal Manufacture	62	61	63	66	68	66	67	71	70	68	66
Engineering, Ship-building, and Electrical Goods	385	365	376	405	434	411	430	480	477	477	475
Vehicles	131	130	138	148	159	162	170	183	184	178	180
Metal Goods not else-where specified	181	172	180	190	189	176	181	193	191	185	180
Precision Instruments, Jewellery, etc.	47	49	52	51	50	51	54	58	57	57	58
Textiles	589	612	633	650	587	612	625	600	584	581	538
Leather, Leather Goods, and Fur	29	28	29	31	28	30	30	31	29	29	27
Clothing	447	476	504	505	475	496	496	486	492	488	468
Food, Drink, and Tobacco	308	327	338	356	367	376	387	400	407	405	409
Manufactures of Wood and Cork	57	58	60	62	59	60	62	65	64	63	62
Paper and Printing	176	182	194	200	194	187	198	205	210	211	209
Other Manufacturing Industries	102	104	108	118	106	108	118	122	119	118	116
Building and Contracting	40	38	38	40	46	48	50	52	60	63	65
Gas, Water, and Electricity	27	30	34	37	38	38	39	40	41	42	42
Transport and Communications	235	230	233	241	252	248	249	252	259	256	252
Distributive Trades	972	1,014	1,021	1,049	1,083	1,126	1,176	1,216	1,259	1,306	1,301
Insurance, Banking and Finance	164	162	161	169	174	179	188	194	203	211	215
Public Administration (b)	424	420	398	394	387	369	369	357	365	371	376
Professional Services	852	868	945	963	993	1,014	1,052	1,088	1,127	1,161	1,192
Miscellaneous Services	1,366	1,281	1,259	1,230	1,228	1,223	1,227	1,223	1,220	1,199	1,192
GRAND TOTAL (d)	6,954	6,954	7,118	7,271	7,286	7,351	7,535	7,689	7,791	7,848	7,778

See p. 42 for footnotes.

D. 1959–65

	Males						
	1959	1960	1961	1962	1963 (c)	1964	1965
Agriculture and Forestry	526	504	480	461	463	439	401
Fishing	27	26	25	26	25	24	23
Mining and Quarrying	817	752	718	698	673	645	611
Bricks, Fireclay, and Refractory Goods	69	71	72	71	68	69	68
Pottery	30	30	29	31	30	30	30
Glass	58	58	59	60	59	60	60
Other Non-Metalliferous Mining Products	98	105	109	112	112	120	124
Chemicals, etc.	379	387	388	381	379	374	379
Metal Manufacture	511	547	561	531	529	552	560
Engineering and Electrical Goods	1,441	1,508	1,583	1,617	1,596	1,617	1,675
Shipbuilding and Marine Engineering	292	278	263	251	230	216	212
Vehicles	759	800	780	771	765	765	758
Metal Goods not elsewhere specified	332	353	366	368	371	378	391
Textiles	403	405	402	396	393	395	391
Leather, Leather Goods, and Fur	38	37	37	37	37	37	36
Clothing	154	156	159	155	151	148	146
Food, Drink, and Tobacco	467	468	475	488	488	485	490
Timber, Furniture, etc.	230	236	234	235	234	238	244
Paper, Printing, and Publishing	374	393	402	409	414	415	421
Other Manufacturing Industries	171	182	184	188	192	199	206
Construction	1,414	1,436	1,480	1,533	1,576	1,628	1,657
Gas, Water, and Electricity	342	337	344	351	359	363	367
Transport and Communications	1,451	1,433	1,445	1,460	1,449	1,431	1,414
Distributive Trades	1,373	1,390	1,384	1,421	1,447	1,441	1,429
Insurance, Banking, and Finance	311	313	321	329	342	352	357
Public Administration	954	947	952	974	1,016	960	966
Professional and Scientific Services	668	680	711	745	771	799	833
Miscellaneous Services	834	840	857	904	932	962	976
GRAND TOTAL (d)	14,565	14,719	14,869	15,064	15,144	15,163	15,243

See p. 42 for footnotes.

D. 1959–65 *(cont.)*

	Females							
	1959	1960	1961	1962	1963	(c)	1964	1965
Agriculture and Forestry	94	93	90	90	93		89	84
Fishing	- -	1	1	1	1		- -	- -
Mining and Quarrying	25	23	24	23	22		23	23
Bricks, Fireclay, and Refractory Goods	7	7	8	7	7		7	7
Pottery	38	38	39	38	36		37	35
Glass	18	19	19	20	19		20	20
Other Non-Metalliferous Mining Products	15	16	16	17	16		17	18
Chemicals, etc.	145	148	147	143	142		143	145
Metal Manufacture	72	76	77	74	74		76	77
Engineering and Electrical Goods	508	555	573	582	582		614	628
Shipbuilding and Marine Engineering	14	14	13	13	12		12	12
Vehicles	118	124	122	119	118		119	117
Metal Goods not elsewhere specified	183	198	199	193	189		200	205
Textiles	515	512	501	469	454		450	438
Leather, Leather Goods, and Fur	27	27	27	27	27		27	26
Clothing	426	441	441	440	427		423	417
Food, Drink, and Tobacco	358	360	366	369	362		361	359
Timber, Furniture, etc.	59	61	61	59	57		59	61
Paper, Printing, and Publishing	205	214	219	223	218		219	222
Other Manufacturing Industries	113	123	126	123	124		128	133
Construction	66	70	76	81	82		83	89
Gas, Water, and Electricity	43	44	45	47	49		51	54
Transport and Communications	249	252	263	264	259		258	264
Distributive Trades	1,430	1,480	1,508	1,554	1,576		1,597	1,627
Insurance, Banking, and Finance	228	237	247	260	275		286	295
Public Administration	350	356	371	382	394		381	389
Professional and Scientific Services	1,302	1,345	1,393	1,458	1,505		1,575	1,638
Miscellaneous Services	1,208	1,196	1,189	1,226	1,224		1,275	1,283
GRAND TOTAL (d)	7,864	8,098	8,242	8,368	8,414		8,543	8,677

(a) As from 1940 women aged 60–64 ceased to be included in the statistics, whilst non-manual workers earning from £250 to £420 per year were included.

(b) The estimates for 1948 and 1949 do not include civil servants stationed overseas.

(c) The estimates for 1964 and 1965 were calculated by a revised method which was described in the *Ministry of Labour Gazette* (March and May 1966). The totals for 1950–1964 were recalculated by this method, and the revised totals are shown here. This was not done, however, for the individual industries for the period before 1964. The break between 1963

and 1964 is negligible except in the case of some of the larger industrial groups for females. Figures for these on the un-revised basis for the year 1964 are as follows:

Engineering and Electrical Goods	611
Textiles	447
Distributive Trades	1,587
Professional and Scientific Services	1,564
Miscellaneous Services	1,268

(d) This includes some unspecified workers not included in the individual items.

Labour Force 3. Total Numbers Registered as Unemployed – Great Britain 1939–65

NOTES

[1]   SOURCE: *Ministry of Labour Gazette.*

[2]   The figures are averages of twelve-monthly figures in each year.

(in thousands)

| | Wholly Unemployed | | Temporarily Stopped | | |
	Males	Females	Males	Females	Total
1939	982·9	315·0	137·2	78·5	1,513·6
1940	507·7 (a)	295·2	100·6 (a)	59·2	962·7 (a)
1941	153·2	139·2	29·3	28·1	349·8
1942	74·0	43·2	3·2	2·8	123·2
1943	53·1	26·9	0·8	0·8	81·6
1944	50·7	22·9	0·4	0·5	74·5
1945	83·7	52·1	0·6	0·7	137·1
1946	257·5	113·5	2·1	1·2	374·3
1947	239·0	86·5	102·7	52·0	480·2
1948	227·5	75·0	4·3	3·2	310·0
1949	223·2	76·9	4·8	3·1	308·0
1950	215·0	90·6	5·1	3·5	314·2
1951	153·4	83·6	8·1	7·8	252·9
1952	196·1	132·6	31·8	53·8	414·3
1953	204·3	115·6	13·9	8·2	342·0
1954	176·5	95·1	7·9	5·3	284·8
1955	137·4	75·7	9·3	9·8	232·2
1956	151·0	78·6	17·8	9·6	257·0
1957	204·3	90·2	12·3	5·7	312·5
1958	293·8	116·3	27·6	19·7	457·4
1959	322·6	121·9	21·2	9·5	475·2
1960	248·3	97·6	11·5	3·0	360·4
1961	226·3	85·8	23·3	5·3	340·7
1962	321·9	110·0	22·9	8·3	463·2
1963	393·8	126·7	46·2	6·4	573·2
1964	279·6	92·6	6·6	1·8	380·6
1965	240·6	76·4	9·7	2·1	328·8

(a) After July 1940 men at Government Training Centres were no longer regarded as unemployed.

44

Labour Force 4. Unemployment among Insured Persons (by Industry) – United Kingdom 1938–65

NOTES

[1] SOURCE: *Ministry of Labour Gazette.*
[2] The figures include both wholly unemployed and temporarily stopped.

[3] The figures are for mid-July up to 1948, and for mid-June subsequently, i.e. they are at the closest possible date to the employment figures given in table 2.

A. 1938–47

	Males					Females				
	1938	1939	1945	1946	1947	1938	1939	1945	1946	1947
Agriculture and Forestry	28,091	27,171	1,739	4,092	4,446	2,775	3,189	410	747	641
Fishing	5,813	5,755	176	643	755	106	120	3	1	2
Mining and Quarrying	203,018	122,351	7,175	13,995	1,820	707	570	47	295	151
Non-Metalliferous Mining Products	6,549	5,260	252	1,020	905	232	167	34	162	134
Brick, Tile, Pipe, etc., Making	8,194	8,368	200	877	813	733	867	28	115	138
Pottery and Earthenware	5,866	4,743	97	335	302	8,580	8,049	43	108	100
Glass	6,059	5,136	135	621	588	904	684	86	387	498
Chemicals, etc.	13,087	10,541	4,014	14,099	6,652	2,878	2,660	6,902	11,508	4,644
Metal Manufacture	71,792	28,978	1,804	5,683	6,493	2,239	1,030	982	3,562	2,611
Engineering, Shipbuilding and Repairing, and Metal Trades	223,101	130,691	24,328	67,353	42,905	35,094	21,021	13,083	20,231	11,093
Textiles	97,892	50,539	1,801	6,603	5,031	182,439	83,580	1,838	3,619	2,919
Leather and Leather Goods	6,416	3,806	129	683	516	2,930	2,150	56	248	240
Clothing	28,803	19,546	492	1,973	3,076	54,752	28,468	1,041	2,765	3,294
Food, Drink, and Tobacco	26,259	23,845	1,760	6,552	4,412	21,328	23,860	1,183	3,671	3,232
Woodworking, etc.	25,989	22,672	1,004	3,343	3,358	3,847	3,377	432	1,423	866
Paper, Printing, etc.	18,602	15,995	552	3,013	2,196	11,471	10,291	391	1,049	1,043
Building and Contracting	256,863	214,164	8,225	33,528	28,740	343	423	117	273	247
Other Manufactures	8,362	6,195	29	3,378	3,543	5,799	3,833	29	1,277	1,442
Gas, Water, and Electricity	17,531	15,016	569	2,304	1,898	197	207	51	468	202
Transport and Communications	115,195	101,152	5,667	21,967	20,342	1,762	2,000	562	5,794	2,814
Distributive Trades	126,493	116,774	4,887	17,228	14,495	47,277	50,323	3,270	11,336	8,907
Commerce, Banking, Finance, and Insurance	8,571	8,581	446	1,882	1,954	1,095	1,436	288	4,981	1,498
Miscellaneous Trades and Services	144,399	136,729	12,350	36,596	35,579	52,852	67,278	7,882	19,693	20,037
GRAND TOTAL (in thousands) (a)	1,410	1,084	81	292	213	438	316	39	100	68

B. 1948–58, Males

	1948	1949	1950	1951	1952	1953	1954	1955	1956	1957	1958
Agriculture and Forestry	8,225	8,511	8,283	6,776	6,830	9,260	8,456	8,271	8,299	9,785	12,621
Fishing	1,382	3,069	5,634	3,233	3,258	3,875	3,852	2,797	3,343	2,942	3,094
Mining and Quarrying	2,904	2,361	2,750	2,434	2,145	2,491	2,194	1,518	2,007	2,623	5,151
Bricks and Fireclay Goods	1,086	857	851	522	806	958	802	765	695	999	1,968
Pottery and Earthenware	388	425	405	204	997	607	373	311	678	960	1,025
Glass	767	751	771	441	1,042	659	459	444	558	715	1,043
Other Non-Metalliferous Mining Products	1,112	1,029	1,057	658	960	1,181	929	727	822	1,128	1,733
Chemicals, etc.	4,934	3,811	3,586	2,246	3,506	3,195	2,705	1,969	2,148	2,810	4,225
Metal Manufacture	5,740	4,812	4,520	4,068	4,431	9,984	5,238	4,931	4,152	5,188	20,433
Engineering, Shipbuilding, and Electrical Goods	27,824	27,166	23,337	14,797	18,987	21,423	15,756	13,129	13,079	16,625	32,907
Vehicles	9,774	7,495	6,460	3,507	6,061	6,355	4,409	3,756	13,715	8,855	10,589
Metal Goods not elsewhere specified	5,277	4,429	3,888	2,252	3,682	5,023	2,846	2,214	2,497	3,890	6,101
Precision Instruments, Jewellery, etc.	948	895	767	521	1,046	817	555	368	457	564	966
Textiles	4,784	4,538	3,820	2,770	48,733	6,221	4,551	9,101	6,896	6,759	19,665
Leather, Leather Goods, and Fur	996	778	672	336	1,585	611	478	353	374	520	1,011
Clothing	4,714	2,340	5,564	2,990	8,100	4,506	4,277	3,146	2,924	2,771	6,834
Food, Drink, and Tobacco	5,666	5,571	6,164	4,109	5,796	6,780	5,811	4,525	5,021	6,893	10,279
Wood and Cork Manufactures	4,157	3,501	6,127	2,681	8,271	5,120	3,603	5,543	4,602	4,186	7,170
Paper and Printing	1,870	1,723	1,640	1,161	3,298	2,158	1,453	1,146	1,471	2,224	2,562
Other Manufacturing Industries	2,834	3,675	2,239	1,299	2,977	2,244	1,680	1,258	2,016	2,230	3,472
Building and Contracting	40,959	36,862	37,245	22,749	33,291	39,537	30,999	23,989	26,091	38,382	53,344
Gas, Water, and Electricity	1,986	1,892	2,162	1,505	2,285	2,603	2,179	1,658	1,727	2,258	3,231
Transport and Communications	24,879	21,902	22,212	15,680	20,112	20,423	18,363	15,390	15,327	18,759	26,417
Distributive Trades	15,323	15,804	16,290	10,867	15,330	16,876	14,402	12,192	12,410	16,858	26,091
Insurance, Banking, and Finance	1,422	1,329	1,391	917	1,280	1,481	1,329	1,171	1,237	1,510	2,147
Public Administration, etc.	19,366	16,735	17,058	12,500	16,650	16,150	13,609	11,086	10,974	14,242	18,007
Professional Services	3,350	3,431	3,381	2,735	3,662	3,837	3,412	2,747	2,735	3,607	4,704
Miscellaneous Services	14,433	16,225	16,889	11,372	14,119	15,333	13,264	10,158	10,397	13,043	18,463
GRAND TOTAL (in thousands) (a)	236	219	222	144	249	220	177	153	166	205	327

See p. 47 for footnote.

45

Labour Force 4. *continued*

C. 1948–58, Females

	1948	1949	1950	1951	1952	1953	1954	1955	1956	1957	1958
Agriculture and Forestry	909	1,460	1,415	1,288	1,521	1,900	1,546	1,275	1,219	1,295	1,548
Fishing	10	16	21	18	16	18	7	11	9	6	10
Mining and Quarrying	118	106	119	102	172	233	134	171	149	114	157
Bricks and Fireclay Goods	111	132	148	101	224	246	197	196	158	222	353
Pottery and Earthenware	94	114	121	89	2,079	642	260	475	1,580	1,118	964
Glass	421	339	404	262	930	587	419	282	367	379	394
Other Non-Metalliferous Mining Products	157	124	143	96	245	212	145	108	120	118	161
Chemicals, etc.	2,344	1,552	1,598	1,197	2,725	2,270	1,740	1,602	1,222	1,556	2,248
Metal Manufacture	1,604	864	802	584	1,055	1,811	914	697	703	912	1,397
Engineering, Shipbuilding, and Electrical Goods	6,055	4,726	4,304	3,204	8,178	5,995	4,269	4,177	5,244	4,496	7,063
Vehicles	1,236	1,009	1,004	721	1,734	1,440	1,058	798	2,787	1,694	2,179
Metal Goods not elsewhere specified	2,709	2,019	2,434	1,723	4,703	3,936	2,105	1,755	1,792	2,405	3,143
Precision, Instruments, Jewellery, etc.	473	339	610	347	1,127	626	440	411	467	593	1,257
Textiles	3,624	5,932	4,609	4,072	104,505	10,216	7,784	18,355	12,641	8,436	34,905
Leather, Leather Goods, and Fur	461	335	341	236	987	446	378	314	397	324	599
Clothing	4,837	2,845	5,698	3,780	18,824	6,558	7,065	6,119	4,992	7,642	11,452
Food, Drink, and Tobacco	3,876	4,493	6,832	5,136	9,768	8,431	7,328	5,932	5,465	6,473	8,468
Wood and Cork Manufactures	779	613	952	598	1,937	1,083	861	978	916	816	1,299
Paper and Printing	846	958	1,116	853	5,137	2,243	1,455	1,175	1,275	1,631	2,204
Other Manufacturing Industries	1,848	1,596	1,770	1,116	3,874	2,106	1,690	1,298	1,433	1,497	2,381
Building and Contracting	305	273	300	236	360	338	307	240	207	292	344
Gas, Water, and Electricity	93	78	94	101	134	153	125	103	111	101	150
Transport and Communications	1,685	1,472	1,627	1,249	2,275	2,096	1,853	1,407	1,506	1,583	1,951
Distributive Trades	7,283	8,117	10,232	8,498	15,488	13,843	11,873	10,133	9,554	11,235	15,812
Insurance, Banking, and Finance	832	585	593	448	677	732	594	479	418	511	651
Public Administration, etc.	4,248	3,786	4,854	3,466	4,882	4,527	2,999	2,241	1,924	2,558	3,006
Professional Services	3,462	3,825	5,122	4,659	7,199	6,421	5,427	4,367	3,965	4,817	6,011
Miscellaneous Services	15,423	18,801	23,228	19,343	29,304	26,877	21,206	17,136	15,637	17,762	22,499
GRAND TOTAL (in thousands) (a)	72	72	86	71	240	114	92	90	84	92	146

D. 1959-65

	Males							Females						
	1959	1960	1961	1962	1963	1964	1965	1959	1960	1961	1962	1963	1964	1965
Agriculture and Forestry	12,663	10,274	9,186	9,432	11,533	9,347	8,483	1,649	1,280	1,117	1,194	1,433	1,186	1,057
Fishing	3,369	3,574	2,871	3,175	3,449	2,611	2,567	8	16	12	10	8	11	16
Mining and Quarrying	8,115	6,303	4,342	6,417	9,537	6,821	5,949	314	227	152	180	242	172	144
Bricks, Fireclay, and Refractory Goods	1,948	1,147	941	1,574	1,924	1,160	1,000	300	212	126	232	247	141	117
Pottery	1,094	613	469	712	918	622	458	809	322	334	385	702	362	225
Glass	1,214	871	733	938	1,358	850	680	607	394	298	381	478	264	246
Other Non-Metalliferous Mining Products	1,423	1,088	875	1,385	1,700	1,101	1,069	156	119	96	151	148	95	96
Chemicals, etc.	4,597	3,388	3,127	4,681	5,760	4,816	4,586	2,071	1,453	1,202	1,581	1,893	1,383	1,001
Metal Manufacture	16,782	5,069	7,083	14,512	14,298	5,740	4,360	1,521	702	572	901	1,063	621	531
Engineering and Electrical Goods	17,320	10,256	10,277	16,454	24,026	13,597	11,567	6,497	4,487	4,054	5,835	7,339	5,008	4,331
Shipbuilding and Marine Engineering	16,479	13,064	12,118	13,368	18,453	11,598	5,840	328	303	242	255	350	260	178
Vehicles	6,036	3,653	4,258	7,781	8,959	5,040	5,765	1,184	786	1,124	1,257	1,196	755	654
Metal Goods not elsewhere specified	5,921	3,669	3,528	6,837	8,332	4,553	3,811	2,925	1,916	1,822	3,022	3,356	1,799	1,417
Textiles	9,822	7,124	5,519	10,351	10,569	5,824	5,235	14,310	9,398	7,598	13,499	11,205	5,722	4,552
Leather, Leather Goods, and Fur	771	611	484	893	980	603	462	431	285	256	382	612	238	197
Clothing	2,968	1,964	1,537	2,524	3,634	1,873	1,614	6,476	4,089	4,443	6,556	8,895	4,503	3,588
Food, Drink, and Tobacco	9,258	6,807	5,863	3,352	10,392	7,267	6,088	8,230	5,789	5,243	6,682	8,236	5,555	4,229
Timber, Furniture, etc.	4,839	4,331	2,975	5,008	5,464	3,392	2,980	988	771	467	812	1,008	568	511
Paper, Printing, and Publishing	2,801	1,809	1,823	2,551	3,418	2,312	2,190	2,178	1,485	1,398	2,142	2,835	1,859	1,405
Other Manufacturing Industries	2,969	2,172	2,247	3,157	4,029	2,805	2,302	2,129	1,390	1,328	2,034	2,470	1,737	1,214
Construction	62,432	46,417	39,320	61,543	75,121	51,386	45,604	559	390	337	468	583	464	475
Gas, Water, and Electricity	3,170	2,557	2,288	3,010	3,676	2,830	2,385	239	172	173	166	219	198	198
Transport and Communications	26,137	21,185	19,236	24,274	28,120	21,746	21,720	2,430	1,721	1,510	1,895	2,412	1,673	1,498
Distributive Trades	30,595	23,647	19,978	28,176	37,454	26,204	22,211	18,342	13,969	11,914	16,326	21,206	14,389	11,995
Insurance, Banking, and Finance	2,839	2,943	3,165	4,227	5,126	5,495	5,872	745	613	570	766	977	808	755
Public Administration, etc.	18,208	15,633	14,028	17,551	20,890	17,057	14,371	2,735	2,206	1,893	2,293	2,878	2,379	2,089
Professional and Scientific Services	4,980	3,889	3,514	4,599	5,873	4,574	4,239	6,593	5,245	4,514	5,831	7,168	5,330	4,598
Miscellaneous Services	25,405	19,387	16,942	22,710	29,647	22,099	19,876	22,897	16,981	14,301	17,346	21,729	15,701	13,342
GRAND TOTAL (in thousands) (a)	324	242	217	319	386	267	233	125	93	82	113	130	87	72

(a) This includes some unspecified workers (e.g. those in government training schemes) not included in the individual items.

Labour Force 5. Numbers and Membership of Trade Unions with Headquarters in the United Kingdom – 1938–65

NOTES

[1] SOURCES: *Abstract* and information kindly supplied by the Department of Employment and Productivity.
[2] These statistics relate to all organisations of employees with head offices in the United Kingdom – including salaried and professional workers – which are known to include

negotiating with employers about conditions of employment among their objectives.
[3] Overseas and H.M. Forces members are included.
[4] There is a negligible amount of double-counting of people who are members of more than one union.

	Total Unions	Members (thousands)		
		Total	Males	Females
1938	1,024	6,053	5,127	926
1939	1,019	6,298	5,288	1,010
1940	1,004	6,613	5,494	1,119
1941	996	7,165	5,753	1,412
1942	991	7,867	6,151	1,716
1943	987	8,174	6,258	1,916
1944	963	8,087	6,239	1,848
1945	781	7,875	6,237	1,638
1946	757	8,803	7,186	1,617
1947	734	9,145	7,483	1,662
1948	749	9,362	7,677	1,685
1949	742	9,318	7,644	1,674
1950	732	9,289	7,605	1,684
1951	735	9,535	7,745	1,790
1952	723	9,588	7,797	1,792
1953	720	9,527	7,749	1,778
1954	711	9,566	7,756	1,810
1955	704	9,741	7,874	1,867
1956	685	9,778	7,871	1,907
1957	685	9,829	7,935	1,894
1958	675	9,639	7,789	1,850
1959	668	9,623	7,756	1,868
1960	664	9,835	7,884	1,951
1961	646	9,897	7,905	1,992
1962	626	9,887	7,860	2,027
1963	607	9,934	7,859	2,075
1964	598	10,079	7,936	2,143
1965	583	10,181	7,973	2,208

Labour Force 6. Financial Summary of Registered Trade Unions – Great Britain 1938–65

NOTE
SOURCE: *Report of the Chief Registrar of Friendly Societies* annually.

	Number of Unions	Members (000s)	Income (£000)	Unemployment Benefit (a)	Dispute Benefit	Provident Benefits	from the Political Fund	Working Expenses	Other Outgoings	Funds at End of Year (£000)
						Expenditure (£000)				
1938	426	4,867	9,581	866	148	2,568	117	3,303	535	20,014
1939	424	5,019	9,702	746	163	2,659	118	3,408	451	22,183
1940	416	5,363	9,918	797	55	2,797	102	3,486	469	24,708
1941	417	5,928	10,243	198	18	2,769	124	3,781	530	27,525
1942	423	6,530	11,416	84	18	2,772	111	4,099	551	31,318
1943	418	6,839	12,113	59	15	2,988	117	4,531	617	35,110
1944	421	6,756	12,548	59	29	3,083	137	4,805	638	38,950
1945	427	6,536	12,881	108	43	3,253	346	5,093	632	42,417
1946	428	7,475	14,617	273	75	3,544	201	5,996	583	46,211
1947	417	7,758	16,663	437	57	3,747	313	6,803	1,350	50,081
1948	416	7,917	17,155	180	250	3,765	375	7,535	810	54,398
1949	417	7,884	17,681	159	74	4,299	517	7,945	1,103	58,119
		----(b)	----(b)						----(b)	
1950	416	7,948	17,624	163	244	4,130	451	8,226	812	62,150
1951	413	8,287	18,248	133	178	4,480	555	9,094	1,400	64,825
1952	406	8,377	19,451	358	351	4,713	357	9,913	1,235	67,607
1953	410	8,323	20,354	172	258	5,046	389	10,338	1,111	70,709
1954	411	8,357	20,898	128	483	5,079	394	10,540	1,129	73,887
1955	405	8,517	22,093	136	649	5,278	611	11,319	1,397	76,565
1956	400	8,549	23,424	184	819	5,539	399	12,129	1,362	79,495
1957	400	8,593	25,707	186	2,971	5,976	516	13,032	1,702	80,796
1958	401	8,405	27,056	328	1,383	6,191	678	13,619	1,414	84,275
1959	398	8,352	27,431	287	2,681	6,532	868	13,905	1,401	86,180
1960	398	8,532	28,631	196	456	6,620	524	14,881	2,033	90,267
1961	393	8,545	30,910	178	539	6,810	605	15,870	2,078	95,134
1962	388	8,532	33,583	309	697	7,183	606	16,981	2,109	100,839
1963	372	8,524	34,753	464	462	7,509	1,063	17,988	1,881	106,179
1964	369	8,620	36,853	209	489	7,527	975	19,199	2,798	111,324
1965	356	8,683	39,069	216	649	8,171	658	20,619	2,539	117,572

(a) Includes travelling and emigration benefits.
(b) From 1950 these columns are adjusted to eliminate duplication in respect of registered unions that are affiliated to a registered federation.

Labour Force 7. Industrial Disputes – United Kingdom 1938–65

NOTES
[1] SOURCE: *Abstract*.
[2] Stoppages involving less than ten workers or lasting less than one day have been omitted, except any in which the aggregate number of working days lost exceeded 100.

A. Number of Disputes beginning in Year

	Total	Building	Mining and Quarrying	Metal, Engineering, and Ship-building	Textiles	Clothing	Transport
1938	875	110	374	138	42	36	49
1939	940	122	417	181	73	25	34
1940	922	81	386	229	60	34	36
1941	1,251	77	482	472	42	20	58
1942	1,303	66	555	476	47	13	51
1943	1,785	71	862	612	52	23	68
1944	2,194	48	1,275	610	48	30	82
1945	2,293	36	1,319	591	41	29	156
1946	2,205	77	1,339	449	36	37	105
1947	1,721	35	1,066	291	25	22	119
1948	1,759	36	1,125	266	40	26	111
1949	1,426	59	879	250	27	20	85
	----	--	---	---	--	--	--
1950 (a)	1,339	71	861	227	15	11	68
1951	1,719	95	1,067	318	14	11	91
1952	1,714 (b)	94	1,226	215	6	11	55
1953	1,746 (b)	80	1,313	194	7	17	73
1954	1,989 (b)	75	1,466	207	15	16	125
1955	2,419 (b)	96	1,784	302	12	12	118
1956	2,648	114	2,078	249	25	7	102
1957	2,859 (b)	126	2,226	268	27	9	121
1958	2,629	178	1,964	301	18	11	83
1959	2,093	171	1,311	396	14	11	88
	----	---	----	---	--	--	--
1960 (a)	2,832 (b)	215	1,669	551	26	15	179
1961	2,686 (b)	286	1,466	547	28	13	138
1962	2,449 (b)	316	1,207	583	32	14	134
1963	2,068 (b)	168	993	568	38	8	133
1964	2,524 (b)	222	1,063	766	38	19	180
1965	2,354 (b)	261	743	854	30	14	179

See p. 51 for footnotes.

B. Number of Working Days lost through Disputes (in thousands)

	Total	Building	Mining and Quarrying	Metal, Engineering, and Ship-building	Textiles	Clothing	Transport
1938	1,334	115	701	243	84	33	40
1939	1,356	131	612	332	100	13	56
1940	940	73	508	163	77	40	13
1941	1,079	36	338	556	36	16	54
1942	1,527	29	862	526	26	19	35
1943	1,808	25	889	635	17	7	181
1944	3,714	7	2,495	1,048	47	5	85
1945	2,835	5	644	528	10	68	1,491
1946	2,158	24	424	1,084	43	111	161
1947	2,433	24	915	579	13	15	627
1948	1,944	27	473	898	56	26	347
1949	1,807	32	755	285	68	10	533
1950 (a)	1,389	64	431	294	44	3	188
1951	1,694	83	351	514	8	8	601
1952	1,792	157	662	791	2	3	32
1953	2,184	101	394	1,525	19	8	69
1954	2,457	233	468	741	3	9	919
1955	3,781	71	1,112	669	15	8	1,687
1956	2,083	78	503	1,017	28	1	35
1957	8,412	84	514	6,592	37	7	998
1958	3,462	151	450	609	10	10	2,116
1959	5,270	138	370	962	54	2	95
1960 (a)	3,024	110	495	1,450	16	9	636
1961	3,046	285	740	1,464	18	5	230
1962	5,798	222	308	4,559	31	6	431
1963	1,755	356	326	854	23	2	72
1964	2,277	125	309	1,338	27	7	312
1965	2,925	135	413	1,763	46	6	305

(*a*) Changes in the Standard Industrial Classification in 1950 and 1960 mean that the figures for industrial groups are not strictly comparable throughout, though for all practical purposes the breaks can be ignored for the groups shown here.

(*b*) In these years there were stoppages involving workers in several industries, and these, though counted in each group of industries, have been counted only once in the total.

CHAPTER III

AGRICULTURE

TABLES

The great majority of the tables in this chapter follows on directly from those in the first *Abstract of British Historical Statistics,* and for the most part it is only necessary to reiterate the major points made there. Clearly the completeness of the statistics was better for the whole of the period covered in this volume than it was for the earlier years of the collection of statistics; and it is probable also that there has been no significant change in the efficiency of collection in recent decades. Nevertheless, it should be noted that the basis of the acreage and livestock figures is returns from individual farmers, and thanks to changes in ownership and the very small size of some holdings, there is little doubt that there is some slight understatement in these figures. Furthermore, the production and yield statistics are estimates based on the evidence of crop reporters, who are generally believed to have a tendency to overestimate in bad harvests and underestimate in good ones. Finally, it is worth drawing attention to the fact that the livestock statistics show stocks rather than flows, and if there have been changes in the rate of turnover caused by changes in the age to which animals are kept these figures will not serve as accurate proxies for output series. Probably, in the period covered here, it is only cattle which have been significantly affected by such changes in the rate of turnover, with a definite speeding-up from the late 1950s.

The statistics of the volume of overseas trade included here do not call for any particular comment, despite the insertion of a new table showing meat imports back into the middle of the nineteenth century. Statistics of the value of imports of the main foodstuffs are given in Chapter XI.

Agriculture 1. Acreage of Crops – Great Britain 1938-65

NOTES
[1]. SOURCES: *Agricultural Statistics* and *A Century of Agricultural Statistics: Great Britain 1866–1966* (London: H.M.S.O., 1968).

[2] To maintain comparability with series published in the first *Abstract of British Historical Statistics* vegetables for human consumption are included throughout under the appropriate heading.

(in thousands of acres)

	Wheat	Barley	Oats	Other Corn (a)	Potatoes	Turnips and Swedes	Mangold	Sugar Beet	Cabbage, Kohl-rabi, and Rape	Bare Fallow	Rotation Grasses for Hay	Rotation Grasses for Grazing	Permanent Pasture for Hay	Permanent Pasture for Grazing	Small Fruit	Orchards	Hops
1938	1,923	984	2,098	386	610	746	218	336	210	370	1,571	1,788	4,402	13,007	58	253	18
1939	1,763	1,010	2,135	381	589	705	215	345	215	374	1,689	1,838	4,786	12,545	56	256	19
1940	1,797	1,321	3,002	518	695	739	229	329	265	306	1,698	1,678	4,398	11,497	51	258	19
1941	2,247	1,457	3,501	990	966	820	265	351	365	219	1,547	1,528	3,883	10,184	45	271	18
1942	2,504	1,513	3,658	1,053	1,116	846	268	425	407	280	1,858 (b)	1,478 (b)	3,343	9,409	43	266	18
1943	3,451	1,771	3,210	1,094	1,193	823	285	417	426	240	2,095	1,633	2,811	8,609	38	267	19
1944	3,215	1,957	3,215	1,087	1,219	818	307	431	468	231	2,266	1,962	2,433	8,376	40	264	20
1945	2,272	2,201	3,305	1,002	1,207	807	307	417	464	347	2,589	2,213	2,524	8,369	36	260	20
1946	2,060	2,203	3,154	988	1,230	751	303	436	441	294	2,640	2,436	2,421	8,641	38	272	21
1947	2,161	2,053	2,927	913	1,149	722	271	395	400	508	2,684	2,345	2,716	8,662	42	272	22
1948	2,275	2,077	2,945	1,067	1,338	661	280	413	405	245	2,477	2,411	2,778	8,618	48	268	23
1949	1,961	2,054	2,878	1,162	1,121	641	274	421	433	309	2,712 (b)	2,437 (b)	2,760	8,885	57	270	22
1950	2,476	1,774	2,760	1,312	1,056	596	276	429	477	269	2,501	2,426	2,891	8,794	61	274	22
1951	2,130	1,906	2,541	1,218	906	593	263	425	481	384	2,746	2,444	2,949	9,041	57	278	22
1952	2,028	2,275	2,580	1,247	854	590	223	408	481	305	2,745	2,410	3,036	8,833	55	279	22
1953	2,215	2,220	2,552	1,265	846	588	214	415	524	225	2,621	2,520	2,996	8,724	51	274	22
1954	2,455	2,058	2,320	1,026	815	569	205	437	535	281	2,655	2,722	2,890	9,095	50	268	20
1955	1,947	2,290	2,330	822	757	566	182	424	547	349	2,774	2,811	3,023	9,261	48	264	20
1956	2,290	2,317	2,309	779	796	526	176	426	556	217	2,637	2,825	3,075	9,173	47	259	20
1957	2,109	2,609	2,109	646	709	511	153	430	565	314	2,819	2,900	3,005	9,266	48	250	20
1958	2,204	2,739	1,999	595	722	496	147	439	559	255	2,907	2,838	3,202	9,045	49	244	21
1959	1,927	3,032	1,833	504	719	483	132	434	529	366	2,960	3,253	3,001	8,975	50	241	20
1960	2,099	3,313	1,771	488	742	455	133	436	552	193	2,924	3,285	3,158	8,522	50	235	20
1961	1,822	3,717	1,550	390	628	421	110	427	510	305	3,129	3,387	2,970	8,660	48	228	20
1962	2,252	3,858	1,357	370	660	395	105	424	489	178	3,074	3,378	2,970	8,549	48	221	20
1963	1,925	4,565	1,149	347	687	370	89	423	432	225	3,130	3,297	2,912	8,497	49	216	21
1964	2,203	4,867	1,000	336	706	359	72	443	392	199	3,123	3,083	3,018	8,284	49	198	21
1965	2,531	5,211	918	337	680	335	59	455	375	167	2,840	3,063	2,865	8,253	47	195	21

(a) This comprises mixed corn, rye, peas, and beans.
(b) From 1943 to 1950 lucerne is included with rotation grasses.
(c) Subsequently fodder beet is included in this column.

Agriculture 2. Acreage of Crops – Northern Ireland 1938–66

NOTE

SOURCES: 6th and 7th *Reports upon the Agricultural Statistics of Northern Ireland* and *Annual General Reports* of the Northern Ireland Ministry of Agriculture.

(in thousands of acres)

	Wheat	Barley	Oats	Other Corn (a)	Potatoes	Turnips	Mangold	Flax	Rotation Grasses	Permanent Grasses
1938	5·5	3·4	297	0·7	123	26·3	1·0	21	607	1,388
1939	2·9	3·5	291	1·0	115	23·4	1·1	21	565	1,442
1940	12·0	17·7	397	6·1	137	26·4	1·7	46	483	1,188
1941	17·6	17·6	449	18·0	157	28·6	2·0	90	451	1,047
1942	12·3	15·3	475	19·4	187	25·6	1·6	73	495	955
1943	13·8	14·4	470	17·9	197	23·6	1·4	93	491	910
1944	5·0	16·1	441	12·0	198	21·9	1·1	125	497	926
1945	1·8	14·3	448	9·7	190	21·4	1·1	80	532	947
1946	2·5	7·8	413	8·4	193	19·7	1·2	36	604	969
1947	1·8	6·5	381	7·2	182	17·3	1·0	17	623	1,026
1948	4·4	5·8	390	9·2	210	15·5	0·9	21	595	1,002
1949	2·0	5·7	374	7·8	188	13·8	0·8	30	577	1,042
1950	2·1	3·8	345	7·6	179	12·4	0·8	22	604	1,085
1951	1·3	2·9	316	5·4	144	11·6	0·9 (b)	21	606	1,143
1952	1·9	5·4	302	6·1	137	10·7	2·4	23	582	1,190
1953	2·3	6·3	288	6·6	139	11·1	1·9	18	552	1,233
1954	2·1	5·1	268	5·6	130	11·0	1·8	11	543	1,228
1955	1·3	5·0	251	4·6	116	10·0	1·1	9	553	1,248
1956	2·7	6·3	256	4·5	125	8·6	1·1	9	561	1,224
1957	3·8	13·0	238	5·4	103	7·6	0·9	3	527	1,231
1958	3·9	16·0	218	5·3	99	7·1	0·8	1	511	1,238
1959	2·4	27·0	199	4·9	96	5·6	0·5	--	551	1,137
1960	3·5	59·0	202	4·2	87	4·6	0·4	--	578	1,129
1961	4·9	111·0	183	2·8	75	3·9	0·3	--	486	1,048
1962	4·1	128·5	162	...	77	3·8	0·3	--	497	1,037
1963	2·5	148·5	146	...	81	2·9	0·2	--	515	1,023
1964	3·1	165·0	125	...	72	2·7	0·2	--	617	1,002
1965	3·8	184·2	96	...	61	2·1	0·2	--	615	1,020
1966	2·9	171·7	82	...	57	1·7	0·1	--	633	1,083

(a) Beans, peas, rye, and dredge corn.
(b) Subsequently includes fodder beet which had not been collected separately previously. In 1952 the fodder beet acreage amounted to 1·7 thousand acres.

NOTE
SOURCE: *Agricultural Statistics.*

(in thousands at 4 June)

	Cattle			Sheep						
	Cows and Heifers	Other Cattle	Total	Shearling Ewes	Ewes Kept for Breeding	Other Sheep	Total	Pigs	Horses	Poultry
1938	3,576	4,454	8,030	2,254	10,406	13,222	25,882	3,822	1,002	64,053
1939	3,615	4,504	8,119	2,240	10,572	13,181	25,993	3,767	987	64,137
1940	3,698	4,662	8,361	2,216	10,309	12,941	25,465	3,631	959	62,121
1941	3,708	4,446	8,153	1,859	8,865	10,722	21,445	2,207	962	49,126
1942	3,883	4,365	8,248	1,769	8,520	10,475	20,764	1,872	917	43,212
1943	3,999	4,428	8,428	1,977	7,899	9,823	19,700	1,571	871	35,299
1944	4,035	4,580	8,616	2,112	7,820	9,503	19,435	1,631	829	38,481
1945	3,996	4,702	8,697	2,071	7,916	9,508	19,496	1,903	796	44,665
1946	4,066	4,649	8,716	2,084	8,018	9,617	19,718	1,644	756	47,276
1947	4,009	4,623	8,633	1,847	6,904	7,436	16,186	1,294	703	48,977
1948	4,108	4,733	8,840	1,554	7,292	8,742	17,589	1,816	635	61,138
1949	4,224	5,038	9,263	1,888	7,473	9,485	18,847	2,364	557	71,257
1950	4,265	5,366	9,630	2,004	7,780	9,929	19,714	2,463	494	75,385
1951	4,145	5,368	9,512	2,046	7,813	9,453	19,311	3,306	432	76,506
1952	4,159	5,144	9,303	1,936	8,183	10,741	20,860	4,287	374	78,519
1953	4,208	5,300	9,508	2,096	8,375	11,089	21,560	4,406	333	77,511
1954	4,255	5,521	9,777	2,120	8,561	11,261	21,943	5,431	300	72,258
1955	4,202	5,563	9,764	2,127	8,840	11,111	22,078	5,157	274	75,585
1956	4,370	5,620	9,989	2,113	9,225	11,384	22,721	4,821	233	80,928
1957	4,417	5,491	9,909	2,192	9,451	12,226	23,868	5,232	208	83,131
1958	4,345	5,631	9,976	2,501	9,903	12,721	25,125	5,695	189	87,474
1959	4,367	5,960	10,328	2,626	10,310	13,665	26,601	5,135	...	94,718
1960	4,506	6,266	10,772	2,467	10,764	13,541	26,772	4,739	157	92,612
1961	4,624	6,237	10,861	2,390	11,001	14,393	27,784	5,009	...	104,075
1962	4,702	6,048	10,749	2,447	11,318	14,523	28,289	5,540	...	99,436
1963	4,632	5,974	10,605	2,410	11,375	14,418	28,204	5,670	...	102,891
1964	4,549	5,966	10,515	2,384	11,475	14,704	28,563	6,227	...	107,820
1965	4,574	6,253	10,826	2,508	11,517	14,812	28,837	6,731	...	107,746

Agriculture 4. Numbers of Livestock – Northern Ireland 1938–65

NOTE

SOURCES: 1938–61 – 6th and 7th *Reports upon the Agricultural Statistics of Northern Ireland*; 1962–65 – *Annual General Reports* of the Ministry of Agriculture.

(in thousands)

| | Cattle | | | Sheep | | | | Horses | | |
	Cows and Heifers	Other Cattle	Total	Ewes for Breeding	Other Sheep	Total	Pigs	for Agricultural Purposes	Total	Poultry
1938	259	473	732	402	491	893	561	80	99	10,193
1939	270	483	753	403	492	895	627	76	97	10,220
1940	259	473	732	379	476	854	475	77	97	9,122
1941	281	506	787	364	448	812	351	80	97	12,933
1942	316	511	827	332	410	742	271	80	95	14,601
1943	325	507	832	301	382	683	257	77	90	15,430
1944	339	546	886	300	371	672	237	75	88	16,646
1945	347	573	919	295	359	654	249	72	85	17,471
1946	356	557	913	324	316	640	312	65	77	19,841
1947	373	561	934	278	249	527	334	65	75	21,029
1948	383	583	966	290	285	575	335	60	68	24,234
1949	375	604	980	321	324	645	458	54	61	24,242
1950	364	626	990	346	371	717	523	49	55	20,724
1951	331	630	961	335	337	672	585	40	45	17,838
1952	314	627	941	372	423	795	676	35	40	16,456
1953	302	634	936	398	496	895	759	33	37	14,608
1954	305	637	942	425	505	930	820	30	...	11,386
1955	288	616	904	437	433	870	686	28	...	11,272
1956	299	619	918	451	423	873	653	24	...	11,536
1957	309	663	972	472	457	929	742	21	...	11,737
1958	303	678	980	504	476	980	790	19	...	12,250
1959	298	666	964	514	497	1,011	848	16	...	11,886
1960	331	667	998	561	538	1,099	985	13	...	10,393
1961	357	718	1,075	586	597	1,183	1,033	11	...	10,214
1962	370	739	1,109	597	612	1,209	1,182	...	...	9,595
1963	372	738	1,110	537	603	1,140	1,190	...	...	9,283
1964	374	737	1,112	520	574	1,094	1,152	...	...	10,557
1965	391	724	1,115	518	556	1,074	1,248	...	...	10,394

Agriculture 5. Agricultural Production – Great Britain 1938–65

NOTE
SOURCES: *Agricultural Statistics* and *A Century of Agricultural Statistics: Great Britain 1866–1966* (London: H.M.S.O., 1968)..

(in thousands of tons, except hops, which are in thousands of hundredweights)

	Wheat	Barley	Oats	Potatoes	Turnips and Swedes (a)	Mangold	Sugar Beet	Rotation Hay	Pasture Hay	Hops
1938	1,959	901	1,702	4,404	10,605	3,689	2,191	1,913	3,389	258
1939	1,642	889	1,733	4,354	9,930	4,050	3,529	2,273	4,783	288
1940	1,628	1,089	2,514	5,375	10,632	4,229	3,176	2,315	3,898	270
1941	2,000	1,127	2,815	6,783	11,780	5,090	3,226	2,139	3,786	262
1942	2,556	1,432	3,125	8,162	13,035	5,404	3,923	2,669	3,233	262
1943	3,435	1,632	2,670	8,537	11,980	5,785	3,760	3,038	2,844	286
1944	3,134	1,737	2,574	8,026	12,070	5,543	3,267	2,894	2,093	254
1945	2,174	2,096	2,862	8,702	12,156	6,508	3,886	3,843	2,659	282
1946	1,965	1,956	2,527	8,614	10,951	6,264	4,522	3,705	2,369	282
1947	1,666	1,614	2,244	6,742	9,220	4,328	2,960	3,654	2,673	290
1948	2,356	2,021	2,571	10,132	9,676	5,901	4,319	3,570	2,873	274
1949	2,202	2,123	2,641	7,605	9,220	5,308	3,962	4,039	2,776	250
1950	2,604	1,707	2,384	8,164	9,230	6,486	5,218	3,113	2,553	368
1951	2,315	1,936	2,321	7,087	9,932	6,068	4,534	3,643	2,823	322
1952	2,305	2,328	2,483	6,775	9,708	4,808	4,236	3,814	2,994	282
1953	2,662	2,514	2,549	7,135	10,789	5,498	5,275	3,615	3,036	272
1954	2,781	2,238	2,201	6,413	9,906	4,498	4,521	3,329	2,584	246
1955	2,598	2,930	2,485	5,521	8,208	3,788	4,556	3,834	3,236	256
1956	2,842	2,793	2,237	6,659	9,034	4,286	5,169	3,161	2,876	184
1957	2,679	2,942	1,941	5,030	8,628	3,549	4,539	3,645	2,929	268
1958	2,707	3,152	1,956	4,982	8,704	3,570	5,742	3,860	3,391	302
					---- (a)					
1959	2,782	3,982	2,000	6,194	7,279	2,669	5,510	7,071		224
1960	2,988	4,168	1,870	6,455	8,760	3,585	7,215	7,402		250
1961	2,568	4,879	1,681	5,638	7,782	2,714	5,936	8,061		204
1962	3,905	5,598	1,585	6,012	7,725	2,655	5,313	7,727		266
1963	2,995	6,430	1,303	5,929	6,874	2,148	5,254	7,822		276
1964	3,729	7,196	1,206	6,411	6,862	1,666	6,218	8,851		252
1965	4,099	7,830	1,124	6,955	6,618	1,508	6,705	7,755		258

(a) With effect from 1959 figures for turnips, swedes, and fodder beet have been collected as a joint item in England & Wales.

Agriculture 6. Agricultural Production – Northern Ireland 1938–66

NOTE
SOURCES: 6th and 7th *Reports upon the Agricultural Statistics of Northern Ireland* and *Annual General Reports* of the Northern Ireland Ministry of Agriculture.

(in thousand tons)

	Wheat	Barley	Oats	Dredge Corn	Potatoes	Turnips	Mangold	Hay (a)
1938	5·7	3·3	290	...	711	320	16·2	825
1939	3·0	3·1	270	0·4	864	385	18·5	734
1940	12·8	15·0	378	4·3	1,030	448	28·7	798
1941	18·2	17·2	432	14·6	1,221	466	30·0	704
1942	11·4	13·9	428	15·7	1,231	380	22·1	758
1943	12·1	12·9	394	13·6	1,285	336	19·7	787
1944	4·4	14·8	379	8·1	1,070	318	16·7	703
1945	1·5	12·5	383	6·3	1,089	324	16·1	690
1946	2·2	7·4	376	5·6	1,552	303	17·6	754
1947	1·4	4·5	265	4·1	1,024	240	13·6	904
1948	4·7	6·5	392	7·3	1,666	262	16·9	784
1949	2·1	6·4	354	5·8	1,430	226	13·1	690
1950	2·0	4·0	308	5·6	1,343	174	11·5	592
1951	1·4	3·3	295	4·4	1,197	178	14·7	746
1952	2·2	6·5	289	5·3	1,073	164	9·5	723
1953	2·5	7·1	272	5·9	1,125	179	10·8	667
1954	2·1	5·9	239	4·7	912	165	14·9	737
1955	1·3	5·8	224	3·6	757	174	11·9	716
1956	3·2	7·4	249	3·9	874	151	12·1	709
1957	4·4	14·7	204	4·8	659	129	10·5	702
1958	4·3	17·8	182	4·3	574	110	8·4	766
								—— (a)
1959	2·9	33·4	187	4·8	722	87	5·8	583
1960	4·3	73·2	188	3·8	555	72	6·3	629
1961	5·5	94·9	141	1·7	544	59	5·0	649
1962	5·8	174·8	162	2·6	563	60	5·5	618
1963	3·3	168·5	135	2·1	550	46	4·4	602
1964	4·3	207·1	119	2·3	455	43	3·6	732
1965	5·7	232·1	90	2·9	430	35	3·1	712
1966	4·2	194·1	72	3·5	399	28	2·3	737

(a) Includes silage grass prior to 1959.

Agriculture 7. Yield per Acre of the Main Agricultural Products – Great Britain 1938–65

NOTE

SOURCES: *Agricultural Statistics* and *A Century of Agricultural Statistics: Great Britain 1866–1966* (London: H.M.S.O., 1968).

	Wheat cwt.	Barley cwt.	Oats cwt.	Potatoes tons	Turnips and Swedes (a) tons	Mangold tons	Sugar Beet (b) tons	Rotation Hay tons	Pasture Hay tons	Hops cwt.
1938	20·4	18·3	16·2	7·2	14·2	17·0	6·6	1·2	0·8	13.9
1939	18·6	17·6	16·2	7·4	14·1	18·9	10·4	1·3	1·0	15·3
1940	18·1	16·5	16·8	7·7	14·4	18·5	9·7	1·4	0·9	14·5
1941	17·8	15·5	16·1	7·0	14·4	19·3	9·3	1·4	1·0	14·5
1942	20·4	18·9	17·1	7·3	15·4	20·3	9·3	1·4	1·0	14·2
1943	19·9	18·4	16·6	7·2	14·6	20·4	9·1	1·5	1·0	14·9
1944	19·5	17·7	16·0	6·6	14·8	18·1	7·7	1·3	0·9	13·0
1945	19·1	19·0	17·3	7·2	15·1	21·3	9·4	1·5	1·1	14·1
1946	19·1	17·8	16·0	7·0	14·6	20·8	10·5	1·4	1·0	13·3
1947	15·4	15·7	15·3	5·9	12·8	16·0	7·6	1·4	1·0	13·2
1948	20·7	19·5	17·5	7·6	14·6	21·1	10·5	1·4	1·0	12·1
1949	22·5	20·7	18·4	6·8	14·4	19·5	9·5	1·5	1·0	11·3
1950	21·0	19·2	17·3	7·7	15·5	23·7	12·3	1·5	1·0	16·6
1951	21·7	20·3	18·3	7·8	16·7	23·3	10·7	1·5	1·1	14·4
1952	22·7	20·5	19·3	7·9	16·5	21·6	10·4	1·6	1·1	12·8
1953	24·0	22·7	20·0	8·4	18·3	25·7	12·8	1·6	1·1	12·5
1954	22·7	21·7	19·0	7·9	17·4	22·0	10·4	1·5	1·1	12·0
1955	26·7	25·6	21·4	7·3	14·5	20·8	10·8	1·6	1·1	12·6
1956	24·8	24·1	19·4	8·4	17·2	24·5	12·2	1·4	1·1	9·3
1957	25·4	22·6	18·4	7·1	16·9	23·3	10·6	1·5	1·1	13·2
1958	24·6	23·0	19·6	6·9	17·1 --- (a)	24·4	13·2	1·6	1·2	14·3
1959	28·9	26·3	21·9	8·6	15·1	20·3	12·8	1·3		11·0
1960	28·5	25·2	21·2	8·7	19·3	26·9	16·7	1·4		12·3
1961	28·2	26·3	21·7	9·0	18·5	24·7	14·0	1·5		10·4
1962	34·7	29·0	23·4	9·1	19·5	25·3	12·6	1·4		13·1
1963	31·1	28·2	22·8	8·6	18·6	24·2	12·5	1·5		13·0
1964	33·8	29·6	24·2	9·1	19·1	23·4	14·2	1·6		12·1
1965	32·4	30·0	24·6	10·2	19·7	25·6	14·9	1·6		12·5

(a) With effect from 1959 figures for turnips, swedes, and fodder beet have been collected as a joint item in England & Wales. Yields for 1955–8 including fodder beet were as follows: 1955 – 14·3; 1956 – 17·1; 1957 – 16·7; 1958 – 17·5.

(b) This column relates to washed and topped beet.

Agriculture 8. Yield per Acre of Main Agricultural Products – Northern Ireland 1938–66

NOTE

SOURCES: 6th and 7th *Reports upon the Agricultural Statistics of Northern Ireland* and *Annual General Reports* of the Northern Ireland Ministry of Agriculture.

	Wheat cwt.	Barley cwt.	Oats cwt.	Potatoes tons	Turnips and Swedes tons	Mangold tons	Hay tons	Grass Silage tons
1938	20·7	19·2	19·5	5·8	12·2	15·5	1·9	
1939	20·4	17·8	18·5	7·5	16·4	16·3	1·7	
1940	21·5	17·0	19·0	7·5	16·9	17·2	1·8	
1941	20·6	19·6	19·2	7·8	16·3	15·3	1·8	
1942	18·5	18·1	18·0	6·6	14·8	14·0	1·7	
1943	17·6	17·9	16·8	6·5	14·2	14·4	1·9	
1944	17·9	18·4	17·2	5·4	14·5	14·6	1·7	
1945	17·5	17·4	17·1	5·7	15·2	14·3	1·6	
1946	18·0	19·2	18·3	8·1	15·4	14·9	1·7	
1947	15·9	13·9	13·9	5·6	13·9	14·3	2·0	
1948	21·2	22·5	20·1	7·9	16·9	18·1	1·8	
1949	21·4	22·5	18·9	7·6	16·3	16·3	1·7	
1950	19·8	20·8	17·8	7·5	14·0	14·0	1·4	
1951	21·6	22·8	18·7	8·3	15·3	16·2	1·7	
1952	22·6	24·2	19·1	7·9	15·3	14·8	1·7	
1953	21·9	22·5	18·9	8·1	16·2	16·1	1·6	
1954	19·9	23·0	17·9	7·0	15·4	16·6	1·8	
1955	20·5	23·1	17·8	6·5	17·4	17·2	1·7	
1956	23·8	23·4	19·5	7·0	17·5	17·7	1·6	
1957	22·9	22·8	17·1	6·4	17·0	18·2	1·6	
1958	22·1	22·3	16·6	5·8	15·7	16·6	1·8	
1959	24·5	24·4	18·8	7·5	15·7	16·5	1·7	7·8
1960	24·3	24·8	18·6	6·4	15·7	17·4	1·8	8·1
1961	22·2	17·1	15·4	7·2	15·2	16·8	1·8	8·0
1962	28·5	27·2	20·0	7·3	15·6	17·0	1·8	8·1
1963	26·0	22·7	18·5	6·8	15·7	18·0	1·7	8·7
1964	27·3	25·1	19·0	6·3	16·3	17·2	1·8	8·7
1965	29·9	25·2	18·7	7·0	16·3	17·2	1·8	8·8
1966	28·9	22·6	17·5	7·0	16·6	17·2	1·8	8·9

Agriculture 9. The Overseas Corn Trade – United Kingdom 1938–65

NOTE
SOURCE: *Annual Statement of Trade.*

(in thousands of hundredweights)

	Imports					Exports and Re-exports of Wheat, Wheat Meal, and Flour	Exports of Barley
	Wheat	Wheat Meal and Flour	Barley	Oats	Maize		
1938	101,626	7,677	19,876	1,576	57,581	3,448	1
1939	106,074	7,333	13,740	1,468	46,399	2,339	1
1940	115,081	11,547	9,146	1,634	41,581	473	1
1941	107,864	14,158	1,277	2	13,458	164	—
1942	69,744	7,488	—	1	2,623	166	—
1943	65,126	14,351	—	—	1,299	110	—
1944	56,474	15,831	—	—	2,341	711	719
1945	71,035	10,857	2,037	2,088	10,207	5,135	715
1946	67,443	10,705	2,195	2,096	2,387	1,334	3,282
1947	83,879	17,876	2,257	2,118	9,540	217	522
1948	84,616	16,217	15,618	5,878	26,599	204	720
1949	95,682	11,783	9,223	1,304	14,014	206	217
						- - - (a)	
1950	65,327	8,616	15,289	1,794	19,514	258	699
1951	81,055	10,285	24,270	2,114	20,460	291	1
1952	78,073	9,989	22,641	2,696	27,435	250	2,288
1953	80,407	9,605	28,702	2,184	27,588	246	2
1954	69,262	7,214	18,602	453	26,094	276	1,986
1955	89,821	6,891	18,554	1,032	29,951	286	1,800
1956	95,626	7,211	16,215	459	30,736	328	2,792
1957	90,599	6,767	20,168	1,004	32,480	230	172
1958	90,343	7,437	26,504	3,358	46,036	329	2,589
1959	85,500	7,528	19,924	2,399	58,569	118	4,893
1960	82,076	7,325	14,083	525	61,688	104	4,411
1961	78,412	7,733	19,474	776	63,126	214	2,710
1962	78,432	7,698	7,003	1,299	91,203	308	6,096
						- - - (a)	
1963	78,713	6,419	6,978	679	68,605	2,821	3,063
1964	75,740	5,518	6,772	492	68,015	329	1,759
1965	86,799	4,677	5,616	411	64,031	342	3,919

(a) Domestic exports of wheat were not distinguished between 1950 and 1962 and cannot therefore be included.

Agriculture 10. Principal Sources of Imports of Wheat – United Kingdom 1938–65

NOTE
SOURCE: *Annual Statement of Trade.*

(in thousands of hundredweights)

	Russia	Canada	U.S.A.	Argentine	Australia
1938	9,543	28,831	15,805	5,811	30,995
1939	—	35,157	13,561	24,962	13,464
1940	—	55,734	4,587	30,537	17,324
1941	—	87,326	614	13,075	6,746
1942	—	56,885	29	6,225	6,605
1943	—	61,736	—	1,476	1,913
1944	—	49,665	215	6,595	—
1945	—	65,290	—	5,745	—
1946	—	57,688	7,525	2,231	—
1947	—	68,761	6,930	7,741	—
1948	—	66,542	183	2,099	15,420
1949	—	73,179	5,548	—	16,321
1950	—	49,217	8,955	—	5,989
1951	—	44,987	21,257	1,686	11,339
1952	3,919	55,360	9,071	—	8,932
1953	41	55,796	8,907	3,653	9,301
1954	1,168	39,223	7,473	6,566	6,150
1955	708	45,079	9,454	7,668	9,919
1956	122	52,661	18,759	6,328	12,031
1957	258	42,589	16,737	9,045	12,793
1958	1,829	47,991	13,801	7,499	5,154
1959	2,744	45,824	9,511	8,100	9,838
1960	3,848	42,598	11,230	5,932	13,620
1961	6,259	41,784	7,941	3,447	12,459
1962	6,861	38,948	6,909	8,811	10,951
1963	5,896	41,594	4,787	3,676	11,133
1964	—	57,642	9,224	3,973	14,411
1965	—	57,514	7,744	12,818	15,253

Agriculture 11. Imports of Meat – United Kingdom 1840–1965

NOTE
SOURCES: 1840–54 *Abstract*; 1855–1965 *Annual Statement of Trade*.

(in thousands of hundredweights)

1840	65	1885	6,712	1930	31,672
			----(b)		
1841	93	1886	6,811	1931	34,849
1842	93	1887	6,691	1932	33,795
1843	95	1888	6,834	1933	31,351
1844	144	1889	8,593	1934	30,654
1845	133	1890	10,068	1935	29,549
1846	264	1891	9,894	1936	29,162
1847	460	1892	10,608	1937	30,813
1848	595	1893	9,408	1938	30,963
1849	895	1894	10,719	1939	31,285
1850	699	1895	12,098	1940	29,245
1851	454	1896	13,518	1941	30,569
1852	302	1897	15,005	1942	32,627
1853	542	1898	16,445	1943	33,577
1854	677	1899	17,658	1944	35,730
---(a)					
1855	679	1900	17,912	1945	23,338
1856	742	1901	18,764	1946	27,141
1857	613	1902	16,971	1947	28,046
1858	456	1903	17,498	1948	22,627
1859	495	1904	17,517	1949	23,420
1860	783	1905	18,680	1950	25,279
1861	807	1906	19,255	1951	20,283
1862	1,765	1907	19,444	1952	21,308
1863	2,440	1908	19,654	1953	26,057
1864	1,647	1909	19,398	1954	24,125
1865	1,192	1910	19,983	1955	26,966
1866	1,228	1911	21,581	1956	28,063
1867	1,048	1912	21,360	1957	29,456
			-----(c)		
1868	1,093	1913	23,557	1958	28,338
1869	1,240	1914	23,811	1959	28,137
1870	1,159	1915	25,432	1960	29,608
1871	1,989	1916	23,485	1961	27,750
1872	2,848	1917	19,702	1962	28,634
1873	3,878	1918	25,263	1963	27,843
1874	3,511	1919	25,694	1964	28,594
			-----(d)		
1875	3,437	1920	24,661	1965	27,935
1876	4,349	1921	27,241		
1877	4,402	1922	26,631		
1878	6,000	1923	31,443		
1879	6,892	1924	30,463		
1880	7,567	1925	30,907		
1881	6,831	1926	30,726		
1882	4,649	1927	31,176		
1883	6,050	1928	30,716		
1884	5,819	1929	29,691		

(a) Unenumerated and preserved meat is not included before 1855, when it amounted to 3 thousand cwt.
(b) Rabbit meat is not included before 1886, when it amounted to 104 thousand cwt.

(c) Poultry is not included before 1913, when it amounted to 278 thousand cwt.
(d) Game is not included before 1920, when it amounted to 17 thousand cwt.

CHAPTER IV

FUEL AND POWER

TABLES

––––––

This chapter is based on the one on coal in the first *Abstract of British Historical Statistics*, but it has been expanded by introducing new tables on other sources of fuel and power. Tables 1 to 6 follow on as closely as possible from those in the first volume, though unfortunately the district figures in tables 1 and 2 are on a different basis. This is the inevitable result of the collection of statistics since nationalisation on the basis of the National Coal Board divisions rather than of counties. Table 5, showing coal and coke used in blast furnaces, follows on directly from the equivalent table in the first volume, despite the fact that it begins in 1927. Figures for 1927–38 were omitted in error in that volume.

Tables 7, 8, and 9 give a selection of the statistics available about electricity production and consumption. The last two are straightforward enough, but it is worth stressing here that the official statistics relate only to authorised – or latterly nationalised – undertakings. In other words they do not include electricity which was not generated by undertakings producing for commercial sale. The main undertakings of this type were the railways, and since they are excluded throughout, the trend indicated by the figures is probably not very greatly affected by this limitation of coverage. However, in the 1920s, and to a less extent the 30s and 40s, there was almost certainly some decline in private generation other than by railway companies, and this served to increase the sales of the authorised undertakings. The same problem is, no doubt, to be found in table 7, but there are others here of perhaps greater importance. There were no official statistics before 1920, and the private publication run by Emil Garcke, which is the source of table 7, had to rely on information supplied voluntarily. As a result there are various omissions, which were roughly allowed for in compiling this table, though the result is probably very approximate until about 1900. Moreover, the accounting years of the undertakings varied to some extent, so that figures could not be obtained for uniform periods. To complicate matters still further, there were changes in these accounting years for some of the undertakings, from time to time, notably when a municipality took over from a private company. However, despite all these draw-backs to the accuracy of the statistics in table 7, they are not without interest as a rough indicator of the early growth of British electricity supply.

Tables 10 and 11 are straightforward and need little comment, except to point out that gas sold to consumers is not quite the same thing as total gas consumption. A series showing the latter is available up to at least 1919 in the original source, and is generally 3 or 4 per cent higher than sales to consumers. As with the electricity statistics, these tables relate to undertakings producing gas for commercial sale, and do not include gas privately produced and consumed – as, for instance, by some iron and steel works.

Fuel and Power 1. Output of Coal in the United Kingdom and in National Coal Board Divisions – 1938–65

NOTE

SOURCES: Ministry of Fuel and Power (later Ministry of Power) *Statistical Digest* and its *Supplement* for 1945. The Division figures for 1946 were not published in these sources and have been obtained from the *Annual Report* of the National Coal Board for 1947 (*S.P.* 1947–8, x) and the *Coal Mining Industry: Annual Statistical Statement for the Year 1946* (*S.P.* 1946–7, xv).

(in millions of tons)

	Scottish	Northern	Durham	North-Eastern	North-Western	East Midlands	West Midlands	South-Western	South-Eastern	Opencast	U.K. Total
1938	30·3	14·9	31·4	43·8	17·0	30·8	19·7	37·4	1·8	—	227·0
1939	30·5	14·4	30·6	45·9	17·0	33·2	20·5	37·4	1·9	—	231·3
1940	29·7	13·6	26·7	46·8	16·0	36·0	19·7	34·3	1·6	—	224·3
1941	26·6	12·0	24·6	44·4	14·4	36·1	17·7	29·2	1·4	—	206·3
1942	26·2	12·0	25·3	42·8	13·8	36·5	17·2	28·5	1·3	1·3	204·9
1943	24·7	11·7	24·3	40·3	13·1	35·5	16·5	26·8	1·4	4·4	198·9
1944	23·4	11·3	23·2	37·9	12·8	34·3	16·0	24·0	1·3	8·7	192·7
1945	21·4	10·5	22·1	36·7	12·4	32·8	15·7	22·0	1·2	8·1	182·8
1946	22·5	11·3	23·2	37·6	12·8	32·7	16·4	22·1	1·3	8·8	190·1 (a)
1947	22·8	11·8	24·3	38·2	13·4	35·1	17·0	22·6	1·4	10·2	197·4
1948	23·5	12·3	25·6	40·1	14·1	37·2	17·7	23·7	1·5	11·7	209·4
1949	23·8	12·8	26·4	42·1	14·4	39·1	18·3	24·2	1·6	12·4	215·1
1950	23·3	13·3	26·5	42·6	14·7	40·1	17·6	24·3	1·7	12·2	216·3
1951	23·6	13·4	27·2	44·4	15·3	43·0	18·0	24·7	1·8	11·0	222·9
1952	22·9	13·2	26·5	44·9	15·5	44·0	18·2	25·0	1·7	12·1	226·4
1953	22·8	13·4	25·9	44·9	15·6	44·5	18·1	25·0	1·7	11·7	224·2
										- - (b)	- - - (b)
1954	22·6	13·5	25·9	45·6	15·6	45·6	18·0	25·1	1·7	10·1	224·1
1955	22·0	13·5	25·6	43·9	15·6	46·1	17·7	24·2	1·5	11·4	221·6
											- - - (c)
1956	21·5	13·7	25·6	43·6	15·7	46·3	17·7	24·1	1·7	12·1	222·0
1957	21·3	13·5	25·2	43·7	15·5	46·9	17·9	24·3	1·7	13·6	223·6
1958	19·5	13·2	24·0	42·7	15·0	45·7	16·9	22·8	1·6	14·3	215·8
1959	18·9	12·8	23·5	42·3	14·2	44·9	16·0	21·2	1·6	10·8	206·1
	- - - (d)	- - - (d)	- - - (d)	- - - (d)	- - - (d)	- - - (d)	- - - (d)	- - - (d)			
1959	18·5	12·7	23·3	41·9	14·0	44·6	15·4	20·5			
1960	17·7	12·0	22·8	40·4	12·9	43·7	13·8	19·1	1·5	7·6	193·6
1961	17·2	11·8	22·3	39·4	11·7	44·1	13·8	17·9	1·4	8·5	190·5
1962	17·5	11·9	22·8	42·3	12·3	46·3	14·3	18·8	1·5	8·1	197·4
		Northumberland & Durham (e)			— (e)						
1963	16·6	33·1		43·5	12·6	47·1	14·7	18·9	1·6	6·1	195·8
1964	15·6	31·2		42·5	12·1	45·3	14·4	19·6	1·5	6·8	195·6
1965	15·2	30·6		39·2	9·9	43·3	14·1	17·5	1·5	7·3	187·5

(a) This is the latest available figure given in the Ministry of Power *Statistical Digest*. The figure of U.K. total output given in the National Coal Board *Annual Report* for 1947 was 188·6 million tons.

(b) Losses of 2 per cent in screening opencast coal were excluded after 1953.
(c) After 1955 there was a change to a 52-week period instead of the calendar year.
(d) Subsequent district figures apply to mines operated by the National Coal Board only.

Fuel and Power 2. Average Number of Wage-Earners on Colliery Books in the United Kingdom and in National Coal Board Divisions – 1938–65

NOTE
SOURCES: as for table 1.

(in thousands)

	Scottish	Northern	Durham	North-Eastern	North-Western	East Midlands	West Midlands	South-Western	South-Eastern	U.K. Total
1938	89·9	51·7	114·5	145·8	68·0	94·8	66·8	143·4	6·6	781·7
1939	88·3	50·9	111·2	145·3	65·7	94·9	66·5	137·1	6·4	766·3
1940	86·4	49·1	105·4	145·4	61·3	95·2	64·5	136·4	5·7	749·2
1941	82·9	45·9	93·0	141·5	56·6	93·2	60·4	119·2	5·0	697·6
1942	83·7	45·6	98·8	142·4	57·4	94·0	60·2	121·8	5·3	709·3
1943	82·8	45·4	100·0	140·8	58·0	93·6	59·6	122·0	5·5	707·8
1944	81·7	45·6	102·0	141·4	58·7	95·0	60·0	120·0	5·8	710·2
1945	80·3	45·6	103·5	141·5	58·8	95·0	60·6	117·6	6·0	708·9
1946	79·1	150·3		137·5	58·1	91·8	58·9	114·9	6·0	696·7
1947	81·1	47·1	108·9	138·5	59·8	94·6	59·5	115·5	6·4	711·4
1948	82·4	48·2	111·0	141·5	61·1	98·2	59·9	115·4	6·3	724·0
1949	82·7	48·5	110·7	140·5	60·1	98·0	59·9	113·0	6·1	719·5
1950	81·5	48·6	108·2	135·5	57·5	95·7	56·2	107·8	6·0	697·0
1951	82·2	49·3	107·1	136·3	57·8	96·6	55·2	107·9	6·2	698·6
1952	84·8	49·9	107·1	140·1	60·6	99·3	57·4	110·0	6·4	715·6
1953	85·2	48·9	105·2	141·1	60·9	100·8	58·3	110·1	6·4	716·9
(a)	---	---	----	----	---	----	---	----	--	----
1953	84·2	47·9	103·7	141·1	60·1	100·5	58·6	110·4	6·4	712·9
1954	83·5	47·1	102·4	140·1	59·5	100·8	58·2	109·1	6·5	707·2
1955	83·7	47·1	102·1	139·3	58·9	101·8	57·4	107·1	6·7	704·1
1956	84·8	47·4	102·3	137·8	58·9	102·2	57·2	105·7	7·1	703·4
1957	86·7	47·6	101·8	138·4	58·4	103·7	59·6	106·7	7·2	710·1
1958	85·8	46·7	100·0	137·0	56·8	103·1	58·0	104·2	7·2	698·8
1959	81·0	44·0	96·1	132·7	52·4	100·4	53·9	97·1	6·9	664·5
(b)	---	---	---	----	---	----	---	---	--	----
1959	79·9	43·7	95·6	132·1	51·9	100·1	53·1	94·9	6·9	658·2
1960	72·2	39·7	90·1	121·9	45·4	94·4	45·5	87·0	5·9	602·1
1961	69·4	37·1	85·3	116·5	41·8	91·3	41·8	81·6	5·7	570·5
1962	63·8	35·2	81·1	115·3	40·0	90·1	40·3	79·6	5·5	550·9
1963	55·8	33·7	75·0	112·8	36·8	88·6	38·4	77·5	5·2	523·8
1964	51·7	32·7 (c)	69·5 (c)	109·5	34·2 (c)	85·5	36·4	73·3	5·0	497·8
1965	48·1	31·3 (c)	63·4 (c)	104·5	32·1 (c)	81·3	33·2	66·7	4·8	465·6

(a) There was a change in the definition used in 1954. The second line of figures for 1953 is on the new basis.
(b) From 1960 the figures relate to mines operated by the National Coal Board only The second line of figures for 1959 is on this basis.

(c) Owing to a reorganisation of the Division areas, these figures, which relate to the old areas, have been partially estimated by reference to the National Coal Board *Annual Reports*.

Fuel and Power 3. Coal Exports – United Kingdom 1938–65

NOTE

SOURCE: Ministry of Fuel and Power (later Ministry of Power) *Statistical Digest*.

(in thousands of tons)

1938	35,856	1948	10,505	1958	4,223
1939	36,917	1949	13,916	1959	3,479
1940	19,646	1950	13,551	1960	5,143
1941	5,084	1951	7,807	1961	5,597
1942	3,574	1952	11,751	1962	4,711
1943	3,625	1953	13,972	1963	7,876
1944	2,606	1954	13,716	1964	5,870
1945	3,325	1955	12,233	1965	3,795
1946	4,455	1956	8,542		
1947	1,057	1957	7,027		

Fuel and Power 4. Consumption of Coal in Great Britain according to Use – 1938–65

NOTE

SOURCES: Ministry of Fuel and Power (later Ministry of Power) *Statistical Digest*, and for Ships from 1959 to 1962 *The Colliery Year Book and Coal Trades Directory*.

(in millions of tons)

	Coke Ovens	Domestic	Electricity	Gasworks	Industry	Mines	Railways	Ships
1938	19·1	...	14·9	19·1	...	11·9	13·2	11·8
1939	20·4	...	15·9	18·9	...	12·1	12·9	10·8
1940	22·3	...	18·1	17·8	...	12·3	13·5	8·2
1941	21·1	...	20·4	19·1	...	12·1	13·8	5·6
1942	21·6	...	22·3	20·7	...	12·0	14·5	4·8
1943	20·9	42·4	22·6	20·8	39·0	11·6	14·8	4·4
1944	20·1	39·6	24·1	20·7	37·0	11·1	15·0	3·6
1945	20·1	36·4	23·5	21·0	35·0	10·5	14·6	4·1
1946	20·1	35·3	26·2	22·7	38·0	10·6	14·8	5·7
1947	19·8	35·8	27·1	22·7	36·0	11·0	14·3	5·4
1948	22·3	36·4	28·8	24·6	38·0	11·2	14·3	6·3
1949	22·6	36·0	30·0	25·3	38·3	10·8	14·4	6·0
1950	22·6	37·3	32·9	26·2	40·1	10·7	14·2	4·9
1951	23·4	37·1	35·4	27·4	40·9	10·6	14·1	4·6
1952	25·1	36·8	35·5	27·7	38·9	10·3	13·9	4·1
1953	25·9	37·1	36·7	27·1	39·4	9·9	13·4	3·7
1954	26·6	38·2	39·6	27·3	40·8	9·5	13·0	3·2
1955	27·0	37·1	42·9	27·9	40·7	8·7	12·2	2·8
1956	29·3	37·5	45·6	27·8	39·5	7·9	12·1	2·2
1957	30·7	35·6	46·4	26·4	37·5	7·2	11·4	1·7
1958	27·8	36·2	46·1	24·8	33·7	6·5	10·3	1·3
1959	25·7	33·4	46·0	22·5	31·7	5·6	9·5	1·1
1960	28·5	34·4	51·1	22·3	31·3	5·0	8·9	0·6
1961	26·8	32·4	54·7	22·2	29·2	4·5	7·7	0·4
1962	23·5	32·7	60·4	22·1	27·4	4·2	6·1	0·3
1963	23·5	32·0	66·8	22·1	25·9	3·9	4·9	...
1964	25·5	27·9	67·4	20·2	24·7	3·7	3·8	...
1965	25·7	27·3	69·3	18·0	24·1	3·4	2·8	...

Fuel and Power 5. Solid Fuel Used in Pig Iron Manufacture – Great Britain 1927–65

NOTES
[1] SOURCE: British Iron and Steel Federation, *Statistical Year Book* (1951) and *Annual Statistics* (1966).
[2] Though the unit is different, this table links with table 7 in the first *Abstract of British Historical Statistics*. Conversion of raw coal to coke equivalent has been made here on the basis of 10 tons of coal equal 6 tons of coke.
[3] Fuel used in the production of blast furnace ferro-alloys is included.

(in thousands of tons of coke equivalent)

1927	9,060·2	1947	8,562·9
1928	8,205·0	1948	9,974·4
1929	9,450·3	1949	9,984·5
1930	7,676·8	1950	9,897·8
1931	4,665·7	1951	10,281·8
1932	4,300·8	1952	11,478·9
1933	4,804·5	1953	11,834·1
1934	6,848·3	1954	11,877·1
1935	7,168·9	1955	12,250·2
1936	8,659·8	1956	12,983·1
1937	9,721·4	1957	13,529·6
1938	7,621·6	1958	11,628·6
1939	8,759·8	1959	10,538·6
1940	9,611·3	1960	12,998·4
1941	9,134·5	1961	12,058·8
1942	9,582·2	1962	10,596·2
1943	8,752·2	1963	10,488·9
1944	8,201·6	1964	12,050·1
1945	8,174·7	1965	11,875·5
1946	8,564·5		

Fuel and Power 6. Percentage of Coal Output Cut Mechanically and Power-Loaded – United Kingdom 1938–65

NOTE
SOURCE: Ministry of Fuel and Power (later Ministry of Power) *Statistical Digest*.

	Mechanically Cut	Power-Loaded (a)		Mechanically Cut	Power-Loaded (a)
1938	59	...	1953	83	6·0
1939	61	...	1954	84	7·4
1940	64	...	1955	87	9·9
1941	66	...	1956	87	15·5
1942	66	...	1957	88	23·1
					- - - (b)
1943	69	...	1958	90	27·8
1944	72	...	1959	90	31·3
1945	72	...	1960	92	37·5
1946	74	...	1961	...	47·7
1947	75	2·4	1962	...	58·8
					- - - (c)
1948	76	2·5	1963	...	68·4
1949	78	3·2	1964	...	75·0
1950	79	3·8	1965	...	80·7
1951	81	4·2			
1952	82	4·9			

(a) Relates to National Coal Board mines only.
(b) Prior to 1958 figures relate to pithead rather than saleable output.

(c) Subsequent figures are for years ended on 31 March following that shown.

Fuel and Power 7. Sales of Electricity – United Kingdom 1895–1920

NOTES
[1] SOURCE: Garcke's *Manual of Electricity Undertakings* (annually from 1896).
[2] The figures relate to authorised undertakings only.
[3] The figures are not of actual sales within the calendar year, but relate to various accounting years ending during a twelve-month period centred on 31 December of the year shown.

(in million British Thermal Units)

1895	20	1910	1,097
1896	30	1911	1,236
1897	43	1912	1,318
1898	60	1913	1,635
1899	85	1914	1,694
1900	125	1915	2,001
1901	196	1916	2,367
1902	247	1917	2,716
1903	345	1918	3,079
1904	448	1919	3,086
1905	554	1920	3,677
1906	713		
1907	817		
1908	955		
1909	1,027		

Fuel and Power 8. Sales of Electricity according to Type of Consumer – Great Britain 1920–65

NOTES

[1] SOURCE: Ministry of Fuel and Power (later Ministry of Power) *Statistical Digest*.

[2] The figures apply to authorised undertakings prior to 1948 and to nationalised ones subsequently.

(in million Kilowatt hours)

	Domestic and Farms	Shops, Offices, etc.	Industry	Public Lighting	Traction	Total
1920	297	398	2,545	48	419	3,707
1921	316	403	2,081	51	391	3,242
1922	370	460	2,456	58	415	3,759
1923	453	543	2,989	67	443	4,495
1924	543	626	3,435	78	486	5,168
1925	635	699	3,709	90	519	5,652
1926	754	812	3,592	96	563	5,817
1927	921	923	4,375	113	649	6,981
1928	1,098	1,042	4,762	126	716	7,744
1929	1,311	1,191	5,318	144	782	8,746
1930	1,532	1,314	5,355	162	806	9,169
1931	1,776	1,439	5,282	181	822	9,500
1932	2,027	1,577	5,518	199	855	10,176
1933	2,296	1,741	6,073	216	947	11,273
1934	2,647	1,963	7,060	240	982	12,892
1935	3,227	2,257	7,853	268	1,036	14,641
1936	3,964	2,619	8,914	298	1,096	16,891
1937	4,687	2,944	10,019	339	1,180	19,169
1938	5,361	3,107	10,320	367	1,249	20,404
1939	5,936	3,117	11,672	248	1,261	22,234
1940	6,228	2,997	13,874	17	1,147	24,263
1941	6,637	3,266	16,244	18	1,143	27,308
1942	6,720	3,256	19,142	20	1,148	30,286
1943	6,709	3,062	20,516	20	1,142	31,449
1944	7,835	3,510	19,976	29	1,169	32,519
1945	8,805	3,482	17,679	161	1,236	31,363
1946	11,663	3,892	17,632	242	1,369	34,798
1947	12,728	3,973	17,606	190	1,361	35,858
1948	13,576	4,469	19,121	257	1,398	38,821
1949	13,657	5,035	20,445	335	1,447	40,919
1950	14,911	5,765	22,920	415	1,463	45,474
1951	16,939	6,354	25,350	441	1,429	50,513
1952	16,869	7,115	26,068	479	1,401	51,950
1953	17,691	7,948	28,000	528	1,401	55,568
1954	19,075	8,746	31,553	576	1,451	61,401
1955	21,146	9,545	34,635	627	1,470	67,423
1956	23,755	10,337	37,224	692	1,512	73,520
1957	24,850	10,733	39,348	742	1,545	77,218
1958	28,227	12,057	41,241	793	1,551	83,869
1959	30,487	12,837	44,695	855	1,630	90,504
1960	35,270	14,526	49,991	922	1,654	102,363
1961	39,968	15,809	51,740	994	1,721	110,232
1962	47,628	18,284	53,529	1,060	1,856	122,357
1963	54,475	20,263	56,106	1,127	1,879	133,850
1964	54,411	21,321	61,604	1,191	1,847	140,374
1965	59,421	23,427	65,040	1,260	1,923	151,071

Fuel and Power 9. Electricity Generated according to Type of Plant – Great Britain 1920–65

NOTES

[1] SOURCE: Ministry of Fuel and Power (later Ministry of Power) *Statistical Digest*.

[2] The figures relate to authorised undertakings prior to 1948 and nationalised ones thereafter.

(in million Kilowatt hours)

	Thermal	Hydro	Total		Thermal	Hydro	Total
1920 (a)	4,263	12	4,275	1943	35,622	1,329	36,951
1921	3,880	10	3,890	1944	37,187	1,176	38,363
1922	4,531	10	4,541	1945	36,140	1,144	37,284
1923	5,276	13	5,289	1946	40,114	1,139	41,253
1924	6,007	15	6,022	1947	41,452	1,128	42,580
1925	6,604	15	6,619	1948	45,148	881	46,029
1926	6,977	15	6,992	1949	47,886	719	48,605
1927	8,421	31	8,452	1950	53,486	1,035	54,521
1928	9,216	108	9,324	1951	58,434	1,142	59,576
1929	10,265	136	10,401	1952	60,723	1,268	61,991
1930	10,597	320	10,917	1953	64,232	1,284	65,516
1931	11,001	416	11,417	1954	71,137	1,759	72,896
1932	11,894	354	12,248	1955	79,001	1,147	80,148
1933	13,228	330	13,558	1956	85,494	1,667	87,161
1934	14,998	464	15,462	1957	88,868	2,098	90,966
1935	16,944	625	17,569	1958	96,389	2,109	98,498
1936	19,554	668	20,222	1959	102,994	2,175	105,169
1937	22,150	755	22,905	1960	116,309	2,539	118,848
1938	23,384	988	24,372	1961	124,393	3,196	127,589
1939	25,427	982	26,409	1962	138,328	3,252	141,580
1940	27,973	800	28,773	1963	150,698	3,074	153,772
1941	31,529	831	32,360	1964	158,758	3,420	162,178
1942	34,557	1,097	35,654	1965	170,743	3,931	174,674

(a) The only reliable figure for an earlier date is contained in the 1907 Census of Production, which gave the public supply as 1,432 million kWh.

Fuel and Power 10. Gas Sold to Consumers – Great Britain 1881–1965

NOTES

[1] SOURCES: 1881–1920 – *Returns* published annually in Parliamentary Papers; 1921–65 – Ministry of Fuel and Power (later Ministry of Power) *Statistical Digest*.
[2] The figures apply to statutory undertakings prior to 1943, and to undertakings later vested in the Gas Boards thereafter, together with a few small transport gasworks until 1954.

[3] The local authority accounting year ended in March or May, and these figures have been attributed to the previous calendar year.

A. in million cubic feet

Year	Value	Year	Value	Year	Value
1881	61,616 (a)	1896	113,940	1911	184,412
1882	64,830	1897	119,099	1912	194,084
1883	68,269	1898	124,123	1913	201,594
				......	
1884	71,639	1899	132,326	1919	222,883
1885	75,260	1900	136,856		
				1920	235,403
1886	78,478	1901	140,421	1921	229,077
1887	81,416	1902	143,990	1922	232,603
1888	84,712	1903	147,702	1923	241,627
1889	87,908	1904	155,141	1924	256,892
1890	92,242	1905	157,322		
				1925	265,757
1891	97,350	1906	163,800	1926	276,569
1892	100,186	1907	168,630	1927	280,202
1893	99,212	1908	169,706	1928	282,429
1894	102,436	1909	173,340	1929	292,598
1895	108,564	1910	178,279		
				1930	289,991

B. in million therms

Year	Value	Year	Value	Year	Value
1923	1,153	1941	1,523	1956	2,591
......				1957	2,537
1925	1,268	1942	1,636		- - - - (c)
......		- - - -		1958	2,551
1930	1,383	1943	1,691	1959	2,540
				1960	2,612
1931	1,390	1944	1,770		
1932	1,373	1945	1,821	1961	2,683
1933	1,366			1962	2,867
	- - - - (b)	1946	2,002	1963	2,924
1934	1,383	1947	2,094	1964	3,169
1935	1,405	1948	2,178	1965	3,310
		1949	2,241		
1936	1,465	1950	2,337		
1937	1,496				
1938	1,500	1951	2,449		
1939	1,499	1952	2,453		
1940	1,443	1953	2,436		
		1954	2,527		
		1955	2,583		

(a) Includes an estimated figure of 3,750 for Scotland.
(b) From 1934 includes gas 'supplied separately for industrial purposes only' through a separate main, which amounted to 11·4 million therms in that year.

(c) Subsequent figures are for years ended on 31 March following that shown.

Fuel and Power 11. Imports and Re-exports of Petroleum –
United Kingdom 1863–1922 and Great Britain 1920–65

NOTES

[1] SOURCES: 1863–1922 *Annual Statement of Trade*; 1920–65 Ministry of Fuel and Power (later Ministry of Power) *Statistical Digest*.

[2] Figures of imports before 1863 are given in the *Annual Statement of Trade* in cwt., and are as follows:

1854	1	1859	11,264
1855	120	1860	35
1856	5,543	1861	25,839
1857	56,544	1862	398,872
1858	65,281		

One cwt. equals approximately 12½ gallons.

A. United Kingdom, in million gallons

	Imports	Re-exports		Imports	Re-exports
1863	7·4	1·0	1893	155·1	1·6
1864	4·4	1·0	1894	163·0	1·9
1865	3·0	0·4	1895	177·1	1·8
1866	6·5	0·6	1896	190·0	2·6
1867	4·7	0·6	1897	185·7	1·8
1868	4·3	0·4	1898	219·3	1·4
1869	5·4	0·3	1899	240·1	1·8
1870	6·9	0·7	1900	255·0	2·0
1871	9·0	0·4	1901	253·8	3·6
1872	6·4	0·1	1902	284·9	4·1
1873	16·7	0·3	1903	285·9	8·7
1874	21·5	0·2	1904	302·1	8·1
1875	19·4	0·1	1905	300·1	7·9
1876	25·2	0·4	1906	299·2	6·9
1877	33·9	0·4	1907	304·1	5·0
1878	30·3	0·8	1908	343·6	5·5
1879	43·3	0·3	1909	358·1	4·5
1880	38·8	0·4	1910	345·5	5·8
1881	59·2	0·4	1911	365·6	7·1
1882	59·7	0·8	1912	414·3	6·7
1883	70·5	0·8	1913	488·1	4·2
1884	53·0	0·8	1914	646·7	5·2
1885	73·9	1·1	1915	588·5	11·6
1886	71·1	0·6	1916	451·6	7·0
1887	77·4	0·5	1917	826·9	5·2
1888	94·4	0·8	1918	1,324·5	1·8
1889	102·9	0·9	1919	713·8	28·2
1890	105·1	1·0	1920	879·4	64·1
1891	130·6	1·2	1921	1,161·0	26·4
1892	130·2	2·4	1922	1,213·3	89·7

Fuel and Power 11. *continued*

B. Great Britain, in thousands of tons

	Crude and Process Oils		Refined Products	
	Imports	Re-exports	Imports	Re-exports
1920	17	1	3,382	252
1921	406	- -	4,046	107
1922	869	- -	3,760	345
1923	1,339	8	3,738	468
1924	1,858	- -	4,157	624
1925	2,276	- -	3,904	858
1926	2,150	- -	5,103	599
1927	2,659	2	5,167	619
1928	1,992	1	5,943	622
1929	1,949	- -	6,241	792
1930	1,844	- -	7,088	657
1931	1,378	- -	6,785	512
1932	1,474	- -	6,831	513
1933	1,571	1	7,444	512
1934	1,904	17	8,274	610
1935	1,954	22	8,368	702
1936	2,047	12	8,724	657
1937	2,109	—	9,132	760
1938	2,272	—	9,390	592
1939	2,166	—	8,733	532
1940	1,564	—	10,001	218
1941	976	—	12,081	53
1942	591	—	9,785	66
1943	527	—	14,452	37
1944	684	—	19,577	79
1945	949	—	14,818	168
1946	2,179	- -	12,232	404
1947	2,474	—	10,592	644
1948	4,641	—	13,196	342
1949	6,048	—	11,453	500
1950	9,246	—	9,896	1,193
	- - - - - (a)		- - - - (a)	
1951	16,702	—	9,786	3,412
1952	22,829	—	5,961	5,441
1953	25,750	15	6,016	7,391
1954	28,075	24	6,612	7,829
1955	27,854	68	8,515	6,274
1956	28,608	69	9,420	7,714
1957	27,967	21	10,829	6,287
1958	33,747	6	11,014	8,390
1959	39,238	121	12,752	8,221
1960	44,615	65	13,802	9,069
1961	48,958	110	11,807	7,701
1962	52,349	991	15,694	9,737
1963	53,868	1,415	18,219	9,724
1964	59,396	396	18,615	9,086
1965 (b)	65,653	268	20,207	10,626

(a) After 1950 refinery feedstock was transferred from refined to crude.

(b) Natural gas is not included

CHAPTER V

IRON AND STEEL

TABLES

The majority of the tables in this chapter follows on directly from those in the first *Abstract of British Historical Statistics*, and do not call for any particular comment. Table 5, giving the numbers employed, is one exception, since there is no exact comparison possible between 1938 and later statistics. As was pointed out in the first volume, these figures have been plagued by changes in the basis of collection since they were first taken in 1920. This has continued to be true since the Second World War. Despite these difficulties, however, the statisticians of the British Iron and Steel Federation managed to compile a postwar series of output per man-year which included a figure for 1938 for comparison. This series is shown here as table 6.

The statistics of the volume of overseas trade in iron and steel show one difference from those in the first volume. An additional import series is given – that of uncoated plates and sheets – which only became of much significance after 1938 at times when home-produced supplies were inadequate for the motor industry. Statistics of the value of overseas trade in iron and steel can be found in Chapter XI, whilst some material on prices is in Chapter XVI.

Iron and Steel 1. Output of Iron Ore in the United Kingdom and its Principal Districts – 1938–65

NOTES

[1] SOURCE: British Iron and Steel Federation, *Statistical Year Book*, subsequently entitled *Annual Statistics*.

[2] The following district output figures are not included in the main table because production ceased after 1947:

	Staffordshire, Shropshire and Warwickshire	Scotland
1938	127	17
1939	138	15
1940	184	33
1941	187	49
1942	150	36
1943	143	10
1944	17	7
1945	2	5
1946	2	4
1947	1	2

(in thousands of tons)

	Total	Cleveland	Lincolnshire	Leicestershire, Northants, Rutland and Oxfordshire	Cumberland and Lancashire	South Wales
1938	11,859	1,514	3,439	5,774	795	188 (a)
1939	14,486	1,550	4,702	7,113	761	205
1940	17,702	1,900	6,076	8,483	781	233
1941	18,974	1,920	6,334	9,575	686	210
1942 (b)	19,906	1,885	6,692	10,317	616	167
1943	18,494	1,757	5,869	9,936	596	125
1944	15,472	1,509	5,279	7,965	535	120
1945	14,175	1,199	4,892	7,529	406	104
1946	12,173	935	4,624	6,103	379	101
1947 (b)	11,091	886	4,409	5,310	369	97
1948	13,089	1,040	5,251	6,381	325	89
1949	13,397	1,028	5,365	6,551	350	102
1950	12,963	1,020	5,012	6,458	343	103
1951	14,777	1,075	5,342	7,786	347	97
1952 (b)	16,232	1,188	5,463	9,074	403	105
1953	15,818	1,219	5,113	9,017	354	115
1954	15,557	871	5,643	8,580	344	118
1955	16,175	625	6,264	8,837	330	120
1956	16,245	581	6,125	9,087	323	129
1957	16,902	556	6,809	9,090	321	126
1958 (b)	14,612	559	6,052	7,548	334	120
1959	14,870	418	6,120	7,883	323	125
1960	17,087	463	6,996	9,194	315	120
1961	16,518	444	7,215	8,446	290	124
1962	15,277	260	7,264	7,376	248	130
1963	14,912	141	7,294	7,083	254	140
1964 (b)	16,326	1	7,757	8,140	274	153
1965	15,415	—	7,596	7,410	261	147

(a) Includes the Denbighshire output of 600 tons.

(b) These were 53-week years.

Iron and Steel 2. Output of Pig Iron in Great Britain and its Principal Districts – 1938–65

(in thousands of tons)

	Total	North Yorkshire and Durham	West Yorkshire, South Lancashire, and North Wales	Cumberland and Furness	Derbyshire, Essex, Leicestershire, Northants and Notts.	Staffordshire, Shropshire, Worcestershire and Warwickshire	Lincolnshire	South Wales	Scotland
1938	6,761	1,833	349	722	1,598	317	868	665	409
1939	7,980	1,983	365	661	1,827	432	1,130	1,101	481
1940	8,205	1,934	401	705	1,787	447	1,308	962	659
1941	7,393	1,678	396	552	1,790	409	1,252	805	511
1942 (a)	7,726	1,799	423	595	1,909	372	1,303	829	496
1943	7,187	1,683	379	526	1,781	347	1,180	804	487
1944	6,737	1,606	323	538	1,681	317	982	778	513
1945	7,107	1,664	349	613	1,697	339	1,039	864	542
1946	7,761	1,902	354	696	1,783	343	1,071	1,011	603
1947 (a)	7,785	1,934	364	703	1,832	287	1,048	1,024	592
1948	9,276	2,410	420	750	2,019	491	1,248	1,173	766
1949	9,499	2,369	414	790	2,108	540	1,306	1,203	769
1950	9,633	2,402	437	824	2,209	551	1,239	1,232	739
1951	9,669	2,338	448	792	2,150	543	1,259	1,351	790
1952 (a)	10,728	2,601	472	933	2,262	523	1,505	1,545	886
1953	11,175	2,646	783	930	2,267	474	1,559	1,653	863
1954	11,883	2,811	873	954	2,276	482	1,647	1,894	947
1955	12,470	2,824	992	964	2,342	567	1,880	1,975	927
1956	13,170	2,761	1,176	1,116	2,581	605	1,804	2,195	931
1957	14,283	3,113	1,272	1,077	2,506	609	2,120	2,526	1,060
1958 (a)	12,975	2,848	1,272	801	2,080	438	2,048	2,511	976
1959	12,583	2,474	1,219	782	2,131	372	2,105	2,682	816
1960	15,763	3,412	1,407	1,028	2,633	553	2,290	3,141	1,299
1961	14,747	3,025	1,463	895	2,308	525	2,334	2,961	1,236
1962	13,692	2,397	1,628	744	1,887	439	2,303	3,428	866
1963	14,591	2,668	1,466	630	1,819	518	2,395	4,207	888
1964 (a)	17,274	3,561	1,646	764	2,084	540	2,723	4,420	1,535
1965	17,460	3,434	1,686	695	1,971	585	2,697	4,718	1,675

NOTES

[1] SOURCE: British Iron and Steel Federation, *Statistical Year Book*, subsequently entitled *Annual Statistics*.

[2] The figures include the output of blast furnace ferro-alloys.

(a) These were 53-week years.

Iron and Steel 3. Output of Pig Iron according to Quality – United Kingdom 1938–65

NOTE
SOURCE: British Iron and Steel Federation, *Statistical Year Book*, subsequently entitled *Annual Statistics*.

(in thousands of tons)

	Hematite	Basic	Foundry	Forge	Blast Furnace Ferro-Alloys	Total (incl. direct castings)
1938	1,484	3,763	1,230	151	130	6,761
1939	1,396	5,108	1,204	167	102	7,980
1940	1,428	5,453	1,062	119	141	8,205
1941	906	5,182	1,082	101	120	7,393
1942 (a)	964	5,553	963	69	175	7,726
1943	927	5,070	1,025	40	124	7,187
1944	1,009	4,792	740	35	160	6,737
1945	1,076	4,884	964	52	131	7,107
1946	1,121	5,288	1,135	66	150	7,761
1947 (a)	1,117	5,183	1,282	70	132	7,785
1948	1,366	6,256	1,396	93	164	9,276
1949	1,437	6,248	1,555	87	168	9,499
1950	1,477	6,478	1,467	61	148	9,633
1951	1,333	6,675	1,417	70	172	9,669
1952 (a)	1,426	7,528	1,522	74	176	10,728
1953	1,392	8,070	1,466	52	194	11,175
1954	1,436	8,772	1,441	45	187	11,883
1955	1,415	9,296	1,509	57	193	12,470
1956	1,547 (b)	9,982	1,412	45	183	13,170
1957	1,571 (b)	11,265	1,259	29	158	14,283
1958 (a)	1,237	10,315	1,229	20	174	12,975
1959	1,021	10,285	1,089	39	148	12,583
1960	1,187	13,072	1,293	5	205	15,763
1961	1,137	12,256	1,196		158	14,747
1962	876	11,568	1,054		194	13,692
1963	817	12,644	1,006		124	14,591
1964 (a)	957	15,069	1,079		168	17,274
1965	877	15,377	1,012		193	17,460

(a) These were 53-week years.

(b) Includes special hematite low silicon iron for basic steelmaking.

Iron and Steel 4. Output of Steel Ingots and Castings by Process – United Kingdom 1938–65

NOTE
SOURCE: British Iron and Steel Federation, *Statistical Year Book*, subsequently entitled *Annual Statistics*.

(in thousands of tons)

	Total	Open Hearth		Bessemer		Electric		Other
		Acid	Basic	Acid	Basic	Arc	Induction	
1938	10,398	1,721	7,743	164	431	223		117
1939	13,221	2,157	9,705	233	702	292		133
1940	12,975	2,174	9,274	176	738	435		179
1941	12,312	1,808	8,945	98	696	573		193
1942 (a)	12,942	1,605	9,394	96	726	860		261
1943	13,031	1,409	9,555	72	731	992		272
1944	12,142	1,173	9,096	85	709	795		284
1945	11,824	1,159	9,026	171	687	542		240
1946	12,695	1,229	9,901	210	724	479		153
1947 (a)	12,725	1,229	9,870	208	678	576		164
1948	14,877	1,398	11,589	218	786	707		178
1949	15,553	1,367	12,230	226	819	740		171
1950	16,293	1,311	12,981	248	846	736		171
1951	15,639	1,259	12,277	241	862	819		179
1952 (a)	16,418	1,239	12,923	246	887	816	114	193
1953	17,609	1,133	14,298	263	798	822	107	188
1954	18,520	995	15,249	265	909	818	112	172
1955	19,791	1,000	16,252	252	1,032	972	127	156
1956	20,659	986	17,018	230	1,078	1,067	131	150
1957	21,699	961	18,075	250	1,058	1,078	133	143
1958 (a)	19,566	762	16,385	229	945	1,011	115	119
1959	20,186	616	16,708	215	1,196	1,225	123	103
1960	24,305	658	19,875	294	1,681	1,540	146	112
1961	22,086	611	17,768	254	1,699	1,507	141	106
1962	20,491	445	16,275	193	2,014	1,371	109	84
1963	22,520	384	16,726	214	3,042	1,955	122	79
1964 (a)	26,230	419	18,070	290	4,432	2,791	148	80
1965	27,006	392	16,822	258	6,026	3,288	149	70

(a) These were 53-week years.

Iron and Steel 5. Numbers Employed in the Iron and Steel Industry –
Great Britain 1940–65

NOTES

[1] SOURCE: British Iron and Steel Federation, *Statistical Year Book*, subsequently entitled *Annual Statistics*.
[2] The figures include workers in iron mines and quarries, coke ovens at blast furnaces, tinplate manufacture, steel foundries, and maintenance and clerical workers. They do not include workers in ferro-alloy manufacture, iron foundries, bolt and nut manufacture, wire-drawing, and scrap merchants.
[3] Two part-time female workers are counted as one full-time worker.

A. Annual Average – 1940–7			B. At a Day in July – 1947–56			C. At a Day in December – 1956–65 (b)		
				(in thousands)				
	Males	Total		Males	Total		Males	Total
1940	295	306	1947	248	269	1956	288	308
1941	291	310	1948	259	278	1957	291	311
1942	289	329	1949	262	282	1958	271	289
1943	286	336	1950	264	286	1959	281	299
	--- (a)	--- (a)	1951	260	280	1960	297	316
1944	269	316	1952	264	286	1961	288	307
1945	253	289	1953	265	285	1962	275	294
1946	256	275	1954	260	280	1963	277	295
1947	266	288	1955	265	285	1964	286	305
			1956	270	290	1965	283	303

(a) After 1943 workers temporarily absent on holiday or sick are excluded.

(b) In Part C workers employed in the production of welded tubes of 16 inches O.D. or more are excluded.

Iron and Steel 6. Output per Man-Year in the Iron and Steel Industry – Great Britain 1938–65

NOTES
[1] SOURCE: British Iron and Steel Federation, *Statistical Year Book*, subsequently entitled *Annual Statistics*.
[2] The index of volume of output reflects activity in the industry as a whole, and allows for changes in the pattern of output. Prior to 1960 no blast furnaces were covered by the indices, but from that date blast furnaces integrated with steel works were so covered.

(1954 = 100)

	Volume of Output	Numbers at Work	Output per Man-Year
1938	51·8	79·0	65·6
1946	66·4	89·0	74·6
1947	68·9	92·5	74·5
1948	80·0	96·2	83·2
1949	80·9	97·8	82·7
1950	83·4	98·0	85·1
1951	86·7	97·6	88·8
1952	93·9	99·2	94·7
1953	96·5	100·2	96·3
1954	100	100	100
1955	108·2	101·8	106·3
1956	113·1	104·1	108·6
1957	117·3	106·6	110·0
1958	103·3	100·4	102·9
1959	104·4 (a)	98·0 (a)	106·5 (a)
1960	124·2	107·5	115·5
1961	115·9	109·3	106·0
1962	106·4	101·5	104·8
1963	113·4	101·8	111·4
1964	130·8	108·2	120·9
1965	138·9	111·1	124·9

(a) See note [2].

Iron and Steel 7. Imports of Iron Ore – United Kingdom 1938–65

NOTES
[1] SOURCE: *Annual Statement of Trade*.
[2] Imports of manganiferous ore are included throughout.

(in thousands of tons and £000)

	Quantity	Value		Quantity	Value		Quantity	Value
1938	5,164	7,303	1948	8,736	24,722	1958	12,899	72,897
1939	5,308	7,039	1949	8,693	25,129	1959	13,350	69,871
1940	4,562	9,650	1950	8,392	24,291	1960	17,969	87,954
1941	2,295	9,109	1951	8,747	37,311	1961	14,966	73,577
1942	1,922	7,602	1952	9,691	57,048	1962	12,897	62,299
1943	1,894	7,890	1953	10,981	62,415	1963	13,940	63,835
1944	2,172	9,134	1954	11,611	59,605	1964	18,001	81,130
1945	4,071	14,796	1955	12,859	68,290	1965	18,300	82,406
1946	6,601	18,751	1956	14,330	83,731			
1947	6,845	18,914	1957	15,912	98,501			

Iron and Steel 8. Imports and Re-exports of Iron and Steel – United Kingdom 1938–65

NOTE
SOURCE: *Annual Statement of Trade.*

(in thousands of tons)

	Pig Iron and Ferro-Alloys	Steel Blooms, Billets and Slabs, (except alloys)	Imports Iron and Steel Bars, Rods, Angles, Shapes, and Sections (except alloys)	Iron and Steel Plates and Sheets (uncoated)	Total Iron and Steel (*a*)	Total Re-exports of Iron and Steel
1938	443	317	352	68	1,342	30·2
1939	427	372	651	80	1,811	2·8
1940	770	1,321	637	196	3,689	1·0
1941	1,071	1,523	648	180	4,177	1·1
1942	424	1,093	316	24	2,509	1·1
1943	497	937	349	319	2,814	4·9
1944	341	699	142	136	1,764	- -
1945	155	80	22	2	313	0·7
1946	64	300	35	9	499	4·4
1947	89	204	33	18	517	1·1
1948	146	174	110	18	568	0·2
1949	346	301	398	52	1,253	0·3
1950	284	161	140	94	757	0·3
1951	402	103	150	92	883	0·4
1952	865	403	460	148	2,457	0·6
1953	784	402	209	102	1,711	3·7
1954	394	70	18	207	780	0·7
1955	798	293	248	520	2,337	1·0
1956	714	266	420	393	2,152	2·5
1957	525	241	125	272	1,312	1·6
1958	269	86	51	255	754	1·4
1959	246	3	50	265	651	1·3
1960	436	220	176	615	1,723	2·9
1961	234	76	64	150	739	3·2
1962	308	152	117	181	1,131	4·0
1963	408	257	277	360	1,654	2·2
1964	611	431	318	479	2,216	2·0
1965	632	16	146	263	1,255	2·3

(*a*) This includes those manufactures of iron and steel which were classified under that heading in the trade accounts up to 1953.

Iron and Steel 9. Iron and Steel Exports – United Kingdom 1938–65

NOTES
[1] SOURCE: *Annual Statement of Trade.*
[2] The 1938 figures for Railway Material and for Total Iron and Steel differ from those given in the first *Abstract of British* *Historical Statistics* through the exclusion here of axles and similar railway parts.

(in thousands of tons)

	Pig Iron (incl. Ferro-Alloys)	Railway Material	Tin- and Terne-Plates and Sheets	Other Plates and Sheets	Tubes, Pipes, and Fittings	Total Iron and Steel (a)
1938	101	158	329	357	312	1,915
1939	78	93	335	315	273	1,582
1940	25	32	394	128	190	1,077
1941	21	9	230	43	42	487
1942	5	16	49	49	24	258
1943	5	11	17	16	15	135
1944	3	25	19	40	55	220
1945	34	85	33	101	102	643
1946	92	268	120	386	357	2,243
1947	3	161	161	283	349	1,877
1948	7	194	207	346	422	2,007
1949	21	202	206	461	496	2,383
1950	41	310	262	584	510	3,088
1951	19	211	251	464	543	2,603
1952	8	204	315	457	578	2,499
1953	9	238	262	568	590	2,637
1954	55	230	302	563	582	2,827
1955	55	284	321	695	683	3,215
1956	149	253	308	637	773	3,350
1957	133	270	418	751	817	3,754
1958	156	272	423	584	746	3,315
1959	169	165	480	672	746	3,812
1960	158	173	499	796	735	3,962
1961	151	180	436	928	634	4,096
1962	226	123	470	1,040	529	4,003
1963	112	94	478	1,319	505	3,925
1964	73	171	412	1,291	542	4,252
1965	127	301	418	1,372	548	4,505

(a) This includes those manufactures of iron and steel which were classified under that heading in the trade accounts up to 1953.

CHAPTER VI

NON-FERROUS METALS

TABLES

1. Output of Non-Ferrous Metals – United Kingdom 1938–65.
2. Imports of Non-Ferrous Ores and Metals – United Kingdom 1938–65.
3. Exports of Smelted, Unmanufactured Non-Ferrous Metals – United Kingdom 1938–65.

The organisation of this chapter differs from the one on tin, copper, and lead in the first *Abstract of British Historical Statistics*, and further metals – aluminium, nickel, and zinc – are included here. But basically the same sort of information is shown as in the first volume. There is, however, a number of differences in definition between the production statistics for the period since the Second World War and those collected earlier, and these often prevent exact comparisons between the series given here and similarly described series in the first volume. One example of this will illustrate the point. In the first volume, figures for the output of tin ore and of white tin in 1938 were given as 3,172 tons and 1,999 tons respectively. In table 1 here tin ore output is shown as two thousand tons – because the figure, like all subsequent ones, relates to metal content, whereas the earlier one related to the concentrated ore. The output of virgin tin metal in 1938 is here given as 32·1 thousand tons, because in the postwar period there has been no distinction made between metal from home-produced and imported ores, and consequently the combined total is the only one available.

There is less difference between the overseas trade volume statistics given here and their equivalents in the first volume of *Historical Statistics*; but even in these there are some differences in definition. The two most notable are the inclusion of brass with copper, which is necessary in order to maintain comparability in the series right through to 1965; and the exclusion here of all except unmanufactured metals.

Information on the value of overseas trade in non-ferrous metals can be found in Chapter XI.

Non-ferrous Metals 1. Output of Non-ferrous Metals – United Kingdom 1938–65

(in thousands of tons)

NOTE
SOURCES: *Abstract*, except for 1938 tin ore figure, which comes from International Tin Council, *Statistical Supplement*, *1967*.

	Virgin Aluminium	Secondary Aluminium	Virgin (or Primary Refined) Copper	Secondary Copper	Lead Concentrates (d)	Refined Lead (b)	Refined Nickel (c)	Tin Ore (a)	Virgin Tin Metal	Zinc Concentrates (d)	Virgin (or Slab) Zinc (e)
1938	23·0	...	...	...	29·7	...	...	2·0	32·1	...	55·3 (e)
1939	25·0	...	...	...	16·6	...	...	1·6	37·3	...	...
1940	19·0	38·1	161·5	...	13·6	...	...	1·6	46·7	...	55·6
1941	22·7	53·2	146·1	...	8·0	...	...	1·5	41·3	8·4	67·5
1942	46·8	78·8	183·0	...	5·4	...	20·3	1·4	37·3	6·8	72·6
1943	55·7	93·5	171·4 —— (f)	...	4·2	15·7	15·4	1·4	31·6	12·8	69·4
1944	35·5	104·5	154·5	...	3·8	13·6	15·0	1·2	28·6	15·8	71·0
1945	31·9	81·0	93·2	...	2·7	13·5	13·4	1·2	27·5	6·8	62·0
1946	31·5	74·9	107·1	73·8	2·6	27·0	11·3	0·8	29·1	0·1	65·4
1947	28·9	97·6	112·5	73·1	2·8	32·1	14·3	0·9	28·1	—	68·3
1948	30·0	80·2	124·9	67·6	2·3	36·2	17·1	0·9	31·0	—	72·0
1949	30·3	75·2	105·1	72·5	2·1	35·8	21·6	0·9	28·4	—	64·1
1950	29·5	79·9	119·3	70·9	3·0	73·1	20·9	0·9	28·5	0·2	70·3
1951	27·7	71·4	132·1	73·8	4·1	73·6	23·3	0·8	27·7	0·2 (d)	69·7
1952	28·0	73·1	146·4	78·9	4·7	86·1	23·8	0·9	29·5	1·7	68·7
1953	30·9	80·5	97·0	88·2	6·6	77·4	23·9	1·1	29·4	2·8	72·7
1954	31·6	84·1	136·5	82·6	6·9	82·1	23·9	0·9	28·0	3·5	81·2
1955	24·4	95·6	123·5	103·7	6·1	82·9	24·3	1·0	27·7	2·8	81·3
1956	27·6	96·2	113·7	102·7	7·5	94·5	24·2	1·0	26·8	1·4	81·5
1957	29·4	97·2	112·3	89·0	8·1	85·7	23·9	1·0	34·5	1·0	76·9
1958	26·4	99·0	98·3	94·9	4·3	79·8	23·1	1·1	33·0	0·3	74·6
1959	24·5	107·3	95·5	96·7	2·4	86·7	24·9	1·3	27·6	—	73·0
1960	28·9	109·6	110·9	104·5	1·4	91·1	33·8	1·2	27·6	—	74·3
1961	32·3	117·2	129·0	105·3	1·5	86·3	37·4	1·2	26·4	—	92·9
1962	34·0	129·7	117·0	111·1	0·4	88·6	37·7	1·2	19·9	—	97·3
1963	30·6	146·6	90·0	120·7	0·2	95·1	37·5	1·2	18·7	—	99·0
1964	31·7	168·9	110·7	130·5	0·2	120·8	37·4	1·2	19·3	—	109·3
1965	35·6	175·2	101·2	131·5	—	125·4	39·8	1·3	18·4	—	105·1

(a) Metal content.
(b) This column relates to lead refined from domestic ores plus unclaimed lead from scrap, etc. Production from imported and domestic ores from 1938 to 1942 was as follows: 1938 – 10·8; 1939 not available; 1940 – 32·2; 1941 – 7·7; 1942 – 5·3.
(c) Including ferro-nickel.

(d) Dry weight up to 1951; estimated gross metal content thereafter.
(e) This figure includes some zinc from scrap.
(f) Subsequently these figures include scrap refined on private account. The corresponding figure for 1943 was 183·3.

Non-ferrous Metals 2. Imports of Non-ferrous Ores and Metals – United Kingdom 1938–65

NOTES
[1] SOURCE: *Annual Statement of Trade.*
[2] The 1965 classification, which excludes manufactures, has been used throughout this table.
[3] Re-exports of non-ferrous metals have ceased to be of much significance since 1938, and therefore a separate table has not been included in this volume. The occasions when the annual re-export of any metal has exceeded 10,000 tons are as follows:

	Copper		Lead
1938	95·2	1938	25·0
1939	18·8	1945	11·0
1945	49·4	1952	33·3
1953	18·1	1953	17·7
1954	21·5		
1955	11·8		
1956	17·4		
1957	13·0		
1959	22·5		
1962	12·4		
1963	11·9		

(in thousands of tons)

	Bauxite	Nickel Ore and Matte	Tin Ore	Zinc Ore	Aluminium and Alloys	Copper, Brass, and other Alloys (a)	Lead	Nickel and Alloys	Tin	Zinc
1938	249·6	29·6	55·5	157·3	51·8	378·2	409·5	22·9	11·8	173·1
1939	302·1	32·2	54·0	175·2	67·7	346·8	341·0	11·2	4·5	175·2
1940	112·4	32·7	83·9	226·2	77·1	513·1	336·8	11·7	1·5	207·4
1941	87·2	27·7	65·5	201·5	142·3	477·6	139·4	8·6	—	209·8
1942	47·8	26·5	43·9	142·7	140·7	459·2	235·7	5·4	—	211·7
1943	241·8	20·3	52·0	97·1	238·3	518·9	226·5	4·9	0·6	187·6
1944	172·1	21·8	32·9	179·0	189·2	465·3	224·9	3·5	—	119·4
1945	162·6	19·4	44·9	156·6	23·2	193·2	176·3	1·5	0·1	97·1
1946	157·0	12·7	47·2	165·5	83·1	297·6	157·0	8·2	0·7	54·9
1947	163·7	21·5	39·3	130·4	96·4	378·1	198·4	13·4	0·2	148·7
1948	308·3	26·4	48·4	156·5	139·4	370·0	161·3	14·4	0·2	167·8
1949	326·6	32·8	46·7	197·9	165·6	323·1	186·4	3·8	0·5	143·3
1950	198·8	25·2	46·1	197·5	141·5	318·8	171·9	3·7	4·6	142·3
1951	345·6	34·3	50·6	180·2	179·7	356·7	175·2	5·6	10·9	122·9
1952	282·9	33·8	55·1	193·0	240·2	385·4	147·0	6·6	2·9	229·1
1953	268·8	33·9	62·4	165·3	179·2	336·3	179·1	9·1	1·0	130·2
1954	370·4	32·9	58·2	192·9	191·3	400·5	196·6	8·8	2·4	155·0
1955	328·1	33·0	61·2	200·3	259·7	411·5	217·8	11·7	1·2	161·6
1956	315·0	34·6	56·9	181·5	233·4	403·2	168·0	10·7	2·2	127·2
1957	354·5	36·0	81·9	207·4	192·7	468·2	158·4	11·5	9·8	147·9
1958	350·9	36·9	64·9	121·2	213·8	461·6	164·9	14·5	13·2	135·4
1959	327·6	33·6	61·5	152·3	256·7	440·0	179·8	14·9	0·7	174·7
1960	375·4	55·1	58·3	189·3	324·8	554·4	210·2	29·6	2·9	190·8
1961	395·0	63·1	51·4	206·2	257·1	504·6	181·0	29·2	1·8	165·0
1962	425·9	53·7	50·1	188·1	272·4	504·3	181·0	17·6	9·2	145·5
1963	331·2	61·6	44·9	212·1	291·5	497·6	180·6	15·6	8·0	160·7
1964	373·6	56·5	43·6	303·5	352·1	528·9	192·5	33·3	8·9	191·1
1965	465·8	63·5	44·7	229·3	340·7	584·4	215·6	28·5	9·3	193·7

(a) Except nickel alloys.

Non-ferrous Metals 3. Exports of Smelted, Unmanufactured Non-ferrous Metals – United Kingdom 1938–65

NOTE
SOURCE: *Annual Statement of Trade.*

(thousand tons)

	Aluminium and Alloys	Brass and Copper Alloys (a)	Copper	Lead	Nickel and Alloys	Tin	Zinc
1938	5·2	15·0	28·5	12·1	13·8	14·6	5·2
1939	5·2	13·7	25·4	10·7	9·7	21·1	5·3
1940	1·7	7·7	18·7	5·8	7·0	17·6	3·1
1941	0·2	5·9	19·0	2·5	1·6	8·9	2·5
1942	0·2	5·3	8·5	2·9	1·3	12·0	0·7
1943	0·1	3·3	4·8	4·8	1·5	12·6	2·3
1944	0·1	3·5	4·6	3·4	1·7	3·8	0·7
1945	6·3	10·1	18·8	10·2	4·7	11·0	3·4
1946	24·5	67·9	70·5	2·4	6·2	22·8	6·2
1947	31·7	42·6	66·6	1·7	7·1	5·1	2·9
1948	57·5	47·1	70·1	2·8	8·4	3·7	4·0
1949	62·4	56·8	87·3	2·4	13·2	5·8	3·9
1950	49·6	47·5	71·6	2·9	11·0	17·8	3·8
1951	44·4	20·7	28·4	3·5	9·0	7·6	2·1
1952	38·1	22·8	29·5	11·4	12·4	15·7	1·7
1953	58·2	39·0	40·0	10·2	15·8	16·7	9·3
1954	44·1	25·0	58·0	11·0	18·0	11·5	4·6
1955	49·0	30·9	72·3	7·6	16·1	12·3	4·2
1956	61·4	44·3	120·5	10·9	14·4	10·3	4·2
1957	48·9	48·9	136·2	14·9	14·7	10·5	4·1
1958	37·5	57·2	182·2	17·9	16·7	12·3	7·5
1959	53·2	57·1	133·7	14·7	24·0	32·0	6·6
1960	53·1	57·1	113·4	21·1	26·7	9·6	10·2
1961	58·6	72·3	109·5	31·5	27·7	11·9	8·1
1962	64·6	73·7	144·3	37·7	20·7	10·0	14·3
1963	63·3	141·0		44·3	23·7	11·4	13·1
1964	53·8	133·5		41·4	33·3	10·0	11·4
1965	68·7	153·7		44·2	33·7	10·2	7·4

(a) Except nickel alloys.

TEXTILES

TABLES

The great majority of the series given in this chapter follows on directly – though sometimes with slight changes in definition – from those in the first *Abstract of British Historical Statistics*, and they do not call for much comment. Table 13, showing the workforce in the textile industries, combines four separate tables given in the first volume. However, exact comparison between the statistics before and after the Second World War is impossible, because there were changes in definition under all headings. Most of the other tables, on the other hand, are straightforward. The only additional table is number 12, showing exports of manufactures of man-made fibres, which became sufficiently large after 1938 to merit inclusion. But this, also, is quite straightforward.

Information on the value of overseas trade in textiles can be found in Chapter XI, and raw cotton, raw wool, and cotton cloth prices are given in Chapter XVI.

Textiles 1. Raw Cotton Consumption – United Kingdom 1938–65

NOTE
SOURCE: *Abstract.*

(in thousand tons)

1938	495	1948	436	1958	287
1939	588	1949	437	1959	284
1940	620	1950	454	1960	274
1941	431	1951	457	1961	246
1942	419	1952	306	1962	218
1943	395	1953	371	1963	222
1944	359	1954	398	1964	233
1945	320	1955	348	1965	226
1946	363	1956	325		
1947	364	1957	339		

Textiles 2. Raw Cotton Imports in Total and from the U.S.A., and Re-exports – United Kingdom 1938–65

NOTE
SOURCE: *Annual Statement of Trade.*

(in million lb.)

	Total Imports	Imports from U.S.A.	Re-exports
1938	1,324	469	49
1939	1,434	560	44
1940	1,587	785	13
1941	888	307	- -
1942	1,329	348	- -
1943	1,118	585	- -
1944	913	256	—
1945	1,020	239	44
1946	910	120	49
1947	897	249	35
1948	956	239	6
1949	1,130	456	3
1950	1,200	333	6
1951	1,166	290	2
1952	719	264	9
1953	871	195	8
1954	1,003	298	8
1955	849	236	14
1956	926	322	25
1957	988	569	13
1958	739	324	7
1959	825	218	14
1960	819	325	12
1961	677	260	13
1962	667	151	13
1963	701	175	13
1964	736	250	20
1965	614	139	11

Textiles 3. Exports of Cotton Manufactures – United Kingdom 1938–65

NOTE
SOURCE: *Annual Statement of Trade.*

	Piece Goods (*a*) (million sq.yd.)	Thread (million lb.)	Twist & Yarn (million lb.)
1938	1,386	13·5	123
1939	1,393	14·3	114
1940	976	14·6	67
1941	783	13·6	29
1942	485	14·2	19
1943	374	13·3	19
1944	434	12·0	20
1945	441	13·8	16
	--- (*b*)		
1946	515	14·9	19
1947	533	10·8	27
1948	762	12·2	59
1949	904	13·9	82
1950	822	13·4	71
1951	864	14·4	65
1952	711	9·4	36
1953	710	10·5	42
1954	637	11·4	40
1955	555	11·1	36
1956	474	11·1	36
1957	456	10·0	38
1958	384	8·0	27
1959	348	7·9	23
1960	327	8·6	21
1961	287	8·3	14
1962	235	6·5	15
1963	223	6·7	14
1964	209	6·3	15
1965	207	5·0	10

(*a*) A series in million linear yards, comparable with figures for earlier years published in the first *Abstract of British Historical Statistics*, is available until 1961. It runs as follows:

1950	867	1953	747	1956	510	1959	370
1951	900	1954	669	1957	491	1960	344
1952	748	1955	587	1958	404	1961	301

1938	1,448	1941	846	1944	466	1947	577
1939	1,462	1942	531	1945	469	1948	817
1940	1,045	1943	399	1946	562	1949	957

(*b*) Knitted, netted, and crocheted piece goods were recorded only in linear yards after 1945. In 1945 they amounted to 17 million square yards or 27 million linear yards.

Textiles 4. Spindles and Looms in Cotton Factories – United Kingdom 1938–65

NOTES

[1] SOURCES: Spindles 1938–9 – *International Cotton Bulletin*; looms in place 1938–41 – *Report of the Cotton Board Committee to Enquire into Post-War Problems* (January 1944); others – *Cotton Board Trade Letter Statistical Supplement*, and its successor from 1952, the *Cotton Board Quarterly Statistical Review*.

[2] Doubling and waste-spinning spindles are not included in this table.

[3] The statistics of looms cover those working on man-made fibres as well as cotton.

| | Spinning Spindles (millions) | | | | | | Looms (thousands) | |
| | in place in all mills | | in place in running mills | | actually running | | in place in all mills | actually running |
	mule	ring	mule	ring	mule	ring		
1938	26·4	10·5	…	…	…	…	495	…
1939	25·8	10·5	…	…	…	…	490	…
1940	…	…	…	…	…	…	490	…
1941	23·41	10·37	13·01	7·58	10·49	6·00	490/497 (a)	293
1942	…	…	…	…	10·27	5·92	505	228
1943	…	…	…	…	9·69	5·68	506	225
1944	…	…	…	…	9·24	5·36	508	228
1945	23·06	10·42	13·25	8·12	9·24	5·20	507	216
1946	22·60	10·41	18·69	9·25	11·91	5·64	500	224·1
1947	21·93	10·26	19·89	9·74	12·93	5·88	…	241·2
1948	21·00	10·09	19·72	9·86	14·56	7·04	…	271·2
1949	19·71	10·19	19·07	10·05	15·23	7·70	…	289·3
1950	18·98	10·33	18·45	10·24	15·22	8·16	…	304·8
1951	18·24	10·57	17·73	10·57	15·01	8·55	…	311·7
1952	17·75	10·81	17·24	10·79	10·33	7·18	…	249·7
1953	17·11	10·97	16·60	10·93	11·25	8·40	…	270·6
1954	…	…	15·76	10·83	11·77	8·78	…	280·7
1955	…	…	14·52	10·85	9·68	8·33	…	252·6
1956	…	…	13·33	10·64	8·52	8·13	…	229·4
1957	…	…	12·28	10·34	8·12	8·24	…	222·7
1958	…	…	10·89	10·23	5·98	7·49	…	192·0
1959	…	…	8·71	9·45	4·90	7·05	…	172·1
1960	…	…	3·33	6·97	2·83	6·22	…	149·4
1961	…	…	2·78	6·84	2·56	6·24	…	150·2
1962	…	…	2·36	6·40	1·80	5·54	…	132·1
1963	…	…	1·56	5·64	1·20	5·01	…	119·3
1964	…	…	1·03	5·19	0·90	4·77	…	116·9
1965	…	…	0·90	4·90	0·76	4·37	…	113·2

(a) The source of the first figure is the *Report of the Cotton Board Committee* and of the second figure is the *Cotton Board Trade Letter*.

Textiles 5. Raw Wool Production – United Kingdom 1938–65

NOTE
SOURCE: *Abstract*.

(estimated clean weight in million lb)

1938	68	1948	50	1958	78
1939	69	1949	56	1959	83
1940	91	1950	58	1960	78
1941	80	1951	56	1961	86
1942	72	1952	62	1962	86
1943	62	1953	64	1963	82
1944	59	1954	71	1964	84
1945	58	1955	67	1965	83
1946	61	1956	69		
1947	50	1957	74		

Textiles 6. Raw Wool Trade – United Kingdom 1938–65

NOTES
[1] SOURCE: *Annual Statement of Trade*.   [2]   This table includes alpaca, vicuna, and llama wool.

(in million lb.)

		Imports			Domestic (a)
	Total	from Australia	from New Zealand	Re-exports	Exports
1938	883·8	365·5	198·0	257·0	42·4
1939	904·2	355·1	223·8	197·3	33·9
1940	1,814·1	675·0	222·5	70·2	15·2
1941	331·7	93·8	158·2	0·6	21·1
1942	412·8	139·0	156·7	—	5·4
1943	270·4	101·3	98·0	—	0·7
1944	508·6	292·7	157·6	—	1·1
1945	505·1	350·5	64·9	76·3	14·2
1946	481·6	229·7	185·7	91·1	41·2
1947	624·1	292·9	211·4	152·5	25·6
1948	678·1	331·9	226·1	153·0	21·8
1949	818·8	472·5	209·4	136·7	32·5
1950	708·5	383·6	180·1	115·7	45·6
1951	507·9	255·9	138·5	75·1	27·6
1952	698·5	320·6	190·0	72·3	42·4
1953	831·5	364·9	191·8	69·0	40·2
1954	686·3	291·7	186·4	65·4	46·3
1955	748·0	346·8	185·4	69·1	48·5
1956	725·2	310·6	163·6	71·7	50·5
1957	700·6	315·3	166·1	63·3	43·1
1958	677·0	292·4	168·2	49·6	45·9
1959	779·9	333·5	170·9	52·2	53·7
1960	670·0	265·2	161·0	51·2	54·8
1961	659·6	224·8	161·1	49·9	63·1
1962	641·4	237·5	163·2	40·5	61·0
1963	654·0	241·5	156·8	29·5	70·5
1964	573·5	217·9	139·4	19·9	57·0
1965	560·7	181·6	135·3	21·0	61·5

(a) Includes wool from imported skins and foreign wool which had been subjected to preliminary processing in the United Kingdom.

Textiles 7. Exports of Wool Manufactures – United Kingdom 1938–65

NOTES
[1] SOURCE: *Annual Statement of Trade.*
[2]   The series for woven fabrics given here differ from those under the headings 'woollen tissues' and 'worsted tissues' in the first *Abstract of British Historical Statistics* in that these latter included knitted, netted or crocheted goods, linings, and lastings.

	Woollen and Worsted Yarn (million lb.)	Noils (m. lb.)	Tops (m. lb.)	Woven Fabrics Woollen (m. sq.yd.)	Worsted (m. sq.yd.)
1938	27·8	11·8	32·5	58·8	29·4
1939	26·3	8·6	33·8	59·2	32·0
1940	17·7	6·7	28·2	45·2	35·6
1941	13·2	4·8	16·2	58·1	27·6
1942	10·2	1·9	11·7	47·5	25·1
1943	9·0	0·4	8·2	27·8	15·9
1944	8·7	0·4	5·0	22·9	10·9
1945	9·0	0·3	16·1	27·5	12·9
1946	15·4	1·1	29·0	51·1	21·5
1947	14·5	5·2	38·5	51·7	23·2
1948	20·9	13·1	59·6	69·9	32·6
1949	29·0	12·3	60·0	70·1	35·9
				- - - (a)	- - - (a)
1950	35·2	16·9	72·9	77·0	40·3
1951	26·6	13·1	49·4	70·2	39·0
1952	25·3	13·4	54·0	58·2	33·6
1953	28·9	15·7	70·2	62·2	34·5
1954	25·5	17·0	67·1	59·2	31·6
				- - - (a)	- - - (a)
1955	26·4	19·9	76·6	68·3	34·3
1956	28·9	17·8	81·5	71·1	33·3
1957	29·9	19·1	83·3	69·6	34·3
1958	25·3	20·8	88·9	59·6	31·5
1959	31·1	21·6	96·4	64·2	33·5
1960	32·8	22·4	91·1	59·1	33·0
1961	29·1	26·2	92·1	53·8	31·8
1962	29·5	20·8	78·2	52·4	31·1
1963	33·9	23·6	96·0	52·4	31·0
1964	32·1	21·6	75·1	53·9	29·8
1965	30·1	20·3	63·9	53·5	30·4

(*a*) From 1950 to 1954 cut lengths containing less than 25 square yards were recorded under a heading which did not discriminate between woollens and worsteds. They are not included in either column here. They amounted to the following (in sq.yd.):

1950	2·7	1953	2·1
1951	2·4	1954	2·2
1952	1·6		

Textiles 8. Spindles and Looms in Wool Factories – United Kingdom 1938–65

NOTES

[1] SOURCE: Commonwealth Economic Committee, *Wool Intelligence* (supplement to June or July issue in each year from 1949).

[2] Doubling and twisting spindles and carpet looms are not included in this table.

[3] The statistics are of spindles and looms installed and capable of operating.

(in thousands)

	Spinning Spindles		
	Worsted	Woollen	Looms
1938	2,283	3,210	78
1943	2,309	3,311	73 (a)
1951	2,949	2,229	64
1952	2,937	2,305	63
1953	2,916	2,180	61
1954	2,899	2,120	60
1955	2,876	2,095	59
1956	2,838	2,050	57
1957	2,844	2,010	56
1958	2,782	1,995	52
1959	2,726	1,909	49
1960	2,719	1,895	47
1961	2,631	1,776	44
1962	2,570	1,750	43
1963	2,416	1,620	40
1964	2,303	1,570	38
1965	2,177	1,520	36

(a) The figure given in the first *Abstract of British Historical Statistics*, p. 198 includes 5,809 non-wool looms which were installed in wool factories.

Textiles 9. Exports of Linen – United Kingdom 1938–65

NOTE

SOURCE: *Annual Statement of Trade.*

	Piece Goods (000 sq.yd.)	Thread (000 lb.)	Yarn (000 lb.)		Piece Goods (000 sq.yd.)	Thread (000 lb.)	Yarn (000 lb.)
1938	51,790	1,822	8,378	1953	47,131	1,596	5,429
1939	77,414	1,890	7,118	1954	47,166	1,797	6,313
1940	45,392	1,895	3,144	1955	45,849	1,855	6,192
1941	27,799	1,546	1,058	1956	46,054	1,774	6,896
1942	22,605	1,778	607	1957	40,621	1,783	9,178
1943	10,528	948	416	1958	34,516	1,593	7,730
1944	6,182	1,473	387	1959	37,206	1,666	7,183
1945	8,814	1,821	772	1960	36,757	1,681	6,280
1946	39,448	2,795	2,084	1961	30,553	1,782	6,144
1947	46,066	2,317	2,763	1962	33,510	1,586	7,008
1948	44,433	1,836	3,091	1963	32,743	1,611	7,242
1949	38,521	1,592	4,461	1964	33,058	1,740	7,732
1950	49,358	1,846	6,324	1965	30,459	1,309	6,021
1951	49,667	2,147	6,579				
1952	38,743	1,387	7,279				

Textiles 10. Imports and Re-exports of Raw Silk and Silk Yarn – United Kingdom 1938–65

NOTE
SOURCE: *Annual Statement of Trade.*

(in thousand lb.)

	Imports		Re-exports	
	Raw Silk and Waste	Thrown and Spun Silk	Raw Silk and Waste	Thrown and Spun Silk
1938	6,837	126	77	15
1939	5,414	148	103	9
1940	7,391	3	24	2
1941	3,895	—	6	- -
1942	1,716	—	17	- -
1943	2,024	—	- -	—
1944	1,605	—	1	—
1945	1,557	—	- -	—
1946	630	234	4	- -
1947	2,243	259	112	1
1948	2,054	270	55	6
1949	1,651	73	96	4
1950	2,046	15	49	5
1951	2,051	11	16	6
1952	318	122	6	- -
1953	894	4	17	5
1954	977	2	25	7
1955	869	6	56	8
1956	1,090	4	56	5
1957	1,077	4	37	7
1958	742	1	25	3
1959	1,140	40	39	8
1960	1,110	21	53	—
1961	1,048	24	50	- -
1962	867	5	64	2
1963	986	6	60	—
1964	931	5	67	- -
1965	884	10	63	- -

Textiles 11. Exports of Silk Manufactures – United Kingdom 1938–65

NOTES
[1] SOURCE: *Annual Statement of Trade.*
[2] This table covers pile fabrics, damasks, tapestries, brocades, etc., and all woven tissues except ribbons. Lace and net are not included.

(in thousand square yards)

1938	2,698	1948	902	1958	551
1939	3,005	1949	704	1959	755
1940	1,735	1950	899	1960	887
1941	945	1951	765	1961	909
1942	656	1952	420	1962	992
1943	100	1953	562	1963	1,040
1944	82	1954	751	1964	831
1945	244	1955	708	1965	940
1946	3,995	1956	792		
1947	1,691	1957	725		

Textiles 12. Exports of Man-Made Fibre Manufactures – United Kingdom 1938–65

NOTE
SOURCE: *Annual Statement of Trade.*

	Yarn (million lb.)	Tissues (a) (million sq.yd.)		Yarn (million lb.)	Tissues (a) (million sq.yd.)		Yarn (million lb.)	Tissues (a) (million sq.yd.)
1938	8·0	62·6	1948	23·5	157·3	1958	37·7	84·1
1939	6·9	74·8	1949	21·5	184·5	1959	45·1	63·7
1940	15·0	85·4	1950	28·4	215·7	1960	48·5	54·3
1941	20·2	90·5	1951	28·2	219·2	1961	53·5	48·9
1942	16·3	116·3	1952	20·9	152·1	1962	67·8	55·0
1943	13·8	75·9	1953	31·5	176·8	1963	81·5	80·4
1944	15·6	91·2	1954	32·3	175·3	1964	96·7	115·4
1945	14·2	94·6	1955	30·8	133·7	1965	90·9	94·5
1946	16·6	113·2	1956	36·2	120·8			
1947	15·3	112·6	1957	44·1	111·3			

(a) Excludes ribbon, lace, etc., but includes tyre cord fabric.

4

MSA

NOTE
SOURCE: *Abstract.*

			(in thousands)			
	Cotton	Wool	Silk and Weaving of Man-Made Fibres	Man-Made Fibre Production	Linen, Hemp, etc. (a)	Jute
1938	414	230	55	27	103	30
1939	395	228	53	26	99	31
1940	383	231	54	26	105	28
1941	297	204	39	21	89	24
1942	236	163	30	20	77	19
1943	224	142	27	19	73	15
1944	214	127	26	18	69	13
1945	209	128	27	19	73	13
1946	240	147	35	21	77	16
1947	252	164	27	37	78	18
	—	—	—	—	— (a)	—
1948 (b)	293	210	48	41	65	21
1949	307	216	52	44	66	18
1950	317	222	58	47	66	18
1951	322	218	61	45	67	19
1952	287	195	52	37	64	18
1953	287	213	52	40	62	20
1954	296	215	54	40	58	21
1955	274	209	54	41	56	20
1956	256	210	55	42	52	20
1957	256	214	53	42	50	20
1958	238	203	50	37	42	18
	Cotton, Linen, and Weaving of Man-Made Fibres					
1959	298	202		40		18
1960	284	204		44		19
1961	270	203		45		18
1962	245	193		45		18
1963	231	193		45		18
1964	228	189		48		18
	- - - (c)	- - - (c)		- - (c)		- -
1965	223	180		51		18

(a) Includes rope, net and twine to 1947, but not thereafter.
(b) As a consequence of the National Insurance Act, there was an increase in the number of insured employees in all industries. Figures on the old basis were collected in 1948 for Great Britain but not for the United Kingdom. These indicate that the increase was from 10 to 15 per cent.
(c) Figures for 1964 on the basis used in 1965 were respectively 229, 190, and 49.

CHAPTER VIII

TRANSPORT AND COMMUNICATIONS

TABLES

This chapter has been considerably expanded in coverage from the equivalent in the first *Abstract of British Historical Statistics*, and there have been changes in many of the series given there. In table 1 the distinction between steam and motor vessels, which was formerly made, has now been dropped, and instead a breakdown by size of ship is given. A more drastic change is made in table 2, with the substitution for separate sail and steam ship series of a breakdown by function of vessels built. However, despite these changes, rough comparisons are possible between periods before and after the Second World War. This is not possible, however, for the index of tramp shipping freights in table 3. The official postwar index begins in 1948, and no attempt has been made to formulate a bridge between that and the Isserlis index which was published in the first volume of *Historical Statistics*. This question was discussed by M. G. Kendall in 'The U.K. Mercantile Marine and its Contribution to the Balance of Payments' in the *Journal of the Royal Statistical Society* (Series A, 1950), and he concluded that 'a comparison of 1948 with 1938 really conveys very little because of some important alterations in the nature of sea transport'. However, his conclusion seems to be excessively cautious, and it is worth noting here that on the base 1938 = 100 he had calculated an index figure for tramp shipping freights in 1948 of 330.

Tables 4 and 5 follow on directly from those in the first volume, but the remainder of the tables in this chapter is new. The mileage of roads series in table 6 are only available in connected and exactly comparable form back to 1922, and since the rate of change of the figures is low, especially up to 1938, they were not given in the earlier volume. However, now that a longer run of years can be covered, it has seemed worthwhile to include them. Various scattered figures of road mileage are, of course, available for much earlier periods, and some of these may be found in W. T. Jackman, *The Development of Transportation in Modern England* (2 vols., Cambridge, 1916; reissued in one volume, London, 1962).

Table 7, showing summary statistics of air traffic, cannot be pushed back before 1937, and was obviously not worth including in the first volume of *Historical Statistics*. Tables 8 and 9, however, go back well into the nineteenth century, and were omitted there because there was not room for them. They contradict rather well the widespread belief that our statistical information on all subjects continually increases and improves over time. On the contrary, they provide some evidence for another widely held view, that the efficiency of the Post Office has declined during the twentieth century.

Transport and Communications 1. Merchant Vessels on the United Kingdom Register – 1938–65

NOTES

[1] SOURCES: *Registrary of Ships* (monthly supplement to Mercantile Navy List) and *Abstract*.

[2] Except for 1938, the figures include vessels of either Commonwealth or foreign countries on bareboat charter to, or requisitioned by, the United Kingdom.

	Steam and Motor Vessels				Sailing Vessels	
	Total Number	Number under 500 Gross Tons	Number over 500 Gross Tons	Thousand Net Tons	Total Number	Thousands Net Tons
1938	13,229	9,491	3,738	10,314	4,017	402
1939	13,303	9,567	3,736	10,511	...	...
1940	13,254	9,545	3,709	10,412	...	...
1941	12,822	9,429	3,393	9,674	...	...
1942	12,185	9,027	3,158	9,000	...	...
1943	12,169	8,969	3,200	9,119	...	...
1944	12,525	9,105	3,420	9,994	...	...
1945	12,700	9,114	3,586	10,341	...	...
1946	12,581	9,057	3,524	10,315	3,610	408
1947	12,481	8,988	3,483	10,371	3,250	380
1948	12,795	9,285	3,510	10,461	3,193	370
1949	13,103	9,549	3,554	10,453	3,149	367
1950	13,429	9,826	3,603	10,738	3,104	365
1951	13,473	9,935	3,538	10,606	3,056	349
1952	13,598	10,078	3,520	10,663	3,065	343
1953	13,649	10,094	3,555	10,811	2,835	321
1954	13,685	10,106	3,579	10,978	2,771	317
1955	13,671	10,096	3,575	10,966	2,676	316
1956	13,764	10,191	3,573	11,053	2,637	312
1957	13,837	10,263	3,574	11,207	2,600	312
1958	14,045	10,501	3,544	11,349	2,588	304
1959	14,202	10,715	3,487	11,627	2,496	294
1960	14,532	11,091	3,441	11,797	2,482	291
1961	15,008	11,632	3,376	12,001	2,493	279
1962	15,580	12,304	3,276	11,501	2,550	276
1963	16,115	12,971	3,144	11,462	2,596	270
1964	16,722	13,685	3,037	11,315	2,622	266
1965	17,483	14,515	2,968	11,426	2,829	272

Transport and Communications 2. Merchant Ships of One Hundred Gross Tons and Over Built – United Kingdom 1938–65

NOTES
[1] SOURCE: *Abstract*.
[2] Vessels exported from 1957 onwards were as follows:

	Number	Thousand Gross Tons			Number	Thousand Gross Tons
1957	65	375		1960	37	119
1958	46	314		1961	41	296
1959	47	173		1962	44	188
				1963	41	280
				1964	39	120
				1965	33	150

	Numbers of Vessels				Thousand Gross Tons			
	All Vessels	Tankers	Passenger and Cargo	Other Vessels	All Vessels	Tankers	Passenger and Cargo	Other Vessels
1938	267	...	...	...	1,030	...	...	...
1939	201	...	...	...	630	...	...	...
1940	172	5	132	35	801	32	731	38
1941	235	41	148	46	1,158	274	816	68
1942	258	44	144	70	1,302	318	930	54
1943	237	36	146	55	1,201	217	939	45
1944	269	79	138	52	1,013	200	769	44
1945	238	37	128	73	743	193	504	46
1946	283	53	130	100	987	326	582	79
1947	293	15	168	110	949	119	772	58
1948	332	24	183	125	1,221	203	947	71
1949	332	42	167	123	1,361	380	885	96
1950	302	58	129	115	1,376	564	694	118
1951	240	69	78	93	1,343	782	485	76
1952	234	58	99	77	1,271	658	520	93
1953	220	61	86	73	1,223	696	449	78
1954	232	61	108	63	1,493	770	673	50
1955	260	46	100	114	1,282	598	611	73
1956	279	36	127	116	1,426	527	842	57
1957	264	30	126	108	1,442	507	870	65
	--- (a)	-- (a)	--- (a)	--- (a)	---- (a)	--- (a)	--- (a)	-- (a)
1957	299	35	132	132	1,448	510	884	54
1958	298	40	128	130	1,453	554	853	46
1959	292	44	101	147	1,388	646	691	51
1960	282	33	89	160	1,303	483	765	55
1961	279	33	81	165	1,390	548	763	79
1962	249	19	75	155	1,022	342	618	62
1963	208	21	77	110	1,127	469	608	50
1964	193	26	50	117	848	403	378	66
1965	202	20	69	113	1,204	479	662	63

(a) Non-propelled vessels are subsequently included, and there was also some rearrangement of categories at this time.

Transport and Communications 3. Index of Tramp Shipping Freights – United Kingdom 1948–65

NOTES

[1] SOURCE: *Abstract*.

[2] This index applies to voyage charter rates.

1948 = 100		*1952 = 100*		*1960 = 100*	
1948	100	1952	100	1960	100
1949	82·3	1953	77·5	1961	106·8
1950	84·0	1954	86·1	1962	89·1
1951	173·7	1955	127·7	1963	109·0
1952	110·6	1956	157·0	1964	112·1
		1957	112·7	1965	126·5
		1958	67·1		
		1959	71·9		
		1960	74·2		

Transport and Communications 4. Railways – Great Britain 1938–65

NOTE
SOURCES: 1938 – *Railway Returns* (in Parliamentary Papers); other physical figures – *Abstract*; other financial figures – *Estimates of the Pooled Revenue Receipts and Expenses of the Controlled Undertakings* (in Parliamentary Papers) for 1939–47; *Annual Reports of* the British Transport Commission for 1948 to 1962, and of the British Railways Board since 1962.

	Miles of Road Open at 31 Dec. (a)	Millions of Passengers Carried		Million Tons of Freight Carried	Train Mileage (millions)		Receipts			Total Working Expenses	Net Working Receipts (+) or Outlays (−) (d)
		Ordinary	Total (b)		Passengers	Goods	Passenger Train (c)	Goods Train	Total Working		
1938	20,007	850·2	1,237·2	265·7	287·4	133·6	75·3 (d)	87·8 (d)	164·7 (d)	137·7 (d)	+27·1 (d)
1939	19,982	844·9	1,225·5	288·3	256·9	239·3	...	...	...	...	...
1940	19,931	691·1	966·6	294·4	201·3	154·5	104·8	140·5	248·0	203·5	+44·5
1941	19,904	778·3	1,023·3	286·7	201·9	151·6	132·1	158·8	293·8	226·6	+67·2
1942	19,892	944·4	1,218·3	295·1	203·2	155·9	163·5	176·7	343·5	251·7	+91·8
1943	19,890	1,036·7	1,334·6	300·9	204·2	156·1	186·3	190·9	381·7	272·2	+109·4
1944	19,880	1,039·1	1,345·3	292·6	202·1	155·0	194·6	196·1	394·4	301·2	+93·2
1945	19,863	1,055·7	1,371·8	266·4	215·8	142·5	210·6	169·7	383·9	317·0	+66·9
1946	19,861	901·1	1,266·0	262·4	236·9	136·5	202·2	155·1	360·7	325·2	+35·5
1947	19,853	768·9	1,139·8	257·3	223·3	131·3	195·7	156·6	355·6	367·2	−11·6
(e)	-----	-----	-----	-----	-----	-----					
1948	19,598	700·3	996·1	273·2	228·1	137·4	151·9	180·5	336·1	328·5	+26·3
1949	19,573	710·5	992·8	280·2	241·4	139·8	142·7	178·9	325·5	327·8	+12·7
1950	19,471	704·0	981·7	281·3	243·1	141·0	137·3	198·9	340·1	324·8	+26·3
1951	19,357	719·6	1,001·3	284·8	234·7	141·7	140·1	227·9	372·7	349·9	+35·0
1952	19,276	710·8	989·0	284·9	235·5	140·9	147·9	250·5	403·4	384·8	+39·6
1953	19,222	710·5	985·3	289·3	237·6	141·6	153·3	263·1	421·4	407·6	+35·1
1954	19,151	744·7	1,020·1	283·5	238·1	140·3	157·4	272·8	435·5	416·4	+16·6
1955	19,061	730·2	993·9	274·2	229·8	133·4	160·1	274·2	440·0	434·1	+2·1
							---- (i)				

Year											
1956	19,025	740·1	1,028·5	277·0	241·1	134·9	175·1 (f)	284·1 (f)	465·5 (f)	481·5 (f)	−16·3 (f)
1956							175·1	300·0	479·3	497·5	−16·5
1957	18,965	788·1	1,101·2	274·3	246·7	135·3	190·3	301·9	499·6	528·6	−27·1
1958	18,848	777·3	1,089·8	242·9	250·3	126·0	189·9	271·5	469·8	519·7	−48·1
1959	18,484	749·2	1,068·8	233·9	249·6	121·4	198·3	254·2	455·6	499·4	−42·0
1960	18,369	721·3	1,036·7	248·5	252·9	122·5	206·7	261·4	476·7	546·2	−67·7
1961	17,903	707·8	1,025·0	238·2	253·5	119·2	213·8	250·4	472·6	561·6	−86·9
1962	17,481	670·5	965·0	228·4	248·2	110·5	218·6	235·7	462·7	571·4	−108·7
									---- (g)	---- (g)	---- (g)
1962									462·4	569·1	−104·0
1963	16,982	646·7	938·4	234·9	... (h)	...	219·3	235·4	463·1	550·2	−87·1
1964	15,991	629·0	927·6	239·6	...	...	225·8	233·0	468·3	541·6	−73·3
1965	14,920	580·5	865·1	228·5	...	...	231·3	225·5	466·2	545·7	−79·5

(a) Total length of running lines irrespective of the number of tracks comprising them. Narrow gauge lines are excluded. In 1960, 1,126 track miles, representing 84 route miles, were transferred from British Railways to British Transport Docks – statistics for 1959 have been revised. In 1963, 126 track miles, representing 10 route miles, were transferred back to British Railways – statistics for 1962 have been revised.

(b) This includes season ticket holders as well as ordinary passengers.

(c) Includes receipts in respect of mail and merchandise carried by coaching trains.

(d) Figures for 1940–7 are taken from the estimates of the pooled revenue receipts and expenses and resultant net revenue of controlled undertakings. These included all major railway companies together with London Passenger Transport Board.

(e) Figures from 1948 onwards refer to British Railways only (i.e. the nationalised undertaking).

(f) From 1957 important changes in the classification of receipts and expenses were introduced.

(g) The break here is caused by the exclusion of the ancillary activities of Rail Catering, Letting of Sites etc., and Commercial Advertising on the transfer of responsibility for the railways from the British Transport Commission to the British Railways Board. Additionally, receipts from collection and delivery and other road freight services were no longer included entirely with goods train receipts but were allocated partly to passenger train receipts (see also note (i)).

(h) British Railways Board ceased publication of these series, and instead provides series of loaded train mileage. These are as follows (in millions) (with the 1962 figure given for purposes of comparison):

	Loaded Passenger Train Mileage	Loaded Goods Train Mileage
1962	239·1	96·2
1963	233·4	91·6
1964	225·8	87·6
1965	212·8	77·5

(i) From 1956 this column includes receipts in respect of collection and delivery and other road freight services (see also note (g)).

Transport and Communications 5. Vehicles in Use – Great Britain 1938–65

NOTE
SOURCE: British Road Federation, *Basic Road Statistics, 1967*.

(in thousands)

	Private Cars	Motor Cycles	Buses and Coaches	Taxis	Goods Vehicles	Other Vehicles	Total (excluding tramcars)	Tramcars
September								
1938	1,944	462	53	35	495	96	3,085	9·0
August								
1939	2,034	418	90		488	118	3,149	7·9
1940	1,423	278	81		444	98	2,325	6·9
1941	1,503	317	85		450	123	2,478	6·5
1942	858	306	85		453	139	1,840	6·4
1943	718	124	87		449	160	1,537	6·3
1944	755	124	90		448	175	1,593	6·3
1945	1,487	309	99		473	185	2,553	6·2
1946	1,770	462	57	48	560	210	3,107	6·1
September								
1947	1,944	528	62	52	670	259	3,515	5·7
1948	1,961	559	68	59	769	312	3,728	5·6
1949	2,131	654	74	60	844	346	4,108	5·3
1950	2,258	752	78	59	895	368	4,409	4·6
1951	2,380	848	79	57	934	379	4,678	4·2
1952	2,508	949	80	53	964	405	4,957	3·6
1953	2,762	1,037	80	36	996	430	5,340	3·0
1954	3,100	1,139	79	28	1,033	447	5,825	2·6
1955	3,526	1,256	78	24	1,109	472	6,465	2·3
1956	3,888	1,326	79	21	1,173	489	6,976	2·0
1957	4,187	1,471	79	19	1,215	513	7,483	1·6
1958	4,549	1,520	79	17	1,268	527	7,959	1·3
1959	4,966	1,733	77	15	1,326	545	8,662	1·1
1960	5,526	1,861	79	15	1,397	562	9,439	0·7
1961	5,979	1,869	78	13	1,451	576	9,965	0·4
1962	6,556	1,866	79	14	1,470	579	10,563	0·3
1963	7,375	1,847	82	14	1,529	599	11,446	0·1
1964	8,247	1,835	82	15	1,576	615	12,369	0·1
1965	8,917	1,707	82	15	1,602	618	12,940	0·1

Transport and Communications 6. Mileage of Roads – Great Britain 1922–66

NOTES
[1] SOURCES: 1922–7 – *Annual Reports of the Road Fund*; 1928–66 – British Road Federation, *Basic Road Statistics, 1968.*

[2] The figures relate to 31 March in the year indicated.

	Trunk Roads	Class I	Class II	Class III	Unclassified	Total
1922	—	22,189	14,400	—	140,717	177,306
1923	—	22,756	14,646	—	139,907	177,309
1924	—	23,230	14,739	—	139,352	177,321
1925	—	24,048	14,638	—	138,996	177,682
1926	—	24,329	14,930	—	138,947	178,206
1927	—	24,552	15,625	—	138,185	178,362
1928	—	25,121	15,683	—	137,933	178,737
1929	—	25,528	15,747	—	137,820	179,095
1930	—	25,996	15,805	—	137,485	179,286
					------(a)	------(a)
1931	—	26,417	15,924	—	134,915	177,256
					------(a)	------(a)
1932	—	26,513	16,482	—	133,796	176,791
1933	—	26,585	16,644	—	134,118	177,347
1934	—	26,663	16,774	—	134,385	177,822
1935	—	26,779	16,837	—	134,891	178,507
					------(a)	------(a)
1936	—	27,015	16,855	—	134,233	178,103
1937	—	27,142	16,930	—	134,832	178,904
1938	2,854	24,405	17,037	—	132,334	179,630
1939	4,456	23,089	17,634	—	135,348	180,527
1940	4,456	23,176	17,715	—	...	...
1941	4,463	23,176	17,715	—	...	...
1942	4,459	23,180	17,729	—	...	...
1943	4,459	23,180	17,729	—	...	...
1944	4,457	23,180	17,731	—	...	...
1945	4,457	23,195	17,750	—	...	...
1946	4,455	23,194	17,748	—	137,666	183,063
1947	8,190	19,517	17,708	48,323	89,313	183,051
1948	8,189	19,538	17,715	48,351	89,684	183,477
1949	8,189	19,583	17,694	48,584	89,608	183,658
1950	8,176	19,599	17,697	48,614	89,735	183,821
1951	8,249	19,533	17,697	48,682	90,676	184,837
1952	8,248	19,563	17,691	48,678	91,343	185,523
1953	8,254	19,551	17,700	48,693	92,063	186,261
1954	8,270	19,585	17,690	48,721	92,774	187,040
1955	8,270	19,606	17,696	48,781	93,742	188,095
1956	8,270	19,670	17,646	48,818	94,633	189,837
1957	8,271	19,736	17,605	48,849	95,690	190,151
1958	8,309	19,706	17,603	48,853	96,675	191,146
1959	8,334 (b)	19,735	17,595	48,875	98,533	193,072
1960	8,438 (b)	19,738	17,606	48,913	99,485	194,180
1961	8,468 (b)	19,747 (c)	17,620	48,927	100,455	195,217
1962	8,484 (b)	19,758 (c)	17,615	48,955	101,323	196,135
1963	8,541 (b)	19,797 (c)	17,608	48,982	103,527	198,455
1964	8,628 (b)	19,823 (c)	17,627	48,987	104,678	199,743
1965	8,695 (b)	19,866 (c)	17,642	48,998	105,855	201,056
1966	8,718 (b)	19,917 (c)	17,632	49,000	106,792	202,059

(a) The reductions between 1930 and 1931, 1931 and 1932, and 1935 and 1936 result from discrepancies discovered by County Councils on transfer of highway functions over the Local Government Act, 1929.

(b) Including the following mileage of motorway:

1958	8	1963	194
1960	95	1964	292
1961	130	1965	346
1962	145	1966	383

(c) Including 6 miles of motorway from 1961 to 1965 and 8 miles in 1966.

NOTES
[1] SOURCE: *Abstract.*
[2] This table covers the United Kingdom Airway Corpora- tions and private companies, but not the associates and over- seas subsidiaries of the Corporations.

	Aircraft Stage Flights (000s)	Aircraft Miles Flown (000s)	Average Length of Flight (miles)	Passengers Carried		Passenger-Miles Flown (millions)	Cargo and Mail Carried (000 short tons)			
				Domestic Services (000s)	International Services (000s)		Domestic Freight	International Freight	Domestic Mail	International Mail
1937	87·0	10,578	120	162	82	49	1·0	1·6	0·4	1·3
1938	91·4	13,220	140	148	72	53	0·7	2·1	0·7	2·9
1939	80·5	11,464	140	132	70	56	0·8	1·4	0·6	1·8
1940	26·6	5,803	220	44	23	42	0·3	0·6	0·5	0·5
1941	28·8	7,559	260	57	26	57	0·1	0·9	0·6	1·0
1942	33·9	10,689	320	64	45	102	0·2	2·4	0·7	1·3
1943	38·4	13,160	340	72	61	125	0·2	4·4	0·7	1·5
1944	45·7	19,480	430	76	93	179	0·2	7·2	0·7	2·2
1945	65·6	28,031	430	117	134	302	0·5	7 5	0·6	2·2
1946	89·6	33,017	369	229	194	363	0·9	3·7	0·6	2·4
1947	114·1	39,522	346	342	244	441	1·1	4·6	0·8	2·6
1948	102·1	44,206	433	381	333	555	1·2	7·8	1·3	3·5
1949	113·9	44,257	388	453	468	615	2·0	13·9	1·4	4·6
1950	131·3	48,299	368	486	671	794	2·6	19·1	1·6	5·7
1951	138·8	52,455	378	528	887	1,065	2·9	34·5	2·4	6·5
1952	158·8	58,134	366	669	1,064	1,243	2·7	32·1	2·4	7·1
1953	177·6	61,720	347	833	1,327	1,434	3·5	59·4	2·4	7·4
1954	180·4	59,570	330	1,002	1,441	1,515	4·3	69·2	2·7	7·6
1955	202·8	69,052	341	1,212	1,782	1,801	8·9	101·2	3·4	8·2
1956	225·8	78,121	346	1,402	2,050	2,102	12·8	88·8	2·8	8·7
1957	234·1	85,073	363	1,588	2,386	2,422	12·7	99·7	2·9	8·8
1958	233·7	86,989	372	1,463	2,522	2,571	8·4	130·7	2·6	9·1
1959	250·7	91,876	366	1,738	2,967	3,091	11·5	183·0	2·7	9·3
1960	284·3	106,533	375	2,240	3,640	3,959	16·2	223·8	3·0	10·9
1961	310·1	116,395	375	2,841	4,010	4,531	19·3	233·4	3·5	11·4
1962	317·3	118,280	373	3,260	4,439	4,870	24·2	270·0	6·2	10·8
1963	313·6	117,778	376	3,673	4,974	5,447	31·3	269·5	6·8	12·2
1964	329·6	127,363	386	4,216	5,539	6,424	40·7	260·6	7·0	13·7
1965	330·5	137,165	415	4,669	6,199	7,417	52·4	252·0	7·5	14·5

NOTES

[1] SOURCES: 1839–1916 – *Annual Reports of the Postmaster General* (in *Sessional Papers* from 1854–5 annually); 1920–66 – *Abstract* (except for letter-post breakdown for 1925–34, which comes from *The Post Office* (G.P.O., 1934)).

[2] Figures from 1878 are for years ended 31 March. Earlier they are for calendar years.

(in millions)

Calendar years	Letters			Postcards			Newspapers, Packets, etc.			Parcels		
	E. & W.	Scot.	Ireland	E. & W.	Scot.	Ireland	E. & W.	Scot.	Ireland	E. & W.	Scot.	Ireland
1839 (*a*)	65	8	9	...	...	...	...	...	...	...	...	...
1840	132	19	18	...	...	...	...	...	...	...	...	...
1841	154	21	21	...	...	...	...	...	...	...	...	...
1842	164	22	22	...	...	...	...	...	...	...	...	...
1843	173	23	23	...	...	...	...	...	...	...	...	...
1844	190	27	26	...	...	...	...	...	...	...	...	...
1845	214	29	29	...	...	...	...	...	...	...	...	...
1846	236	31	33	...	...	...	...	...	...	...	...	...
1847	253	33	35	...	...	...	...	...	...	...	...	...
1848	260	34	35	...	...	...	...	...	...	...	...	...
1849	267	35	36	...	...	...	...	...	...	...	...	...
1850	276	35	35	...	...	...	...	...	...	...	...	...
1851	288	37	36	...	...	...	...	...	...	...	...	...
1852	304	38	37	...	...	...	...	...	...	...	...	...
1853	330	41	40	...	...	...	...	...	...	...	...	...
1854	358	44	41	...	...	...	...	...	...	...	...	...
1855	369	46	42	...	...	...	...	...	...	...	...	...
1856	388	48	42	...	...	...	51	11	12	...	...	...
1857	410	52	43	...	...	...	54	11	12	...	...	...
1858	428	51	44	...	...	...	56	11	12	...	...	...
1859	446	52	47	...	...	...	59	11	12	...	...	...
1860	462	54	48	...	...	...	60	10	12	...	...	...
1861	487	56	50	...	...	...	62	11	12	...	...	...
1862	497	57	51	...	...	...	63	11	13	...	...	...
1863	529	61	52	...	...	...	66	11	12	...	...	...
1864	560	64	55	...	...	...	72	11	13	...	...	...
1865	597	67	56	...	...	...	73	11	13	...	...	...
1866	623	70	57	...	...	...	75	11	13	...	...	...
1867	640	76	59	...	...	...	78	11	13	...	...	...
1868	670	78	60	...	...	...	81	12	13	...	...	...
1869	683	79	62	...	...	...	83	12	14	...	...	...
1870	704	79	64	...	...	...	102	14	15	...	...	...
1871	721	80	66	...	...	...	160	21	21	...	...	...
1872	737	82	66	64	8	4	177	25	21	...	...	...
1873	756	84	67	60	8	4	204	28	22	...	...	...
1874	802	90	70	66	9	4	206	29	23	...	...	...
1875	847	91	71	73	9	5	227	30	23	...	...	...
1876	856	91	72	78	10	5	242	33	24	...	...	...
Years ended 31 March												
1878	884	100	74	86	11	5	256	36	26	...	...	...
1879	922	99	76	94	12	5	265	36	27	...	...	...

See p. 111 for footnotes.

Transport and Communications 8. *continued*

(in millions)

	Letters			Postcards			Newspapers, Packets, etc.			Parcels		
	E. & W.	Scot.	Ireland	E. & W.	Scot.	Ireland	E. & W.	Scot.	Ireland	E. & W.	Scot.	Ireland
1880	950	102	76	97	12	6	281	37	27	...	...	...
1881	981	105	79	104	13	6	307	39	28	...	...	...
1882	1,037	110	82	114	15	6	338	43	31	...	...	...
1883	1,078	117	86	121	16	7	353	45	31	...	...	...
1884	1,112	122	88	129	17	8	359	48	30	...	...	...
1885	1,148	123	89	134	18	8	380	51	33	19	2	1
1886	1,187	126	90	144	20	8	402	54	34	22	3	2
1887	1,240	129	91	151	20	8	429	56	35	27	3	2
1888	1,287	132	93	159	21	9	451	56	35	30	4	2
1889	1,327	136	96	170	22	9	471	57	36	33	4	3
1890	1,413	140	97	184	23	10	505	59	38	35	5	3
1891	1,463	143	100	195	24	11	540	61	41	38	5	3
1892	1,516	147	105	205	25	11	554	62	42	41	5	3
1893	1,532	152	106	206	27	11	584	69	45	43	6	4
1894	1,549	154	109	209	27	12	620	74	46	45	6	4
1895	1,502	156	113	272	29	13	640	78	48	47	6	4
1896	1,559	163	113	268	32	14	682	88	51	50	7	4
1897	1,607	169	118	287	34	15	700	93	56	53	7	4
1898	1,711	177	124	309	36	15	730	94	54	56	7	4
1899	1,860	191	137	327	39	16	709	93	54	60	8	5
1900	1,909	197	141	343	41	17	720	94	52	62	8	5
1901	1,977	202	144	359	42	18	747	97	56	67	9	5
1902	2,085	218	149	380	46	19	784	96	56	72	9	6
1903	2,208	222	150	416	54	20	820	108	58	75	10	6
1904	2,218	226	153	517	72	24	827	108	61	78	10	6
1905	2,239	230	156	617	87	31	848	113	62	81	10	6
1906	2,313	238	156	677	91	33	897	119	61	84	11	7
1907	2,398	248	158	705	92	35	936	125	62	87	11	7
1908	2,444	256	165	729	92	37	950	127	63	91	12	7
1909	2,483	256	168	732	91	37	962	127	66	94	12	7
1910	2,517	257	173	746	85	37	975	128	70	98	13	7
1911	2,606	265	177	748	87	37	1,034	135	72	101	13	8
1912	2,730	274	183	780	88	38	1,058	135	73	104	13	8
1913	2,827	284	188	776	86	37	1,069	136	76	108	14	8
1914	2,986	296	196	801	88	37	1,160	141	78	113	15	9
1915	2,926	291	192	763	82	35	1,028	130	73	121	15	9
1916–19	...	...	...	...	...	...	...	...	...	...	...	...
1920	3,290	333	209	503	53	25	1,099	142	76	120	15	10
1921	2,976	300	184	507	49	21	1,300	165	77	113	15	9
1922	2,814	285	176	415	39	17	1,249	160	76	104	14	9
			N.I.			N.I.			N.I.			N.I.
1923	2,959	289	52	432	38	5	1,478	175	27	104	14	2·3
1924	2,991	297	52	427	38	5	1,553	194	28	109	15	2·4
1925	3,135	311	54	422	38	5	1,640	205	30	119	16	2·6

(in millions)

	Letters			Postcards			Newspapers, Packets, etc.			Parcels		
	E. & W.	Scot.	Ireland	E. & W.	Scot.	Ireland	E. & W.	Scot.	Ireland	E. & W.	Scot.	Ireland
1926		3,575			460			2,025		125	17	2·6
1927		3,560			400			1,840		122	16	2·4
1928		3,630			423			2,147			140·0	
1929		3,642			421			2,167			151·5	
											---- (*b*)	
1930		3,700			420			2,280			160·5	
1931		3,745			430			2,300			161·9	
1932		3,750			410			2,380			158·1	
1933		3,810			405			2,425			151·7	
1934		3,890			410			2,453			153·3	
1935				6,935							149·7	
1936				7,345							162·2	
1937				7,690							174·4	
1938				7,990							179·5	
1939				8,150							184·8	
				—— (*c*)								
1940				7,460							192·7	
1941				6,310							187·6	
1942				6,150							198·2	
1943				6,390							204·7	
1944				6,480							235·3	
1945				6,600							284·0	
1946				6,550							257·3	
1947				7,300							238·7	
1948				7,600							243·5	
1949				8,050							239·6	
1950				8,350							243·3	
1951				8,500							232·7	
1952				8,750							223·6	
1953				8,800							243·2	
1954				9,100							241·6	
1955				9,500							242·8	
1956				9,700							237·6	
1957				9,700							249·0	
1958				9,600							247·4	
1959				9,700							243·3	
1960				10,200							234·7	
1961				10,600							248·2	
1962				10,500							233·4	
1963				10,600							224·2	
1964				11,000							229·9	
1965				11,200							216·0	
1966				11,300							235·3	

(*a*) This is an estimate based on one week in November, and applies to the year ended 5 December. It includes franked letters.
(*b*) Subsequent figures refer to parcels handled, not parcels delivered. Figures of parcels handled for 1928 and 1929 were 153·1 and 154·5 respectively.

(*c*) Subsequent figures refer to mail posted in the United Kingdom, not mail delivered. Figures for mail posted for 1938 and 1939 were 8,080 and 8,240 respectively. Figures of mail delivered for 1940–6 were as follows:

| 1940 | 7,360 | 1942 | 6,105 | 1944 | 6,270 | 1946 | 6,230 |
| 1941 | 6,250 | 1943 | 6,270 | 1945 | 6,250 | | |

Transport and Communications 9. Telegraph and Telephone Services – United Kingdom 1870–1966

NOTES

[1] SOURCES: 1870–1916 – *Annual Reports of the Postmaster General* (in *Sessional Papers* from 1854–5 annually); 1917–66 – *Abstract*.

[2] Figures from 1878 are for years ended 31 March. Earlier they are for calendar years.

(in millions)

Calendar years	Telegrams Sent			Telephone Calls Made, U.K.	
	E. & W.	Scot.	Ireland	Trunk Service	Local Service
1870 (a)	7·1	1·0	0·5		
1871	9·7	1·3	0·8		
1872	12·1	1·7	1·1		
1873	14·1	1·9	1·3		
1874	15·6	2·1	1·4		
1875	17·1	2·3	1·4		
1876	17·7	2·4	1·5		
Years ended 31 March					
1878	18·1	2·5	1·6		
1879	20·4	2·5	1·6		
1880	22·2	2·7	1·6		
1881	25·2	3·0	1·7		
1882	26·3	3·2	1·9		
1883	26·9	3·2	1·9		
1884	27·6	3·2	1·9		
1885	28·1	3·3	1·9		
1886	33·1	3·8	2·2		
1887	42·3	5·1	2·8		
1888	44·9	5·4	3·0		
1889	48·5	6·0	3·2		
1890	52·4	6·5	3·4		
1891	55·7	7·1	3·7		
1892	58·8	7·2	3·8		
1893	58·9	7·1	3·9		
1894	59·6	7·3	4·0		
1895	60·2	7·3	4·0		
1896	66·4	8·1	4·3		
1897	67·0	8·1	4·4		
1898	70·0	8·5	4·6	5·9	…
1899	73·2	9·1	4·7	7·1	…
1900	76·1	9·4	4·9	8·1	…
1901	75·4	9·3	4·9	9·0	…
1902	75·8	9·7	4·9	10·1	…
1903	77·8	9·6	5·1	11·6	…
1904	75·6	9·3	5·1	13·5	…
1905	74·8	9·1	5·1	15·5	…
1906	75·1	9·1	5·2	18·1	…
1907	75·0	9·2	5·3	19·9	…
1908	71·6	9·0	5·4	22·1	…
1909	70·8	8·7	5·3	23·6	…

See p. 114 for footnotes.

(in millions)

Year	Telegrams Sent			Telephone Calls Made, U.K	
	E. & W.	Scot.	Ireland	Trunk Service	Local Service
1910	72·7	8·7	5·5	26·7	...
1911	72·5	8·7	5·5	30·2	...
1912	74·3	9·0	5·9	33·7	...
1913	73·6	9·2	5·7	36·0	797
1914	72·3	9·1	5·7	38·2	834
1915	75·8	9·3	6·1	40·7	815
1916	70·0	8·8	5·4	40·4	776
1917		79		38·8	701
1918		80		43·7	700
1919		89		46·5	716
1920		101		54·2	848
1921		88		57·8	843
1922		83		52·4	682
		— (a)		— (a)	— (a)
1923		80		59·5	730
1924		78		70·3	832
1925		79		77·7	852
1926		77		86·5	930
1927		75		95·3	1,006
1928		74		102·9	1,071
1929		72		110·5	1,155
1930		71		118·3	1,205
1931		66		122·8	1,248
1932		61		125·7	1,305
1933		57		129·8	1,361
1934		58		140·5	1,440
				— (b)	— (b)
1935		55		85·9	1,595
1936		65		99·2	1,725
				— (c)	— (c)
1937		72		100·7	1,882
1938		71		106·9	2,060
		— (d)			
1938		57			
1939		58		113·0	2,124
1940		63		117·4	2,098
1941		61		118·0	1,974
1942		67		134·0	1,901
1943		76		161·0	1,942
1944		71		181·0	1,970
1945		71		189·1	2,039
1946		74		193·2	2,175
1947		63		205·2	2,509
1948		58		217	2,681
1949		54		227	2,820

See p. 114 *for footnotes.*

Transport and Communications 9. *continued*

(in millions)

	Telegrams Sent			Telephone Calls Made, U.K.	
	E. & W.	Scot.	Ireland	Trunk Service	Local Service
1950		52		235	2,940
1951		65		250	3,076
1952		62		262	3,230
1953		58		264	3,165
1954		56		278	3,370
1955		48		306	3,615
1956		43		333	3,865
1957		39		321	3,743
1958		37		327	3,671
1959		35		343	3,700
1960		35		387	3,900
1961		35		426	4,300
1962		34		477	4,500
1963		33		545	4,750
1964		31		624	5,100
1965		32		736	5,600
1966		31		841	6,050

a) Subsequently excludes Southern Ireland.
(*b*) Subsequently all calls of value fourpence or under were counted as local, instead of twopence and under as previously. Estimated figures on the new basis for 1934 are 76·6 and 1,504 respectively.

(*c*) Some calls were subsequently reallocated. Estimated figures on the new basis for 1936 are 89·8 and 1,734 respectively.
(*d*) Subsequently excludes telegrams sent via private cable companies.

Transport and Communications 10. Broadcast Receiving Licences – United Kingdom 1923–66

NOTES
[1] SOURCE: *Abstract*.

[2] The figures are of licences current at 31 March.

(in 000s)

	Sound		Sound	Television		Sound	Television
1923	125	1938	8,589		1953	10,750	2,142
1924	748	1939	8,968		1954	10,188	3,249
1925	1,350	1940	8,951		1955	9,477	4,504
1926	1,960	1941	8,752		1956	8,522	5,740
1927	2,270	1942	8,683		1957	7,559	6,966
1928	2,483	1943	9,242		1958	6,556	8,090
1929	2,730	1944	9,555		1959	5,481	9,255
1930	3,091	1945	9,711		1960	4,535	10,470
1931	3,647	1946	10,396		1961	3,909	11,268
1932	4,620	1947	10,763	15	1962	3,538	11,834
1933	5,497	1948	11,134	46	1963	3,256	12,443
1934	6,260	1949	11,621	127	1964	2,999	12,885
1935	7,012	1950	11,876	344	1965	2,794	13,253
1936	7,618	1951	11,605	764	1966	2,611	13,567
1937	8,131	1952	11,304	1,449			

BUILDING

TABLES

Tables 1 and 2 follow on directly from equivalent tables in the first *Abstract of British Historical Statistics*, and table 4 is a substitute covering the same topic – building costs. Table 3 gives a more detailed breakdown of the total houses built, according to whether local authority or private enterprise was responsible, and the only reason for not including it in the first volume was the short run of years which would have been covered then. None of these tables calls for any particular comment.

Building 1. Number of Houses at Censuses – United Kingdom 1931–66

NOTES
[1] SOURCE: *Abstract* based on the Census *Reports*.
[2] The definition of the term 'house' has changed slightly from time to time. Details can be found in *Guides to Official Sources*, no. 2, and in the 1961 Census Housing Tables Part I, general explanatory notes. The figures here relate to all houses, whether classed as occupied or unoccupied.

(in thousands)

	England & Wales	Scotland	Northern Ireland
1931	9,400	1,197	...
1937	...	...	322
1951	12,389	1,442	346
1961	14,646	1,627	387
1966	15,449	1,691	419

Building 2. Houses Built – Great Britain 1938–65

NOTE
SOURCE: *Abstract*.

(in thousands)

Year	Built	Year	Built	Year	Built
1938	359·1	1948	245·9	1958	273·7
1939	255·6	1949	197·7	1959	276·7
1940	95·1	1950	198·2	1960	297·8
1941	23·4	1951	194·8	1961	296·1
1942	12·9	1952	239·9	1962	305·4
1943	9·5	1953	318·8	1963	298·9
1944	8·1	1954	347·8	1964	373·7
1945	13·8	1955	317·4	1965	382·3
1946	138·5	1956	300·6		
1947	186·0	1957	301·1		

Building 3. Local Authority and Private House-Building – United Kingdom 1920–65

NOTES

[1] SOURCE: *Abstract*.
[2] The following categories of houses are not covered by this table: (i) Private houses having a rateable value exceeding £78 (£105 in the Metropolitan Police District) up to 1945; (ii) houses built for government departments; (iii) war-destroyed houses rebuilt; and (iv) temporary houses.

[3] In the *Abstract* before World War II the series were headed 'Built by Local Authorities' and 'Built by Private Enterprise'. These are apparently equivalent to the postwar headings used here.

1 April–31 March	Houses Built in England & Wales		Houses Built in Scotland		Houses Built in Northern Ireland	
	For Local Authorities	For Private Owners	For Local Authorities	For Private Owners	For Local Authorities	For Private Owners
1919/20	576	...	—	...	—	...
1920/1	15,585	...	1,201	...	—	...
1921/2	80,783	...	5,796	...	—	...
1922/3	57,535	...	9,527	...	—	...
1923/4	14,353	71,857	5,233	...	—	...
1924/5	20,624	116,265	3,238	3,638	73	...
1925/6	44,218	129,208	5,290	5,639	882	...
1926/7	74,093	143,536	9,621	7,496	123	...
1927/8	104,034	134,880	16,460	6,137	91	...
1928/9	55,723	113,809	13,954	5,024	198	...
1929/30	60,245	141,815	13,023	5,011	300	...
	- - - - - (a)					
1930/1	55,874	127,933	8,122	4,571	144	...
1931/2	70,061	130,751	8,952	4,766	37	...
1932/3	55,991	144,505	12,165	6,596	15	...
1933/4	55,840	210,782	16,503	10,760	20	...
1934/5	41,593	287,513	15,733	6,096	50	1,392
			——— (b)	——— (b)		
1935/6	52,357	272,503	18,814	7,086	20	4,132
1936/7	71,740	274,313	16,044	7,757	213	5,239
1937/8	77,970	259,632	13,341	8,187	350	355
1938/9	101,744	230,616	19,162	7,311	1,126	207
1939/40	50,452	145,510	19,118	6,411	(169) (c)	(96) (c)
1940/1	15,408	27,090	10,474	3,732	400	—
1941/2	2,913	5,601	4,714	692	206	—
1942/3	1,378	2,494	3,072	224	—	—
1943/4	2,539	1,079	2,717	92	—	—
1944/5	2,432	1,852	2,383	170	—	10

See p. 118 for footnotes.

Calendar Years	Houses Built in England & Wales		Houses Built in Scotland		Houses Built in Northern Ireland	
	For Local Authorities	For Private Owners	For Local Authorities	For Private Owners	For Local Authorities	For Private Owners
1945	(508) (d)	(937) (d)	1,428	141	—	21
1946	21,202	29,720	3,811	499	232	347
1947	86,567	39,626	10,773	1,354	688	507
1948	170,821	31,210	19,547	1,541	3,180	1,639
1949	141,766	24,688	24,180	1,102	4,860	2,667
1950	139,356	26,576	24,314	782	4,247	2,882
1951	141,587	21,406	20,997	1,145	3,899	2,934
1952	165,637	32,078	27,623	2,242	5,917	2,350
1953	202,891	60,528	35,992	2,393	6,033	1,946
1954	199,642	88,028	35,331	2,608	4,345	1,787
1955	162,525	109,934	29,278	3,523	4,221	2,636
1956	139,977	119,585	26,290	4,576	4,443	2,270
1957	137,584	122,942	28,326	3,513	3,719	2,329
1958	113,146	124,087	27,373	4,061	2,764	2,072
1959	99,456	146,476	22,709	4,232	2,380	2,458
1960	103,235	162,100	21,503	6,529	3,478	2,776
1961	92,880	170,366	19,541	7,147	3,697	3,214
1962	105,302	167,016	18,788	7,784	4,487	3,411
1963	97,015	168,242	21,164	6,622	5,724	2,923
1964	119,468	210,432	29,156	7,662	6,130	3,170
1965	133,024	206,246	26,584	7,553	5,349	3,363

(a) Figures up to this point exclude a small number of houses built by local authorities without state assistance.
(b) Subsequent figures are for the calendar year indicated first in the stub.

(c) Houses built from 1 April to 31 December 1939.
(d) Houses built from 1 April to 31 December 1945.

Building 4. Index of Building Costs – Great Britain 1939–66

NOTES
[1] SOURCE: Building Research Station, *Collection of Construction Statistics*.
[2] This is the 'combined index', which is based on the average of the Venning index (published in *Building*), the B.R.S. Measured Work index, and the Ministry of Public Building & Works Current Cost index since 1955 and the Board of Inland Revenue indices up to then.

Average of 1958–60 = 100

1939	29	1949	67	1959	99
1940	33	1950	69	1960	101
1941	38	1951	80	1961	106
1942	41	1952	88	1962	110
1943	42	1953	86	1963	113
1944	44	1954	88	1964	117
1945	50	1955	92	1965	123
1946	56	1956	97	1966	128
1947	61	1957	99		
1948	65	1958	100		

CHAPTER X

MISCELLANEOUS PRODUCTION STATISTICS

TABLES

———————

This chapter contains both some of the most simple and the most complicated tables in this book. The first three tables are straightforward enough, and are all that remain of the extensive statistics based on the excise, which were given in the first *Abstract of British Historical Statistics*. A particular interest attaches to table 2, showing British spirits charged with duty for consumption in the various parts of the United Kingdom, since this is practically unique in going back in an almost unbroken series to the seventeenth century. It is a pity that the Commissioners of Customs and Excise have, in the 1960s, ceased to publish the regional breakdown in this series, and also in the statistics of spirits distilled shown in table 3. These detailed figures are still available, however, for a fee.

Table 4, showing patents, is a straightforward continuation from the first volume. To it have been added, in table 5, the statistics relating to designs and trade marks, from their inception in 1884. These were omitted in the earlier volume because of the shortage of space.

Table 6 gives a brief summary of some of the mass of statistics available in the main Censuses of Production since 1935 which cover the whole of the United Kingdom. The principal difficulty in using these statistics is the lack of any exact comparability between Censuses; though it is fair to say that each Census does provide this for at least its immediate predecessor. The main problems in achieving a longer period of comparison are alluded to in the notes to the table. Very much more information is, of course, available in the original sources.

The indices of industrial production since 1938, shown in the last table, are extremely complicated in origin, and this is not the place to comment on them. Anyone who requires details of their construction must consult Lomax's article in the *Journal of the Royal Statistical Society* (Series A, 1959) for his index, or the *Board of Trade Journal* for the official indices since 1950.

Miscellaneous Production Statistics 1. Beer on which Duty was Paid – United Kingdom 1938–66

NOTE
SOURCE: *Annual Report of H.M. Commissioners of Customs and Excise.*

(in millions of barrels)

Years ended 31 March		Years ended 31 March		Years ended 31 March	
1938	18·0	1948	17·9	1958	16·8
1939	18·3	1949	16·6	1959	16·3
1940	18·9	1950	16·1	1960	17·5
1941	18·4	1951	16·8	1961	18·2
1942	19·3	1952	17·0	1962	19·1
1943	18·2	1953	16·6	1963	19·0
1944	19·1	1954	16·6	1964	19·8
1945	19·6	1955	16·2	1965	20·1
1946	20·8	1956	16·6	1966	20·4
1947	17·6	1957	16·7		

Miscellaneous Production Statistics 2. British Spirits Charged with Duty for Consumption – 1938–65

NOTES

[1] SOURCES: *Report of the Commissioners of Customs and Excise*, with the regional breakdown since 1960 supplied by the Statistical Office of the Board of Customs and Excise.
[2] The modern heading for the series shown in this table is 'Dutiable Spirits – Quantities Retained for Consumption'.

[3] The series include spirits granted rebate of duty in respect of medical or scientific use, but do not include spirits delivered for re-distillation, methylation, use in art or manufacture, or in fortifying wines.

(in thousands of gallons)

Years ended 31 March	England & Wales	Scotland	Northern Ireland	United Kingdom
1938	7,344	1,733	163	9,239
1939	7,282	1,728	167	9,176
1940	7,468	2,001	196	9,665
1941	5,555	1,923	185	7,662
1942	5,318	1,499	182	6,999
1943	5,608	1,952	173	7,733
1944	5,975	1,803	161	7,938
1945	5,214	1,418	133	6,764
1946	5,353	1,425	134	6,913
1947	5,344	1,493	121	6,958
1948	4,024	1,078	96	5,197
1949	3,908	895	90	4,893
1950	4,783	1,226	90	6,098
1951	6,223	1,413	115	7,751
1952	5,506	1,287	101	6,893
1953	5,953	1,459	104	7,517
1954	6,243	1,802	121	8,166
1955	6,939	1,948	142	9,028
1956	7,620	1,952	147	9,718
1957	7,769	2,195	152	10,116
1958	8,073	2,254	166	10,493
1959	7,888	2,497	176	10,561
1960	8,672	2,475	215	11,363
1961	7,415	4,925	193	12,533
1962	7,027	5,191	202	12,420
1963	7,139	5,354	233	12,726
1964	7,875	6,158	251	14,285
1965	7,731	6,721	258	14,710

Miscellaneous Production Statistics 3. British Spirits Distilled — 1938–65

NOTES

[1] SOURCES: *Reports of the Commissioners of Customs and Excise*, with the regional breakdown since 1960 supplied by the Statistical Office of the Board of Customs and Excise.

[2] This account relates to all spirits, whether potable or not, produced in the different kingdoms.

(in thousands of gallons)

Years ended 31 March	England & Wales and Northern Ireland	Scotland	United Kingdom
1938	45,878	32,503	78,381
1939	45,925	32,581	78,507
1940	47,586	27,023	74,609
1941	40,028	20,091	60,119
1942	48,979	8,030	57,009
1943	22,322	9,880	32,203
1944	19,060	3,927	22,987
1945	46,726	11,319	58,046
1946	33,459	19,219	52,678
1947	38,485	8,962	47,447
1948	42,091	23,783	65,874
1949	38,346	29,156	67,502
1950	44,525	32,301	76,826
1951	60,295	38,078	98,372
1952	49,354	39,576	88,931
1953	29,129	41,572	70,701
1954	32,838	44,316	77,154
1955	43,523	53,157	96,681
1956	48,212	57,493	105,706
1957	46,467	65,783	112,250
1958	31,582	83,595	115,178
1959	23,417	82,310	105,726
1960	31,143	84,785	115,928
1961	30,369	105,717	136,086
1962	27,091	112,138	139,228
1963	27,431	119,504	146,935
1964	28,539	140,673	169,212
1965	37,415	159,092	196,507

Miscellaneous Production Statistics 4. Patents – United Kingdom 1938–65

NOTE

SOURCE: *Reports of the Comptroller General of Patents, Designs and Trade Marks.*

	Applications	Patents Sealed		Applications	Patents Sealed		Applications	Patents Sealed
1938	37,973	19,314	1948	33,626	15,558	1958	42,277	18,531
1939	33,109	17,605	1949	33,347	20,703	1959	44,495	18,157
				----- (a)	----- (a)			
1940	18,254	11,453	1950	31,686	13,509	1960	44,914	26,775
1941	16,847	11,179	1951	30,513	13,761	1961	46,811	28,871
1942	18,624	7,969	1952	33,142	21,380	1962	49,187	27,721
1943	21,944	7,945	1953	36,401	17,882	1963	51,468	30,148
1944	26,200	7,712	1954	37,871	17,985	1964	53,104	32,619
1945	35,332	7,465	1955	37,551	20,630	1965	55,507	33,864
1946	38,181	8,971	1956	39,730	19,938			
1947	35,378	11,727	1957	40,498	25,205			

(a) Under the Patents Act of 1949 an application claiming two or more Convention priorities is now filed as a single application with additional fees, whereas, prior to 1950, the former Acts required a separate application in respect of each Convention priority.

NOTE
SOURCE: *Reports of the Comptroller General of Patents, Designs and Trade Marks.*

	Designs		Trade Marks	
	Applications	Registered	Applications	Registered
1884	19,753	19,687	7,104	4,523
1885	20,725	20,602	8,026	4,332
1886	24,041	23,838	10,677	4,725
1887	26,043	25,314	10,586	4,740
1888	26,239	25,135	13,315	5,520
1889	24,705	23,989	11,316	5,053
1890	22,553	21,107	10,258	6,014
1891	21,950	20,880	10,787	4,225
1892	19,527	18,501	9,101	3,649
1893	19,480	18,338	8,675	3,522
1894	22,255	20,847	8,013	2,905
1895	21,417	20,192	8,272	2,821
1896	22,849	21,727	9,466	2,917
1897	20,417	19,301	10,624	3,358
1898	20,049	18,830	9,767	3,437
1899	19,495	18,470	8,927	3,777
1900	16,952	16,282	7,937	3,223
1901	16,934	16,217	8,775	3,246
1902	17,825	17,106	8,899	3,377
1903	21,104	20,426	9,467	3,748
1904	23,531	22,604	9,972	3,842
1905	23,938	23,138	10,521	4,261
1906	22,001	21,212	11,414	4,731
1907	24,928	24,039	10,796	6,255
1908	24,907	24,389	10,645	5,965
1909	26,412	25,754	10,880	6,112
1910	32,745	32,212	10,623	5,722
1911	43,057	41,581	9,743	4,868
1912	43,015	42,077	10,014	4,942
1913	40,429	39,275	9,689	5,071
1914	34,354	33,362	8,317	4,408
1915	18,130	17,390	6,057	3,241
1916	15,399	14,766	5,837	2,878
1917	13,208	12,729	5,502	2,744
1918	10,019	9,597	6,968	3,055
1919	14,094	13,049	12,479	4,837
1920	13,669	13,071	14,064	7,122
1921	13,387	12,313	11,959	7,518
1922	15,736	14,419	12,397	7,099
1923	19,085	17,807	12,571	7,694
1924	22,155	20,155	12,597	7,968
1925	23,801	22,308	12,387	7,464
1926	23,206	21,874	13,007	7,734

	Designs		Trade Marks	
	Applications	Registered	Applications	Registered
1927	22,707	21,009	12,381	7,543
1928	24,746	23,899	12,684	6,818
1929	23,648	22,072	11,753	7,455
1930	21,463	20,169	10,830	6,728
1931	18,886	17,685	9,870	6,016
1932	22,374	19,887	10,322	6,060
1933	25,015	20,767	9,845	5,472
1934	20,681	17,830	10,016	5,533
1935	21,229	18,269	9,169	5,783
1936	20,292	17,523	9,163	5,337
1937	19,343	16,831	8,836	5,027
1938	16,118	16,544	8,493	5,265
1939	11,588	10,595	6,690	4,643
1940	4,473	4,632	3,507	2,529
1941	3,118	2,576	3,726	2,090
1942	2,301	2,254	4,082	2,386
1943	2,824	2,049	5,471	2,739
1944	3,525	2,436	6,943	3,340
1945	4,755	3,103	9,341	3,341
1946	6,524	4,285	11,690	4,167
1947	5,463	5,196	10,365	4,476
1948	5,725	5,060	10,326	7,397
1949	6,631	4,800	9,362	8,006
1950	7,327	5,362	9,791	7,777
1951	9,155	8,412	8,649	7,828
1952	9,671	8,447	9,913	6,846
1953	8,270	7,435	11,734	7,261
1954	9,215	7,316	12,384	8,285
1955	9,792	8,121	11,793	7,884
1956	9,964	7,821	11,356	7,737
1957	10,512	8,320	11,756	8,217
1958	10,891	8,680	12,938	7,250
1959	9,098	7,893	14,166	6,987
1960	9,237	7,840	16,128	9,894
1961	9,427	8,361	13,997	10,841
1962	7,780	7,431	14,210	9,754
1963	7,915	6,722	15,024	10,121
1964	8,327	6,866	15,388	11,462
1965	8,105	6,800	14,995	9,814

Miscellaneous Production Statistics 6. Output at the Main Censuses of Production – United Kingdom 1935–63

NOTES

[1] SOURCE: *Abstract*.

[2] There is no exact comparability from one Census to the next, for a variety of reasons, and the vertical 'break' line between the two sets of figures for 1954 should not be taken to mean that this is the only significant failure of continuity. Recent *Abstracts* are the best source of reasonably comparable runs of figures. Even so the following points should be noted: (i) The 1935 figures cover only firms employing more than 10 persons; (ii) in the last three censuses especially, there is a substantial amount of duplication represented by the total value of partly-manufactured goods sold by one industrial establishment to another; (iii) gross output at the last two censuses includes goods for merchanting and canteen supplies; and (iv) the Mining and Quarrying figures are for Great Britain only, except in 1935 when they cover Northern Ireland also.

Gross Output

(in £ million)

	1935	1951	1954	1954	1958	1963
Food, Drink, and Tobacco	665	3,227	3,819	3,235	3,751	4,477
Chemicals and Allied Industries	206	1,283	1,687	1,663	2,197	2,692
Metal Manufacture	245	1,479	1,879	1,778	2,258	2,479
Engineering and Allied Industries	710	4,408	5,644	5,297	7,052	9,013
Textiles, Leather, and Clothing	656	3,339	2,934	2,892	2,686	3,081
Other Manufactures	413	2,174	2,297	2,305	2,807	3,771
All Manufacturing Industries	2,900	15,909	18,259	17,170	20,751	25,512
Mining and Quarrying	167	617	775	746	929	1,031
Construction	295	1,600	2,053	1,997	2,723	3,930
Gas, Electricity, and Water	181	607	810	795	1,093	1,593
All Census Industries	3,543	18,733	21,897	20,709	25,496	32,066

Net Output

	1935	1951	1954	1954	1958	1963
Food, Drink, and Tobacco	203	608	742	645	917	1,248
Chemicals and Allied Industries	89	372	529	538	736	1,016
Metal Manufacture	88	443	519	533	689	826
Engineering and Allied Industries	357	1,989	2,622	2,489	3,227	4,388
Textiles, Leather, and Clothing	249	935	968	964	967	1,272
Other Manufactures	237	924	1,058	1,066	1,313	1,955
All Manufacturing Industries	1,226	5,271	6,438	6,234	7,849	10,705
Mining and Quarrying	136	471	577	575	726	772
Construction	150	770	983	933	1,245	1,857
Gas, Electricity, and Water	128	327	437	438	621	982
All Census Industries	1,640	6,838	8,435	8,180	10,441	14,316

Miscellaneous Production Statistics 7. Indices of Industrial Production – United Kingdom 1938–65

NOTE

SOURCES: Part A – K. S. Lomax, 'Production and Productivity Movements in the United Kingdom since 1900', *J.R.S.S.* series A (1959); Parts B and C – *Abstract*.

Part A. 1938–57 (1924 = 100)

| | Total All Industries | Mining and Quarrying | Manufacturing Industry | | | Metals | | | | |
			Total	Building Materials	Chemicals	Ferrous	Non-ferrous	Engineering	Vehicles	Precision Instruments, etc.
1938	146·4	90·7	147·8	168·5	141·0	118·3	174·6	145·2	224·7	158·3
1946	149·4	70·6	153·6	168·7	209·8	138·6	264·7	179·2	244·9	175·2
1947	158·7	72·7	164·3	194·3	213·3	145·0	304·2	202·9	255·8	203·9
1948	171·7	76·9	178·4	213·0	232·9	167·4	297·7	220·1	279·9	208·1
1949	182·5	79·4	190·5	223·2	253·6	174·8	279·8	233·7	309·8	221·6
1950	195·1	80·1	206·6	237·3	289·3	182·8	304·5	256·2	339·2	229·7
1951	201·2	82·9	215·2	247·9	313·9	189·2	345·3	279·7	348·2	234·9
1952	195·9	83·8	206·2	245·8	310·5	195·2	344·1	279·3	347·6	208·3
1953	207·9	83·5	219·8	256·0	356·1	198·2	295·3	284·4	385·4	225·4
1954	222·5	84·4	237·6	263·7	392·4	208·6	349·2	308·4	434·7	256·6
1955	234·5	83·4	253·1	274·1	415·7	224·1	388·8	340·5	480·9	262·8
1956	234·4	84·0	249·9	271·1	431·1	229·5	369·4	331·5	449·0	249·3
1957	237·6	84·1	254·4	264·3	448·1	235·5	361·4	342·9	461·8	254·5

Manufacturing Industries

	Metal Goods n.e.s.	Textiles	Leather	Clothing	Food, Drink, and Tobacco	Paper and Printing	Timber	Other Manufactures	Building and Contracting	Gas, Electricity, and Water Supply
1938	180·5	111·3	110·0	129·5	146·7	141·7	178·7	...	171·8	216·3
1946	208·9	86·5	102·1	85·2	162·8	132·9	133·0	208·7	131·9	289·8
1947	222·6	93·5	116·2	90·9	162·1	141·5	126·0	256·5	137·6	300·6
1948	232·1	108·3	166·5	95·3	168·9	147·7	139·7	306·4	149·9	319·5
1949	232·8	117·3	117·5	103·9	175·5	170·3	157·2	314·7	156·9	341·2
1950	242·5	128·2	119·8	109·9	180·7	196·7	169·9	357·9	157·1	371·6
1951	262·5	128·4	113·0	105·8	177·5	207·2	178·1	376·3	150·9	395·5
1952	257·4	104·2	100·0	100·2	182·4	174·9	160·8	341·0	155·4	407·4
1953	239·5	123·4	110·3	108·9	192·5	196·3	173·6	371·4	166·7	427·8
1954	257·9	127·1	112·1	108·8	196·3	229·1	203·0	426·8	173·0	462·6
1955	289·2	125·0	111·8	112·7	198·3	249·3	204·8	469·1	174·3	488·2
1956	285·5	124·3	106·1	114·9	204·0	246·4	196·0	453·8	184·5	511·5
1957	269·9	123·9	106·8	114·1	206·9	250·4	200·3	486·6	184·5	519·5

Miscellaneous Production Statistics 7. *continued*

Part B. 1950–8 (1954 = 100)

	Total All Industries	Mining and Quarrying	Total	Bricks, Pottery, Glass, Cement, etc.	Chemicals	Metals		Engineering (excl. Ships)	Ship-building and Marine Engineering	Vehicles
						Ferrous	Non-ferrous			
Weights										
	1,000	*72*	*760*	*30*	*63*	*54*	*15*	*164*	*22*	*78*
1950	88·3	94·8	87·8	88·8	79·7	88·0	87·4	84·5	93·5	76·4
1951	91·3	98·0	91·6	93·7	83·7	91·8	98·4	90·5	96·2	79·9
1952	89·2	99·3	88·2	92·3	79·6	95·4	97·5	92·4	99·2	79·5
1953	94·3	98·8	93·7	96·9	89·1	96·1	84·8	93·6	105·1	90·4
1954	100	100	100	100	100	100	100	100	100	100
1955	105·1	99·0	106·4	103·9	106·2	107·8	110·6	107·4	108·5	114·6
1956	105·6	99·2	105·9	102·4	110·6	110·8	107·5	107·0	117·4	107·2
1957	107·5	98·5	108·3	99·3	115·0	112·7	106·5	111·0	107·9	114·9
1958	106·3	94·3	106·9	98·0	115·0	99·9	105·5	111·5	108·8	118·4

Part C. 1958–65 (1958 = 100)

	Total All Industries	Mining and Quarrying	Total	Bricks, Pottery, Glass, Cement, etc.	Chemicals	Ferrous	Non-ferrous	Engineering (excl. Ships)	Ship-building and Marine Engineering	Vehicles
Weights										
	1,000	*72*	*748*	*28*	*68*	*55*	*13*	*167*	*22*	*79*
1958	100	100	100	100	100	100	100	100	100	100
1959	105·1	97·4	106·0	106·4	110·7	103·8	107·3	105·4	93·6	109·3
1960	112·5	93·9	114·6	118·4	122·6	120·8	122·6	113·7	84·8	118·0
1961	113·9	92·6	114·8	123·5	124·5	113·5	116·4	121·2	85·7	109·8
1962	115·1	95·1	115·3	125·6	129·0	106·3	113·6	123·2	86·6	112·0
1963	119·0	95·0	120·0	129·6	138·2	111·3	118·7	126·1	77·4	121·0
1964	128·2	95·3	129·5	148·4	151·1	127·1	131·5	137·2	74·9	126·4
1965	131·9	91·8	133·8	150·6	158·1	133·6	133·7	144·1	74·0	129·3

Part B, 1950–58 (*cont.*)

Manufacturing Industries

	Metal Goods, n.e.s.	Textiles	Leather	Clothing	Food, Drink, and Tobacco	Paper and Printing	Timber	Other Manufactures	Construction	Gas, Electricity, and Water Supply
Weights	*42*	*77*	*5*	*33*	*81*	*53*	*22*	*22*	*120*	*48*
1950	95·0	100·1	110·1	101·2	90·1	86·5	84·1	86·8	90·8	80·4
1951	101·2	99·8	106·8	95·7	93·1	91·3	90·6	91·6	87·3	85·5
1952	97·5	81·9	94·2	91·7	94·7	76·7	80·2	81·9	90·0	88·1
1953	91·8	97·4	101·5	100·3	98·5	85·7	89·0	88·3	96·3	92·5
1954	100	100	100	100	100	100	100	100	100	100
1955	111·6	97·5	99·7	103·7	102·7	107·7	100·1	110·8	100·3	105·4
1956	108·1	96·4	93·5	105·8	105·5	106·3	94·0	105·6	105·8	110·2
1957	108·6	96·5	93·3	105·1	106·9	109·1	96·0	111·9	105·5	114·3
1958	106·0	87·1	88·0	101·5	109·4	111·2	93·6	112·6	105·0	119·4

Part C, 1958–65 (*cont.*)

Weights	*42*	*58*	*4*	*30*	*86*	*55*	*20*	*22*	*126*	*54*
1958	100	100	100	100	100	100	100	100	100	100
1959	99·8	105·6	103·3	111·5	103·6	107·0	111·9	108·2	105·6	102·6
1960	112·2	110·4	101·6	119·6	106·7	119·4	114·0	120·1	111·5	110·5
1961	104·7	106·6	102·4	121·9	110·2	119·7	115·8	116·0	119·5	115·6
1962	101·1	104·6	96·8	118·1	112·2	122·1	111·1	118·2	120·7	124·8
1963	108·3	109·6	98·8	120·0	115·0	127·8	112·6	125·8	121·0	133·0
1964	120·6	116·2	101·9	125·6	118·3	138·5	127·8	136·7	135·3	137·4
1965	123·5	118·1	103·2	129·3	121·0	141·7	127·4	144·1	138·0	145·3

CHAPTER XI

OVERSEAS TRADE

TABLES

All the tables in this chapter follow on more or less directly from those in the first *Abstract of British Historical Statistics,* and whilst they are not without their problems, these are mostly of the kind to be dealt with in the notes. Table 1, showing the overall values of imports, exports, and re-exports may be subject to revision in its later years, owing to the under-recording of exports which was discovered in 1968. This applies also to individual series in the balance of payments table, number 8, though allowance has been made for this in the overall balance shown in that table. It is perhaps worth pointing out that the differences between the similarly-described series in these two tables are caused by different coverage and methods of valuation. The main difference is the deduction in table 8 of freight and insurance charges from the value of imports.

Tables 2, 3, and 4 show only slight breaks in a few of the series from those given in the first volume, and these are explained in the footnotes. In the cases where these breaks would have been large if a later classification had been used instead of the one current in 1938, figures have been given both according to the latter and according to the one in use in 1965. Some commodity groups which have only become significant since 1938 have been added to these tables, one or two items which have ceased to be important have been dropped, and a different arrangement has been adopted.

In table 5, showing trade with different regions and with the major countries, there have been certain changes from volume 1 in the makeup of the regions shown, mostly to take account of developments since the Second World War. The old division of Europe, used for pre-war statistics, no longer seemed to have a great deal of significance, and instead a division showing the trade with E.F.T.A., E.E.C., and the Communist Bloc has been substituted. Some other failures of comparability between postwar and earlier statistics are inevitable, because of boundary changes.

Tables 6 and 7 are straightforward indices based on the trade figures, and do not call for comment. On the other hand, the complexities of table 8 are such that any explanations beyond those given in the notes cannot be given here, but must be sought in the *Balance of Payments* 'pink books'.

Figures of the volume of certain major imports and exports which are reasonably homogeneous can be found in Chapters III to VII.

Overseas Trade 1. Values at Current Prices of Overseas Trade – United Kingdom 1938–65

NOTES
[1] SOURCES: *Annual Statement of Trade* and *Abstract*.　　　　[2] The value of bullion, specie, and diamonds is excluded.

(in £000,000)

	Imports	Domestic Exports	Re-exports		Imports	Domestic Exports	Re-exports
1938	919·5	470·8	61·5	1951	3,892·1	2,566·4	
1939	885·5	439·5	46·0	1952	3,464·8	2,566·7	142·0
1940	1,082·1 (a)	392·6 (a)	25·9 (a)				
1941	986·1 (a)	323·8 (a)	8·3 (a)	1953	3,328·1	2,558·0	103·1
1942	996·7 (a)	271·3 (a)	4·5 (a)	1954	3,359·2	2,649·9	98·3
				1955	3,860·8	2,876·7	116·4
1943	1,233·9 (a)	233·5 (a)	6·0 (a)	1956	3,861·5	3,143·3	143·7
1944	1,309·3 (a)	266·3 (a)	15·6 (a)	1957	4,043·7	3,295·0	129·8
1945	1,103·7 (a)	399·3 (a)	51·0 (a)				
1946	1,301·0	914·7	50·3	1958	3,747·5	3,176·2	141·2
1947	1,794·5	1,138·3	59·8	1959	3,983·4	3,330·1	130·9
	- - - - - (b)	- - - - - (b)		1960	4,540·7	3,554·8	141·2
1947	1,798·4	1,141·8		1961	4,395·1	3,681·5	158·6
				1962	4,487·0	3,791·0	157·6
1948	2,075·4	1,578·3	64·7				
1949	2,277·5	1,787·4	58·6	1963	4,812·7	4,081·0	153·8
1950	2,606·6	2,174·2	84·7	1964	5,506·7	4,253·4	153·4
1951	3,901·9	2,581·6	127·0	1965	5,751·1	4,728·0	172·8
	- - - - - (c)	- - - - - (c)					

(a) These figures exclude munitions. If these are included the series are as follows:

1940	1,152·1	411·2	26·0
1941	1,145·1	365·4	12·7
1942	1,206·2	391·1	10·6
1943	1,885·4	337·1	13·4
1944	2,359·8	327·1	18·2
1945	1,516·9	434·5	51·1

(b) This break is apparently caused by a revaluation of non-ferrous metal ores and manufactures. Revised figures back to 1949 were published in the 1953 *Annual Statement of Trade*, and back to 1947 in the 1954 *Abstract*.

(c) This break is caused by, firstly, a new system of valuing the parcel post, and secondly, the subsequent treatment of Channel Islands trade as part of the internal trade of the United Kingdom. Revised figures back to 1951 were published in the 1960 *Abstract* and have been used here.

Overseas Trade 2. Values at Current Prices of Principal Imports – United Kingdom 1938-65

NOTES

[1] SOURCE: *Annual Statement of Trade.*

[2] As from 1959 trade with the Channel Islands was not included as part of the overseas trade of the United Kingdom. The only significant break caused by this change is mentioned in footnote (g).

[3] The classification current in 1938 has been used so far as possible for categories which appeared in the first *Abstract of British Historical Statistics*. For categories which assumed importance only after 1938, the 1965 classification was used except as indicated in the footnotes.

(in £000,000)

	Butter and Margarine	Coffee	Fruit and Vegetables	Grain and Flour (a)	Meat and Meat Preparations	Live Animals for Food	Sugar	Tea	Wine	Metalliferous Ores and Scrap (b)	Timber	Raw Cotton
1938	51·0	1·4	54·2	74·4	90·7	9·2	19·2	30·8	5·3	25·9	42·9	29·6
1939	48·5	2·0	54·7	55·4	93·3	11·0	22·0	24·4	5·5	26·6	37·1	34·2
1940	33·0	3·5	43·2	93·7	97·2	10·9	23·7	27·5	4·7	40·2	37·9	50·3
1941	27·8	0·4	18·8	89·6	118·7	7·1	26·0	30·3	0·8	35·4	24·8	35·8
1942	17·8	1·7	18·8	53·6	148·8	13·1	15·1	23·5	0·4	31·2	20·4	52·7
1943	20·8	3·0	14·5	66·0	167·0	11·4	29·4	36·0	0·5	33·6	32·6	53·8
1944	21·2	3·4	30·0	65·5	167·9	11·6	23·8	35·1	0·9	29·8	36·0	42·0
1945	31·7	4·2	29·9	81·4	113·7	12·6	24·1	33·4	2·9	34·6	45·8	48·8
1946	37·3	3·3	72·0	90·2	139·7	11·8	37·1	35·2	7·3	42·0	55·1	46·4
1947	42·9	5·7	119·8	141·5	147·2	12·1	59·2	44·8	10·3	43·7	113·6	58·8
1948	67·8	6·0	132·1	201·2	125·9	11·8	58·3	55·7	10·6	60·7	93·9	106·7
1949	86·9	5·6	130·0	182·8	152·9	18·2	65·7	66·3	8·3	72·3	99·4	121·5
1950	91·4	11·0	134·2	159·9	203·7	19·9	80·1	57·4	9·5	86·2	93·8	160·6
1951	90·5	13·9	166·8	245·9	213·9	20·9	105·7	76·2	12·2	119·8	220·4	258·8
1952	82·4	14·1	159·6	262·2	221·3	23·2	93·3	79·4	9·7	157·1	163·7	128·3
1953	94·9	10·9	171·5	238·6	263·3	24·7	119·1	83·0	10·3	141·0	166·2	107·2
1954	101·4	14·2	199·6	185·5	252·2	33·9	96·7	127·2	11·9	137·0	162·4	125·9
				----(f)		---(f)						
1955	112·0	12·7	214·9	227·1	289·3	36·2	95·3	125·8	13·5	163·0	201·1	98·6
1956	120·6	15·5	232·2	241·0	287·5	32·8	100·7	114·5	14·0	182·1	167·7	104·2
1957	101·5	16·1	225·5	221·5	302·8	45·0	146·5	134·2	16·4	205·2	181·2	108·4
1958	97·8	14·7	258·2	233·0	307·6	38·6	95·6	127·5	15·7	137·7	148·4	71·6
			---(g)									
1959	134·7	14·2	233·7	239·6	310·2	29·7	80·8	112·3	18·1	133·7	149·3	67·9
1960	122·5	12·5	239·8	227·3	339·9	32·9	75·8	116·1	21·7	182·5	194·0	73·5
1961	106·3	12·7	250·8	218·0	306·5	43·7	70·0	115·3	25·6	164·0	185·2	62·2
1962	117·8	14·4	293·0	252·0	312·8	37·4	56·7	115·5	24·7	138·9	163·3	59·7
											---(f)	
1963	135·8	17·2	282·2	226·0	312·9	41·7	164·6	114·2	28·1	143·9	174·9	60·1
1964	157·7	23·5	282·6	226·6	368·4	50·9	134·9	109·0	31·4	185·3	223·3	65·1
1965	148·0	14·8	288·0	239·8	367·7	38·0	94·6	107·5	29·6	202·7	227·2	53·7

See p. 133 for footnotes.

131

Overseas Trade 2. *continued*

(in £000,000)

	Raw Wool	Flax and Hemp	Jute	Tobacco	Undressed Hides, Skins, and Furs	Rubber	Oils, Oil-seed, Gums, Resin, Tallow, etc. (c)	Paper-making Materials	Petroleum	Dyewoods and Dyestuffs	Chemicals (b)
1938	41·6	6·4	3·7	23·3	18·2	11·5	25·4	16·0	46·0	2·8	21·6
1939	39·3	8·0	4·0	13·6	15·5	9·5	26·1	15·7	47·1	3·4	24·3
1940	65·8	11·1	7·4	8·8	15·7	23·8	39·1	13·1	72·6	4·2	28·1
1941	21·3	5·3	3·1	18·0	8·6	22·2	34·9	7·8	93·7	3·1	23·3
1942	27·2	5·2	4·6	20·6	12·5	9·1	36·0	10·5	99·4	2·6	45·2
1943	18·8	6·6	4·4	42·2	10·5	13·3	51·5	9·4	153·5	2·1	61·0
1944	35·5	7·4	3·6	32·7	11·7	25·7	49·0	8·8	222·3	2·3	50·4
1945	35·5	8·4	4·3	53·4	14·5	11·7	42·0	15·4	145·6	2·8	38·2
1946	37·9	9·3	3·7	68·1	27·3	42·3	52·2	18·8	86·6	3·0	28·5
1947	60·3	14·3	5·5	47·4	39·9	27·8	105·4	27·3	98·5	4·6	46·1
1948	87·0	16·3	9·0	42·6	34·6	30·0	112·8	52·3	154·9	5·1	46·7
1949	127·8	14·3	10·1	52·5	38·0	22·4	131·3	48·4	146·9	4·3	42·2
1950	186·9	22·3	13·2	64·6	49·2	59·9	136·1	53·0	193·5	5·3	60·3
1951	242·2	33·4	17·2	81·4	68·5	160·3	192·2	144·4	300·0	9·9	106·6
1952	172·9	24·6	13·7	51·9	40·4	103·3	167·5	111·3	332·5	5·0	77·9
1953	231·8	19·0	14·3	77·8	50·2	56·3	131·5	73·3	307·4	6·5	77·5
1954	186·6	18·7	12·2	76·2	43·8	50·0	125·3	93·2	307·4	8·0	104·8
			– – – (f)								– – (f)
1955	179·2	18·4	13·3	86·5	45·7	95·8	118·0	114·9	328·3	7·7	115·4
1956	170·0	17·2	10·8	80·6	44·0	88·5	123·3	114·7	364·1	7·0	110·2
1957	191·4	17·1	14·9	85·6	48·0	84·2	129·3	110·7	433·6	7·8	117·4
1958	135·2	13·0	12·4	86·9	39·0	75·8	105·2	102·1	424·2	5·8	121·4
										– – (f)	
1959	148·5	17·0	13·3	84·7	48·7	63·8	112·6	103·9	458·6	6·4	139·3
1960	135·7	19·1	15·6	103·6	49·9	77·7	109·3	126·3	472·9	6·6	176·7
1961	128·4	16·5	14·6	100·6	46·8	72·0	100·5	122·4	475·5	7·1	169·0
1962	124·6	17·7	15·5	80·8	46·4	61·5	95·0	109·3	518·7	7·5	173·5
1963	141·6	21·9	12·7	99·5	58·8	52·7	102·0	119·3	545·6	8·7	205·8
1964	147·4	22·7	11·5	91·1	57·1	50·5	106·5	141·1	576·1	11·9	252·2
1965	116·8	17·3	12·8	84·0	55·7	47·3	117·4	142·6	591·7	11·0	282·1

Overseas Trade 2. *continued*

(in £000,000)

	Iron and Steel (d)		Non-ferrous Metals (d)		Machinery (e)	Road Vehicles and Aircraft	Paper Manufactures	Textiles	Footwear and Clothing	Man-made Fibres, Yarns, and Manufactures	Hats, Haberdashery, Apparel, etc. (e)
	1938 class.	1965 class.	1938 class.	1965 class.							
1938	14·5	12·4	40·8	39·9	21·8	4·0	14·7	16·5	10·8	4·2	8·5
1939	17·6	15·8	38·7	39·9	24·5	7·4	15·5	16·2	8·3	4·7	8·3
1940	48·2	46·3	59·5	58·1	41·2	43·6	16·1	22·1	2·6	7·6	7·5
1941	69·1	66·8	57·7	56·9	53·8	104·3	4·9	6·1	1·4	10·7	8·1
1942	47·0	45·1	60·9	58·9	41·7	125·4	4·4	7·3	1·1	16·0	7·7
1943	59·0	55·6	84·0	82·8	56·4	239·3	3·8	9·0	1·4	12·6	3·4
1944	32·9	31·2	66·6	66·4	55·8	459·0	6·2	16·0	5·6	16·3	4·7
1945	6·4	5·4	22·1	21·9	24·2	231·5	11·4	14·1	5·5	17·1	11·2
1946	9·4	9·1	40·8	40·4	13·5	2·3	11·8	18·7	2·4	23·8	30·5
1947	15·0	14·3	79·2	78·0	29·6	4·4	21·7	49·8	6·0	27·7	31·9
1948	19·7	18·4	88·8	87·1	44·0	8·0	23·9	70·2	5·3	37·8	31·4
1949	37·5	35·6	93·5	92·0	47·8	22·0	20·1	73·2	6·3	40·4	29·5
1950	24·7	23·3	109·8	104·1	44·5	18·2	29·7	81·2	10·9	48·5	35·6
1951	41·7	37·4	167·7	160·5	54·9	11·9	83·9	153·8	11·3	62·6	46·1
1952	125·2	115·7	207·4	202·8	109·1	16·8	43·7	81·6	8·3	40·1	32·8
1953	63·8	61·0	157·9	154·6	94·3	47·9	35·9	48·3	8·5	44·9	32·6
1954	30·4	28·2	180·1	175·0	70·4	23·9	56·5	70·7	13·1	45·1	31·2
1955	101·8	98·8	238·5	233·2	86·2	27·8	72·6	74·1	17·7	38·2	31·1
			--- (f)		--- (f)						
1956	110·3	105·6	231·3	225·1	103·6	24·4	70·4	75·5	22·6	35·5	32·1
1957	84·4	79·2	205·8	199·1	112·3	29·6	77·8	89·2	25·5	37·0	32·8
1958	51·7	46·5	182·2	177·3	117·9	28·0	77·9	85·3	29·1	32·3	29·6
			--- (f)	--- (f)							
1959	46·0	40·1	202·1	195·7	134·4	36·1	81·7	98·0	40·1	31·4	29·2
1960	110·2	100·6	290·1	262·4	183·8	76·3	96·1	136·9	58·2	35·1	30·2
1961	61·2	49·0	234·5	226·3	225·1	37·8	98·7	147·4	65·1	37·6	29·0
1962	66·1	53·6	233·3	225·2	226·1	40·9	105·0	135·0	71·3	45·8	30·9
						--- (f)					
1963	87·4	75·0	241·9	224·5	230·3	53·3	113·9	144·7	84·3	54·7	35·3
1964	120·9	105·9	339·2	298·5	313·7	70·6	132·5	177·0	96·9	67·2	39·3
1965	96·3	78·0	380·9	347·3	349·1	82·1	122·9	151·5	75·3	67·2	45·2

(a) This series differs from that in the first *Abstract of British Historical Statistics* in that the latter does not include rice, sago, etc.

(b) These two series depart from the 1965 classification in that calcined bauxite (refractory grade) is included with metalliferous ores, not with chemicals.

(c) Excluding petroleum.

(d) The 1938 classification includes many manufactures of metal. In the case of non-ferrous metals the 1965 classification has been amended so as to exclude silver.

(e) This includes heavy electrical machinery.

(f) These are all negligible breaks, usually caused by the discontinuation of separate records for items which had ceased to be important enough to merit it.

(g) The size of the break caused by the exclusion of the Channel Islands from the trade figures is indicated in this case by the figure for imports thence in 1958, which came to £11·7 million.

Overseas Trade 3. Values at Current Prices of Principal Domestic Exports – United Kingdom 1938–65

(in £000,000)

Year	Coal	Iron and Steel (a) 1938 class.	Iron and Steel (a) 1965 class.	Hardwares and Cutlery	Machinery (b)	Non-Ferrous Metals (a) 1938 class.	Non-Ferrous Metals (a) 1965 class.	Electrical Goods	Road Vehicles and Aircraft (c)	Chemicals	Leather Goods	Cotton Goods	Wool Goods	Linen Goods	Silk Goods	Hats, Haberdashery, Apparel, etc.	Man-made Fibres, Yarns and Manufactures
1938	40·7	41·6	30·0	5·7	57·9	12·3	9·9	13·4	25·4	22·1	2·5	49·7	23·7 (d)	6·3	1·3	8·5 (e)	4·2
1939	42·3	32·8	23·7	4·9	47·4	12·7	10·5	11·3	23·5	22·8	2·5	49·1	23·5	7·0	1·2	8·3	4·7
1940	27·5	31·0	23·7	6·3	36·5	12·4	10·4	13·2	22·8	27·7	2·4	49·3	24·2	7·1	1·1	7·5	7·6
1941	9·2	18·9	13·0	5·6	30·9	7·6	6·0	11·4	29·1	25·0	5·9	44·7	26·9	5·7	1·0	8·1	10·7
1942	6·8	9·8	5·5	4·5	29·9	7·0	5·6	11·2	43·0	24·0	1·9	40·1	23·1	6·0	0·4	7·7	16·0
1943	7·4	6·1	3·0	4·1	28·0	6·8	5·5	11·1	49·2	27·9	1·0	34·2	16·8	3·7	0·1	3·4	12·6
1944	5·3	8·5	4·9	4·7	41·2	4·7	3·1	12·6	41·7	29·4	1·0	37·1	14·1	2·9	0·1	4·7	16·3
1945	7·1	20·8	13·6	6·5	47·1	12·1	10·2	13·8	34·1	38·2	1·5	42·7	18·5	4·0	0·1	11·2	17·1
1946	10·1	80·0	54·4	17·7	114·7	37·6	30·7	37·4	78·6	66·1	6·3	63·2	38·7	14·7	3·5	30·5	23·8
1947	2·7	84·4	50·3	23·1	180·9	40·3	27·8	49·4	118·1	67·4	8·0	77·9	49·8	20·0	1·9	31·9	27·7
1948	43·6	105·3	65·5	26·4	254·2	54·6	37·7	72·5	180·4	83·6	8·8	131·1	79·1	18·4	1·5	31·4	37·8
1949	59·7	126·3	80·5	27·3	279·3	63·6	48·8	79·2	214·7	86·1	6·9	159·1	85·5	16·2	1·5	29·5	40·4
1950	60·5	155·7	102·4	29·9	317·3	76·9	61·8	84·0	305·7	107·5	10·9	158·4	108·4	19·7	1·7	35·6	48·5
1951	34·1	159·3	103·6	37·3	365·3	70·5	50·4	96·6	363·2	142·4	15·0	209·1	136·7	25·6	1·6	46·1	62·6
1952	65·9	191·6	130·5	37·0	421·8	82·3 (f)	61·5	109·7	369·7	138·1	11·9	148·0	97·8	22·2	0·9	32·8	40·1
1953	70·8	196·7	134·5	30·7	405·0	83·1	71·7	105·0	359·1	130·0	13·4	130·2	102·5	20·6	1·0	32·6	44·9
1954	68·0	195·4	136·4	33·1	407·3	75·4	64·9	101·1	388·1	149·7	12·0	126·1	101·1	20·5	1·1	31·2	45·1
1955	63·9	217·9	155·9	38·7 (f)	440·2	98·4	87·5	119·7	440·0	170·1	13·0	112·7	105·4	19·9	1·0	31·1	38·2
1956	62·4	236·0	172·7	40·8 (f)	479·6	131·3	118·5	141·9	483·7	179·0	14·6	102·7	104·4	19·2	1·0	32·1	35·5
1957	61·8	290·4	212·5	41·2	513·3	123·9	111·0	149·0	546·1	196·6	15·5	103·0	109·9	19·2	1·0 (f)	32·8	37·0
1958	32·7	263·2	187·9	38·6	508·6	115·2	101·7	142·6	616·8	191·5	15·6	84·4	93·2	16·1	0·6	29·6	32·3
1959	23·9	261·0	191·3	40·4	531·2	135·6	122·3	152·6	686·2	213·6	16·5	76·0	94·6	15·6	0·7	29·2	31·4
1960	28·4	285·1	215·2	45·9	580·3	135·5	112·5	153·9	739·6	233·1	17·1	75·7	101·8	16·1	0·7	30·2	35·1
1961	29·3	280·6	211·2	47·3	668·4	131·9	116·7	176·3	698·2	239·3	16·5	68·6	95·2	14·2	0·7	29·0	37·6
1962	31·2	269·5	200·1	50·6	701·1	138·8	122·5	191·3	735·6	251·3	16·1	57·2	93·6	15·4	0·8	30·9	45·8
1963	47·8	273·9	204·5	46·6	773·3	131·5	115·6	218·5	796·7	258·8	17·2	54·3	97·8	15·2	0·9	35·3	54·7
1964	36·9	295·9	217·4	50·2	783·1	142·6	125·9	219·4	813·1	288·9	19·0	51·8	102·6	17·0	0·8	39·3	67·2
1965	25·4	317·2	234·4	54·2	846·2	176·4	155·7	227·9	897·7	307·7	20·1	49·7	103·7	15·6	0·9	45·2	67·2

NOTES

SOURCE: *Annual Statement of Trade.*

[1] As from 1959 trade with the Channel Islands not included as part of the overseas trade of the United Kingdom. This causes no significant break in the export series.

[2] The classification current in 1938 has been used so far as possible for categories which appeared in the first *Abstract of British Historical Statistics*. For categories which assumed importance only after 1938 the 1965 classification was used, except as indicated in footnote (a).

(a) The 1938 classification includes many manufactures of metal. In the case of non-ferrous metals the 1965 classification has been amended to exclude silver. The 1938 figure for iron and steel on the 1938 classification differs from that in the first *Abstract of British Historical Statistics* through the exclusion here of railway axles etc.
(b) This includes heavy electrical machinery. The 1938 figure differs from that in the first *Abstract of British Historical Statistics* through the exclusion here of certain vehicle parts.
(c) This covers only mechanically propelled vehicles.

(d) The 1938 figure differs from that in the first *Abstract of British Historical Statistics* through the inclusion here of yarn and fabrics of mohair, angora, etc., and the exclusion here of gloves and hosiery of wool.
(e) The 1938 figure differs from that in the first *Abstract of British Historical Statistics* through the inclusion here of hosiery and gloves of wool and cotton.
(f) These are all negligible breaks, usually caused by the discontinuation of separate records for items which had ceased to be important enough to merit it.

Overseas Trade 4. Values at Current Prices of Principal Re-exports – United Kingdom 1938–65

NOTES
[1] SOURCE: *Annual Statement of Trade.*
[2] As from 1959 trade with the Channel Islands was not included as part of the overseas trade of the United Kingdom. This causes no significant break in the re-export series.

(in £000,000)

	Coffee	Tea	Raw Cotton	Raw Wool	Hides, Skins, and Furs	Non-ferrous Metals and Manufactures	Rubber	Petroleum
1938	0·4	4·6	1·3	12·5	9·6	9·1	2·7	0·8
1939	0·2	4·0	1·2	8·6	7·8	2·7	3·6	0·8
1940	0·1	3·7	0·5	4·8	3·6	0·7	1·2	1·1
1941	--	1·2	--	0·1	0·3	1·1	1·2	0·3
1942	--	0·6	--	—	0·1	0·6	--	0·6
1943	--	0·7	--	—	0·2	0·3	0·2	0·4
1944	0·5	0·8	—	—	0·2	0·9	0·8	0·6
1945	0·6	1·7	2·3	7·2	0·3	5·4	0·9	1·5
1946	0·1	4·8	2·6	8·2	3·9	1·1	7·2	2·5
1947	0·2	1·6	3·0	18·4	3·7	0·2	13·3	3·1
1948	0·2	1·1	0·6	23·1	6·2	0·2	4·6	1·7
1949	0·5	1·6	0·4	22·0	5·8	0·2	4·0	1·3
1950	0·7	3·1	1·1	28·9	10·8	0·7	8·7	1·4
1951	0·4	3·2	0·5	34·9	16·7	1·5	28·8	2·2
1952	1·3	4·1	1·4	18·2	18·9	12·7	48·3	0·6
1953	2·4	7·2	1·1	20·2	15·5	7·4	10·0	1·4
1954	2·1	8·2	0·9	19·0	14·6	6·4	3·1	2·7
1955	1·3	9·7	2·1	16·3	19·5	5·4	11·3	2·4
1956	0·7	8·4	3·9	15·3	19·9	8·1	33·1	4·8
1957	0·7	8·2	1·6	16·1	19·0	8·6	18·5	3·5
1958	0·9	8·6	0·7	9·2	18·9	3·6	32·0	5·2
1959	0·5	10·1	1·1	10·0	21·3	10·0	11·2	5·5
1960	0·5	8·4	1·2	10·4	22·5	3·6	23·5	2·3
1961	1·1	8·9	1·3	9·2	22·1	7·9	29·0	1·1
1962	0·3	9·9	1·4	7·7	27·6	8·5	18·3	1·6
1963	0·2	9·6	1·3	6·5	31·5	6·9	9·9	1·9
1964	0·9	10·5	2·0	5·2	26·3	10·0	3·2	0·9
1965	0·7	11·2	1·3	4·6	29·7	13·0	1·9	0·3

Overseas Trade 5. Values at Current Prices of Overseas Trade According to Regions and Principal Countries – United Kingdom 1938–65

(in £000,000)

	E.F.T.A. Countries (a)			E.E.C. Countries (b)			Eastern Europe (c)			Southern Europe and North Africa (d)			Turkey and the Middle East (e)		
	Imports	Exports	Re-exports	Imports	Exports	Re-exports	Imports	Exports	Re-exports	Imports	Exports	Re-exports	Imports	Exports	Re-exports
1938	84·7	41·8	3·0	111·1	64·1	21·4	55·0	22·3	12·3	16·5	12·1	1·0	27·9	21·8	0·4
1939	87·0	48·4	3·3	103·0	51·4	16·2	36·9	16·7	4·1	17·7	9·1	0·7	29·0	20·6	0·4
1940	39·6	19·6	1·5	41·4	28·1	8·1	14·1	3·3	0·7	18·4	7·9	0·5	31·7	23·9	0·3
1941	9·3	5·2	0·2	0·1	—	—	1·5	23·4	5·9	10·2	7·7	0·3	17·3	23·6	0·2
1942	9·5	5·0	0·1	0·1	0·4	—	3·3	67·8	7·3	9·4	4·2	0·2	20·2	23·2	0·2
1943	10·7	11·0	0·2	0·1	0·3	- -	1·8	54·3	4·6	16·8	10·9	0·6	14·8	23·1	0·3
1944	10·4	7·5	0·2	7·5	8·8	4·4	2·1	49·9	6·2	21·4	11·0	0·8	24·5	18·1	0·1
1945	40·8	17·5	2·3	12·2	68·0	35·4	3·8	34·4	3·4	24·5	11·2	1·2	25·9	29·4	0·5
	- - - (n)	- - - (n)	- - - (n)	- - - (n)	- - - (n)	- - - (n)									
1946	72·2	108·7	5·5	66·0	116·8	23·8	5·9	33·1	5·2	31·2	28·2	1·4	50·9	77·1	0·9
1947	99·3	117·3	5·4	137·7	115·1	21·3	18·9	34·6	8·4	39·1	31·4	1·1	58·4	93·7	0·9
1948	137·2	167·2	6·9	189·0	155·0	27·6	56·6	24·1	8·6	44·5	47·8	1·5	123·0	122·2	4·2
1949	185·2	185·4	5·9	257·6	167·8	25·9	54·0	32·7	6·7	52·1	47·2	1·6	111·2	125·3	1·3
1950	223·3	250·5	8·1	331·9	241·3	36·9	74·4	31·7	6·2	55·0	51·2	2·0	159·3	134·8	1·8
				- - - (o)	- - - (o)	- - - (o)									
1951	353·4	278·7	10·0	512·6	267·7	45·6	102·7	26·6	25·3	110·6	59·8	2·9	245·0	144·2	2·3
1952	319·8	263·4	8·1	426·2	291·5	39·4	97·8	25·4	37·8	101·1	71·7	3·2	276·4	161·9	2·0
1953	330·5	283·4	9·5	346·9	336·7	43·7	81·2	23·1	11·6	86·4	71·9	2·2	254·3	145·3	2·4
1954	332·6	298·3	9·9	390·6	349·0	42·8	79·5	30·5	9·8	89·3	75·5	1·9	239·6	129·1	1·8
1955	371·4	302·2	9·4	482·1	375·6	46·8	110·0	45·5	14·0	96·2	85·9	2·3	236·8	155·7	2·7
1956	384·9	330·6	10·9	492·8	428·9	49·3	103·9	49·5	33·6	97·8	103·4	3·0	245·5	166·5	3·2
1957	397·8	340·7	12·3	491·0	459·9	46·2	115·7	67·2	19·7	99·9	97·5	3·2	248·4	173·1	5·2
1958	365·9	319·4	12·3	534·8	419·1	43·4	111·8	54·1	30·8	94·0	94·5	3·0	295·5	183·4	3·0
1959	391·9	346·8	12·9	558·7	465·7	46·0	125·2	68·4	11·3	93·7	86·4	2·8	311·5	185·0	3·0
1960	464·0	383·0	14·3	661·7	519·8	47·3	148·1	84·2	19·2	118·6	99·1	3·1	334·7	187·1	3·4
1961	460·5	430·9	16·0	677·1	613·3	52·8	168·2	111·4	30·4	117·4	111·2	3·7	331·2	208·9	2·7
1962	463·0	462·8	13·9	707·5	720·0	61·3	171·2	119·7	18·9	139·6	130·9	3·3	348·7	198·9	2·9
1963	506·3	501·7	14·9	768·6	826·4	66·5	179·3	133·2	10·2	153·0	153·4	3·7	350·8	220·3	3·4
1964	621·7	511·3	17·0	914·1	841·9	64·5	194·0	116·7	4·0	184·8	166·6	4·0	355·7	210·9	3·8
1965	666·9	555·0	18·2	994·7	904·8	75·4	222·4	125·2	3·7	202·9	195·0	4·4	325·4	243·1	4·6

NOTE
SOURCE: *Annual Statement of Trade.*

(in £,000,000)

	The Remainder of Africa (f)			Asia (g)			West Indies			Central and South America			Russia (h)		
	Imports	Exports	Re-exports	Imports	Exports	Re-exports	Imports	Exports	Re-exports	Imports	Exports	Re-exports	Imports	Exports	Re-exports
1938	43·9	63·0	1·4	108·2	67·4	1·3	31·5	7·9	0·2	70·7	36·2	0·8	29·2	11·2	11·4
1939	48·4	55·2	1·1	99·6	59·7	1·3	32·9	7·0	0·2	77·8	36·2	0·6	17·2	8·0	3·5
1940	73·7	58·5	0·8	149·1	65·2	0·8	44·4	7·4	0·1	108·4	36·5	0·5	1·9	0·8	0·5
1941	75·8	60·9	1·5	118·6	61·4	0·7	71·6	6·7	0·1	88·8	29·7	0·2	1·2	23·4	5·9
1942	84·8	58·7	0·1	84·1	28·6	0·1	49·2	6·7	– –	83·6	26·6	0·1	3·2	67·2	7·3
1943	87·5	58·5	0·4	85·5	20·7	0·1	57·6	6·5	– –	98·6	22·6	0·1	1·8	54·3	4·6
1944	102·7	59·9	0·5	86·3	28·1	0·1	52·6	5·5	0·1	113·4	11·2	0·1	2·1	49·9	6·2
1945	78·3	70·7	0·2	87·1	42·3	0·4	50·4	7·0	– –	87·9	17·4	0·2	3·8	28·4	1·2
1946	95·4	129·4	0·7	130·9	134·9	1·0	74·7	13·9	0·1	127·1	54·6	1·0	5·0	9·9	1·2
1947	134·6	163·2	0·7	170·3	190·7	1·0	109·4	16·4	0·1	195·6	82·1	0·6	7·5	12·3	2·2
1948	197·3	238·8	0·9	196·3	225·3	1·0	122·9	25·3	0·3	194·3	121·8	0·8	27·1	5·3	1·7
1949	228·0	283·7	1·2	206·8	268·8	1·2	101·8	29·1	0·3	159·3	138·0	1·3	16·1	8·6	1·7
1950	271·1	284·8	1·8	265·0	274·6	1·6	124·5	37·3	0·6	210·9	154·5	1·7	34·2	11·6	2·6
1951	393·9	369·3	3·2	475·9	363·6	3·4	164·6	48·2	0·6	269·8	158·1	2·8	60·1	3·7	20·5
1952	407·8	412·9	2·6	351·4	381·5	2·8	129·0	54·2	0·6	142·4	152·8	1·7	58·1	3·8	33·6
1953	387·3	421·8	2·8	290·3	355·8	3·4	134·4	51·4	0·8	211·2	114·0	1·5	39·9	3·3	9·0
1954	403·9	413·8	3·2	335·7	347·7	2·7	117·3	57·4	1·0	211·7	121·2	2·2	41·8	10·1	4·6
1955	412·9	451·2	3·8	404·9	370·0	4·7	113·1	68·9	1·0	232·4	118·5	1·7	62·6	22·9	9·0
1956	417·3	448·7	4·0	377·8	440·4	6·5	126·7	81·5	1·4	254·4	135·7	1·6	55·1	26·3	29·6
1957	372·8	467·6	5·1	394·9	460·6	4·7	156·0	89·9	1·1	308·9	167·3	1·5	70·5	37·4	14·3
1958	339·3	459·5	5·8	386·2	415·7	4·7	113·1	95·4	1·2	278·9	144·0	1·9	59·5	23·7	28·3
1959	387·2	420·3	6·8	398·5	451·6	5·4	111·6	103·5	1·9	315·4	148·6	1·9	63·1	27·4	7·4
1960	404·4	443·0	6·9	430·4	456·5	7·1	113·1	91·7	1·5	304·1	176·2	1·6	74·9	37·2	16·1
1961	400·9	441·3	7·2	428·3	468·0	6·6	100·9	81·9	1·6	278·0	173·6	1·7	85·0	43·4	26·1
1962	399·6	411·3	6·8	434·1	426·9	6·7	92·9	79·3	1·3	299·2	167·7	2·2	84·2	41·9	15·6
1963	449·5	472·0	5·4	437·6	460·9	6·7	135·0	74·8	1·4	299·6	147·7	1·6	90·8	55·4	8·5
1964	471·9	499·5	5·6	475·4	458·1	7·3	128·6	87·8	1·7	294·6	149·9	2·7	90·1	38·0	1·7
1965	604·7	550·8	7·4	456·5	473·3	9·8	98·7	97·1	1·8	289·7	157·7	3·0	118·8	46·9	0·5

See p. 140 for footnotes.

Overseas Trade 5. *continued*

(in £000,000)

	Germany (i)			Netherlands			Belgium			France		
	Imports	Exports	Re-exports	Imports	Exports	Re-exports	Imports	Exports	Re-exports	Imports	Exports	Re-exports
1938	31·9	21·8	6·6	29·3	13·1	1·7	18·6	8·2	4·4	23·6	15·1	8·2
1939	19·4	12·3	3·9	30·2	13·5	1·6	18·8	7·2	3·3	26·9	13·6	7·0
1940	—	—	—	11·8	5·8	1·1	9·4	3·0	0·8	14·7	16·4	6·1
1941	—	—	—	—	—	—	—	—	—	0·1	—	—
1942	—	—	—	—	—	—	—	0·4	—	0·1	—	—
1943	—	—	—	—	0·3	—	—	—	—	—	—	—
1944	—	—	—	—	0·5	—	—	0·9	—	0·1	6·8	4·2
1945	2·1	2·8	0·1	1·3	5·9	3·9	2·8	31·0	17·4	2·1	26·0	13·7
1946	6·4	17·8	5·8	11·6	30·9	4·8	3·1	27·0	3·7	14·2	34·3	4·5
1947	19·3	21·1	6·9	26·2	31·3	1·7	14·7	33·6	3·1	31·4	23·8	5·4
1948	29·6	25·2	6·0	44·3	45·3	3·1	38·2	37·1	5·3	45·9	34·1	10·5
1949	37·6	26·7	6·9	65·4	52·9	3·0	37·5	35·9	4·3	75·0	33·4	8·7
1950	41·6	44·0	11·6	85·8	71·8	4·6	42·5	51·7	6·2	109·8	44·1	11·2
	— — — (i)	— — — (i)	— — — (i)									
1951	74·8	50·0	10·2	128·1	73·8	6·6	87·7	56·4	6·5	134·8	55·1	18·1
1952	90·1	50·7	12·9	102·3	70·5	7·9	92·0	57·5	3·2	86·9	61·5	10·6
1953	69·8	59·2	17·1	88·9	93·8	6·4	58·9	56·3	4·2	82·1	65·6	10·6
1954	77·6	70·6	16·8	109·6	99·6	6·7	52·8	54·7	5·5	97·1	64·2	9·6
1955	91·3	76·9	18·6	132·9	106·1	7·7	63·6	62·9	4·3	136·5	71·6	11·4
1956	109·9	92·1	19·3	137·3	118·8	8·2	72·9	69·2	4·0	112·2	88·8	13·3
1957	124·6	105·0	18·7	131·8	117·7	4·9	60·1	77·7	3·6	110·4	88·0	13·9
1958	136·0	123·2	17·5	159·3	97·9	7·5	61·7	59·5	4·7	100·5	71·8	9·3
1959	144·3	142·0	20·8	160·0	113·0	7·9	57·5	61·0	3·5	103·7	76·9	9·0
1960	181·5	163·4	20·7	180·3	115·9	7·1	68·2	64·7	3·5	131·9	87·5	10·2
1961	194·3	171·2	21·7	172·5	137·6	6·5	64·8	77·2	4·1	142·8	112·2	12·0
1962	193·6	199·3	25·6	197·1	151·0	7·2	72·5	91·9	4·7	131·3	138·0	14·3
1963	208·3	213·1	27·2	208·7	167·7	7·7	87·0	99·8	6·1	153·5	180·7	13·7
1964	265·8	219·0	26·7	235·0	192·2	7·6	95·5	113·6	4·3	184·2	184·9	15·5
1965	265·4	255·0	30·4	270·8	193·1	9·9	121·8	169·2	4·6	190·5	177·2	16·2

(in £000,000)

	Irish Republic			India (j)			Australia			New Zealand		
	Imports	Exports	Re-exports	Imports	Exports	Re-exports	Imports	Exports	Re-exports	Imports	Exports	Re-exports
1938	23·0	20·3	5·7	49·9	33·8	0·5	71·8	38·2	0·8	46·9	19·2	0·3
1939	25·3	22·9	5·5	48·5	29·7	0·5	62·0	32·3	0·8	41·8	16·0	0·2
1940	31·7	23·2	5·4	72·9	33·3	0·4	96·8	46·3	0·4	55·8	16·5	0·2
1941	32·1	19·0	1·8	57·3	31·6	0·4	46·4	38·0	0·2	56·4	14·8	--
1942	34·0	18·0	1·5	60·2	22·3	0·1	40·2	64·0	0·2	60·3	25·0	0·1
1943	28·4	11·6	1·6	60·1	17·6	--	32·8	44·3	0·1	49·8	19·4	0·2
1944	30·8	12·0	1·8	69·5	23·5	0·1	53·8	50·5	0·1	57·2	17·1	--
1945	35·0	18·6	2·6	67·6	33·1	0·3	52·8	49·6	0·2	62·9	14·8	0·1
1946	37·1	39·6	3·9	69·0	79·7	0·7	67·4	55·2	0·3	74·4	27·9	0·1
1947	35·1	56·0	3·5	94·7 — (j)	91·5 — (j)	0·6 — (j)	97·1	71·9	0·5	90·0	43·2	0·2
1948	43·3	75·4	3·8	96·3	96·1	0·4	168·9	144·7	0·5	108·7	52·5	0·1
1949	55·5	76·6	3·2	99·0	117·1	0·3	212·9	188·5	0·7	117·1	64·6	0·2
1950	62·5	86·7	3·5	98·3	96·7	0·5	219·7	255·8	1·0	133·9	86·5	0·3
1951	70·0	97·0	5·1	152·6	115·2	0·7	254·4	323·8	2·0	164·7	110·5	0·7
1952	90·6	89·0	4·1	114·7	112·6	0·6	226·7	220·9	0·9	165·7	115·3	0·4
1953	104·8	92·6	4·8	113·4	114·5	0·6	294·2	212·9	1·2	169·8	100·3	0·4
1954	103·3	100·7	4·6	148·4	114·8	0·4	235·9	277·6	1·6	176·0	125·9	0·7
1955	97·3	108·3	5·6	159·0	130·2	1·2	263·9	284·3	2·1	179·9	139·3	0·8
1956	89·7	103·0	5·8	141·4	167·9	1·9	236·1	239·8	1·4	197·0	127·2	0·6
1957	109·4	102·7	7·7	157·5	176·4	1·2	248·0	235·5	2·0	183·1	139·9	0·7
1958	108·8	108·2	8·2	139·4	160·7	1·0	199·1	235·4	2·0	160·5	128·0	0·9
1959	103·8	107·2	7·6	142·6	171·4	1·3	222·9	223·4	1·7	182·9	97·8	0·6
1960	121·9	110·9	7·4	148·5	150·5	1·3	197·2	259·9	2·3	183·0	120·8	0·8
1961	145·8	133·1	6·4	144·9	151·8	1·1	174·1	201·1	1·9	159·6	124·1	0·6
1962	138·8	135·0	6·9	135·9	116·5	1·7	185·2	228·4	2·3	169·4	107·2	0·7
1963	151·8	148·8	7·7	140·7	136·6	1·3	206·1	235·8	2·1	173·1	115·2	0·8
1964	170·4	164·5	9·3	140·7	126·8	1·5	250·2	255·7	1·9	207·8	117·2	0·6
1965	170·4	175·8	9·9	128·3	114·1	2·3	219·5	281·4	3·0	208·2	125·0	1·1

See p. 140 for footnotes.

Overseas Trade 5. continued

(in £000,000)

	U.S.A. (k)			Canada (l)			Argentina			South Africa (m)		
	Imports	Exports	Re-exports	Imports	Exports	Re-exports	Imports	Exports	Re-exports	Imports	Exports	Re-exports
1938	118·2	20·5	8·3	81·3	23·5	1·1	38·5	19·3	0·4	15·2	39·6	0·6
1939	117·5	28·4	8·1	82·1	23·4	0·9	46·8	20·4	0·2	16·7	36·3	0·6
1940	275·5	33·0	4·9	153·0	33·3	0·9	61·4	17·8	0·1	24·0	38·3	0·4
1941	409·0	31·8	1·1	193·8	39·2	0·3	52·2	15·5	0·1	16·1	39·2	1·3
1942	535·6	26·0	0·3	178·4	32·6	0·1	49·4	13·3	- -	16·9	38·2	- -
1943	1,103·8	20·4	5·0	284·9	31·5	0·2	58·3	9·6	- -	14·7	31·7	0·1
1944	1,391·4	19·0	4·0	389·5	26·5	0·1	80·8	4·1	- -	18·7	28·5	- -
1945	610·3	19·2	3·5	323·3	27·7	0·1	47·6	6·4	0·1	16·0	37·1	0·1
1946	229·6	35·5	4·2	201·3	33·5	0·8	66·7	20·5	0·4	15·4	75·4	0·2
1947	297·2	48·0	13·3	239·1	44·9	1·0	130·6	34·8	0·2	26·7	92·1	0·3
1948	183·2	66·2	4·6	223·4	72·8	1·7	121·8	52·5	0·3	32·7	120·6	0·5
1949	222·1	57·1	5·5	225·2	79·8	1·8	77·1	51·1	0·5	34·3	125·1	0·5
1950	211·0	113·1	14·3	180·2	125·9	2·5	95·6	38·5	0·4	55·2	121·2	0·8
1951	380·0	136·7	16·9	260·5	137·2	2·9	86·2	28·1	0·9	65·6	165·7	1·8
1952	314·6	146·3	34·8	319·7	129·7	2·7	53·1	21·2	0·4	69·9	145·5	1·0
1953	252·7	159·0	13·2	305·5	156·8	4·2	99·1	14·6	0·6	78·7	159·1	1·2
1954	282·4	150·4	10·4	272·8	131·9	3·7	81·1	22·8	0·9	90·5	156·9	1·3
1955	420·0	183·1	15·8	343·7	140·8	3·9	86·7	23·5	0·5	88·8	167·7	1·3
1956	408·0	243·2	15·9	347·5	177·7	4·6	91·6	17·3	0·3	99·4	155·2	1·4
1957	482·5	244·3	14·6	320·2	195·3	4·5	108·0	32·9	0·3	102·1	173·8	1·7
1958	351·7	272·7	20·9	308·6	188·1	5·4	104·4	32·5	0·4	99·5	188·1	1·8
1959	370·7	360·8	21·3	312·0	207·6	6·0	105·6	40·2	0·2	97·3	150·2	1·9
1960	565·8	325·5	17·2	374·9	214·6	6·1	97·7	41·9	0·2	105·4	155·5	1·8
1961	484·4	280·4	17·7	349·4	221·8	6·4	75·0	50·5	0·2	110·8	149·0	1·7
1962	476·4	327·0	20·5	348·9	187·9	6·4	93·2	46·9	0·2	114·8	148·2	2·0
1963	498·4	340·3	20·1	368·5	172·6	6·9	89·0	25·0	0·2	129·6	197·2	2·2
1964	639·1	356·0	22·8	452·0	186·9	5·9	78·2	27·6	0·4	145·3	224·2	2·7
1965	671·4	493·7	21·0	458·2	200·6	7·4	71·5	26·8	0·7	199·8	263·5	3·9

(a) I.e. Austria (from 1946 only), Denmark (including Faroe Islands and Greenland), Liechtenstein (from 1946 only), Norway (including Spitzbergen), Portugal (including Azores and Madeira), Sweden, and Switzerland.

(b) I.e. Belgium, France, Germany (including Austria and Liechtenstein to 1945, and East Germany from 1946 to 1950), Italy, Luxemburg, and Netherlands.

(c) I.e. Albania, Bulgaria, Czechoslovakia, Hungary, Poland, Romania, Russia (including the Baltic Republics), and Yugoslavia.

(d) I.e. Algeria, Cyprus, Gibraltar, Greece (including the Dodecanese), Libya, Malta, Morocco, Spain (including Canary Islands and Spanish ports in North Africa), and Tunisia. This group is not precisely the same as that under the same heading in the first Abstract of British Historical Statistics.

(e) I.e. Aden, Egypt, Iraq, Iran, Israel, Jordan, Lebanon, the Persian Gulf states, Saudi Arabia, Syria, Turkey, and Yemen. This group is not precisely the same as that under the same heading in the first Abstract of British Historical Statistics.

(f) I.e. all Africa except Algeria, Egypt, Libya, Morocco, Spanish ports in North Africa, and Tunisia. It includes all islands off the African coast except Azores, Canary Islands, and Madeira.

(g) I.e. all parts of Asia from Afghanistan and Pakistan eastwards, except Russia. The Australian parts of New Guinea and islands in the Pacific are not included.

(h) Includes Estonia, Latvia and Lithuania during the period when they were separately recorded.

(i) From 1951 East Germany is not included. The figures in 1951 were as follows: Imports 2·9, Exports 0·3, Re-exports 0·3.

(j) From 1948 Pakistan was recorded separately; and is not included here. The figures in 1948 were as follows: Imports 113, Exports 179, Re-exports negligible.

(k) Includes Alaska and Hawaii. This causes a slight difference from the imports figure for 1938 given in the first Abstract of British Historical Statistics.

(l) Includes Newfoundland and Labrador.

(m) Includes South-West Africa.

(n) Austria and Liechtenstein were included in E.E.C. rather than E.F.T.A. up to 1945

(o) East Germany excluded from 1951: (see footnote (i)).

Overseas Trade 6. Indices of the Volume of Overseas Trade – United Kingdom 1938–65

NOTE
SOURCE: *Abstract.*

	Imports	Domestic Exports		Imports	Domestic Exports		Imports	Domestic Exports
1938 = 100 (a)			*1954 = 100*			*1961 = 100*		
1938	100	100	1950	89	101	1956	81	92
1947	70	99	1951	100	100	1957	84	93
			1952	92	94	1958	84	90
1950 = 100			1953	99	96	1959	90	93
1947	89	62	1954	100	100	1960	102	98
1948	93	78						
1949	100	86	1955	111	107	1961	100	100
1950	100	100	1956	110	113	1962	103	102
1951	112	101	1957	114	116	1963	107	108
1952	103	95	1958	114	111	1964	119	111
			1959	122	116	1965	120	117

(a) Whilst all the other indices are weighted by the base-year prices, this one is weighted by 1947 prices.

Overseas Trade 7. Terms of Trade – United Kingdom 1938–65

NOTE
SOURCE: *Abstract.*

	Index Numbers of Average Values		Net Terms of Trade
	Imports	Exports	
1950 = 100			
1938	30	38	79
1947	77	84	92
1948	86	92	93
1949	87	95	92
1950	100	100	100
1951	133	117	113
1952	129	124	105
1954 = 100			
1950	85	85	100
1951	113	100	113
1952	111	105	106
1953	101	101	100
1954	100	100	100
1955	103	102	101
1956	105	106	99
1957	107	111	96
1958	99	110	90
1959	98	109	90
1961 = 100			
1956	110	95	87
1957	111	100	89
1958	103	99	96
1959	102	98	96
1960	102	100	97
1961	100	100	100
1962	99	101	102
1963	103	104	101
1964	107	106	99
1965	107	108	102

Overseas Trade 8. Balance of Payments – United Kingdom 1938–65

NOTES

[1] SOURCES: 1938–45 – London and Cambridge Economic Service, *The British Economy: Key Statistics 1900–66*; 1946–65 – Central Statistical Office, *United Kingdom Balance of Payments, 1966*.

[2] The 1938–45 figures are estimates of the net change in external assets and liabilities, and are not closely comparable with subsequent figures in the same column. In the source they are described as figures of the current account balance.

[3] The Central Statistical Office say of the estimates of 1946–51 that 'the very limited data available did not permit estimates of equivalent standing to be produced for years prior to 1952'. They are, however, 'reasonably consistent' with later figures.

[4] Items which are shown net have a sign: + = net inflow, – = net outflow.

(in £ million)

	Current Account									Capital Account						
	Exports and Re-exports	Imports	Visible Balance (a)	Services and Transfers Government	Services and Transfers Private	Interest, Dividends, Profits Private Sector	Interest, Dividends, Profits Government Sector	Invisible Balance	Current Account Balance	Inter-Government Loans (b)	Other Official Long-term Capital	Private Investment Abroad	Private Investment in U.K. (c)	Long-term Capital Balance	Balance on Current and Capital Account	Balancing Item (c)
1938	...	...	...	...	...	...	...	...	...	...	...	...	...	...	–70	...
1939	...	...	...	...	...	...	...	...	...	...	...	...	...	...	–250	...
1940	...	...	...	...	...	...	...	...	...	...	...	...	...	...	–804	...
1941	...	...	...	...	...	...	...	...	...	...	...	...	...	...	–816	...
1942	...	...	...	...	...	...	...	...	...	...	...	...	...	...	–663	...
1943	...	...	...	...	...	...	...	...	...	...	...	...	...	...	–680	...
1944	...	...	...	...	...	...	...	...	...	...	...	...	...	...	–659	...
1945	...	...	...	...	...	...	...	...	...	...	...	...	...	...	–875	...
1946	960	1,063	–103	–327	+115	...	+85	–127	–230	—	+214	...	+34	(+248) (d)	(+18) (d)	...
1947	1,180	1,541	–361	–152	–18	...	+150	–20	–381	+30	+629	...	–362	(+297) (d)	(–84) (d)	...
1948	1,639	1,790	–151	–82	+25	...	+235	+177	+26	+138	+304	...	–163	(+279) (d)	(+305) (d)	...
1949	1,863	2,000	–137	–140	+57	...	+219	+136	–1	+154	–30	...	–171	(–47) (d)	(–48) (d)	...
1950	2,261	2,312	–51	–136	+98	...	+396	+358	+307	+140	–14	...	–70	(+56) (d)	(+363) (d)	...
1951	2,735	3,424	–689	–158	+136	...	+342	+320	–369	+43	–68	...	–295	(–320) (d)	(–689) (d)	...
1952	2,769	3,048	–279	–61	+253	...	+252	+442	+163	—	–20	–127	+13	–134	+29	+66
1953	2,683	2,927	–244	–66	+215	...	+229	+389	+145	–30	–19	–173	+28	–194	–49	+32
1954	2,785	2,989	–204	–131	+192	...	+250	+321	+117	–20	–8	–238	+75	–191	–74	+57
1955	3,073	3,386	–313	–138	+124	...	+174	+158	–155	–52	–10	–182	+122	–122	–277	+121
1956	3,377	3,324	+53	–175	+119	...	+229	+155	+208	–50	–18	–258	+139	–187	+21	+21
1957	3,509	3,538	–29	–144	+177	...	+249	+262	+233	+75	–9	–298	+126	–106	+127	+80
1958	3,406	3,377	+29	–219	+241	+434	–141	+315	+344	–44	–6	–310	+164	–196	+148	+15
1959	3,522	3,639	–117	–227	+227	+388	–128	+260	+143	–118	–6	–303	+172	–255	–112	–13
1960	3,732	4,138	–406	–282	+192	+379	–148	+141	–265	–92	–11	–322	+233	–192	–457	–72
1961	3,891	4,043	–152	–332	+228	+416	–164	+148	–4	–16	–29	–313	+426	+68	+64	+75
1962	3,993	4,095	–102	–360	+241	+480	–147	+214	+112	–91	–13	–242	+248	–98	+14	–25
1963	4,282	4,362	–80	–382	+184	+524	–132	+194	+114	–97	–8	–320	+276	–149	–35	+15
1964 (a)	4,466	5,003	–519	–432	+163	+523	–116	+138	–381	–101	–15	–399	+152	–363	–744	–22
1965 (a)	4,777	5,042	–237	–447	+165	+662	–133	+187	–50	–66	–19	–354	+237	–202	–252	+67

(a) The visible balance in 1964 and 1965 incorporates the following items:

	1964	1965
Net under-recording of exports	20	40
Payments for U.S. Military Aircraft	2	12

(b) For the period 1946–51 the heading is 'special grants' which are described, as 'grants to or from the U.K. government which, because they were of a non-recurrent financial nature, are not appropriate to the current account'.

(c) For the period 1946–51 'Private Investment' includes 'miscellaneous capital' and the balancing item.

(d) These figures are not given in the original source, but have been computed from the items shown here. The inclusion of the balancing item invalidates any close comparison with later figures.

CHAPTER XII

WAGES AND THE STANDARD OF LIVING

TABLES

The coverage and representativeness of wage indices has improved a great deal since the Second World War, so that whilst the first two tables in this chapter follow on from equivalents in the first *Abstract of British Historical Statistics*, they provide more sensitive indices of changes in weekly wage rates than exist for earlier periods. Moreover, they are now supplemented by new tables, numbers 3 and 4, showing average weekly earnings of manual workers in manufacturing and certain other industries, and of coal miners.

The statistics in these four tables are all in terms of money wages. Real wages may be calculated from them by using the cost of living indices shown in Chapter XVI. By doing this one probably gets the best available indicator at the present day of movements in the standard of living. The *per capita* consumption statistics of coffee, tea, sugar, and tobacco, which are given in table 5, do not nowadays tell us much about living standards, though they have a certain intrinsic interest, especially as they continue series which go back into the late eighteenth or early nineteenth century, and which were included in the first volume of *Historical Statistics*.

Further information on wages is available in an excellent volume of historical labour statistics recently produced by the Department of Employment and Productivity.

Wages and the Standard of Living 1. Indices of Average Weekly Wage Rates of All Workers – United Kingdom 1938–65

NOTE
SOURCE: *Ministry of Labour Gazette.*

A. 1 September 1939 = 100		B. 30 June 1947 = 100		C. 31 January 1956 = 100	
1938	99	1947	101	1956	105
1939	101	(June to Dec.)		1957	110
1940	111	1948	106	1958	114
1941	122	1949	109	1959	117
1942	130	1950	111	1960	120
		1951	120		
1943	136			1961	125
1944	143	1952	130	1962	130
1945	149	1953	136	1963	134
1946	162	1954	142	1964	141
1947	168	1955	152	1965	147
(Jan. to Nov.)		1956	163		

Wages and the Standard of Living 2. Indices of Weekly Wage Rates in Certain Industry Groups – United Kingdom 1938–65

NOTE

SOURCES: 1938 – E. C. Ramsbottom, 'The Course of Wages in the United Kingdom', *J.R.S.S.* (1939); 1939–58 – information kindly supplied by the Department of Employment and Productivity; 1959–65 – *Ministry of Labour Gazette.*

A. 1938–47: 1924 = 100

	Agriculture		Coal Mining	Iron and Steel	Engineering	Shipbuilding and Repairing	Cotton	Woollen and Worsted	Printing and Bookbinding	Furniture	Building	Gas Supply	Railway Service
	E. & W.	Scot											
1938	123	100	97·5	116·5	113	124	92	89	100	101	101·5	100	99
1939	124	103	99	117	115	126	93	90·5	100	102	103	100	100·5
1940	156	127	113	130·5	125	137·5	110	107·5	102·5	110	110·5	116·5	112·5
1941	178	145·5	130	142	133	145·5	120·5	115	107	117·5	119	124·5	121
1942	214·5	181·5	150	143	141	154	124	119·5	113	120	123	132	130·5
1943	216	181·5	160·5	152	150·5	165·5	134	123·5	116	124	127	139	140·5
1944	232	192·5	166·5	157·5	157	172	143·5	128	124	131	129·5	147·5	148·5
1945	247	208·5	166·5	163·5	166	179	153·5	134	124	133	137·5	152	158
1946	268	219·5	166·5	170·5	176	190·5	169·5	141	137·5	140·5	161·5	168	165
1947	300·5	250	166·5	175	178	193	170	147·5	148·5	145	165	172·5	171·5

Wages and the Standard of Living 2. (continued)

B. 1948–55: June 1947 = 100

	Agriculture, Forestry, and Fishing	Mining and Quarrying	Treatment of Non-Metalliferous Mining Products Other than Coal	Chemicals and Allied Trades	Metals	Textiles	Leather, Leather Goods, and Fur	Clothing	Food, Drink, and Tobacco
1948	112·5	105·5	102	106	102	107	102	108	105·5
1949	117	106	105	109	105·5	112	105	111·5	110
1950	119	106·5	106	112	107	115·5	107	112	112·5
1951	127·5	114	116	123	117	128·5	118·5	120	120·5
1952	138	124	126·5	134·5	127	135	127·5	126	131·5
1953	144·5	127	132	140	133	140	135·5	134·5	138·5
1954	150	132·5	138	145·5	139	145	140·5	143	144·5
1955	159	144·5	147·5	155·5	149	151·5	149	150·5	153·5

C. 1956–65: 31 January 1956 = 100

	Agriculture, Forestry, and Fishing	Mining and Quarrying	Bricks, Pottery, Glass, Cement, etc.	Chemicals and Allied Trades	Metals	Textiles	Leather, Leather Goods, and Fur	Clothing and Footwear	Food, Drink, and Tobacco
1956	102	107	104	100	106	102	103	104	105
1957	107	112	111	106	112	117	109	111	111
1958	113	115	112	109	114	110	114	116	116
1959	117	118	115	112	117	112	118	118	119
1960	120	119	120	115	119	116	121	123	123
1961	127	126	126	118	125	121	122	124	128
1962	132	129	131	124	127	124	126	132	132
1963	138	135	138	131	139	128	131	135	138
1964	143	139	146	139	136	133	135	144	144
1965	152	145	155	144	140	139	142	151	150

B. 1948–55 (*cont.*)

	Manufactures of Wood and Cork	Paper and Printing	Other Manufactures	Building and Contracting	Public Utilities	Transport and Communication	Distributive Trades	Public Administration and Professional Services	Miscellaneous Services
1948	105	108	102·5	109·5	105	106·5	110	103·5	105
1949	109	111	106	112	108·5	107·5	111	106·5	109·5
1950	112·5	115	107	115·5	111·5	108	116·5	107·5	112
1951	123	127·5	118	125·5	120	118·5	123	115	117·5
1952	137	143·5	127·5	137	130	126	133	125·5	124·5
1953	142·5	150	131	144·5	136·5	130·5	141	131	131·5
1954	147	152·5	137·5	152	143	138	146·5	136·5	135
1955	155	160	146	161·5	155·5	149	154·5	147	142

C. 1956–65 (*cont.*)

	Timber, Furniture, etc.	Paper, Printing, and Publishing	Other Manufactures	Construction	Gas, Water, and Electricity	Transport and Communication	Distributive Trades	Public Administration and Professional Services	Miscellaneous Services
1956	105	106	101	106	101	103	104	106	104
1957	111	111	105	112	105	109	109	112	109
1958	116	116	109	117	109	112	115	116	114
1959	118	118	112	120	112	115	117	119	118
1960	122	122	115	122	115	121	121	123	120
1961	126	126	120	125	120	125	128	129	125
1962	134	133	128	133	125	129	132	134	132
1963	138	137	135	138	132	135	138	140	137
1964	143	143	142	144	141	144	143	148	143
1965	149	152	146	148	156	153	150	156	147

Wages and the Standard of Living 3. Average Weekly Earnings and Hours of Manual Workers in Manufacturing and Certain Other Industries – Great Britain 1938–65

NOTES

[1] SOURCE: *Ministry of Labour Gazette.*

[2] The figures apply to one week in October in each year, except for 1940–5 when the month was July.

	Men aged 21 and over		Women aged 18 and over: Full time	
	Earnings s. d.	Hours	Earnings s. d.	Hours
1938	69 0	47·7	32 6	43·5
	-----	---	-----	---
1939	...	...	...	...
1940	89 0	...	38 11	...
1941	99 5	...	43 11	...
1942	111 5	...	54 2	...
1943	121 3	52·9	62 2	45·9
1944	124 4	51·2	64 3	44·6
1945	121 4	49·7	63 2	43·3
----	-----	---	-----	---
1946	120 9	47·6	65 3	42·6
1947	128 1	46·6	69 7	41·5
	----- (a)	--- (a)	----- (a)	--- (a)
1948	137 11	46·7	74 6	41·6
1949	142 8	46·8	78 9	41·7
1950	150 5	47·6	82 7	42·0
1951	166 0	47·8	90 1	41·5
1952	178 6	47·7	96 4	41·8
1953	189 2	47·9	102 5	42·0
1954	204 5	48·5	108 2	42·0
1955	222 11	48·9	115 5	41·8
1956	237 11	48·5	123 2	41·5
1957	251 7	48·2	129 6	41·2
1958	256 7	47·7	133 11	41·2
1959	270 9	48·5	140 4	41·6
	----- (b)	--- (b)	----- (b)	--- (b)
1959	271 1	48·5	140 11	41·4
1960	290 8	48·0	148 4	40·5
1961	306 10	47·4	154 6	39·7
1962	317 3	47·0	160 10	39·4
1963	334 11	47·6	168 3	39·7
1964	362 2	47·7	179 1	39·4
1965	391 9	47·0	191 11	38·7

(a) 1948 and subsequent figures are not completely comparable with earlier ones owing to changes associated with the use of the 1948 Standard Industrial Classification.

(b) The first figures for 1959 are based on the 1948 S.I.C., the second on the 1958 S.I.C.

Wages and the Standard of Living 4. Average Weekly Earnings in Coal Mines – Great Britain 1938–66

NOTE
SOURCE: Ministry of Fuel and Power (later Ministry of Power) *Statistical Digest*.

	All Ages s. d.	Adult Males s. d.		All Ages s. d.	Adult Males s. d.		All Ages s. d.	Adult Males s. d.
1938	57 11		1948	163 10	170 4	1958	300 3	315 4
1939	61 9		1949	174 7	181 11	1959	300 3	313 11
1940	71 2		1950	182 4	190 0	1960	311 8	324 0
1941	82 9		1951	203 7	212 10	1961	331 1	343 0
1942	96 2		1952	225 0	236 2	1962	345 4	357 9
1943	103 3		1953	232 1	244 6	Year ended		
1944	113 0		1954	245 11	258 8	March		
1945	116 11		1955	261 0	274 6	1964 (a)	366 1	377 10
1946	123 2		1956	284 8	299 1	1965	382 7	396 8
1947	138 9	147 1	1957	304 11	320 0	1966	407 1	421 2

(a) Fifteen-month period.

Wages and the Standard of Living 5. *Per Capita* Consumption of Coffee, Tea, Sugar, and Tobacco – United Kingdom 1934/8 to 1965

NOTES
[1] SOURCE: *Abstract*.
[2] The series for coffee, tea and sugar are of estimated supplies per head of the population (civil population 1941–7) and do not exactly correspond with the series on pp. 355–8 of the first *Abstract of British Historical Statistics*.

[3] The series for tobacco is derived by the same method as the series in the first *Abstract of British Historical Statistics*, i.e. net duty-paid clearances divided by the mid-year population. However, total population estimates have been used instead of *de facto* population, since the latter are not available for the war period.

	Coffee	Tea	Sugar	Tobacco
		(in lb.)		
1934–8	0·7	9·3	103·9	
1938	...	...	...	3·98
1939	...	...	...	4·17
1940	1·2	8·6	71·8	3·96
1941	1·2	8·1	67·4	4·60
1942	1·2	8·2	69·2	4·83
1943	1·0	7·0	69·3	4·55
1944	1·2	7·4	74·0	4·51
1945	1·2	8·2	70·8	4·76
1946	1·4	8·8	79·5	5·08
1947	1·6	8·5	83·8	4·54
1948	1·7	8·0	85·1	4·28
1949	1·8	8·3	93·1	4·19
1950	1·5	8·5	85·3	4·23
1951	1·7	8·1	95·0	4·37
1952	1·5	8·5	90·4	4·30
1953	1·3	9·5	98·7	4·40
1954	1·3	9·7	106·1	4·56
1955	1·3	9·3	108·8	4·61
1956	1·5	10·1	109·8	4·59
1957	1·6	9·8	111·7	4·70
1958	1·7	9·9	115·5	4·74
1959	1·9	9·7	112·3	4·89
1960	2·1	9·3	112·0	4·97
1961	2·1	9·9	115·2	4·89
1962	2·7	9·4	112·6	4·71
1963	2·9	9·5	112·4	4·76
1964	2·5	9·4	109·1	4·67
1965	2·7	8·9	110·4	4·38

CHAPTER XIII

NATIONAL INCOME AND EXPENDITURE

TABLES

Despite the fact that there has recently been a great deal of work done in this field for the nineteenth century – and especially on capital formation – we have decided not to include any of it here. The aggregate estimates which have so far been published (or which we have seen before publication) reveal too great a measure of disagreement amongst the experts for it to be safe to publish them in a volume of this nature, where discussion of their provenance would necessarily be limited. The reader who wants estimates of this kind should consult Phyllis Deane, 'New Estimates of Gross National Product for the United Kingdom, 1830–1914', *The Review of Income and Wealth* (June 1968), and C. H. Feinstein, *National Income, Expenditure and Output of the United Kingdom, 1855–1964* (Cambridge University Press, forthcoming). There are, of course, certain estimates for particular sectors of the economy which have been reasonably well established, but there does not seem to be a place for them here on their own. The tables in this chapter, therefore, are confined to material for the period since the Second World War which has been derived from the *National Income and Expenditure* Blue Books or the Central Statistical Office. This does not call for any comment, except perhaps to note that revisions are frequently made to these series, sometimes covering a good many years. It is always advisable, therefore, to consult the latest Blue Book if precise up-to-date figures are required.

NOTE
SOURCE: *National Income and Expenditure 1968 and 1969.*

(in £ million)

	G.D.P. at factor cost		G.N.P. (a) at factor cost		National Income (b)	
	Current Prices	1963 Prices	Current Prices	1963 Prices	Current Prices	1963 Prices
1946	8,770	...	8,855	...	...	...
1947	9,308	...	9,458	...	...	...
1948	10,282	17,943	10,517	18,276	9,669	16,928
1949	10,914	18,492	11,133	18,795	10,240	17,398
1950	11,341	19,039	11,737	19,522	10,784	18,074
1951	12,616	19,761	12,958	20,078	11,857	18,583
1952	13,757	19,769	14,009	20,007	12,769	18,475
1953	14,836	20,684	15,065	20,924	13,776	19,336
1954	15,678	21,402	15,928	21,664	14,588	20,009
1955	16,809	22,099	16,983	22,276	15,522	20,549
1956	18,197	22,474	18,426	22,705	16,842	20,927
1957	19,295	22,890	19,544	23,135	17,853	21,295
1958	20,115	22,701	20,408	23,005	18,617	21,102
1959	21,151	23,476	21,411	23,746	19,567	21,772
1960	22,563	24,613	22,794	24,849	20,861	22,791
1961	24,139	25,492	24,391	25,749	22,326	23,605
1962	25,230	25,763	25,563	26,104	23,366	23,882
1963	26,826	26,826	27,218	27,218	24,900	24,900
1964	28,966	28,226	29,373	28,620	26,881	26,186
1965	30,895	28,948	31,364	29,397	28,667	26,851

(a) I.e. G.D.P. plus net property income from abroad.

(b) I.e. G.N.P. less capital consumption. Net national product at factor cost for the fixed price series.

National Income and Expenditure 2. Consumers' Expenditure – United Kingdom 1946–65

NOTES

[1] SOURCES: *National Income and Expenditure 1964, 1965, 1966, 1967, 1968, and 1969*. The food figures for 1946–51 and the catering component of 'Other Goods and Services' have been estimated by Dr C. H. Feinstein, who kindly allowed me to use them. Certain revisions which were not published in the Blue Books were made available to Dr Feinstein by the Central Statistical Office.

[2] Latest revisions have always been used, except in the 'Food' column, where the 1968 and earlier definition was preferred to that used in the 1969 Blue Book. In all cases where revised figures were published in the 1969 Blue Book they were converted to 1958 prices on the basis of the price index implicit in the figures published in the 1965 Blue Book.

A. At Current Prices

(in £ million)

	Food (Household Expenditure)	Alcoholic Drink	Tobacco	Housing	Fuel and Light	Clothing	Motor Cars and Motor Cycles	Other Durable Goods	Other Household Goods	Vehicle Running Costs	Other Travel and Communications	Other Goods and Services (a)	Consumers' Expenditure Abroad	*Less* Expenditure of Foreign Tourists, etc.	Total Consumers' Expenditure
1946	1,580	696	602	692	280	638	36	197	214	88	360	1,782	124	16	7,273
1947	1,826	726	689	757	300	736	49	269	245	101	378	1,852	124	24	8,028
1948	1,975	802	764	787	327	902	48	310	269	57	413	1,888	103	36	8,609
1949	2,148	755	753	801	335	1,013	61	360	300	81	422	1,884	103	47	8,969
1950	2,371	734	766	841	356	1,063	64	424	325	111	423	1,936	116	69	9,461
1951	2,599	774	800	886	392	1,116	74	480	351	132	454	2,094	152	89	10,215
1952	2,857	779	821	934	424	1,097	117	462	355	152	497	2,229	150	108	10,766
1953	3,156	795	837	1,001	451	1,115	186	528	364	171	517	2,324	152	122	11,475
1954	3,327	794	855	1,056	490	1,205	234	603	388	191	525	2,450	175	130	12,163
1955	3,615	832	880	1,122	528	1,297	310	624	419	244	549	2,648	192	150	13,110
1956	3,820	866	935	1,183	597	1,378	268	616	441	273	600	2,802	207	165	13,821
1957	3,962	906	981	1,276	618	1,439	320	685	472	289	646	2,951	216	179	14,582
1958	4,054	908	1,031	1,449	689	1,454	425	750	478	357	657	3,087	222	186	15,375
1959	4,184	917	1,061	1,559	686	1,516	506	873	504	405	677	3,254	234	199	16,187
1960	4,255	954	1,140	1,660	751	1,647	568	852	515	454	712	3,452	259	225	16,994

Year														
1961	4,399	1,054	1,217	1,775	796	1,709	515	873	543	526	751	3,699	276	231	17,902
1962	4,595	1,115	1,242	1,955	911	1,751	569	907	561	614	790	3,939	292	236	19,005
1963	4,727	1,175	1,286	2,161	1,010	1,845	733	970	575	682	832	4,148	326	242	20,228
1964	4,932	1,317	1,343	2,343	1,000	1,938	843	1,040	610	778	884	4,466	359	245	21,608
1965	5,105	1,415	1,428	2,586	1,087	2,059	801	1,093	642	914	944	4,774	390	249	22,989

B. At 1958 Prices

Year														
1946	3,098	869	1,051	1,205	537	926	71	282	328	135	557	2,911	210	28	12,152
1947	3,320	872	920	1,261	560	1,043	84	367	348	152	591	2,905	172	38	12,557
1948	3,365	832	890	1,261	563	1,156	71	398	356	77	625	2,831	161	55	12,531
1949	3,492	805	864	1,259	559	1,248	91	468	387	115	636	2,764	147	70	12,765
1950	3,648	816	870	1,282	583	1,293	94	530	406	146	633	2,762	153	100	13,116
1951	3,580	843	898	1,272	601	1,171	90	526	373	156	648	2,724	179	120	12,941
1952	3,545	835	915	1,281	595	1,153	124	476	381	162	655	2,719	170	135	12,876
1953	3,747	849	929	1,306	600	1,182	215	560	404	183	657	2,793	173	148	13,450
1954	3,811	845	949	1,340	625	1,367	271	653	431	204	656	2,902	194	153	13,995
1955	3,902	879	973	1,378	640	1,359	354	664	460	259	657	2,996	207	169	14,559
1956	3,963	899	986	1,404	661	1,413	282	615	460	283	667	3,010	217	178	14,682
1957	4,017	914	1,012	1,420	646	1,452	325	680	482	283	679	3,038	222	185	14,985
1958	4,054	908	1,031	1,449	689	1,454	425	750	478	357	657	3,087	222	186	15,375
1959	4,136	966	1,054	1,490	683	1,524	522	887	499	402	669	3,221	235	196	16,092
1960	4,226	1,015	1,092	1,532	744	1,634	600	865	507	447	675	3,359	257	214	16,739
1961	4,304	1,078	1,108	1,565	761	1,667	546	873	524	502	678	3,463	268	211	17,126
1962	4,347	1,080	1,067	1,622	840	1,660	620	892	525	567	683	3,561	275	210	17,529
1963	4,396	1,112	1,101	1,681	908	1,724	891	964	532	623	700	3,687	296	211	18,404
1964	4,466	1,189	1,081	1,717	879	1,783	1,032	1,003	555	702	726	3,864	314	205	19,106
1965	4,470	1,167	1,042	1,820	940	1,855	978	1,022	563	762	749	3,980	328	199	19,477

(a) Includes income in kind.

National Income and Expenditure 3. Gross Domestic Fixed Capital Formation by Industry Group – United Kingdom 1948–65

NOTE
SOURCE: *National Income and Expenditure 1963, 1964, 1965, 1966, 1967, 1968, and 1969.*

(in £ million)

	Agriculture, Forestry, and Fishing		Mining and Quarrying		Manufacturing		Construction		Gas, Electricity, and Water	
	Current Prices	1958 Prices	Current Prices	1958 Prices	Current Prices	1958 Prices	Current Prices	1958 Prices	Current Prices	1958 Prices
1948	93	136	28	45	328	520	22	34	138	206
1949	94	134	35	55	377	588	25	38	171	252
1950	93	128	33	51	444	676	25	38	195	282
1951	94	117	34	47	519	724	33	44	217	284
1952	97	109	46	58	553	689	36	43	239	284
1953	94	106	62	75	551	672	35	41	265	309
1954	100	113	79	96	591	713	44	52	304	356
1955	110	122	86	99	689	792	50	57	344	384
1956	102	108	91	99	854	925	53	57	342	359
1957	114	117	103	106	947	978	57	58	359	367
1958	134	134	105	105	922	922	62	62	387	387
1959	151	151	116	117	867	871	62	63	429	431
1960	157	157	95	94	1,021	1,016	70	72	427	429
1961	168	165	106	103	1,239	1,195	86	85	455	447
1962	163	157	99	93	1,168	1,098	74	73	523	503
1963	176	168	90	83	1,055	974	110	107	647	612
1964	177	167	102	92	1,216	1,092	130	125	757	700
1965	181	166	106	92	1,401	1,203	145	133	823	735

	Transport and Communications (a)		Distribution and Other Services (b)		Social and Public Services (c)		Dwellings		Total G.D.F.C.F. (d)	
	Current Prices	1958 Prices	Current Prices	1958 Prices	Current Prices	1958 Prices	Current Prices	1958 Prices	Current Prices	1958 Prices
1948	217	344	131	187	82	123	337	485	1,422	2,135
1949	233	355	160	231	101	151	332	476	1,577	2,333
1950	226	334	179	251	123	182	331	465	1,700	2,459
1951	212	297	200	250	150	201	376	458	1,889	2,469
1952	219	273	217	248	160	191	494	546	2,106	2,479
1953	279	329	233	267	170	202	630	711	2,359	2,748
1954	292	345	280	324	174	206	645	736	2,552	2,982
1955	310	347	358	398	195	219	640	689	2,829	3,150
1956	393	428	365	388	224	240	634	650	3,103	3,294
1957	499	519	397	407	247	255	616	621	3,381	3,469
1958	531	531	457	457	264	264	586	586	3,492	3,492
1959	581	578	534	543	285	289	661	674	3,736	3,768
1960	626	616	617	630	302	306	750	758	4,120	4,132
1961	613	595	702	704	364	363	829	813	4,619	4,524
1962	577	549	735	712	444	424	891	839	4,731	4,500
1963	578	538	786	757	473	441	944	857	4,916	4,591
1964	707	651	935	882	561	509	1,210	1,087	5,854	5,360
1965	746	654	971	890	601	597	1,271	1,097	6,303	5,622

(a) Includes highways and bridges, but not road goods transport, and not taxi and private hire car businesses until 1960.
(b) Includes road haulage and, before 1960, taxi and private hire car businesses.
(c) Excludes highways and bridges.
(d) Includes transfer costs of land and buildings, which are not included in the component industries.

National Income and Expenditure 4. Domestic Fixed Capital Formation by Type of Asset – United Kingdom 1948–65

NOTES

[1] SOURCES: All figures from 1953 onwards, all earlier total figures, and all earlier figures by asset of gross capital formation at current prices – *National Income and Expenditure 1963, 1964, 1965, 1966, 1967, 1968,* and *1969*; remaining figures are calculations by Dr C. H. Feinstein, which he has kindly made available to us.

[2] The figures of total gross domestic fixed capital formation include the transfer costs of land and buildings, which are not included in the individual asset figures.

(in £ million)

	Vehicles, Ships, and Aircraft				Plant and Machinery				Dwellings				Other New Buildings and Works				Total Domestic Fixed Capital Formation			
	Gross		Net		Gross		Net		Gross		Net		Gross		Net		Gross		Net	
	Current Prices	1958 Prices	Current Prices	1958 Prices	Current Prices	1958 Prices	Current Prices	1958 Prices	Current Prices	1958 Prices	Current Prices	1958 Prices	Current Prices	1958 Prices	Current Prices	1958 Prices	Current Prices	1958 Prices	Current Prices	1958 Prices
1948	249	416	125	204	500	757	185	284	337	485	176	254	290	423	88	126	1,422	2,135	574	868
1949	272	446	140	219	562	828	220	333	332	476	166	240	362	580	158	228	1,577	2,333	684	1,020
1950	262	389	96	147	643	931	276	411	331	478	161	238	413	609	212	302	1,700	2,459	747	1,098
1951	256	350	53	96	752	1,024	340	478	376	458	176	215	451	588	219	275	1,889	2,469	788	1,064
1952	260	308	26	42	795	975	321	406	494	546	270	298	512	612	249	293	2,106	2,479	866	1,039
1953	308	363	60	78	832	986	330	394	630	711	405	457	549	652	275	326	2,359	2,748	1,070	1,255
1954	332	390	71	88	927	1,096	399	477	645	736	417	475	605	719	325	386	2,552	2,982	1,212	1,426
1955	369	431	82	106	1,054	1,188	480	542	640	689	392	422	719	799	414	457	2,829	3,150	1,368	1,527
1956	426	469	112	137	1,147	1,221	513	546	634	650	368	377	852	914	526	563	3,103	3,294	1,519	1,623
1957	498	518	165	179	1,288	1,323	599	615	616	621	341	343	937	966	585	603	3,381	3,469	1,690	1,739
1958	530	530	178	178	1,328	1,328	590	590	586	586	303	303	1,004	1,004	630	630	3,492	3,492	1,701	1,701
1959	574	583	217	222	1,388	1,384	614	613	661	674	377	385	1,063	1,076	684	691	3,736	3,768	1,892	1,911
1960	641	653	268	272	1,502	1,480	680	670	750	758	460	465	1,172	1,187	779	789	4,120	4,132	2,187	2,196
1961	605	608	204	205	1,763	1,682	864	825	829	813	533	522	1,365	1,367	953	953	4,619	4,524	2,554	2,505
1962	525	524	102	99	1,766	1,656	807	759	891	839	581	548	1,492	1,429	1,044	1,001	4,731	4,500	2,544	2,407
1963	519	547	90	103	1,885	1,739	859	797	944	857	617	561	1,511	1,394	1,032	951	4,916	4,591	2,598	2,412
1964	634	659	174	185	2,161	1,942	1,037	940	1,210	1,087	869	780	1,790	1,617	1,282	1,158	5,854	5,360	3,362	3,064
1965	633	649	142	153	2,418	2,071	1,183	1,014	1,271	1,097	904	781	1,923	1,684	1,377	1,206	6,303	5,622	3,606	3,154

National Income and Expenditure 5. Gross Capital Stock at 1958 Replacement Cost – United Kingdom 1948–65

NOTES

[1] SOURCES: *National Income and Expenditure 1968* and information kindly supplied by Mr V. H. Woodward.

[2] For an account of the principles of valuation see *National Accounts Statistics, Sources and Methods*, pp. 383–7.

[3] A breakdown by type of asset is available for a more limited number of years, namely:

	1948	1951	1954	1958	1961	1962	1963	1964	1965
Road Vehicles	1·0	1·4	1·8	2·1	2·5	2·7	2·8	3·1	3·3
Other Vehicles, Ships, and Aircraft	3·4	3·6	3·7	4·0	4·4	4·4	4·4	4·4	4·4
Plant and Machinery	15·2	17·0	18·8	21·9	24·7	25·7	26·7	28·1	29·6
Dwellings	21·3	22·5	24·2	26·3	28·1	28·7	29·4	30·3	31·3
Other Buildings and Works	24·3	25·0	26·4	28·6	31·1	32·3	33·4	34·5	35·8

(in £ thousand million)

	1948	1949	1950	1951	1952	1953	1954	1955	1956	1957	1958	1959	1960	1961	1962	1963	1964	1965
Agriculture (a)	0·4	0·5	0·5	0·5	0·5	0·6	0·6	0·6	0·6	0·6	0·6	0·7	0·7	0·7	0·7	0·8	0·8	0·8
Mining and Quarrying	1·0	1·0	1·0	1·0	1·0	1·1	1·1	1·2	1·2	1·3	1·3	1·4	1·4	1·5	1·5	1·5	1·5	1·5
Manufacturing (excluding textiles)	11·1	11·5	12·0	12·5	13·1	13·6	14·1	14·6	15·2	15·9	16·6	17·2	17·9	18·8	19·6	20·3	21·1	21·9
Construction	0·3	0·4	0·4	0·4	0·5	0·5	0·5	0·6	0·6	0·6	0·7	0·7	0·8	0·9	0·9	1·0	1·1	1·2
Gas	0·7	0·7	0·7	0·7	0·8	0·8	0·8	0·9	0·9	1·0	1·0	1·0	1·0	1·0	1·1	1·1	1·2	1·2
Electricity	2·5	2·6	2·8	2·9	3·0	3·1	3·3	3·5	3·7	3·9	4·1	4·4	4·6	4·9	5·2	5·5	6·0	6·5
Water	2·0	2·0	2·0	2·0	2·0	2·1	2·1	2·1	2·1	2·1	2·1	2·1	2·2	2·2	2·2	2·2	2·3	2·3
Railways	5·7	5·6	5·5	5·5	5·4	5·4	5·4	5·3	5·3	5·4	5·4	5·4	5·4	5·5	5·5	5·5	5·5	5·4
Roads (b)	1·6	1·6	1·6	1·6	1·6	1·6	1·6	1·6	1·6	1·7	1·7	1·8	1·8	1·9	2·1	2·2	2·3	2·5
Other Transport and Communications (c)	4·9	5·0	5·2	5·2	5·3	5·4	5·6	5·7	5·8	5·9	6·0	6·2	6·4	6·5	6·6	6·7	6·8	7·0
Distribution and Other Services (d)	4·9	4·9	5·1	5·3	5·5	5·7	5·9	6·2	6·4	6·6	7·0	7·4	7·9	8·4	9·0	9·6	10·3	11·0
Private Dwellings	17·0	17·0	17·1	17·0	17·0	17·1	17·3	17·5	17·7	17·9	18·1	18·4	18·8	19·2	19·6	20·0	20·5	21·0
Public Dwellings	4·3	4·7	5·1	5·5	5·9	6·4	6·9	7·3	7·6	7·9	8·2	8·5	8·7	8·9	9·1	9·4	9·8	10·3
Other Public and Social Services (e)	4·0	4·1	4·2	4·3	4·5	4·6	4·7	4·9	5·0	5·2	5·4	5·5	5·7	6·0	6·2	6·5	6·8	7·2
Other Industries (f)	4·6	4·7	4·7	4·8	4·9	4·9	5·0	4·9	4·8	4·7	4·6	4·5	4·5	4·5	4·5	4·5	4·5	4·6
TOTAL GROSS CAPITAL STOCK	65·2	66·5	67·9	69·5	71·0	72·9	74·9	76·9	78·5	80·6	82·9	85·2	86·8	90·8	93·8	96·7	100·4	104·4

(a) Plant and machinery only.
(b) Excluding the non-renewable element more than 75 years old.
(c) Excluding taxis and private hire cars.
(d) I.e. distributive trades, insurance, banking and finance, professional and scientific services, miscellaneous services, road haulage, taxis and private hire cars, miscellaneous transport services, and storage.
(e) I.e. education (except as in note (f)), sewerage, prisons, etc.
(f) I.e. hospitals, universities, private schools, agricultural buildings and vehicles, and textiles.

CHAPTER XIV

PUBLIC FINANCE

TABLES

Except where a break is unavoidable or makes for a longer subsequent run of comparable figures, all the tables in this chapter follow on directly from those in the first *Abstract of British Historical Statistics*, and do not require comment other than that in the notes and footnotes. One noteworthy omission is in table 2, where most of the detailed items of government civil expenditure are not shown. This is the result of the very large number of changes in the categorisation and allocation of these items, which prevent the compilation of comparable figures for all except very short periods.

Public Finance 1. Gross Public Income – United Kingdom 1938–65

NOTE
SOURCE: *Finance Accounts of the United Kingdom.*

(in £ million)

Principal Constituent Items

	Total Gross Income	Customs	Excise	Stamps	Property and Income Tax	Surtax	Death Duties	Profits Tax (a)	Motor Vehicle Duties	Post Office (b)	Telegraph Service (b)	Telephone Service (b)	Broadcast Receiving Licences (c)
1938	948.7	221.6	113.7	24.2	298.0	57.1	89.0	1.4	34.6	47.0	7.8	31.8	...
1939	1,006.2	226.3	114.2	21.0	335.9	62.5	77.4	21.9	35.6	47.3	7.8	33.4	...
1940	1,132.2	262.1	137.9	17.1	390.1	69.8	77.7	26.9	34.1	43.9	8.0	35.1	...
1941	1,495.3	304.9	224.1	13.7	523.9	76.1	80.8	96.2	38.0	54.5	8.7	38.5	...
1942	2,174.6	378.4	325.7	14.1	769.7	74.9	90.9	269.1	38.4	56.7	8.6	49.0	...
											– – (c)		
1943	2,922.4	549.5	425.3	15.3	1,006.8	75.4	93.3	377.5	28.5	58.6	5.7	50.6	4.6
1944	3,149.2	560.8	482.2	17.7	1,183.6	76.0	99.5	500.1	27.3	65.6	4.9	40.5	4.8
1945	3,354.7	579.4	469.9	17.0	1,316.9	73.5	110.9	510.4	29.0	68.0	5.3	43.3	4.8
1946	3,401.2	569.8	540.8	25.1	1,361.3	69.1	120.3	466.4	43.2	63.8	5.7	46.0	5.2
1947	3,622.7	620.7	563.5	38.3	1,156.2	75.8	148.0	357.5	49.5	71.0	5.5	54.5	9.9
1948	4,011.3	791.1	629.7	56.3	1,189.7	91.2	172.0	288.7	49.1	76.3	5.5	61.5	11.2
1949	4,168.0	823.3	733.5	56.4	1,367.6	97.9	177.1	278.9	52.7	81.0	5.4	66.3	11.7
1950	4,098.0	813.3	706.4	51.5	1,438.4	114.7	189.6	297.0	55.8	85.3	5.1	71.8	12.6
1951	4,157.2	905.2	724.8	54.5	1,404.4	121.1	185.2	267.7	61.4	86.3	7.8	78.0	13.0
1952	4,629.0	998.5	753.3	61.9	1,668.7	129.6	183.0	315.4	65.2	97.3	10.0	82.8	14.2
1953	4,653.8	1,024.5	739.1	50.2	1,736.2	131.2	151.8	379.1	67.7	108.4	10.5	91.0	14.8
1954	4,666.0	1,042.4	722.0	56.6	1,731.0	132.4	164.5	254.3	73.1	112.5	13.3	106.2	16.4
1955	4,986.7	1,100.0	771.6	75.1	1,893.0	134.7	187.9	249.3	79.0	119.7	14.0	115.0	22.3
1956	5,160.4	1,148.6	864.5	70.6	1,942.9	138.6	175.7	211.0	87.0	122.6	15.4	126.9	25.8
1957	5,462.4	1,198.9	901.7	63.0	2,114.2	158.0	169.0	200.0	90.6	140.7	15.4	152.4	28.4
1958	5,678.7	1,207.5	942.4	63.7	2,208.3	157.4	170.6	255.2	100.7	154.8	16.1	172.4	30.7
1959	5,850.1	1,261.5	929.8	65.4	2,321.8	166.6	186.9	274.8	106.8	164.7	17.8	187.7	33.7
1960	6,015.6	1,373.3	908.6	97.3	2,242.6	181.3	226.5	261.8	108.4	173.3	18.5	201.1	36.1
1961	6,343.6	1,456.3	933.3	90.2	2,433.1	189.4	235.6	263.1	126.0	182.0	18.9	209.0	37.9
1962	6,644.9	1,616.3	978.4	96.6	2,726.7	224.1	262.2	335.1	141.0	...	...	...	39.5
1963	6,794.1	1,639.4	1,028.4	95.7	2,818.0	184.2	270.2	383.1	152.5	...	...	...	40.7
1964	6,890.2	1,723.0	1,042.9	88.2	2,745.1	177.4	310.2	390.4	171.1	...	...	...	50.4
1965	7,727.0	2,007.7	1,165.7	78.9	3,088.0	184.0	297.5	422.6	186.8	...	...	...	55.4

(a) This includes National Defence Contribution, Excess Profits Tax, and Excess Profits Levy.
(b) The Post Office Act (1961) separated the finances of the Post Office from the Exchequer from 1 April 1961.
(c) Until 1943, broadcast receiving licence receipts were included under the Telegraph Service.

Public Finance 2. Gross Public Expenditure – United Kingdom 1938–66

(in £ million)

NOTES

SOURCES: *Finance Accounts* and *Abstract*.

[1] Because of the exceptionally large number of changes in the administration of civil expenditures since 1938, only continuous series of some length have been included here. Further details of the composition of civil expenditures are most conveniently found in the *Abstract*.

[3] Expenditures for debt redemption, other than through the payment of terminable annuities, are excluded throughout.

[4] The column 'Total Gross Expenditure' is not equal to the sum of the 'Payments to Northern Ireland', 'Grand Total Debt Charges', and 'Grand Total Supply Services' owing to the exclusion of other Consolidated Fund services and some incidental expenditures.

[5] The figures are for years ended 31 March.

	Total Gross Expenditure	Payments to Northern Ireland	Grand Total Debt Charges	Charges met from		Constituent Items			
				Revenue	Receipts under Certain Acts	Interest on Funded Debt (a)	Interest on Unfunded Debt	Terminable Annuities	Management and Expenses
1938	909·4	8·9	216·2	216·2	—	116·6	98·2	0·4	1·0
1939	1,005·7	9·5	218·7	216·8	1·9	116·6	100·5	0·4	1·1
1940	1,401·0	9·6	228·6	222·8	5·8	116·6	110·5	0·4	1·0
1941	3,953·7	9·7	233·6	212·9	20·6	116·6	115·0	0·5	1·5
1942	4,876·3	9·1	278·0	257·2	20·7	116·6	157·7	0·5	3·1
1943	5,725·7	9·2	331·6	310·8	20·8	116·6	211·9	0·5	2·5
1944	5,899·0	9·0	385·1	364·7	20·4	116·6	265·7	0·5	2·3
1945	6,174·4	10·0	434·9	415·0	20·0	116·6	315·5	0·4	2·3
1946	5,591·5	12·3	474·9	455·4	19·4	116·6	355·1	0·5	2·7
1947	4,191·9	20·3	501·9	498·8	3·1	118·4	380·7	0·4	2·4
1948	3,353·6	24·3	511·4	502·6	8·8	127·7	381·6	0·4	1·7
1949	3,314·2	32·3	497·1	477·2	19·9	130·3	364·7	0·4	1·7
1950	3,530·6	37·0	499·7	472·2	27·5	130·3	367·4	0·4	1·6
1951	3,417·3	37·7	514·9	477·8	37·1	130·2	374·0	0·4	10·3
1952	4,221·8	39·4	561·3	513·6	47·7	130·1	429·1	0·4	1·6
1953	4,530·5	44·7	640·6	576·4	64·2	129·6	505·1	0·4	5·5
1954	4,476·8	50·1	667·1	579·8	87·3	128·9	528·4	0·4	9·4
1955	4,517·4	50·2	673·7	569·7	103·9	128·2	539·9	0·4	5·2
1956	4,726·8	59·2	757·1	637·8	119·2	127·6	625·2	0·4	4·0
1957	5,135·7	66·4	857·4	710·6	146·7	126·9	718·4	0·4	11·6
1958	5,218·2	71·6	832·4	663·0	169·4	126·2	699·8	0·4	6·1
1959	5,434·8	76·5	868·8	662·7	206·1	125·4	726·8	0·3	16·3
1960	5,590·3	80·2	858·3	614·7	243·6	124·7	712·8	0·3	20·4
1961	6,157·1	89·0	934·6	660·8	273·8	124·0	797·1	0·3	13·2
1962	6,194·7	97·4	1,035·8	710·8	324·9	123·2	878·8	0·3	33·5
1963	6,400·5	101·8	981·7	589·1	392·6	122·5	831·0	0·3	27·8
1964	6,775·7	118·6	1,045·1	647·9	397·3	121·8	893·7	0·3	29·3
1965	7,264·6	138·6	1,065·5	635·5	430·1	121·1	911·6	0·2	32·6

	Grand Total Supply Services	Defence					Costs of Collection			Civil Expenditures			
		Army and Ordnance (b)	Navy (b)	Air (b)	Central Defence Expenditure (c)	Total Defence	Customs and Excise	Inland Revenue	Post Office	Grand Total (d) Civil Votes	Law and Justice (e)	Colonial, Consular, and Foreign (f)	Education and Broadcasting
1938	681·1	63·0	78·0	56·3	—	197·3	5·9	7·8	72·9	397·2	22·7	8·6	59·9
1939	774·7	85·7	95·9	72·8	—	254·4	6·0	8·2	75·3	430·8	28·3	11·8	61·6
1940	1,161·3	81·9	69·4	66·6	—	626·4	6·1	8·3	79·3	441·2	30·9	17·4	63·1
1941	3,723·5	-- (g)	-- (g)	-- (g)	—	3,200·0	6·2	8·6	81·7	407·0	20·5	12·9	63·3
1942	4,602·2	-- (g)	-- (g)	-- (g)	—	4,085·0	6·3	9·7	93·7	407·4	20·7	11·8	65·6
1943	5,398·3	-- (g)	-- (g)	-- (g)	—	4,840·0	6·0	12·1	102·5	437·7	20·6	23·1	77·5
1944	5,518·2	-- (g)	-- (g)	-- (g)	—	4,950·0	5·6	13·1	110·6	438·8	20·5	14·9	79·5
1945	5,742·2	-- (g)	-- (g)	-- (g)	—	5,125·0	5·8	13·7	123·4	474·4	20·2	28·3	85·3
1946	5,114·6	-- (g)	-- (g)	-- (g)	—	4,410·0	6·1	14·4	124·3	559·7	23·4	36·4	117·7
1947	3,463·5	717·0	266·9	255·5	414·0	1,653·4	8·0	16·7	133·8	1,651·6	29·0	92·6	149·6
1948	2,796·2	383·6	194·3	181·9	94·1	853·9	7·9	19·3	146·0	1,769·1	31·4	59·1	182·1
1949	2,786·5	346·7	162·7	186·9	56·9	753·2	8·3	20·8	159·4	1,844·8	41·8	67·3	213·0
1950	2,998·9	291·8	186·8	201·6	60·5	740·7	9·2	21·8	168·2	2,059·0	52·2	63·9	241·7
1951	2,883·8	309·0	190·0	225·1	53·3	777·4	9·3	24·0	171·1	1,901·8	51·6	78·0	252·9
1952	3,651·6	422·3	271·3	322·3	94·3	1,110·2	10·4	28·1	198·4	2,304·4	57·3	74·4	273·7
1953	3,893·7	525·0	333·4	421·3	124·0	1,403·7	11·3	30·5	217·6	2,230·6	75·6	91·1	288·0
1954	3,831·7	487·8	324·1	416·4	136·2	1,364·5	12·3	31·9	232·9	2,190·1	80·4	84·7	303·0
1955	3,883·5	477·0	345·8	463·6	149·5	1,435·9	12·9	33·4	243·6	2,157·7	82·9	102·3	338·0
1956	4,017·2	462·9	337·7	431·1	173·2	1,404·9	13·6	35·4	277·4	2,285·9	82·1	115·0	377·5
1957	4,348·3	498·9	342·6	471·5	212·1	1,525·1	15·6	39·6	304·0	2,464·1	90·1	91·5	434·1
1958	4,473·3	387·0	353·0	474·0	214·8	1,429·7	16·4	41·8	335·5	2,649·9	100·4	90·7	480·7
1959	4,687·0	433·0	373·7	465·7	195·3	1,467·7	17·3	44·7	370·0	2,787·3	104·0	100·9	523·2
1960	4,886·3	428·2	364·6	485·1	197·8	1,475·7	18·5	49·1	384·5	2,958·5	95·1	104·7	215·3
1961	5,398·6	482·8	389·2	532·0	191·8	1,595·8	20·7	52·0	409·9	3,315·1	107·2	119·1	204·1
1962	5,367·8	508·4	413·8	547·3	219·2	1,688·7	20·9	60·2	— (h)	3,598·0	121·2	144·6	246·9
1963	5,695·3	528·5	438·1	569·7	230·3	1,766·6	21·2	60·8	—	3,846·7	134·0	154·9	— (i)
1964	5,999·8	489·5	433·6	499·2	369·9	1,791·7	22·3	63·4	—	4,122·4	150·0	170·6	—
1965	6,479·5	506·0	473·9	491·8	436·7	1,909·0	24·7	66·5	—	4,479·3	160·4	239·0	—
1966	7,139·9	553·6	512·0	533·0	457·2	2,055·9	26·9	74·9	—	4,982·2	180·1	225·9	—

(a) This column differs from the equivalent in the first *Abstract of British Historical Statistics* in that it excludes management and expenses of the debt, which are here shown separately.

(b) These columns differ from the equivalents in the first *Abstract of British Historical Statistics* in that they exclude amounts issued under the Defence Loans Act.

(c) This column consists of an aggregate of expenditures by the Ministry of Supply (later called Ministry of Aviation) and the Ministry of Defence. The Ministry of Supply component includes expenditures which should properly be included with Civil Expenditures. They are as follows:

1947 414·0	1951 49·3	1955 133·0	1959 181·0	1963 212·0
1948 94·1	1952 83·0	1956 157·9	1960 181·3	1964 207·5
1949 56·3	1953 111·8	1957 195·3	1961 176·4	1965 254·5
1950 59·8	1954 119·1	1958 200·6	1962 203·9	1966 269·8

(d) This total excludes expenditures by the Ministry of Supply (later called Ministry of Aviation) which should properly be included here. See footnote (c).

(e) This includes a small element of expenditure on the courts which is not included in the Total.

(f) Now called 'Commonwealth and Foreign'.

(g) During these years all military payments, except purely nominal amounts, were made from votes of credit, and are shown only in the Total.

(h) The Post Office Act (1961) separated the finances of the Post Office from the Exchequer from 1 April 1961.

(i) This column ends owing to administrative changes. Expenditures under the new categories can be found in the *Abstract*.

Public Finance 3. Nominal Amount of the Unredeemed Capital of the Public Debt of the United Kingdom at the End of Each Financial Year – 1938–66

NOTES

[1] SOURCES: *Return relating to the National Debt* and material kindly supplied by the National Debt Office.
[2] All figures relate to 31 March in the year shown.
[3] All figures exclude the amounts of Funding Loan and Victory Bonds tendered for duties under Section 3 (3) of the War Loan Act (1919), and held by the National Debt Commissioners.
[4] Except for columns 1 and 6 the figures given here do not compare exactly with those in the first *Abstract of British Historical Statistics* owing to the exclusion here of external debt arising from the 1914–18 War.

(in £ million)

| | | Unfunded | | | Net Total National Debt (a) | Outstanding Investment Borrowing | Aggregate Liabilities of the State |
	Funded	Internal	External	Total			
1938	3,364·8	3,616·4		3,616·4	6,993·7	122·8	7,116·5
1939	3,364·6	3,752·6	—	3,752·6	7,130·8	138·0	7,268·7
1940	3,364·4	4,520·2	—	4,520·2	7,899·2	151·6	8,050·8
1941	3,364·3	6,985·1	2·3	6,987·4	10,366·4	153·9	10,520·3
1942	3,364·3	9,552·5	109·9	9,662·4	13,041·1	152·9	13,193·9
1943	3,364·2	12,181·2	263·1	12,444·3	15,822·6	151·1	15,973·7
1944	3,364·2	14,929·1	255·1	15,184·2	18,562·2	148·3	18,710·5
1945	3,364·1	17,752·0	236·1	17,988·1	21,365·9	142·9	21,508·8
1946	3,422·3	19,831·5	369·1	20,200·6	23,636·5	137·4	23,773·9
1947	3,903·4	20,946·4	767·5	21,713·9	25,630·6	139·9	25,770·6
1948	3,902·0	20,151·0	1,554·8	21,705·8	25,620·8	151·9	25,772·7
1949	3,900·8	19,658·7	1,595·3	21,254·0	25,167·6	164·2	25,331·8
1950	3,899·3	19,700·5	2,189·9	21,890·4	25,802·3	184·0	25,986·3
1951	3,897·9	19,819·2	2,192·1	22,011·3	25,921·6	203·5	26,125·1
1952	3,887·1	19,823·5	2,167·9	21,991·4	25,890·5	227·0	26,117·5
1953	3,866·4	20,101·4	2,162·5	22,172·9	26,051·2	263·5	26,314·7
1954	3,846·9	20,610·1	2,114·5	22,724·6	26,583·0	304·9	26,887·9
1955	3,828·4	20,963·4	2,130·4	23,093·8	26,933·7	300·1	27,233·8
1956	3,809·2	21,144·0	2,074·7	23,218·7	27,038·9	281·1	27,320·0
1957	3,789·1	21,142·6	2,065·3	23,207·9	27,007·5	261·2	27,268·7
1958	3,768·2	21,290·8	2,163·1	23,453·9	27,232·0	241·5	27,473·5
1959	3,748·3	21,432·0	2,186·5	23,618·5	27,376·3	222·3	27,598·6
1960	3,726·9	21,953·6	2,043·0	23,996·6	27,732·6	204·1	27,936·7
1961	3,706·0	22,558·0	1,979·1	24,537·1	28,251·7	186·8	28,438·5
1962	3,683·7	23,060·5	1,922·2	24,982·7	28,674·4	0·1	28,674·5
1963	3,664·0	24,301·4	1,874·6	26,176·0	29,847·6	—	29,847·6
1964	3,645·9	24,738·6	1,835·0	26,573·6	30,226·3	—	30,226·3
1965	3,627·4	25,000·6	1,806·4	26,807·0	30,440·6	—	30,440·6
1966	3,606·2	25,933·4	1,795·0	27,728·4	31,340·7	—	31,340·7

(a) This column includes a small amount representing the estimated capital liability of terminable annuities.

Public Finance 4. Receipts of Local Authorities – England and Wales 1938–66

NOTES
[1] SOURCE: *Abstract.*   [2] The figures are for years ended 31 March.

(in £ million)
Principal Constituent Items

Year	Total Receipts	Loans	Rates (a)	Government Grants etc. (b)	House Rents (d)	Receipts from Trading Services					
						Water	Gas	Electricity	Transport	Harbours, Docks, etc.	Other Trading Services (e)
1938	659·2	122·7	177·3	136·1	23·4	21·4	18·0	52·5	24·5	13·7	
1939	692·3	129·8	191·4	140·2	24·9	21·7	17·7	56·9	25·2	13·6	7·1
1940	711·8	89·4	201·3	181·9	26·7	22·3	18·3	59·3	25·3	13·4	...
1941	734·9	51·6	203·9	226·0	27·6	23·7	20·9	64·9	27·0	11·7	...
1942	787·8	25·4	198·9	278·3 (c)	27·3	24·9	24·1	74·4	31·4	13·4	8·4
1943	769·0	21·8	200·4	248·1 (c)	27·6	25·6	26·3	76·2	34·3	13·3	12·1
1944	766·8	17·8	204·1	228·4 (c)	27·6	26·2	28·5	82·4	35·3	18·9	15·2
1945	786·3	14·8	206·7	230·3 (c)	27·5	27·0	30·5	88·1	36·7	20·9	15·5
1946	835·7	31·0	222·6	235·8	27·8	26·9	33·0	93·9	37·8	18·0	16·3
1947	1,034·8	149·9	243·2	252·1	30·1	28·6	37·1	107·8	41·3	20·0	18·4
1948	1,253·7	266·9	283·3	269·7	34·0	30·2	40·6	115·6	44·9	23·3	17·9
1949	1,196·1	287·3	284·4	284·9	42·3	32·6	46·8	—	47·0	23·8	19·0
1950	1,204·5	307·5	294·3	294·4	50·1	34·3	3·8	—	49·2	25·4	19·2
1951	1,261·3	340·4	304·9	304·6	58·2	34·5	—	—	49·9	26·0	18·1
1952	1,421·8	397·9	331·9	349·9	67·7	36·0	—	—	55·4	29·8	18·9
1953	1,579·1	473·9	351·0	384·8	77·9	38·0	—	—	59·7	29·2	19·5
1954	1,709·2	494·8	392·5	414·2	91·9	40·5	—	—	61·8	32·9	19·6
1955	1,784·8	491·4	410·5	452·9	105·3	42·6	—	—	62·9	33·4	21·0
1956	1,901·3	511·9	421·1	500·4	125·6	45·1	—	—	66·2	37·0	22·7
1957	2,097·4	501·0	513·5	568·0	148·1	50·8	—	—	70·7	38·1	23·7
1958	2,205·1	470·7	552·1	615·9	165·2	53·4	—	—	73·4	40·3	25·3
1959	2,311·0	463·7	579·3	658·8	182·9	55·3	—	—	75·7	41·1	27·0
1960	2,530·9	513·5	649·9	705·6	200·8	58·7	—	—	76·5	44·0	28·9
1961	2,701·2	530·4	696·7	756·0	216·3	62·1	—	—	78·2	46·0	30·4
1962	3,000·2	648·1	747·4	830·6	240·2	65·2	—	—	81·4	46·7	33·3
1963	3,303·7	704·7	831·3	907·0	268·2	69·2	—	—	84·1	51·6	35·3
1964	3,730·7	829·2	923·1	1,022·4	297·7	75·8	—	—	88·9	54·5	38·3
1965	4,214·2	1,069·5	991·2	1,103·0	325·6	83·4	—	—	90·5	57·7	40·5
1966	4,690·4	1,151·6	1,131·5	1,260·0	370·4	87·2	—	—	94·4	61·3	44·1

(a) Including, from 1948/9, payments made in lieu of rates by the British Transport Commission and Central Electricity Authority.
(b) Including local taxation licence duties, and the following grants and reimbursements for services arising solely from the war:

1938/9	2·8	1940/1	84·5	1942/3	83·7	1944/5	65·5
1939/40	42·5	1941/2	101·5	1943/4	69·6		

(c) Including grants to certain local authorities which lost rate income owing to war conditions.
(d) Including interest, etc., in connection with the Small Dwelling Acquisition Acts.
(e) Including corporation estates, ferries, markets, and civic restaurants.

Public Finance 5. Expenditure of Local Authorities other than on Capital Works – England & Wales 1938–65

(in £ million)

Principal Constituent Items

	Total Expenditure	Education	Libraries and Museums	Poor Relief (a, b)	Housing (c)	Highways and Bridges	Public Lighting	Fire Service	Sewerage	Refuse Disposal	Police	Public Baths etc.
1938	505·6	98·0	3·0	34·3	42·3	49·6	5·6	3·0	12·5	8·3	25·3	3·0
1939	532·8	100·4	3·2	35·5	44·9	50·4	5·8	3·1	12·7	8·5	26·1	3·1
1940	578·8	98·6	3·2	35·3	47·5	44·7	3·1	3·4	12·8	8·7	31·0	3·1
1941	631·1	99·5	3·2	31·2	48·0	39·3	1·6	3·7	13·0	10·0	34·0	3·1
1942	707·4	105·4	3·5	28·3	48·1	38·9	1·5	29·4	13·3	11·2	37·4	3·2
1943	694·3	113·4	3·6	27·6	47·7	39·8	1·5	14·0	13·4	12·5	37·4	3·3
1944	698·1	120·5	3·9	28·4	47·6	38·9	1·5	6·9	13·7	12·8	36·1	3·4
1945	729·1	128·1	4·1	30·0	48·5	39·8	2·4	5·0	13·8	13·1	34·9	3·5
1946	779·9	156·3	4·4	32·5	49·1	43·4	4·8	3·5	13·8	14·0	35·1	3·7
1947	873·7	183·2	5·5	37·3	53·7	56·6	5·5	3·4	14·9	16·1	36·1	4·4
1948	959·9 (i)	209·4	6·5	42·5	61·0 / - - - (h)	61·2	5·7	3·5	15·6	18·3	41·1	4·9
1949	866·2 (i)	236·4	7·6	11·7	70·1	58·6	7·2	12·2	16·6	19·8	44·1	5·2
1950	849·1	257·1	8·3	—	80·8	62·8	8·5	13·8	17·7	20·6	48·6	5·5
1951	887·4	268·7	8·8	—	91·2	62·8	9·1	14·9	18·0	21·7	54·4	5·6
1952	987·7	318·2	10·0	—	104·2	70·0	10·0	16·5	19·2	24·3	61·5	6·0
1953	1,062·3	345·4	10·7	—	122·2	74·4	11·0	17·9	20·8	26·2	66·3	6·3
1954	1,127·5	364·5	11·2	—	143·4	77·8	11·7	18·6	22·2	26·9	69·1	6·6
1955	1,225·3	409·1	12·1	—	163·7	84·6	12·2	19·1	23·7	28·0	71·8	6·7
1956	1,330·8	451·3	13·2	—	198·0 / - - - (j)	90·3	13·4	20·4	25·8	30·8	78·8	7·4
1957	1,497·1	527·1	15·1	—	221·9	96·4	14·7	22·2	29·8	33·6	91·6	8·3
1958	1,630·2	587·0	16·5	—	244·9	103·9	15·7	24·1	33·4	35·3	95·2	8·8
1959	1,731·3	633·9	17·7	—	262·7	105·7	16·8	25·5	36·7	36·9	102·6	9·1
1960	1,865·7	696·8	19·6	—	279·1	112·8	17·6	27·1	40·0	38·1	108·2	9·4
1961	2,018·5	752·4	21·8	—	301·2	119·9	18·6	29·2	43·9	41·0	122·2	9·8
1962	2,232·3	830·7	24·1	—	332·7	133·7	19·9	32·0	49·2	45·2	136·8	11·0
1963	2,446·9	929·7	26·3	—	355·8	149·3	21·2	36·2	53·8	47·9	146·5	12·1
1964	2,667·5	1,019·3	28·8	—	386·5	165·8	22·1	38·7	58·3	50·9	162·4	12·9
1965	2,902·8	1,101·1	32·0	—	435·4	178·0	23·7	42·7	66·0	54·8	176·1	14·2

NOTE

SOURCE: *Abstract.*

(in £ million)

Principal Constituent Items

	Commons Parks etc.	Lunacy (a, b)	Health Services (d)	Welfare Services (e)	Municipal Health (f)	Water Supply (d)	Gas Supply (a)	Electricity Supply (a)	Transport Services	Harbours, Docks, Piers, etc.	Loan Charges (g)
1938	6.9	14.3	30.2	—	—	22.5	17.9	52.5	24.2	14.1	114.7
1939	7.1	15.0	33.3	—	—	23.4	18.1	56.9	25.0	13.9	118.1
1940	6.7	15.3	32.8	—	—	24.4	18.8	59.6	25.1	14.3	118.8
1941	6.2	15.8	31.7	—	—	25.4	20.8	64.7	26.9	13.1	120.9
1942	6.1	16.6	33.0	—	—	27.0	23.9	74.0	30.5	14.2	120.6
1943	6.3	17.1	35.4	—	—	27.4	26.1	76.3	33.1	15.0	120.8
1944	6.6	17.9	39.6	—	—	27.2	28.1	81.4	35.0	18.3	121.2
1945	7.0	19.0	42.9	—	—	28.6	30.6	87.6	36.4	21.2	120.4
1946	7.8	19.9	49.4	—	—	29.2	32.9	94.2	37.7	19.4	112.2
1947	9.6	23.1	60.4	—	—	30.4	37.2	108.3	40.7	20.5	111.4
1948	11.3	26.6	72.7 (d)	—	—	32.1	40.6	119.0	44.4	22.8	117.0
1949	12.5	7.5	24.4 (d)	16.3	24.5	33.3	46.9	—	48.3	23.7	101.6
1950	13.8	—	9.6	25.0	32.1	35.5	3.8	—	49.9	25.4	111.2
1951	14.6	—	9.6	27.1	36.0	36.6	—	—	51.9	26.1	122.5
1952	15.8	—	10.5	31.7	38.5	38.4	—	—	56.7	29.8	136.8
1953	16.9	—	11.0	35.5	42.9	41.0	—	—	60.3	29.5	157.4
1954	17.6	—	11.3	37.9	43.0	44.0	—	—	61.2	32.9	183.5
1955	18.5	—	11.5	39.9	45.1	45.8	—	—	62.9	33.5	209.1
1956	20.4	—	12.7	42.6	49.1	49.9	—	—	66.2	37.2	236.5
1957	22.3	—	14.3	46.6	54.1	53.7	—	—	70.5	38.3	270.7
1958	24.1	—	15.4	50.4	57.8	58.7	—	—	73.6	40.3	311.5
1959	26.3	—	16.6	53.9	61.7	60.4	—	—	75.0	41.2	342.8
1960	27.1	—	17.7	57.3	68.1	63.8	—	—	76.1	43.8	372.3
1961	28.9	—	18.5	62.1	72.5	67.7	—	—	78.7	45.8	415.0
1962	30.7	—	20.8	68.9	81.3	72.0	—	—	82.8	48.2	466.4
1963	32.5	—	22.7	75.9	87.3	77.3	—	—	83.9	51.4	508.4
1964	36.1	—	24.6	84.6	95.7	80.8	—	—	89.1	53.9	561.9
1965	38.7	—	27.1	91.8	104.5	87.8	—	—	90.9	57.7	645.6

(a) Owing to legislative changes in the postwar years, these items disappear or emerge under other headings between 1948 and 1950.

(b) Maintenance of pauper lunatics is included under the heading 'Lunacy'.

(c) Including amounts advanced under the Small Dwellings Acquisition Acts.

(d) Prior to 1949 this column was an aggregate of 'Maternity and Child Welfare', 'Hospitals, Sanitoria, Dispensaries, etc.', and 'Other Items' under the general heading 'Public Health'. Following the establishment of the National Health Service on 5 July 1948, the first two elements disappear or emerge under other headings.

(e) This column is an aggregate of 'Care of Aged, Handicapped, and Homeless', and 'Protection of Children'. In the earlier years these were called 'National Assistance — Accommodation and Welfare', and 'Child Welfare and Child Life Protection'.

(f) I.e. Local Health Authority Services (e.g. care of mothers and young children, ambulances, health visiting).

(g) Figures under this heading are only included in total expenditure in so far as they are not already included under some other heading.

(h) This break is apparently caused by the subsequent exclusion of expenditure on town planning.

(i) These breaks result from the transfer of various items from local authorities to nationalised industry boards and the National Health Service.

(j) After 1956 this column includes expenditure in respect of requisitioned houses.

Public Finance 6. Expenditure of Local Authorities on Capital Works – England & Wales 1938–66

(in £ million)

NOTE
SOURCE: *Abstract.*

Years ended 31 March	Total Expenditure	Education	Workhouses etc. (a)	Housing etc. (b)	Highways and Bridges	Lunatic Asylums (a)	Hospitals and Other Public Health (c)	Sewerage	Water Supply	Gas Supply (a)	Electricity (a)	Transport Services	Harbours, Docks, etc.	Commons, Parks, etc.	Welfare Services (d)
1938	142·1	11·1	1·2	53·7	12·2	2·2	2·9	6·3	6·2	2·2	19·5	4·0	2·2	3·5	—
1939	150·8	14·8	1·5	55·1	13·5	2·3	3·6	7·5	7·2	1·8	18·3	2·9	1·4	3·0	—
1940	117·0	14·4	1·0	29·3	9·8	1·9	3·5	5·7	6·3	1·8	14·9	2·1	1·5	1·4	—
1941	62·0	6·8	0·3	9·1	3·1	0·8	1·5	2·4	3·8	1·0	11·1	0·3	0·8	0·4	—
1942	47·3	1·9	0·2	5·4	1·5	0·3	0·9	1·3	2·8	0·9	11·8	0·1	0·9	0·1	—
1943	38·2	0·8	0·1	6·0	1·8	0·1	0·5	1·2	2·1	1·3	12·1	0·4	1·1	0·1	—
1944	25·4	0·6	0·1	7·2	0·6	0·1	0·3	0·7	1·6	1·0	8·0	0·5	0·5	0·1	—
1945	23·8	0·4	0·1	7·8	1·4	0·1	0·2	0·4	1·2	0·9	6·7	0·7	0·6	0·1	—
1946	46·5	0·8	0·1	24·9	0·5	0·2	0·5	0·6	1·6	1·3	11·2	1·1	1·8	0·2	—
1947	162·4	2·0	0·4	114·2	1·7	0·2	0·9	1·9	5·0	3·0	22·8	1·9	1·8	0·8	—
1948	303·5	8·3	0·7	221·0	3·4	0·5	1·6	4·5	6·3	4·2	31·4	5·0	1·8	1·0	1·2
1949	329·5	18·4	0·3	252·3	3·3	0·3	— (c)	7·3	11·2	6·0	—	8·1	3·5	1·0	—
1950	331·1	28·0	—	233·8	5·1	—	1·9	9·5	15·3	0·7	—	8·9	3·3	1·3	2·9
1951	368·8	39·8	—	248·8	5·8	—	1·9	11·0	17·5	—	—	7·3	4·4	1·5	3·5
1952	426·5	53·5	—	281·7	5·8	—	2·4	15·3	20·8	—	—	4·8	4·6	2·1	4·3
1953	497·8	58·0	—	342·9	6·3	—	2·0	17·6	23·5	—	—	3·7	4·6	2·0	4·2
1954	543·6	58·7	—	373·8	6·5	—	2·0	18·9	24·8	—	—	4·8	5·2	1·4	3·7
1955	525·7	60·1	—	360·2 — — (e)	8·1	—	2·2	19·5	23·8	—	—	3·0	5·0	2·1	3·3
1956	541·1	68·8	—	349·2	10·8	—	2·2	23·7	24·4	—	—	3·7	5·7	2·6	3·9
1957	555·0	86·0	—	338·3	13·5	—	2·0	26·5	28·3	—	—	4·4	6·7	2·2	3·3
1958	528·6	96·3	—	309·9	15·1	—	1·9	27·3	25·8	—	—	3·2	5·4	1·3	3·1
1959	511·9	92·0	—	286·0	21·0	—	2·5	28·3	26·1	—	—	3·0	7·5	1·6	3·4
1960	571·5	89·2	—	321·2	26·5	—	3·5	35·2	28·1	—	—	2·3	7·4	2·6	4·9
1961	620·8	88·2	—	345·6	31·7	—	5·1	37·0	31·7	—	—	1·7	6·2	3·8	5·6
1962	741·2	111·0	—	399·4	35·7	—	7·1	46·4	34·4	—	—	1·7	7·8	5·7	7·3
1963	793·7	122·3	—	414·0	43·9	—	8·6	53·2	36·9	—	—	3·0	6·8	5·6	9·4
1964	979·4	123·9	—	556·0	59·7	—	10·1	58·4	39·0	—	—	3·6	6·0	6·8	10·2
1965	1,225·8	134·6	—	723·4	72·6	—	11·8	62·8	42·1	—	—	2·9	10·1	9·2	15·7
1966	1,289·3	129·3	—	779·9	69·4	—	10·8	62·0	43·8	—	—	3·8	14·2	9·5	15·5

(a) Owing to legislative changes these items disappear or emerge under other headings between 1948 and 1950.

(b) Includes Town and Country Planning.

(c) Until the establishment of the National Health Service this column is an aggregate of 'Maternity & Child Welfare', 'Hospitals, Sanitoria and Dispensaries', and 'Other items', all of which came under the general heading of 'Public Health'. After 1949 the first two of these constituents disappear from local authority accounts or are included in the last column. From 1950 various local authority health services are included (e.g. ambulances, health visiting, care of mothers and young children). The equivalent figure for 1949 is £11·1 m.

(d) This column is an aggregate of welfare services provided by local authorities since the legislative changes of the postwar years. It consists of 'Care of Aged, Handicapped, and Homeless', and 'Protection of Children'.

(e) From 1955/6 expenditure in respect of requisitioned houses is included in this column.

Public Finance 7. Receipts of Local Authorities – Scotland 1938–66

NOTE
SOURCE: *Abstract*.

(in £ million)

Years ended 15 May	Total Receipts	Loans	Rates (a)	Government Grants etc.	Housing Rents (b)	Principal Trading Services			
						Water	Gas	Electricity	Transport
1938	84·4	17·0	21·8	21·4	4·1	0·9	4·7	4·3	5·1
1939	89·0	19·2	22·4	22·0	4·4	0·9	4·6	4·6	5·4
1940	87·4	13·1	23·5	25·1	4·7	0·9	4·9	4·8	5·2
1941	88·4	8·3	23·7	27·3	5·0	1·1	5·9	5·4	5·9
			--- (c)	--- (c)					
1942	90·9	4·7	23·9	30·6	5·1	1·1	6·4	5·9	6·4
1943	89·5	2·9	24·0	28·5	5·3	1·2	7·0	6·0	6·8
1944	90·4	3·1	24·2	27·0	5·4	1·3	7·5	6·5	7·0
1945	91·4	3·6	25·8	25·3	5·5	1·2	8·3	6·7	7·2
1946	102·8	6·7	27·8	29·5	5·4	1·2	9·0	6·7	7·4
1947	127·1	22·7	29·7	32·6	5·8	1·3	9·9	7·6	7·9
1948	148·5	32·7	32·8	38·3	6·6	1·5	10·9	6·8 (d)	8·2
1949	146·9	37·0	31·2 (e)	36·6	7·3	1·5	11·3 (d)	—	8·7
1950	143·3	39·3	31·7	38·2	8·0	1·5	—	—	8·9
1951	152·2	42·5	33·3	39·9	8·7	1·5	—	—	9·5
1952	177·9	54·0	38·2	44·9	9·5	1·6	—	—	10·8
1953	210·2	70·1	46·0	48·8	10·4	1·9	—	—	12·1
1954	225·1	71·7	50·7	54·6	11·6	2·2	—	—	13·0
1955	226·6	63·9	51·2	60·6	12·8	2·3	—	—	13·1
1956	247·1	70·2	55·6	66·8	13·5	2·8	—	—	15·2
1957	261·8	63·1	64·9	74·3	14·8	2·8	—	—	15·5
1958	270·1	60·7	68·8	84·1	10·9	2·9	—	—	15·6
1959	293·2	69·5	73·1	91·8	11·8	3·1	—	—	15·6
1960	304·4	67·0	76·9	96·5	13·7	2·9	—	—	16·1
1961	320·5	66·0	79·7	103·6	14·8	3·2	—	—	17·9
1962	360·2	81·6	94·6	112·6	16·4	3·2	—	—	16·9
1963	387·3	91·7	99·4	119·0	21·3	3·4	—	—	17·9
1964	444·4	119·2	107·9	135·2	23·4	3·5	—	—	17·2
1965	483·2	133·4	116·1	142·9	25·9	3·7	—	—	18·0
1966	530·8	145·1	126·5	157·4	29·7	3·9	—	—	19·4

(a) Including water rates.
(b) Gross income from council houses, apart from rates and grants, but including interest on advances under Small Dwellings Acquisition Acts.
(c) Up to 1941 'Government Grants etc.' includes Exchequer grants under Local Government (Scotland) Acts and compensation for loss of rates due to the derating provisions of the Acts of 1929. After 1941 these amounts are included under 'Rates'.

(d) Owing to legislative changes these services disappear or emerge under other headings in the years 1949–50.
(e) From 1949 this heading includes payments in lieu of rates made by the British Transport Commission, British Electricity Authority (later South of Scotland Electricity Board), and the North of Scotland Hydro-Electric Board.

Public Finance 8. Expenditure of Local Authorities other than out of Loans – Scotland 1938–66

(in £000)

Principal Constituent Items

	Total Expenditure	Education	Libraries and Museums	Highways and Bridges	Public Lighting	Police (a)	Sewerage	Refuse Disposal	Commons, Parks, etc.	Lunacy	Hospitals, Clinics, etc. (b)	Individual Health (c)
1938	66,309	13,888	258	6,063	970	2,709	1,139	1,396	871	1,490	1,561	—
1939	68,994	14,139	264	6,330	1,003	2,757	1,229	1,423	893	1,553	1,960	—
1940	74,505	13,861	272	5,190	612	3,020	1,360	1,608	900	1,603	1,984	—
1941	78,637	13,971	276	4,565	583	3,423	1,294	1,752	850	1,987	2,429	—
1942	85,331	14,880	298	4,663	570	3,792	1,247	1,986	644	2,137	2,625	—
1943	84,409	15,695	302	4,631	582	3,860	1,276	2,046	827	2,113	2,723	—
1944	87,000	16,906	318	4,481	613	3,811	1,265	2,201	853	2,191	3,008	—
1945	88,967	18,143	329	4,423	726	3,768	1,285	2,190	945	2,311	3,450	—
1946	95,914	23,080	364	4,973	1,002	3,895	1,297	2,281	1,055	2,430	3,648	—
1947	105,233	25,043	404	6,564	1,093	4,188	1,428	2,721	1,244	2,711	4,090	—
1948	115,712	28,482	459	6,862	1,247	4,620	1,702	2,864	1,450	3,297	4,681	2,005
1949	105,801	30,865	566	6,518	1,452	4,880	1,692	3,153	1,529	408	739	2,649
1950	100,337	32,848	608	7,016	1,803	5,423	1,743	3,269	1,719	—	—	3,320
1951	108,446	34,573	637	7,184	1,939	5,756	2,161	3,618	1,833	—	—	3,528
1952	122,773	40,444	731	8,096	2,036	6,541	2,067	4,074	2,036	—	—	—
1953	133,486	43,669	787	8,631	2,397	6,775	2,431	4,302	2,195	—	—	3,978
1954	141,956	45,489	814	8,714	2,468	7,121	2,639	4,523	2,207	—	—	4,081
1955	156,468	51,181	858	9,286	2,656	7,896	2,846	4,848	2,423	—	—	4,400
1956	170,767	55,934	962	10,210	2,906	8,522	3,233	5,348	2,818	—	—	4,728
1957	194,988	67,825	1,088	11,160	3,251	9,948	3,712	5,701	2,941	—	—	5,315
1958	202,270	71,738	1,177	12,248	3,378	10,563	3,407	6,176	3,081	—	—	5,956
1959	213,063	75,221	1,220	12,334	3,592	11,389	3,589	6,466	3,400	—	—	6,093
1960	221,211	79,722	1,276	12,872	3,661	12,014	3,720	6,759	3,694	—	—	6,500
1961	241,557	86,546	1,336	14,739	3,816	13,758	3,961	7,049	3,790	—	—	6,710
1962	264,430	96,693	1,469	15,891	4,047	15,209	4,583	7,788	4,300	—	—	6,988
1963	281,878	103,198	1,596	16,991	4,304	16,205	4,697	8,206	4,406	—	—	7,676
1964	307,720	113,783	1,632	20,113	4,560	17,919	5,212	9,398	4,589	—	—	8,217
1965	333,264	122,642	1,806	19,606	4,856	19,638	5,740	9,551	5,024	—	—	8,966
1966	365,840	134,033	2,032	21,595	5,225	21,606	6,529	10,685	5,532	—	—	10,133

NOTE

Source: *Abstract.*

(in £000)
Principal Constituent Items

	Housing	Poor Relief (b)	L.A. Welfare Services (d)	Water Supply	Gas Supply (b)	Electricity Supply	Transport Services	Harbours etc.	Loan Charges
1938	7,245	5,653	—	2,438	4,738	4,354	5,060	1,960	12,575
1939	7,887	5,394	—	2,479	4,819	4,596	5,447	1,909	13,345
1940	8,694	5,441	—	2,634	4,905	4,837	5,355	1,925	14,232
1941	9,080	4,416	—	2,690	5,779	5,401	5,859	2,245	14,635
1942	9,492	4,016	—	2,757	6,436	5,923	6,138	2,457	15,683
1943	9,363	3,854	—	2,813	7,027	6,013	6,418	2,500	14,610
1944	9,511	3,995	—	2,914	7,564	6,517	7,130	2,915	14,893
1945	9,765	4,405	—	2,846	8,393	6,607	7,503	2,727	14,525
1946	9,890	4,650	—	2,945	9,086	6,961	7,578	2,580	14,767
1947	10,913	4,925	—	3,042	9,982	7,619	7,916	2,390	14,466
1948	12,506	5,263	—	3,323	10,863	7,027	8,495	2,819	14,552
1949	13,796	673	2,222	3,657	11,423	—	9,140	2,862	14,430
1950	15,150	—	2,659	3,608	—	—	9,487	3,066	14,061
1951	16,691	—	2,886	3,702	—	—	10,187	3,153	16,358
1952	19,079	—	3,219	4,089	—	—	11,315	3,348	19,249
1953	23,130	—	3,493	4,716	—	—	12,069	3,526	20,716
1954	26,930	—	3,966	5,166	—	—	12,893	3,651	24,656
1955	30,046	—	4,222	5,413	—	—	13,134	3,946	28,148
1956	33,675	—	4,483	6,350	—	—	14,111	4,271	31,735
1957	39,073	—	4,853	7,085	—	—	15,320	4,682	36,834
1958	36,924	—	5,268	7,454	—	—	15,850	5,021	42,170
1959	38,857	—	5,679	8,170	—	—	15,771	5,002	45,943
1960	41,014	—	5,931	8,369	—	—	15,781	4,957	49,374
1961	44,387	—	6,223	8,938	—	—	16,906	5,733	55,428
1962	48,942	—	6,963	9,583	—	—	16,753	6,132	63,009
1963	52,501	—	7,255	10,464	—	—	17,093	6,245	67,011
1964	56,033	—	8,273	11,241	—	—	17,861	6,062	72,883
1965	64,036	—	9,113	11,763	—	—	18,480	6,393	85,867
1966	71,715	—	10,170	12,916	—	—	19,276	6,667	95,095

(a) Includes 'Administration of Justice'.
(b) Owing to legislative changes these items disappear or emerge under other headings between 1948 and 1950.
(c) I.e. Local Authority Health Services under the N.H.S. since 5 July 1948.
(d) This comprises National Assistance, Child Welfare and Child Life Protection, etc.

Public Finance 9. Expenditure of Local Authorities on Capital Works – Scotland 1938–66

(in £ooo)

Principal Constituent Items

Years ended 15 May	Total Expenditure	Education	Highways and Bridges	Sewerage	Commons, Parks, etc.	Lunatic Asylums (a)	Health Services (b)	Housing
1938	18,650	1,231	798	1,051	158	161	188	10,297
1939	20,441	1,155	770	1,188	124	204	324	12,003
1940	15,931	1,261	608	943	101	180	344	8,106
1941	7,249	740	168	317	24	92	231	3,269
1942	4,469	347	107	136	9	35	107	1,875
1943	3,990	92	32	180	5	20	94	1,730
1944	2,975	94	22	43	9	22	56	1,594
1945	3,698	151	20	56	10	13	41	2,278
1946	8,332	135	42	325	11	12	46	5,691
1947	21,735	215	365	963	35	57	77	16,354
1948	34,521 (d)	861	337	1,456	85	73	130	26,654
1949	42,423 (d)	1,741	676	1,636	119	7	54 (b)	32,510
1950	44,928	2,517	747	2,300	167	—	223	32,431
1951	47,375	3,429	782	1,871	199	—	285	33,720
1952	58,325	4,261	638	2,087	142	—	220	41,079
1953	69,191	5,519	820	3,098	168	—	230	49,420
1954	74,196	5,252	1,038	3,043	207	—	307	53,423
1955	73,176	6,704	1,159	3,484	202	—	283	49,038
1956	72,279	8,810	1,911	3,096	325	—	368	45,594
1957	70,657	10,365	2,110	2,401	294	—	205	44,035
1958	71,270	12,059	2,647	2,321	180	—	198	42,319
1959	71,319	12,786	4,254	2,143	167	—	304	40,042
1960	72,206	13,751	6,714	2,500	419	—	362	35,936
1961	78,422	14,131	8,999	2,747	498	—	479	38,441
1962	91,011	15,676	11,475	3,968	418	—	471	42,504
1963	99,630	18,684	9,783	4,265	479	—	436	47,686
1964	130,140	21,025	10,430	4,090	491	—	1,206	72,106
1965	146,914	22,307	11,764	5,776	803	—	988	78,315
1966	154,849	20,532	11,396	5,762	701	—	1,168	82,254

NOTE
SOURCE: *Abstract.*

170

(in £000)

Principal Constituent Items

Years ended 15 May	Work-houses (a)	Water Supply	Gas Supply (a)	Electricity Supply (a)	Transport Services	Harbours, Docks, etc.	Welfare Services (c)
1938	118	810	383	1,658	686	68	—
1939	138	763	625	1,518	412	328	—
1940	82	906	669	1,252	316	256	—
1941	17	467	375	593	92	138	—
1942	3	446	252	384	130	432	—
1943	8	468	319	584	70	223	—
1944	1	151	254	432	98	45	—
1945	3	113	420	325	75	21	—
1946	8	412	602	654	101	43	—
1947	32	786	996	1,225	156	47	—
1948	52	1,358	954	1,599	65	135	58
1949	5	1,951	936	—	1,304	532	199
1950	—	3,095	—	—	1,608	575	329
1951	—	3,845	—	—	925	789	444
1952	—	6,726	—	—	163	890	
1953	—	6,053	—	—	344	956	307
1954	—	6,116	—	—	403	1,161	362
1955	—	5,230	—	—	3,087	1,010	271
1956	—	6,103	—	—	2,085	638	288
1957	—	4,652	—	—	1,828	1,202	360
1958	—	3,757	—	—	1,654	1,710	422
1959	—	3,703	—	—	1,753	2,097	245
1960	—	4,965	—	—	1,574	1,222	247
1961	—	5,973	—	—	990	707	276
1962	—	5,447	—	—	1,321	2,063	380
1963	—	5,197	—	—	1,472	2,299	423
1964	—	6,181	—	—	981	2,284	508
1965	—	9,662	—	—	903	1,971	630
1966	—	9,522	—	—	482	3,560	809

(a) Owing to legislative changes these services disappear or emerge under other headings between 1948 and 1950.

(b) Formerly called 'hospitals, clinics, etc.', this consists of expenditures on general hospitals, hospitals for infectious diseases, and hospitals for the treatment of tuberculosis until 1949. Thereafter it consists of expenditure on 'individual health' and 'other items' under the general heading of 'public health'. The corresponding figure for 1949 was £161,000.

(c) This column is an aggregate of expenditure on capital works for those welfare services provided by local authorities since the legislative changes of the post-war years. It consists of 'Care of the Aged, Handicapped, and Homeless', and 'Protection of Children'.

(d) Nationalisation of municipal services affects comparability before and after these years.

Public Finance 10. Income Tax Rates and Yields – United Kingdom 1938–66

NOTE
SOURCE: *Report of the Commissioners of Inland Revenue.*

	Net Receipt (a)	Net Produce (b)	Standard Rate in the Pound (c)	Net Produce per Penny of Standard Rate (c)
		(in £ million)		
1938	297·9	296	5/–	4·9
1939	336·1	331	5/6	5·0
1940	391·6	403	7/–	4·8
1941	530·8	603	8/6	5·9
1942	775·5	962	10/–	8·0
1943	1,007·3	1,108	10/–	9·2
1944	1,182·8	...	10/–	...
1945	1,309·6	...	10/–	...
1946	1,371·4	1,405	10/–	11·7
1947	1,155·6	1,120	9/–	10·4
1948	1,194·5	1,211	9/–	11·2
1949	1,360·4	1,333	9/–	12·3
1950	1,436·7	1,447	9/–	13·4
1951	1,414·2	1,409	9/–	13·0
1952	1,682·3	1,730	9/6	15·2
1953	1,751·2	1,709	9/6	15·0
1954	1,716·4	1,684	9/–	15·6
1955	1,874·2	1,870	9/–	17·3
1956	1,945·6	1,927	8/6	18·9
1957	2,132·5	2,124	8/6	20·8
1958	2,222·2	2,268	8/6	22·2
1959	2,317·8	2,323	8/6	22·8
1960	2,215·5	2,145	7/9	23·1
1961	2,428·9	2,440	7/9	26·2
1962	2,719·8	2,752	7/9	29·6
1963	2,820·6	2,850	7/9	30·6
1964	2,750·4	2,771	7/9	29·8
1965	3,088·3	3,139	7/9	33·8
1966	3,682·5	3,759	8/3	38·0

(a) The amount of tax actually collected in the year ended 5 April less refunds.

(b) The yield of the tax assessed in the year ended 5 April.
(c) In the year ended 5 April.

Public Finance 11. Gross Assessments (or Gross Income Reviewed) for Income Tax, by Schedule – United Kingdom 1938–66

NOTE
SOURCE: *Report of the Commissioners of Inland Revenue.*

(in £ million)

	A	B	C	D	E
1938	573	47	171	1,415	1,784
1939	586	47	173	1,499	1,853
1940	594	47	169	1,409	2,000
1941	593	47	167	1,530	2,562
1942	585	35	182	1,712	3,309
1943	582	50	200	1,897	3,930
1944	582	50	216	1,985	... (a)
1945	580	50	228	2,051	4,027 (b)
1946	580	50	240	2,097	4,144 (b)
1947	584	49	246	2,284	4,688 (b)
1948	600	49	268	2,696	5,710
1949	613	49	238	3,254	6,162
				- - - - (c)	
1950	620	(c)	232	3,636	6,643
1951	630		222	3,708	7,069
1952	642		218	4,215	7,985
1953	658		232	4,687	8,375
1954	675		257	4,739	8,900
1955	691		265	5,131	9,685
1956	709		269	5,621	10,621
1957	727		265	6,032	11,606
1958	745		278	6,395	12,250
1959	763		296	6,576	12,665
1960	797		299	6,922	13,530
1961	830		303	7,378	14,727
1962	880		320	8,262	15,874
1963	925		365	8,536	16,686
1964	610 (d)		387	8,658	17,653
				- - - - (d)	
1965	35 (d)		388	10,097	19,165
1966	—		392	10,476	20,755

(a) Owing to the introduction of the Pay as You Earn scheme of collection, comparative figures are not available for Schedule E for 1943/4.
(b) For these years the figures relate to income charged under P.A.Y.E. only and exclude pay, pensions, etc., in respect of service with the Armed Forces.

(c) From 1949/50 the profits from lands occupied for farming or other commercial use were all assessed under Schedule D.
(d) Schedule A taxation was abolished in the Finance Act (1963). Rents and other receipts from land in the United Kingdom were charged under Schedule D after 1964. Assessments made under Schedule A in 1964 and 1965 relate to earlier years.

CHAPTER XV

BANKING AND INSURANCE

TABLES

The majority of the tables in this chapter follows on directly from those in the first *Abstract of British Historical Statistics*, and they do not call for much further comment. The only new banking table is one which covers a fairly short period in the middle of the nineteenth century, to which our attention was drawn by Professor J. R. T. Hughes. In the absence of much other connected material for commercial banks at that time it is felt that this may be useful. For more recent periods, additional statistics to those given here are available in the Bank of England *Quarterly Review*, and there is a good deal in the Radcliffe Report (*S.P.* 1958–9, XVII).

The Yield on Consols is again included as the best available indicator of the long-term rate of interest, though it may be questioned how well it has conformed since the Second World War to the measure required for that theoretical abstraction – a loan of infinite duration without risk of default. The virtually constant fall in the value of money, and the general expectation of its continuation, may well be held to constitute a species of default.

Tables 9 and 10, showing the market rate of discount and capital issues respectively, have both been expanded compared with their equivalents in the first volume of *Historical Statistics*. Table 9 shows monthly rather than yearly averages, and more detail is given about capital issues. This latter is carried back as far as it is available. Finally, an additional table, number 11, has been included at the suggestion of Professor Barry Supple, showing selected life assurance statistics back to 1881.

Banking and Insurance 1. The Bank of England – 1938–65

NOTES
[1] SOURCE: *Abstract*.
[2] Gold Coin and Bullion held by the Issue Department are not given here, because the amounts held since September 1939 have been negligible. The average holding for 1938 was £326·4 million and the holding on 30 August 1939 was £263·0 million, which was practically all transferred to the Treasury. Issue Department holdings of other securities and of coin other than gold coin have also been negligible. Since 1938 the highest yearly averages have been: Other securities – £3·4 million (in 1940), and coin other than gold coin – £3·3 million (in 1951).

(in £ million)

	Issue Department Circulation	Banking Department						Reserves of Notes
		Deposits			Securities			
		Total	Public (a)	Bankers (b)	Government	Other		
1938	485·6	160·7	18·2	106·2	103·2	30·6		43·9
1939	507·3	161·9	21·3	102·5	107·0	31·4		40·6
1940	574·7	185·0	27·3	110·3	141·4	27·1		33·4
1941	651·1	192·1	16·8	122·4	144·3	30·8		33·6
1942	808·3	197·5	10·8	136·9	150·3	27·8		36·4
1943	966·3	223·4	8·7	158·9	179·8	23·5		36·8
1944	1,135·7	250·5	9·9	184·4	214·0	22·3		30·9
1945	1,284·2	285·7	12·8	217·9	251·8	24·2		26·6
1946	1,357·8	322·5	12·6	254·7	260·2	33·9		45·4
1947	1,383·3	397·8	12·8	295·9	313·1	35·0		66·4
1948	1,253·7	422·1	24·8	304·6	340·8	39·2		59·0
1949	1,269·0	432·0	41·0	296·4	354·3	45·5		45·7
1950	1,287·4	596·8	210·2	292·2	519·8	49·0		41·3
1951	1,342·4	406·2	20·2	297·6	341·4	41·6		40·6
1952	1,435·2	376·7	25·6	277·2	314·8	37·8		40·7
1953	1,531·9	390·4	43·2	277·6	341·4	26·3		38·7
1954	1,630·3	368·8	20·6	281·1	327·4	25·1		32·1
1955	1,760·0	340·6	19·2	254·0	283·4	37·9		35·1
1956	1,875·1	317·5	16·1	228·0	257·8	39·5		36·4
1957	1,966·3	303·6	13·3	216·2	239·4	47·9		32·2
1958	2,034·6	303·0	12·6	217·9	245·4	40·1		33·7
1959	2,104·5	313·9	13·0	236·0	258·0	37·0		36·2
1960	2,210·7	403·0	12·0	248·3	331·9	48·2		40·2
1961	2,306·2	516·2	13·0	250·0	423·8	74·7		35·0
1962	2,327·3	502·3	13·1	246·2	403·7	69·3		46·7
1963	2,398·2	334·3	12·5	249·3	227·7	81·3		42·5
1964	2,561·7	342·2	12·4	250·6	251·2	67·8		40·6
1965	2,727·4	424·9	12·3	266·6	311·1	82·7		48·5

(a) From 1948 to 1955 this includes a Special Account of H.M. Treasury established in August 1948 under the Economic Co-operation Agreement between the United States and the United Kingdom. The amounts in this account were as follows:

1948	10·8	1951	4·2	1954	5·8
1949	28·6	1952	12·5	1955	3·9
1950	195·6	1953	29·7		

(b) From 1960 onwards this sometimes included an element of 'Special Deposits' called from the London Clearing Banks and the Scottish Banks and not at their free disposal. The amounts were as follows:

1960	77·1	1965	56·4
1961	182·1		
1962	172·0		

Banking and Insurance 2. Liabilities and Assets of London Clearing Banks – 1938-65

NOTES

[1] SOURCE: *Abstract.*

[2] Up to 1958 the figures are averages of balances on the third Wednesday in the month, except for 30 June and 31 December. Subsequently the figures are averages of balances on the third Wednesday in the month except for December 1960 to December 1962 when the second Wednesday was used, and May 1963 when the fourth Wednesday was used.

[3] After 1960 the figures exclude the business of Lloyds Bank: Eastern Branches.

(in £ million)

	Total Assets or Liabilities	Deposits	Cash and Balances at Bank of England	Balances at Other Banks	Money at Call and Short Notice	Bills Discounted	Treasury Deposit Receipts	Investments	Advances to Customers and Other Accounts	Acceptances, Endorsements, etc.	Outstanding Advances to Nationalised Industries	Special Deposits with Bank of England (a)
1938	2,536	2,277	241	60	151	280	—	637	976	118	—	—
1939	2,513	2,248	244	67	149	255	—	608	991	125	—	—
1940	2,765	2,506	268	87	148	370	73	666	955	118	—	—
1941	3,216	2,970	311	107	134	231	495	894	858	104	—	—
1942	3,512	3,275	345	116	133	234	642	1,069	797	95	—	—
1943	3,918	3,677	386	123	152	185	1,002	1,147	747	98	—	—
1944	4,396	4,153	437	131	180	171	1,387	1,165	750	99	—	—
1945	4,942	4,692	492	141	206	188	1,811	1,156	768	104	—	—
1946	5,397	5,097	523	165	300	457	1,492	1,345	888	153	—	—
1947	6,032	5,650	473	186	450	723	1,308	1,474	1,107	233	—	—
1948	6,311	5,913	486	199	473	744	1,284	1,479	1,319	248	—	—
1949	6,387	5,974	496	202	510	914	983	1,505	1,440	259	—	—
1950	6,476	6,014	497	203	550	1,298	430	1,505	1,603	307	—	—
1951	6,787	6,162	511	232 (b)	569	1,228	247	1,624	1,822	468	70	—
1952	6,667	6,083	505	301	529	1,062	7	1,983	– – – (c) 1,776	427	84	—
1953	6,754	6,256	509	310	472	1,219	—	2,163	1,666	336	70	—
1954	7,014	6,495	528	343	457	1,206	—	2,321	1,731	349	102	—
1955	7,095	6,454	529	361	439	1,130	—	2,149	1,941	462	120	—
1956	6,902	6,288	516	367	431	1,270	—	1,978	1,820	432	87	—
1957	7,122	6,432	526	394	439	1,291	—	2,008	1,868	503	58	—
1958	7,339	6,636	543	406	434	1,277	—	2,149	1,923	506	68	—
1959	7,783	6,935	565	436	489	1,223	—	1,836	2,522	601	73	—
1960	8,259	7,236	588	493	562	1,149	—	1,407	3,123	745	72	74
					– – –	– – – (d)			– – – (d)			
1961	8,471	7,395	607	486	606	1,225	—	1,122	3,357	767	66	174
					– – – (e)	– – – (d)			– – – (d) (e)			
1962	8,443	7,611	623	527	718	1,205	—	1,194	3,408	461	59	159
1963	8,856	7,971	647	563	748	1,140	—	1,244	3,880	455	67	—
1964	9,479	8,550	696	658	738	1,155	—	1,220	4,328	490	67	—
1965	10,044	8,989	739	673	910	1,114	—	1,087	4,653	541	58	56

(a) The amounts of Special Deposits are calculated as percentages of the latest available monthly total deposits of each bank (excluding certain banks' deposits with branches outside England & Wales). Calls were made as follows: on 28 April 1960 – 1% by 15 June; on 23 June 1960 – a further ½% by 20 July and ¼% by 17 August; on 25 July 1961 – a further ½% by 16 August and ½% by 20 September. In 1962 releases of 1% were announced on 31 May, 27 September and 29 November and were affected by repayments of ½% on each of 12 June, 18 June, 8 October, 15 October, 10 December, and 17 December. Calls of 1% were made on 29 April 1965.

(b) The definition of this column up to 1951 is 'Balances with, and cheques in course of collection on, other banks in the United Kingdom and the Irish Republic'. Subsequently there was added 'items in transit between offices of the same bank'. Figures on the old definition for later years were: 1952 – 226; 1953 – 232; 1954 – 256; 1955 – 269.

(c) Figures from 1952 onwards exclude items in transit between eight banks. Figures for later years which compare with earlier ones were: 1952 – 1,838; 1953 – 1,732; 1954 – 1,804; 1955 – 2,019.

(d) From February 1961 Bills Discounted included, and Advances to Customers excluded, refinanceable export credits.

(e) In October 1961 certain assets were reclassified and approximately £40 million was transferred from Advances to Customers, to Money at Call and Short Notices.

Banking and Insurance 3. Deposits at Certain Joint Stock Banks – London 1834–57

NOTES
[1] SOURCE: Select Committee on Bank Acts, Q. 1134 (*S.P.* 1857-8, v).

[2] The figures relate to 31 December except for the Union and Commercial Banks, which are taken at 30 June.

(in £)

	London and Westminster	London Joint Stock	Union	Commercial	London and County	City	Bank of London	Unity
1834	180,380	—	—	—	—	—	—	—
1835	266,884	—	—	—	—	—	—	—
1836	643,332	—	—	—	—	—	—	—
1837	793,148	594,101	—	—	—	—	—	—
1838	1,387,855	1,145,421	...	...	186,477	—	—	—
1839	1,266,845	1,035,088	...	...	351,275	—	—	—
1840	1,361,545	1,170,893	377,755	...	437,995	—	—	—
1841	1,499,328	1,403,188	503,550	168,977	581,279	—	—	—
1842	2,087,757	1,771,739	745,988	246,824	858,802	—	—	—
1843	2,219,624	2,046,285	956,467	216,948	996,082	—	—	—
1844	2,676,741	2,245,330	1,591,200	239,622	1,231,412	—	—	—
1845	3,590,014	2,460,475	2,012,548	500,728	1,489,738	—	—	—
1846	3,280,864	2,446,017	2,170,310	440,721	1,588,585	—	—	—
1847	2,733,753	1,971,912	2,510,064	409,925	1,225,120	—	—	—
1848	3,089,659	2,328,056	2,644,728	406,217	1,354,730	—	—	—
1849	3,680,623	2,792,507	2,835,617	541,805	1,675,494	—	—	—
1850	3,969,648	2,949,869	2,963,583	612,596	2,030,238	—	—	—
1851	4,677,298	3,157,575	3,094,316	764,541	2,465,768	—	—	—
1852	5,581,706	3,591,506	4,268,438	964,177	3,281,603	—	—	—
1853	6,259,540	5,010,623	4,878,731	1,246,824	3,417,130	—	—	—
1854	7,177,244	6,161,154	7,031,477	1,265,903	3,779,944	—	—	—
1855	8,744,095	6,241,594	8,363,460	1,317,554	4,443,359	—	—	—
1856	11,438,461	7,224,527	9,045,606	1,536,361	3,543,824	944,475	—	—
1857	13,889,021	10,737,580	10,874,640 (a)	936,724 (b)	3,533,425	1,388,933	1,114,846	117,380

(a) 9,645,913 at 31 December 1857.

(b) 821,626 at 31 December 1857.

Banking and Insurance 4. Bank Clearings – London 1938–65

NOTES
[1] SOURCE: *Abstract*.
[2] Changes in the composition of the clearing whilst the Clearing Banks Emergency Operations were in force (September 1939 to August 1946) may preclude strict comparability throughout.

(in £ million)

	London	Provinces	Total
1938	39,611	1,258	40,869
1939	36,642	1,269	37,911
1940	40,019	1,408	41,427
1941	43,011	1,471	44,482
1942	48,657	1,480	50,137
1943	57,107	1,168	58,275
1944	62,645	943	63,588
1945	66,944	1,030	67,974
1946	69,011	1,258	70,270
1947	73,330	1,413	74,743
1948	80,210	1,737	81,947
1949	86,060	1,886	87,946
1950	94,241	2,076	96,317
1951	108,773	2,284	111,057
1952	110,584	2,053	112,637
1953	123,373	2,140	125,513
1954	144,288	2,346	146,634
1955	152,613	2,470	155,083
1956	160,889	2,397	163,286
1957	172,702	2,471	175,173
1958	180,914	2,448	183,362
1959	199,183	2,621	201,804
1960	225,417	2,758	228,175
1961	242,384	2,799	245,183
1962	272,850	2,767	275,617
1963	302,338	2,816	305,155
1964	355,744	2,926	358,669
1965	408,562	3,014	411,576

NOTES
[1] SOURCE: *Abstract*.
[2] The figures for 1938 and 1939 do not correspond exactly   with those given in the first *Abstract of British Historical Statistics* because of a difference in the method of averaging.

(notes held by the public to the nearest £ million)

	Bank of England (a)	Scottish Banks (b)	Northern Irish Banks (b)
1938	484·6	23·5	5·3
1939	506·4	24·7	5·6
1940	573·7	28·7	7·6
1941	649·8	33·9	10·8
1942	807·4	43·9	14·2
1943	965·1	53·5	16·0
1944	1,134·5	61·1	16·3
1945	1,283·2	64·9	15·7
1946	1,356·6	68·1	16·0
1947	1,382·3	71·8	14·7
1948	1,252·5	66·0	12·2
1949	1,264·4	68·5	11·2
1950	1,282·6	70·1	10·0
1951	1,341·5	74·1	9·2
1952	1,433·6	81·2	8·9
1953	1,529·7	90·0	8·2
1954	1,627·9	95·5	8·3
1955	1,757·6	101·8	8·4
1956	1,873·0	109·0	9·5
1957	1,963·9	116·8	9·9
1958	2,032·7	119·4	9·4
1959	2,103·6	120·5	8·9
1960	2,209·8	124·9	8·7
1961	2,305·4	128·0	8·5
1962	2,326·4	125·8	7·9
1963	2,397·3	126·1	7·4
1964	2,560·8	128·8	7·2
1965	2,726·5	130·3	7·4

(a) Average of Wednesdays.
(b) Average of Saturdays in the thirteen four-week periods as   published in *The London Gazette* or *The Belfast Gazette* with as close a correspondence as possible to the calendar year.

Banking and Insurance 6. Savings Bank Deposits – United Kingdom 1938–65

NOTES
[1] SOURCES: *Post Office Savings Bank* (H.M.S.O., annually), and *Trustee Savings Bank Year Book*.
[2] Figures for the Post Office Savings Bank are taken at 31 December, and for the Trustee Savings Banks at 20 November.

[3] The Trustee Savings Bank figures are for cash only, and do not include stock owing to depositors.

(amount due to depositors in £ million)

| | Post Office | Trustee Savings Banks | |
		Ordinary Departments	Special Investment Departments
1938	509·3	142·4	96·5
1939	551·4	152·3	99·4
1940	654·4	173·6	101·9
1941	822·9	214·8	108·6
1942	1,005·4	264·6	113·9
1943	1,240·6	333·0	115·2
1944	1,493·9	411·0	115·8
1945	1,776·6	488·5	114·6
1946	1,981·9	557·7	112·6
1947	1,943·2	621·9	109·6
1948	1,948·1	688·7	110·5
1949	1,947·6	744·4	112·5
1950	1,934·3	793·7	115·2
1951	1,875·9	816·6	115·7
1952	1,812·3	831·3	122·4
1953	1,746·8	824·9	143·7
1954	1,727·4	827·1	192·6
1955	1,700·0	827·3	226·2
1956	1,687·9	811·6	282·8
1957	1,676·6	823·3	316·8
1958	1,645·6	822·8	342·6
1959	1,679·0	858·6	380·5
1960	1,710·2	880·6	434·0
1961	1,736·6	902·4	499·0
1962	1,760·1	913·6	603·5
1963	1,791·6	951·6	733·4
1964	1,814·4	995·6	885·1
1965	1,822·5	1,028·0	994·0

180

Banking and Insurance 7. Yield on Consols 1938–65

NOTE
SOURCE: *Abstract*.

(per cent)

1938	3·4	1948	3·2	1958	5·0
1939	3·7	1949	3·3	1959	4·8
1940	3·4	1950	3·5	1960	5·4
1941	3·1	1951	3·8	1961	6·2
1942	3·0	1952	4·2	1962	6·0
1943	3·1	1953	4·1	1963	5·6
1944	3·1	1954	3·8	1964	6·0
1945	2·9	1955	4·2	1965	6·4
1946	2·6	1956	4·7		
1947	2·8	1957	5·0		

Banking and Insurance 8. Changes in Bank Rate, 1938–67

NOTE
SOURCE: *Abstract*.

(per cent)

1938		2	1960	27 October	$5\frac{1}{2}$
1939	24 August	4	1960	8 December	5
1939	28 September	3	1961	26 July	7
1939	26 October	2	1961	5 October	$6\frac{1}{2}$
1951	8 November	$2\frac{1}{2}$	1961	2 November	6
1952	12 March	4	1962	8 March	$5\frac{1}{2}$
1953	17 September	$3\frac{1}{2}$	1962	22 March	5
1954	13 May	3	1962	26 April	$4\frac{1}{2}$
1955	27 January	$3\frac{1}{2}$	1963	3 January	4
1955	24 February	$4\frac{1}{2}$	1964	27 February	5
1956	16 February	$5\frac{1}{2}$	1964	23 November	7
1957	7 February	5	1965	3 June	6
1957	19 September	7	1966	14 July	7
1958	20 March	6	1967	26 January	$6\frac{1}{2}$
1958	22 May	$5\frac{1}{2}$	1967	16 March	6
1958	19 June	5	1967	4 May	$5\frac{1}{2}$
1958	14 August	$4\frac{1}{2}$	1967	19 October	6
1958	20 November	4	1967	9 November	$6\frac{1}{2}$
1960	21 January	5	1967	19 November	8
1960	23 June	6			

Banking and Insurance 9. Rates for Three-Months Bank Bills – London 1938–65

NOTES
[1] SOURCE: *Abstract*.   [2] The figures are the means of the market buying rate on working days as quoted in *The Times*.

(discounts in per cent per year)

	Jan.	Feb.	Mar.	Apr.	May	June	July	Aug.	Sept.	Oct.	Nov.	Dec.
1938	0·53	0·53	0·53	0·53	0·53	0·59	0·53	0·53	0·91	0·69	0·66	0·94
1939	0·56	0·53	0·63	1·41	0·72	0·75	0·78	1·59	3·53	1·88	1·19	1·22
1940	1·09	1·03	1·03	1·03	1·03	1·03	1·03	1·03	1·03	1·03	1·03	1·03
1941	1·03	1·03	1·03	1·03	1·03	1·03	1·03	1·03	1·03	1·03	1·03	1·03
1942	1·03	1·03	1·03	1·03	1·03	1·03	1·03	1·03	1·03	1·03	1·03	1·03
1943	1·03	1·03	1·03	1·03	1·03	1·03	1·03	1·03	1·03	1·03	1·03	1·03
1944	1·03	1·03	1·03	1·03	1·03	1·03	1·03	1·03	1·03	1·03	1·03	1·03
1945	1·03	1·03	1·03	1·03	1·03	1·03	1·03	1·03	1·03	1·03	0·53	0·53
1946	0·53	0·53	0·53	0·53	0·53	0·53	0·53	0·53	0·53	0·53	0·53	0·53
1947	0·53	0·53	0·53	0·53	0·53	0·53	0·53	0·53	0·53	0·53	0·53	0·53
1948	0·54	0·56	0·56	0·56	0·56	0·56	0·56	0·56	0·56	0·56	0·56	0·56
1949	0·56	0·56	0·56	0·58	0·63	0·63	0·63	0·67	0·69	0·69	0·69	0·69
1950	0·69	0·69	0·69	0·69	0·69	0·69	0·69	0·69	0·69	0·69	0·69	0·69
1951	0·69	0·69	0·69	0·69	0·69	0·69	0·93	1·00	1·00	1·00	1·38	1·50
1952	1·50	1·50	2·48	3·00	3·00	3·00	3·00	3·00	3·00	3·00	3·00	3·00
1953	3·00	3·00	3·00	3·00	3·00	3·00	3·00	3·00	2·67	2·19	2·19	2·19
1954	2·19	2·15	2·16	2·17	1·89	1·66	1·60	1·61	1·64	1·62	1·62	1·78
1955	2·02	2·58	3·81	3·83	3·94	3·99	4·00	4·06	4·15	4·16	4·21	4·22
1956	4·22	4·77	5·34	5·27	5·14	5·20	5·10	5·08	5·17	5·15	5·08	5·07
1957	4·84	4·44	4·25	4·18	4·04	4·08	4·06	4·17	5·40	6·81	6·77	6·67
1958	6·51	6·17	5·96	5·47	5·24	4·64	4·31	3·98	3·82	3·79	3·67	3·34
1959	3·28	3·23	3·41	3·40	3·44	3·54	3·57	3·60	3·59	3·58	3·55	3·72
1960	4·14	4·69	4·74	4·80	4·76	5·03	5·76	5·75	5·71	5·62	4·98	4·63
1961	4·44	4·48	4·61	4·63	4·55	4·64	5·10	6·91	6·84	6·32	5·67	5·61
1962	5·65	5·65	5·13	4·50	4·14	3·99	4·09	4·02	3·93	3·92	4·03	3·86
1963	3·69	3·63	3·70	3·88	3·88	3·84	3·87	3·85	3·88	3·86	3·91	3·91
1964	3·91	4·00	4·53	4·53	4·56	4·65	4·73	4·84	4·84	4·88	5·42	6·84
1965	6·84	6·75	6·74	6·78	6·73	6·04	5·97	5·97	5·97	5·92	5·91	5·91

Banking and Insurance 10. Capital Issues – United Kingdom 1927–65

NOTES

[1] SOURCES: 1927–39 – Bank of England *Statistical Summary*; 1946–65 – *Abstract*.

[2] The main difference between the 1927–60 series and the later one is that the latter does not include nationalised industries' stock issues. For a fuller account of the differences between the two series see Bank of England *Quarterly Bulletin*, vol. 1, no. 5 (Dec. 1961).

[3] Government stock is not included.

Part A. 1927–60 (in £ million)

	Total New Issues (a)	'Industrial' Issues (b)	Other U.K. Issues	Overseas Issues	Investment Trust Issues
1927	316·7	121·4	...	150·8	19·5
1928	360·6	159·4	...	150·1	33·9
1929	269·2	134·7	...	107·3	26·0
1930	244·8	92·9	...	112·8	9·5
1931	94·5	32·9	7·2	49·6	4·9
1932	117·8	77·5	10·2	29·4	0·7
1933	136·9	70·2	24·9	40·6	1·2
1934	164·6	91·0	28·2	42·0	3·4
1935	199·2	141·1	22·6	21·3	14·2
1936	244·6	165·6	41·5	32·4	5·2
1937	187·2	113·8	33·2	32·9	7·0
1938	131·8	76·7	26·0	28·1	1·1
1939	(72·3) (c)	38·9	14·5	18·9	...
1946	153·6	136·0	—	16·8	0·7
1947	187·3	154·2	—	32·5	0·6
1948	277·8	238·8	—	38·1	0·9
1949	157·1	113·1	—	41·9	2·1
1950	360·2	307·2	—	52·2	0·8
1951	292·2	239·7	—	50·2	2·3
1952	387·2	332·5	—	52·4	2·2
1953	435·1	350·4	19·4	57·4	7·8
1954	530·6	406·9	18·2	79·2	26·3
1955	634·5	539·0	8·8	63·6	23·1
1956	365·5	234·8	53·9	52·6	24·3
1957	367·3	261·6	25·7	65·1	14·9
1958	359·5	209·8	60·9	74·0	14·8
1959	541·4	413·9	45·2	48·8	33·6
1960	607·5	459·3	52·5	48·1	47·6

Part B. 1954–65

	Gross Issues	Gross Redemptions	Net Issues Loan Capital	Net Issues Pref. Shares	Net Issues Ordinary Shares
1954	335·4	70·3	154·5	17·3	93·3
1955	355·1	80·3	113·0	16·7	145·1
1956	305·0	36·2	108·6	7·8	152·4
1957	391·5	50·8	185·3	−1·1	156·5
1958	387·4	92·5	194·1	0·1	100·7
1959	511·6	86·4	163·6	7·6	254·0
1960	573·5	91·0	144·5	4·1	333·9
1961	699·4	69·6	184·7	−1·1	446·2
1962	638·7	65·7	308·7	2·7	261·6
1963	660·9	108·5	347·8	10·0	194·6
1964	757·9	82·0	443·0	7·5	225·4
1965	825·9	150·1	602·7	−14·4	87·5

(a) Investment trust issues were not included in the heading 'total new issues' in the source until 1946. They have been included here, but since the addition was of rounded figures there may be an error in the last digit.

(b) The heading was later changed to 'Public Corporation' and 'Public Companies' issues.

(c) Excludes investment trust issues.

Banking and Insurance 11. Life Assurance Premiums and Funds –
Great Britain 1881–1965

NOTES

[1] SOURCES: Board of Trade, *Summary of Statements of Insurance Business* and *Report of the Industrial Assurance Commissioner* annually.

[2] The statistics relate only to companies established within Great Britain.

(in £ million)

	Ordinary Business		Industrial Business by Companies		Industrial Business by Collecting Societies	
	Premiums Income (a)	Life Fund at 31 Dec. (b)	Premiums Income	Life Fund at 31 Dec.	Premiums Income	Life Fund at 31 Dec.
1881	12·5	127·7	...	...	...	...
1882	12·8	131·9	...	...	...	...
1883	12·9	135·6	...	...	...	...
1884	13·2	139·5	...	...	...	...
1885	13·4	142·8	...	...	...	...
1886	13·7	146·1	...	...	...	...
1887	14·4	149·9	...	...	...	...
1888	15·0	154·9	...	...	...	...
1889	15·5	160·5	...	...	...	...
1890	16·0	165·9	...	...	...	...
1891	15·7	170·5	...	...	...	...
1892	17·9	176·4	...	...	...	...
1893	18·3	183·0	...	...	...	...
1894	19·4	190·2	...	...	...	...
1895	21·0	199·3	...	...	...	...
1896	21·9	209·2	...	...	...	...
1897	22·2	219·8	...	...	...	...
1898	23·2	228·9	...	...	...	...
1899	23·4	238·2	...	...	...	...
1900	23·5	246·1	...	...	...	...
1901	24·4	255·3	...	...	...	...
1902	25·0	265·0	...	...	...	...
1903	25·8	274·2	...	...	...	...
1904	27·3	284·5	...	...	...	...
1905	27·5	296·0	...	...	...	...
1906	28·1	306·4	...	...	...	...
1907	28·9	315·4	...	...	...	...
1908	30·0	325·9	...	...	...	...
1909	31·9	336·4	...	...	...	...
1910	31·3	348·6	...	...	...	...
1911	31·9	359·8	...	...	...	...
1912	32·8	370·5	...	...	...	...
1913	33·9	381·5	...	...	...	...
1914	34·3	390·1	18·0	58·7	...	...
1915	33·8	390·5	18·6	61·4	...	...
1916	34·0	395·2	19·6	65·0	...	...
1917	34·5	396·4	21·0	69·4	...	...
1918	38·6	411·0	22·4	74·0	...	...
1919	43·5	425·9	25·4	80·5	...	...
1920	47·5	437·5	29·3	89·7	...	...

See p. 185 for footnotes.

(in £ million)

	Ordinary Business		Industrial Business by Companies		Industrial Business by Collecting Societies	
	Premiums Income (a)	Life Fund at 31 Dec. (b)	Premiums Income	Life Fund at 31 Dec.	Premiums Income	Life Fund at 31 Dec.
1921	49·0	456·6	31·1	100·3	...	...
1922	51·5	479·5	31·6	111·5	...	...
1923	54·3	506·3	33·2	123·2	...	...
1924	58·8	532·7	34·1	136·4	8·1	29·3
1925	65·8	570·1	36·6	151·8	8·6	31·8
1926	65·4	605·6	36·8	165·8	8·6	34·7
1927	71·4	640·4	38·8	179·1	9·2	37·7
1928	76·0	674·3	40·9	192·0	9·6	40·9
1929	78·0	710·1	42·0	203·1	10·0	43·6
1930	75·5	734·5	43·8	217·3	10·4	46·8
1931	75·4	754·3	45·4	226·3	10·7	50·4
1932	86·4	793	46·4	243·0	11·0	53·4
1933	90·1	833	47·7	259·3	11·3	56·9
1934	91·9	868	50·1	277·5	11·8	60·6
1935	95·6	903	51·5	296·7	12·2	63·9
1936	98·1	943	53·6	317·1	12·8	68·0
1937	99·7	984	55·8	337·3	13·4	72·4
1938	102·1	1,023	58·0	359·2	13·8	76·2
1939	99·5	1,042	59·8	374·4	14·3	80·7
1940	96·4	1,054	62·2	388·6	14·6	84·9
1941	95·5	1,081	63·6	407·0	15·0	90·0
1942	99·8	1,115	68·0	430·4	15·9	95·5
1943	103·6	1,153	72·2	456·0	17·0	102·4
1944	109·5	1,193	75·7	484·9	17·8	109·3
1945	117·5	1,244	79·4	526·9	18·4	116·6
1946	134·5	1,313	83·6	568·6	19·6	123·8
1947	158·9	1,391	91·2	604·1	21·2	132·5
1948	173·0	1,478	97·1	640·0	22·8	141·7
1949	185·8	1,573	100·3	671·1	23·8	150·4
1950	203·9	1,675	103·5	703·0	24·1	159·3
1951	232·4	1,786	108·2	724·9	24·9	167·2
1952	253·6	1,914	112·0	746·5	25·6	172·5
1953	274·7	2,078	116·6	786·5	26·4	182·6
1954	290·8	2,273	120·9	840·1	27·5	194·2
1955	331·0	2,484	127·4	889·9	28·6	203·4
1956	357·4	2,681	134·5	936·5	29·3	213·7
1957	396·9	2,907	140·1	972·1	30·3	225·3
1958	438·3	3,211	146·6	1,026·9	31·3	235·8
1959	478·5	3,557	153·5	1,090·6	32·6	249·0
1960	532·3	3,951	161·0	1,162·5	34·5	263·0
1961	589·4	4,385	168·6	1,227·5	35·0	274·5
1962	651·0	4,840	181·2	1,296·6	34·9	280·5
1963	759·1	5,408	185·1	1,368·7	36·1	296·1
1964	836·1	6,046	194·2	1,458·5	37·4	312·4
1965	849·3	6,680	204·0	1,561·2	38·8	329·4

(a) Includes considerations for annuities.   (b) Includes Annuity Fund.

CHAPTER XVI

PRICES

TABLES

With the exception of table 8, showing the average export value of cotton piece-goods back to 1821, this chapter does not attempt a coverage greater than that in the first *Abstract of British Historical Statistics*. The price indices given there have, where possible, been continued. *The Statist* index, table 1, goes back with little break to 1846, which gives it a certain usefulness; but the representativeness of the commodities which it comprises has suffered severely of late years. The Board of Trade wholesale price indices in table 2 suffer from the opposite complaint. Their coverage is up-to-date, but there are three separate bases for the period since 1938. The same applies to the indices of retail prices in table 4. In both cases, of course, there has been an immense increase in the level of sophistication of the indices. Even the index of agricultural prices, which is a new table in this volume (number 3), has two bases for this period.

In the tables of actual prices, as opposed to indices, the series shown in the first volume have been continued, with the addition of the cotton cloth prices already referred to and of a series of steel prices. Of the old series, the only ones about the inclusion of which there was some doubt in our minds were the two of coal prices. The representativeness of these particular series is certainly not what it used to be; but there seemed to be some value in continuing long-running comparable series.

186

Prices 1. *The Statist* Price Indices, 1938–65

NOTES

[1] SOURCE: Annual article by the editor of *The Statist* in the *Journal of the Royal Economic Society*, series A.

[2] These indices are based on wholesale prices and the unit value of imports.

(average of 1867–77 = 100)

	Food				Raw Materials				Overall Index
	Vegetable (a)	Animal (b)	Sugar, Tea, and Coffee	Total	Minerals (c)	Textile Fibres (d)	Sundry (e)	Total	
1938	81	111	43	84	136	75	83	95	90
1939	74	115	47	83	137	93	88	102	94
1940	112	141	58	111	167	149	117	140	128
1941	140	142	65	125	181	162	131	154	142
1942	170	148	66	140	184	163	142	160	151
1943	156	156	72	138	187	166	156	167	155
1944	152	156	73	137	197	182	161	178	160
1945	155	156	78	139	209	189	159	182	164
1946	155	154	88	140	239	231	198	219	186
1947	191	149	100	156	304	295	263	284	230
1948	217	155	107	171	368	348	279	324	260
1949	240	185	151	201	382	356	273	328	274
1950	268	204	224	235	416	491	299	390	324
1951	305	227	249	265	516	639	394	501	401
1952	336	285	227	294	532	475	363	443	380
1953	365	317	261	325	473	430	329	399	366
1954	330	325	320	326	476	429	298	386	361
1955	313	367	281	329	529	410	310	400	370
1956	319	351	282	326	581	400	352	428	384
1957	295	343	298	313	570	408	338	422	376
1958	314	347	251	313	539	346	319	386	355
1959	303	350	230	305	528	369	324	393	356
1960	277	356	230	296	518	416	325	405	359
1961	274	322	207	277	524	433	322	411	354
1962	311	343	213	301	541	404	314	416	360
1963	308	343	285	328	552	417	324	413	374
1964	316	397	280	339	649	441	318	445	401
1965	308	404	221	326	706	429	331	462	404

(a) Viz. English wheat, Canadian wheat, flour, barley, oats, maize, potatoes, and rice.
(b) Viz. prime beef, middling beef, prime mutton, middling mutton, pork, bacon, and butter.
(c) Viz. pig iron, bar iron, copper, tin, lead, and coal.
(d) Viz. middling American cotton, East Indian (from 1959 Sudan) cotton, flax, hemp, jute, English wool, merino wool, and silk.
(e) Viz. hides, leather, tallow, palm oil, olive oil, linseed oil and seeds, motor spirit, kerosene, gas oil, soda crystals, sodium nitrate, indigo, and timber.

Prices 2. Board of Trade Wholesale Price Indices – 1938–65

NOTE
SOURCE: *Board of Trade Journal.* The full revised series for 1938–50 was kindly supplied by the Statistics Division of the Board of Trade.

A. 1938–50: 1930 = 100

	Food, Drink, and Tobacco				Industrial Materials and Manufactures									Total Index (All Articles)
	Cereals	Meat and Fish	Other Foods and Tobacco	Total	Coal	Iron and Steel	Non-ferrous Metals	Cotton	Wool	Other Textiles	Chemicals and Oils	Miscellaneous	Total	
1938	109·9	85·9	97·5	97·3	123·2	139·1	94·4	83·6	101·4	68·7	94·7	93·2	103·5	101·4
1939	96·5	88·7	104·6	97·3	121·1	131·5	100·4	88·5	105·8	79·7	95·3	98·7	105·5	102·8
1940	138·0	114·6	143·3	132·7	140·1	159·2	123·2	125·3	157·3	108·5	117·1	142·6	138·4	136·6
1941	150·4	118·1	166·5	146·1	159·5	181·1	123·9	138·2	170·1	120·2	126·9	169·1	155·8	152·6
1942	188·8	116·7	171·3	157·5	171·1	182·5	125·8	140·9	172·9	128·4	136·0	172·0	160·1	159·4
1943	179·3	121·7	179·0	159·8	185·8	182·8	126·0	136·7	177·3	132·8	146·3	177·1	164·0	162·8
1944	167·3	121·8	182·4	157·8	209·1	184·1	127·8	153·6	183·7	134·3	151·4	184·2	170·2	166·2
1945	164·7	121·8	184·7	157·9	237·0	188·8	127·1	161·9	185·2	139·1	149·3	188·6	174·7	169·0
1946	166·9	123·5	181·6	158·1	244·0	209·2	150·9	173·3	186·5	151·1	148·3	188·7	184·2	175·2
1947	172·2	121·6	197·9	164·6	251·7	221·5	222·5	199·9	212·1	165·8	175·6	210·9	207·0	191·7
1948	176·7	136·0	225·1	180·8	297·4	235·6	241·7	300·4	276·3	167·8	190·7	266·6	241·8	219·3
1949	196·7	156·1	230·6	196·3	303·8	252·9	255·3	322·1	304·9	169·8	191·1	256·6	249·1	230·0
1950	235·3	173·6	251·3	221·1	304·5	260·8	337·1	397·5	505·6	197·2	208·4	293·6	285·8	262·4

B. 1946–57: 30 June 1949 = 100

	Materials Used in Broad Sectors of Industry							Output of Broad Sectors of Industry						
	All Non-Food Manufacturing	Mechanical Engineering	Electrical Machinery	Textiles	Building and Civil Engineering	House Building	Fuel Used in all Manufacturing Industry	All Non-Food Manufactured Products	Chemicals	Iron and Steel	Textiles	Clothing and Footwear	Food	Paper
1946	...	83·2	82·5	...	83·2	83·6	...	...	...	...	...	...	...	...
1947	...	93·6	98·9	...	94·3	93·7	...	...	...	...	...	...	...	...
1948	...	97·4	101·9	...	100·6	100·8	...	...	...	90·4	...	...	...	...
1949	...	101·5	104·2	...	102·0	101·8	...	...	...	97·7	...	...	...	...
1950	138·6	113·2	122·0	155·0	106·1	105·2	103·0	106·8	103·7	101·0	131·1	103·7	...	101·4
1951	193·3	134·3	151·9	211·0	125·6	123·0	112·2	124·8	120·9	113·2	178·5	124·7	118·0	168·4
1952	162·1	149·9	165·4	154·7	133·6	130·6	124·1	127·8	131·0	136·5	136·4	114·9	132·5	160·9
1953	145·8	145·7	155·2	145·7	130·4	128·7	130·8	125·2	130·4	139·8	129·4	113·7	138·6	131·0
1954	143·5	150·4	160·5	147·4	131·4	130·7	136·2	125·5	130·8	141·3	130·3	114·2	139·1	133·3
1955	152·4	168·1	185·7	140·7	137·3	137·1	147·2	129·6	133·1	148·1	126·1	113·6	143·9	140·3
1956	156·2	177·3	190·0	144·1	142·4	142·3	163·2	135·6	138·8	158·9	126·7	115·3	148·1	146·0
1957	154·7	183·9	181·7	148·1	146·9	146·4	175·4	139·9	143·2	176·5	131·8	118·3	156·3	147·7

188

C. 1955–65: 1954 = 100

Materials Purchased by Broad Sectors of Industry

	All Basic Materials and Fuel Used in Manufacturing Industry	Basic Materials Used in Manufacturing Industry	Fuel Used in Manufacturing Industry	Food Manufacturing	Mechanical Engineering	Electrical Machinery	Textiles	Construction Materials	House Building Materials
				Materials and Fuel Used in					
1955	103.0	102.7	106.1	97.8	110.2	110.2	96.0	104.7	105.2
1956	106.7	105.3	116.9	100.1	116.5	114.3	98.0	109.5	109.4
1957	107.4	105.3	123.4	97.3	121.9	114.9	103.1	113.7	112.3
1958	100.8	97.1	129.0	96.7	123.5	114.5	88.7	114.2	111.9
1959	101.7	98.4	127.5	98.6	124.5	115.6	88.1	113.4	111.0
1960	101.8	98.5	127.6	96.1	126.2	116.9	91.6	115.1	114.0
1961	100.6	96.4	133.0	93.0	128.1	118.3	92.9	118.2	118.0
1962	100.6	95.9	136.5	95.3	130.1	120.0	91.3	120.4	120.2
1963	103.0	98.5	137.8	99.6	130.8	120.9	96.6	121.9	121.7
1964	107.0	103.0	138.3	103.8	135.3	125.0	98.7	125.8	126.2
1965	107.5	103.1	141.6	102.3	140.5	131.2	94.5	130.4	131.5

Output of Broad Sectors of Industry

	All Manufactured Products		Food Manufactures	Chemicals		Iron and Steel		Textiles		Clothing and Footwear	Paper
	Total Sales	Home Sales	Home Sales	Total Sales	Home Sales	Total Sales	Home Sales	Total Sales	Home Sales	Home Sales	Home Sales
1955	103.4	102.6	102.1	99.9	99.5	104.0	104.7	98.3	97.7	100.1	104.9
1956	106.7	107.0	105.8	102.9	103.1	112.1	112.8	98.1	97.5	101.7	109.2
1957	110.2	110.4	107.1	105.9	106.5	123.9	125.2	101.1	100.9	104.4	110.3
1958	111.0	111.1	104.9	104.6	105.6	127.7	129.9	98.9	97.9	105.5	109.7
1959	111.4	111.5	106.9	105.3	106.6	125.4	129.0	96.5	96.0	105.2	107.6
1960	113.1	113.0	106.9	104.4	106.0	125.6	128.5	101.4	100.8	107.1	107.6
1961	115.7	116.0	107.2	103.1	105.1	126.1	129.7	104.3	103.3	108.9	109.8
1962	118.0	118.6	111.1	102.6	104.5	128.7	133.3	103.8	102.5	110.4	111.0
1963	119.5	119.9	114.2	103.3	104.6	128.8	133.7	105.7	103.9	110.7	111.6
1964	123.2	123.9	118.1	105.4	106.8	129.3	134.3	110.1	107.9	112.6	114.3
1965	128.4	129.7	120.6	108.1	109.4	131.6	136.6	111.6	110.1	115.3	118.7

Prices 3. Index of Agricultural Prices – England & Wales, 1938–65

NOTE
SOURCE: *Abstract*.

Part A. 1936/8 = 100

	All Products	Cereals and Farm Crops	Livestock and Livestock Products (a)	Fruit, Vegetables, and Glasshouse Produce
1938	102	93	104	111
1939	103	99	106	94
1940	143	138	143	153
1941	173	169	162	237
1942	184	201	178	197
1943	187	194	180	216
1944	191	192	185	216
1945	197	198	192	204
1946	207	198	208	211
1947	241	214	233	302
1948	249	238	252	244
1949	260	239	267	259
1950	270	250	281	249
1951	296	283	310	254
1952	306	279	323	273
1953	312	283	331	275
1954	310	282	325	281
1955	327	299	340	310
1956	328	319	331	335
1957	319	290	325	334
1958	327	353	322	317
1959	317	321	319	295
1960	302	276	313	287

Part B. 1954/5 to 1956/7 = 100

	All Products	Farm Crops	Fatstock	Livestock Products and Poultry	Fruit and Vegetables
1954/5	99·7	98·6	99·7	100·7	97·8
1955/6	102·2	106·6	98·7	101·8	107·4
1956/7	98·1	94·9	101·6	97·5	94·7
1957/8	101·6	112·6	98·0	96·7	113·7
1958/9	101·2	117·0	100·0	95·4	98·1
1959/60	96·4	96·9	99·3	92·1	104·8
1960/1	93·5	93·6	98·1	90·2	91·8
1961/2	97·4	105·7	99·1	86·1	127·3
1962/3	97·2	108·8	98·0	87·7	113·8
1963/4	95·9	98·9	100·5	88·7	106·2
1964/5	98·2	96·8	104·2	90·8	116·5
1965/6	99·5	95·1	104·9	93·3	118·5

(a) Excluding store stock.

Prices 4. Indices of Retail Prices – United Kingdom 1938–65

NOTE
SOURCE: *Abstract.*

Part A. Working Class Cost of Living Index

	All Items	Food	Clothing	Fuel and Light	Rent and Rates
	July 1914 = 100	1 September 1939 = 100			
1938	156	102	100	99	99
1939	158	102	103	101	100
1940	184	119	137	115	101
1941	199	122	177	125	101
1942	200	117	192	129	101
1943	199	120	169	134	101
1944	201	122	166	141	101
1945	203	123	167	149	102
1946	203·5	122	166	152	103
1947 (June)	203	117	166	155	108

Part B. Interim Index of Retail Prices

17 June 1947 = 100

	All Items	Food	Clothing	Fuel and Light	Rent and Rates	Household Durable Goods	Miscellaneous Goods	Services	Alcoholic Drink	Tobacco
Weights 1947	*1,000*	*348*	*97*	*65*	*88*	*71*	*35*	*79*	*217*	
1948	108	108·2	109·3	110·9	99·5	107·9	109·7	104·7	109·1	
1949	111	114·1	117·7	113·0	100·0	108·5	112·1	105·4	108·3	
1950	114	122·7	119·8	116·5	101·1	112·3	113·1	108·4	105·1	
1951	125	136·3	138·3	128·0	103·3	132·1	128·2	117·9	106·3	
1952 (15 Jan.)	132	149·7	147·1	140·1	104·2	136·6	137·3	123·9	108·5	

15 January 1952 = 100 (All Items: *17 June 1947 = 100*)

	All Items	Food	Clothing	Fuel and Light	Rent and Rates	Household Durable Goods	Miscellaneous Goods	Services	Alcoholic Drink	Tobacco
Weights 1952	*1,000*	*399*	*98*	*66*	*72*	*62*	*44*	*91*	*78*	*90*
1952	136	105·4	97·7	101·3	102·2	98·6	102·5	103·8	100·7	100·0
1953	140	111·3	95·6	106·5	107·7	96·1	100·9	108·2	101·2	100·3
1954	143	114·2	96·2	111·3	111·7	95·3	100·0	110·6	101·6	100·3
1955	149	122·8	96·5	117·6	115·0	96·8	101·9	115·1	102·8	100·9
1956	153·4	125·4	98·7	127·6	117·9	102·5	106·6	119·1	103·1	102·9

Prices 4. *continued*

Part C. Index of Retail Prices

	All Items	Food	Alcoholic Drink	Tobacco	Housing	Fuel and Light	Household Durable Goods	Clothing and Footwear	Transport and Vehicles	Miscellaneous Goods	Services
					17 January 1956 = 100						
Weights 1956	1,000	350	71	80	87	55	66	106	68	59	58
1956	102·0	102·2	101·3	103·5	102·8	101·3	101·0	100·6	102·1	102·4	103·5
1957	105·8	104·9	104·3	106·1	110·1	107·9	101·1	102·2	110·2	107·7	109·4
1958	109·0	107·1	105·8	107·8	121·7	113·3	100·5	103·0	112·9	113·0	114·5
1959	109·6	108·2	100·0	107·9	127·8	114·5	98·5	102·6	114·7	113·5	116·1
1960	110·7	107·4	98·2	111·9	131·7	117·3	98·3	103·9	118·1	115·0	120·1
1961	114·5	109·1	102·5	117·7	137·6	124·7	100·3	105·6	123·0	124·3	126·2
1962 (16 Jan.)	117·5	110·7	108·2	123·6	140·6	130·6	102·1	106·6	126·7	128·2	130·1
					16 January 1962 = 100						
Weights 1962	1,000	319	64	79	102	62	64	98	92	65	56
1962	101·6	102·3	100·3	100·0	103·3	101·3	100·4	102·0	100·5	100·6	101·9
Weights 1963	1,000	319	63	77	104	63	64	98	93	63	56
1963	103·6	104·8	102·3	100·0	108·4	106·0	100·1	103·5	100·5	101·9	104·0
Weights 1964	1,000	314	63	74	107	66	62	95	100	63	56
1964	107·0	107·8	107·9	105·8	114·0	109·3	102·3	104·9	102·1	105·0	106·9
Weights 1965	1,000	311	65	76	109	65	59	92	105	63	55
1965	112·1	111·6	117·1	118·0	120·5	114·5	104·8	107·0	106·7	109·0	112·7

Prices 5. Average Prices of Coal in London and for Export – 1938–65

NOTE
SOURCE: Article by the editor of *The Statist* in the *Journal of the Royal Statistical Society* annually.

(per ton)

Year	Best Yorks. House (a) s. d.	Average of all Exports shillings	Year	Best Yorks. House (a) s. d.	Average of all Exports shillings	Year	Best Yorks. House (a) s. d.	Average of all Exports shillings
1938	25 8	21·32	1948	54 9	74·07	1958	82 10	105·31
1939	25 4	21·12	1949	54 9	72·97	1959	81 7	87·06
1940	28 1	27·23	1950	53 0	73·65	1960	84 5	73·40
1941	30 10	32·22	1951	58 6	74·88	1961	89 9	72·04
1942	32 6	34·87	1952	64 11	94·38	1962	88 9	85·58
1943	34 11	36·91	1953	69 6	89·03	1963	89 11	87·4
1944	38 10	39·19	1954	62 6	86·75	1964	88 8	92·3
1945	42 8	40·27	1955	66 4	86·96	1965	88 1	96·3
1946	45 2	40·94	1956	74 3	105·41			
1947	48 2	47·61	1957	79 9	116·23			

(a) Rounded up to the nearest penny.

Prices 6. Average Prices of British Corn – England & Wales 1938–65

NOTES
[1] SOURCE: *Agricultural Statistics* (1965/6).
[2] The figures are straight averages of 52/3-weekly average prices as calculated from returns from towns prescribed under the Corn Returns Act, 1882.

[3] Subsidies, payments under the Cereal Deficiency Payments Scheme, etc., are excluded.

(per cwt.)

Year	Wheat s. d.	Barley s. d.	Oats s. d.	Year	Wheat s. d.	Barley s. d.	Oats s. d.
1938	6 9	10 2	7 7	1953	31 2	30 1	24 7
1939	5 0	8 10	6 11	1954	28 3	25 9	22 7
1940	10 0	18 2	13 4	1955	22 11	26 0	26 3
1941	14 8	24 0	14 8	1956	25 6	25 8	24 8
1942	15 11	45 8	14 11	1957	21 7	23 2	22 10
1943	16 3	31 5	15 8	1958	21 9	22 11	23 10
1944	14 11	26 5	16 3	1959	21 0	22 7	22 7
1945	14 5	24 5	16 5	1960	21 4	21 3	22 6
1946	14 10	24 3	16 3	1961	20 7	19 10	19 5
1947	16 9	24 0	18 3	1962	21 10	23 0	23 0
1948	21 0	26 10	20 10	1963	20 11	20 8	21 0
1949	23 3	25 10	21 0	1964	21 11	21 2	21 5
1950	25 10	27 11	21 7	1965	22 6	22 10	22 8
1951	28 8	38 10	26 2				
1952	29 7	32 7	26 9				

Prices 7. Average Prices of Middling American Raw Cotton Imports –
United Kingdom 1938–65

NOTE
SOURCE: Article by the editor of *The Statist* in the *Journal of the Royal Statistical Society* annually.

(pence per lb.)

1938	4·93	1948	23·23	1958	24·21
1939	5·95	1949	24·85	1959	21·49
1940	8·10	1950	36·15	1960	21·66
1941	9·14	1951	46·01	1961	23·27
1942	8·83	1952	38·92	1962	23·66
1943	7·83	1953	31·83	1963	22·80
1944	11·32	1954	32·72	1964	22·48
1945	12·75	1955	31·70	1965	22·49
1946	14·87	1956	26·95		
1947	21·21	1957	25·35		

Prices 8. Average Value of Cotton Piece Goods Exported – United Kingdom 1821–1965

NOTES

[1] SOURCES: 1821–84 – T. Ellison, *The Cotton Trade of Great Britain* (London, 1886), pullout table 2; 1885–1965 – *Annual Statement of Trade*.

[2] Exports ceased to be measured in linear yards after 1961, and that series cannot be continued subsequently. The values per square yard, shown here for 1961–5, can be taken back to 1920 from the original source.

(pence per linear yard, except as indicated)

1821	11·73	1860	3·49	1898	2·20	1935	4·71
1822	10·96	1861	3·38	1899	2·24	1936	4·86
1823	10·32	1862	4·07	1900	2·50	1937	5·31
1824	10·06	1863	5·28	1901	2·53	1938	5·30
1825	10·15	1864	6·01	1902	2·49	1939	5·25
1826	8·87	1865	5·34	1903	2·57	1940	7·38
1827	8·50	1866	5·39	1904	2·75	1941	8·48
1828	8·24	1867	4·50	1905	2·74	1942	11·03
1829	7·46	1868	4·05	1906	2·89	1943	12·21
1830	7·62	1869	4·18	1907	3·09	1944	12·45
1831	6·92	1870	3·90	1908	3·05	1945	14·71
1832	5·99	1871	3·73	1909	2·86	1946	17·57
1833	6·02	1872	3·97	1910	3·14	1947	21·12
1834	6·10	1873	3·86	1911	3·26	1948	25·69
1835	6·53	1874	3·63	1912	3·18	1949	26·89
1836	6·47	1875	3·61	1913	3·32	1950	28·28
1837	5·75	1876	3·28	1914	3·31	1951	35·85
1838	5·41	1877	3·26	1915	3·27	1952	32·91
1839	5·37	1878	3·17	1916	4·06	1953	28·83
1840	4·95	1879	3·01	1917	5·44	1954	30·05
1841	4·79	1880	3·06	1918	8·99	1955	29·79
1842	4·21	1881	2·95	1919	12·20	1956	26·42
1843	3·96	1882	3·03	1920	(16·32) *(a)*	1957	27·49
1844	4·04	1883	2·92	1921	10·83	1958	31·15
1845	3·96	1884	2·81	1922	7·93	1959	30·35
1846	3·76	1885	2·65	1923	7·67	1960	31·66
1847	4·13	1886	2·48	1924	8·03	1961	33·57
1848	3·44	1887	2·53	1925	7·80	(pence per sq.yd.) *(b)*	
1849	3·37	1888	2·50	1926	7·10	1961	34·23
1850	3·63	1889	2·47	1927	6·30	1962	33·70
						1963	33·58
1851	3·43	1890	2·54	1928	6·49		
1852	3·41	1891	2·56	1929	6·33	1964	35·79
1853	3·60	1892	2·40	1930	5·91	1965	36·34
1854	3·33	1893	2·44	1931	5·00		
1855	3·24	1894	2·27	1932	4·55		
1856	3·36	1895	2·23	1933	4·56		
1857	3·49	1896	2·49	1934	4·64		
1858	3·31	1897	2·29				
1859	3·46						

(a) Exports were measured in square yards only in 1920. The 1921 ratio between square and linear yards has been used to convert the 1920 figure to linear yards in order to calculate this figure. The 1920 average value in pence per square yard was 17·08.

(b) The series in pence per square yard does not include a small quantity of knitted, netted, and crocheted piece goods which continue to be measured in linear yards only.

Prices 9. Prices of Iron and Steel – Great Britain 1938–65

NOTES

[1] SOURCES: First three columns – Article by the editor of *The Statist* in the *Journal of the Royal Statistical Society* annually; last column – British Iron and Steel Federation, *Statistical Yearbook* (later known as *Annual Statistics*).

[2] The series of steel prices, which was not given in the first *Abstract of British Historical Statistics*, can be taken back to 1923 in the source, and run as follows:

	£	s.	d.		£	s.	d.		£	s.	d.
1923	8	8	8	1928	6	5	0	1933	5	6	11
1924	7	19	5	1929	6	10	3	1934	5	10	2½
1925	7	5	1	1930	6	2	9	1935	5	10	0
1926	6	14	11	1931	5	6	4	1936	6	0	2½
1927	6	12	1	1932	5	5	5	1937	7	6	8

[3] The series of steel prices are stated in the source to be indicative of trends rather than based on actual sale prices.

(per ton)

	Scottish Pig Iron		Cleveland No. 3 Pig Iron		Common Iron Bars			Steels Billets (soft, basic)		
	s.	d.	s.	d.	£	s.	d.	£	s.	d.
1938	118	0	109	0	13	5	0	8	7	6
1939	104	3	100	7	12	7	6	7	15	10
1940	114	10	116	4	14	6	3	10	7	11
1941	123	0	128	0	15	12	6	12	10	0
1942	123	0	128	0	15	12	6	12	10	0
1943	123	0	128	0	15	12	6	12	10	0
1944	123	0	128	0	16	10	0	12	10	0
1945	139	11	140	6	18	0	0	12	10	0
1946	167	0	165	6	19	12	6	12	19	5
1947	176	9	175	5	20	8	9	13	6	3
1948	194	6	193	6	21	5	0	14	4	7
1949	228	11	204	7	20	0	0	16	8	2
1950	239	6	209	1	20	0	0	17	1	6
1951	252	1	221	10	21	17	6	19	3	6
1952	291	10	255	8	26	16	0	25	3	2
1953	328	9	274	10	28	7	6	26	0	11
1954	344	8	296	3	31	5	0	26	2	0
1955	372	4	324	7	38	17	6	26	9	1
1956	428	2	350	5	43	7	6	28	16	4
1957	464	6	401	0	45	0	0	32	1	5
1958	464	6	401	0	45	0	0	33	7	0
1959	464	6	401	0	45	0	0	32	13	9
1960	469	4	423	0	43	5	0	32	5	6
1961	470	0	426	0	43	0	0	32	8	11
1962	488	4	447	0	44	2	6	32	19	2
1963	488	3	445	2	44	0	0	33	0	6
1964	492	0	449	0	44	3	0	32	12	9
1965	492	0	449	0	44	3	0	32	14	10

Prices 10. Raw Wool Prices – United Kingdom 1938–65

NOTE

SOURCES: Lincoln and Port Philip – Article by the editor of *The Statist* in the *Journal of the Royal Statistical Society* annually import value – *Annual Statement of Trade*.

(pence per lb.)

	Lincoln Half-Hogg	Port Philip Merino Average Fleece	Average Import Value		Lincoln Half-Hogg	Port Philip Merino Average Fleece	Average Import Value
1938	11·9	18·6	11·2	1953	60·0	126·25	66·6
1939	12·2	17·9	10·3	1954	63·25	111·25	64·8
1940	19·4	29·6	14·5	1955	61·75	99·4	58·9
1941	21·0	32·0	15·3	1956	61·9	102·6	57·6
1942	21·0	32·0	15·7	1957	68·5	100·75	67·1
1943	21·0	32·0	16·6	1958	53·5	70·75	48·8
1944	21·0	32·0	16·7	1959	55·2	75·75	46·9
1945	21·1	31·6	16·8	1960	57·8	71·25	50·0
1946	20·7	35·2	19·0	1961	58·5	79·5	48·2
1947	22·7	58·2	23·2	1962	58·25	85·5	47·5
1948	33·0	91·2	30·7	1963	59·75	64·3	53·4
1949	38·4	92·4	37·4	1964	66·83	63·62	61·2
1950	65·75	157·45	63·2	1965	53·7	87·3	49·6
1951	99·0	177·25	113·1				
1952	49·5	120·0	59·0				

CHAPTER XVII

MISCELLANEOUS STATISTICS

TABLES

1. Crimes (Indictable Offences) Known to the Police – England & Wales 1857–1965, and Scotland 1868–1965.
2. Proceedings and Convictions in Courts of Summary Jurisdiction – England & Wales 1857–1965, and Scotland 1868–1965.
3. Trials and Convictions in Superior Courts – England & Wales 1805–1965, and Scotland 1830–1965.
4. Bankruptcies – Great Britain 1870–1965.
5. General Elections – United Kingdom 1885–1966.
6. Primary Schools – England & Wales, and Scotland 1850–1966.
7. Secondary Schools – England & Wales 1905–66, and Scotland 1899–1966.
8. Direct Grant and Independent Schools – England & Wales 1946–66.
9. University Education – Great Britain 1922–65.

The tables in this chapter all cover topics which were not included in the first *Abstract of British Historical Statistics*. The first three tables give the main summary aggregates from the vast array of criminal statistics available from 1857 onwards, and the smaller number going back still earlier. The most important sources of these statistics are referred to in the notes to each table, and much more information is to be found there, especially on the nature of offences and on local statistics. These statistics – and especially those of crimes known to the police, given in table 1 – have been subjected to considerable criticism, both n the nineteenth century and more recently. They were much discussed in articles in the *Journal of the Statistical Society*, especially up to the 1860s, but again also in the 1890s, and, by Lodge, in 1953 (Series A). A recent critic, J. J. Tobias, *Crime and Industrial Society in the 19th Century* (London, 1967), thinks that their defects 'are enough to rule out any use of national totals'. But he bases his conclusion largely on the belief that 'the national totals are as strong only as the weakest component'. For most statistical purposes this is surely not true. The weaknesses of the statistics of different areas at different times can be expected to have some mutually offsetting effect, at any rate once the system of reporting and recording has been established for a few years. It is, at any rate, in the belief that the law of large numbers will operate in the case of the criminal statistics that they have been included here: but the user is warned to take care.

Tables 4 and 5, showing respectively bankruptcies and electoral statistics, bear no direct relation to any others, and are in any case fairly straightforward, so no further comment is made here. Further electoral statistics may be found in the sources mentioned in the notes to table 5, and additionally in the following books and articles: H. B. Berrington, 'The General Election of 1964', *Journal of the Royal Statistical Society* (series A, 1965); D. E. Butler and J. Freeman, *British Political Facts* (2nd edition, London, 1968); D. E. Butler and Donald Stokes, *Political Change in Britain* (London, 1969); F. W. S. Craig, *British Parliamentary Election Statistics, 1918–1968* (Glasgow, 1969); B. R. Mitchell and Klaus Boehm, *British Parliamentary Election Results, 1950–1964* (Cambridge, 1966); the Nuffield Studies of general elections from 1950, written first by H. G. Nicholas and then by D. E. Butler (recently with co-authors).

Finally there are four tables of educational statistics, selected from the much greater amount of badly organised material which is available in the sources. We hesitated for some time before deciding to include the nineteenth-century education statistics, because the material is far from easily tractable. The authorities changed the coverage of the statistics which they collected, and their methods of calculation too, on numerous occasions, often with little to indicate to the user what changes had taken place. We have attempted to compile consistent series and to indicate the major breaks so far as possible; but it is certain that we have not been wholly successful. Moreover, the figures for this period do not include privately financed schools even though they were at that time a relatively important part of the educational system. The statistics up to about 1900, then, must be taken only as rough indicators of the growth of the public educational system. Coverage after 1900 was greatly improved, and changes were much more clearly indicated; though privately financed schools continued to be excluded. Finally, after the Second World War, comprehensive statistics become available.

Whilst the schools statistics up to the twentieth century are incomplete but usable, those for universities have too many gaps before 1922 to be worth including here. Accordingly table 9 begins at that date.

Miscellaneous Statistics 1. Crimes (Indictable Offences) Known to the Police – England & Wales 1857–1965, and Scotland 1868–1965

NOTES

[1] SOURCE: *Judicial Statistics* (later called *Criminal Statistics*) published for each year, separately for England & Wales and for Scotland, in Sessional Papers.

[2] The English figures for years up to and including 1892, and the Scottish figure for 1868, are for twelve months ended 29 September in the year indicated. All other figures are for calendar years.

[3] The Scottish figures up to 1896 are for crimes and offences, i.e. they include the equivalent of non-indictable offences in England.

[4] The English figures do not include certain offences which may be tried either on indictment or summarily.

	Total		Against the Person		Against Property with Violence		Against Property without Violence	
	E. & W.	Scot.	E. & W.	Scot.	E. & W.	Scot.	E. & W.	Scot.
1857	91,671	...	2,787	...	6,471	...	77,795	...
1858	92,511	...	2,709	...	5,723	...	80,261	...
1859	85,459	...	2,579	...	4,433	...	74,811	...
1860	82,859	...	2,200	...	4,065	...	73,605	...
1861	88,480	...	2,473	...	5,062	...	77,913	...
1862	94,538	...	2,536	...	5,746	...	82,504	...
1863	92,768	...	2,966	...	5,433	...	80,358	...
1864	89,948	...	3,091	...	5,022	...	78,371	...
1865	92,522	...	3,123	...	5,160	...	80,655	...
1866	89,302	...	2,861	...	5,088	...	78,484	...
1867	96,085	...	2,799	...	5,911	...	84,278	...
1868	101,369	103,999	2,964	...	6,355	...	88,791	...
1869	100,400	108,357	2,956	7,113	6,046	24,758	88,079	...
1870	90,532	118,105	2,707	7,351	5,197	23,886	79,615	...
1871	81,973	121,571	2,626	7,625	4,209	22,486	72,398	...
1872	81,261	129,812	2,586	8,277	3,940	22,309	72,142	...
1873	83,230	133,356	2,542	8,690	4,029	23,423	73,991	...
1874	86,171	132,207	2,881	9,055	4,176	23,567	76,204	...
1875	82,316	123,169	3,219	9,139	4,124	22,722	72,265	...
1876	85,423	124,803	3,236	8,844	4,135	23,618	75,299	...
1877	88,882	128,042	3,006	8,865	4,546	26,014	78,637	...
1878	93,743	124,963	2,869	8,182	6,744	26,078	81,019	...
1879	91,137	111,862	2,579	7,439	5,926	26,034	79,611	...
1880	98,440	122,656	2,855	8,522	6,782	25,999	85,289	...
1881	97,105	123,730	2,879	8,514	6,698	25,187	84,237	...
1882	100,258	127,093	3,237	9,059	7,112	25,364	86,635	...
1883	95,757	130,006	2,809	...	6,126	...	83,536	...
1884	92,342	126,643	3,165	...	6,078	...	79,575	...
1885	86,905	114,865	3,073	...	5,999	...	74,308	...
1886	87,206	115,830	3,626	...	6,630	...	73,530	...
1887	85,370	120,404	3,470	...	6,637	...	71,850	...
1888	88,152	124,215	3,567	...	6,884	...	74,601	...
1889	86,880	128,354	3,424	...	6,545	...	73,864	...
1890	81,773	136,565	3,513	...	6,095	...	69,175	...
1891	79,734	134,000	3,352	...	5,938	...	67,568	...

See p. 202 for footnotes.

Miscellaneous Statistics 1. *continued*

	Total		Against the Person		Against Property with Violence		Against Property without Violence	
	E. & W.	Scot.	E. & W.	Scot.	E. & W.	Scot.	E. & W.	Scot.
1892	85,200	136,014	3,461	...	6,780	...	71,755	...
1893	86,396	134,185	3,919	...	7,978	...	71,242	...
1894	86,052	139,288	3,877	...	7,854	...	71,110	...
1895	81,323	134,357	3,873	...	7,889	...	66,270	...
1896	78,614	143,684	3,832	...	7,631	...	63,929	...
		——— *(a)*						
1897	78,905	32,632	3,768	5,775	7,999	3,205	63,826	19,184
1898	82,426	33,118	3,867	5,712	8,768	3,171	66,317	19,639
1899	76,025	32,632	3,668	5,312	7,354	3,150	61,447	19,420
1900	77,934	33,492	3,490	5,059	7,764	3,509	63,604	19,841
1901	80,962	34,940	3,664	5,040	8,753	4,097	65,088	20,770
1902	83,260	34,515	3,551	5,125	9,093	3,977	66,878	20,345
1903	86,172	35,735	3,521	5,115	9,920	4,736	68,645	21,046
1904	92,907	38,833	3,384	4,626	10,857	4,751	74,443	24,766
1905	94,654	39,804	3,512	4,533	11,082	4,681	75,828	25,791
1906	91,665	40,397	3,758	4,761	10,868	4,540	72,840	26,507
1907	98,822	42,115	3,916	4,862	11,745	4,481	78,799	27,871
1908	105,279	42,161	3,821	4,666	13,485	5,172	83,514	27,699
1909	105,287	39,599	3,893	3,656	13,799	5,637	83,130	26,327
1910	103,132	38,376	3,934	3,798	13,692	4,354	80,894	25,618
1911	97,171	36,774	4,185	4,260	12,294	4,141	76,044	23,862
1912	101,997	38,506	4,613	4,647	12,292	4,836	80,607	24,427
1913	97,933	38,569	4,710	5,002	12,291	4,641	76,523	24,280
1914	89,387	37,594	4,218	4,663	10,850	4,891	70,124	23,586
1915	77,972	33,915	3,450	3,502	7,384	3,642	63,941	21,183
1916	80,653	31,526	3,202	2,485	8,567	4,094	66,874	21,764
1917	88,864	31,524	2,733	1,923	10,388	5,181	73,881	21,200
1918	87,762	29,187	2,950	1,701	11,224	5,071	71,979	19,124
1919	87,827	33,922	4,187	2,689	13,736	6,540	67,357	20,957
1920	100,827	39,444	4,616	4,234	15,863	6,924	77,417	24,620
1921	103,258	39,943	4,239	3,332	16,408	7,560	79,724	25,205
1922	107,230	36,876	4,288	2,792	18,040	6,818	82,201	23,861
1923	110,206	35,369	4,299	2,893	18,033	6,129	84,791	23,011
1924	112,574	32,527	4,419	3,014	18,312	5,933	86,775	20,173
1925	113,986	33,070	4,621	3,001	18,072	6,618	88,058	19,990
1926	133,460	38,478	5,147	2,964	19,733	7,848	104,842	23,251
1927	125,703	31,204	5,379	2,847	19,648	7,673	96,191	17,397
1928	130,469	33,506	5,295	3,004	22,172	8,831	98,624	18,173
1929	134,581	35,301	5,461	3,000	22,897	9,765	101,400	18,938
1930	147,031	36,723	5,669	3,096	26,248	10,327	110,159	19,455
1931	159,278	38,410	5,283	2,965	31,671	12,360	117,099	19,348
1932	208,175	48,734	5,180	2,865	40,509	16,007	156,639	26,201
1933	227,285	49,834	5,614	2,927	37,414	16,266	178,241	26,946
1934	233,359	51,951	6,236	2,984	36,994	16,395	183,940	28,604
1935	234,372	59,753	6,266	3,238	36,475	16,492	185,660	35,434
1936	248,803	59,407	6,903	3,368	38,702	15,169	197,121	34,759

See p. 202 for footnotes

Miscellaneous Statistics 1. *continued*

	Total		Against the Person		Against Property with Violence		Against Property without Violence	
	E. & W.	Scot.	E. & W.	Scot.	E. & W.	Scot.	E. & W.	Scot.
1937	266,265	58,860	7,369	3,370	45,448	13,902	207,342	34,225
1938	283,220	58,976	7,739	3,643	49,565	14,909	219,481	33,789
1939	303,771	60,104	7,914	3,081	52,655	15,548	237,036	34,482
1940	305,114	62,266	7,050	2,636	49,752	15,757	242,669	36,473
1941	358,655	67,494	8,335	2,779	53,417	16,940	290,130	40,654
1942	364,889	69,127	9,816	2,833	56,925	17,920	288,868	41,460
1943	372,760	70,944	11,216	2,983	59,330	19,643	293,150	42,012
1944	415,010	71,583	12,241	3,051	74,778	21,394	319,852	40,203
1945	478,394	86,075	13,289	2,701	109,386	32,168	346,564	42,900
1946	472,489	76,608	13,391	2,489	115,698	27,224	332,860	39,837
1947	498,576	75,195	14,407	2,496	112,893	25,744	358,353	39,987
1948	522,684	81,683	16,105	2,425	113,889	30,090	377,728	41,912
1949	459,869	70,646	17,250	2,354	92,578	25,573	336,155	36,639
1950	461,435	74,640	19,434	2,423	93,978	27,026	334,222	38,529
1951	524,506	83,008	21,149	2,756	96,820	27,901	392,538	44,695
1952	513,359	82,282	21,964	2,691	99,063	28,420	377,930	43,867
1953	472,989	76,866	23,400	2,931	89,695	27,151	344,127	39,517
1954	434,327	74,974	23,602	2,967	76,804	27,355	317,934	37,426
1955	438,085	74,773	24,962	2,810	75,822	25,938	325,017	39,195
1956	479,710	79,753 ----- (*b*)	26,410	2,848	86,852	28,636	353,805	41,290
1957	545,562	80,231 ----- (*c*)	29,595	3,242	106,357	32,745	395,839	42,290
1958	626,509	91,983	29,828	3,481	132,988	42,949	448,805	43,436
1959	675,626	95,672	33,900	3,744	136,022	43,687	490,203	45,998
1960	743,713	102,617	35,696	4,298	153,633	45,813	537,003	50,012
1961	806,900	108,920	38,005	4,216	167,540	49,882	584,858	52,181
1962	896,424	117,824	37,958	4,508	195,069	54,847	648,487	55,324
1963	978,076	128,399	40,601	4,604	221,878	61,517	699,227	58,688
1964	1,067,963	133,654	43,373	5,517	237,277	60,869	769,852	63,538
1965	1,133,882	140,141	45,703	6,345	256,848	64,232	811,869	65,155

(*a*) See note [3] above. The figure for 1897 which compares with the earlier series is 143,188.
(*b*) Subsequently no longer includes petty cases of malicious injury to property and cases of false fire alarms.

(*c*) Subsequently no longer includes cases of taking a motor vehicle without the owner's consent.

Miscellaneous Statistics 2. Proceedings and Convictions in Courts of Summary Jurisdiction – England & Wales 1857–1965, Scotland 1868–1965

NOTES

[1] SOURCE: *Judicial Statistics* (later called *Criminal Statistics*) published for each year, separately for England & Wales and for Scotland in Sessional Papers.

[2] The English figures for years up to and including 1892, and the Scottish figures for 1868, are for twelve months ended 29 September in the year indicated. All other figures are for calendar years.

(in thousands)

	England & Wales				Scotland			
	Persons Dealt with Summarily for Offences		Convictions		Persons Proceeded against Summarily for		Convictions	
	Indictable	Non-indictable	Indictable	Non-indictable	Crimes (i.e. indictable)	Offences (i.e. non-indictable)	Crimes	Offences
1857	34·4	329·0	233·8					
1858	34·6	355·5	260·3					
1859	33·4	343·9	257·8					
1860	32·5	338·7	255·8					
1861	37·7	343·2	263·5					
1862	41·3	352·9	273·0					
1863	40·6	365·0	283·6					
1864	38·9	386·5	300·7					
1865	40·3	402·6	312·9					
1866	38·8	427·1	339·1					
1867	40·5	417·1	335·4					
1868	42·3	430·0	347·5		87·2		81·9	
1869	42·0	457·5	372·7		90·8		84·8	
1870	38·6	467·4	389·7		101·5		95·2	
1871	36·8	482·2	407·9		95·0		87·9	
1872	37·1	499·7	423·6		101·1		94·6	
1873	38·6	530·6	456·7		103·8		97·4	
1874	38·3	559·4	486·8		109·9		103·1	
1875	35·3	589·6	512·4		124·2		117·2	
1876	35·9	599·9	526·9		120·8		114·0	
1877	38·0	590·1	519·8		120·8		113·1	
1878	39·7	606·4	538·2		119·6		112·3	
1879	38·7	573·9	506·3		104·5		96·9	
1880	46·0	589·1	517·4		117·0		108·7	
1881	45·9	595·3	531·0		117·2		108·7	
1882	48·1	637·6	575·6		120·5		111·9	
1883	46·2	651·7	588·7		104·3		96·3	
1884	45·3	648·9	583·3		105·1		97·0	
1885	42·9	613·2	548·4		95·4		88·0	
1886	42·3	572·0	509·1		97·7		90·1	
1887	43·0	594·9	529·4		101·4		93·9	
1888	44·8	598·4	538·9		106·1		98·9	
1889	45·6	616·2	559·0		108·4		101·0	
1890	43·1	667·8	605·9		113·0		105·3	
1891	42·5	663·2	602·6		112·3		104·8	
1892	46·2	640·6	579·9		113·8		105·2	
	--- (a)	---- (a)	—— (b)					

See p. 205 for footnotes.

(in thousands)

	England & Wales				Scotland			
	Persons Dealt with Summarily for Offences		Convictions		Persons Proceeded against Summarily for		Convictions	
	Indictable	Non-indictable	Indictable	Non-indictable	Crimes (i.e. indictable)	Offences (i.e. non-indictable)	Crimes	Offences
1893	45·1	600·2	34·1	471·1	113·7		105·0	
1894	44·2	630·3	34·0	494·7	119·1		112·1	
1895	39·3	624·6	30·6	490·2	114·1		107·2	
1896	39·6	666·0	31·0	525·7	122·3		115·3	
1897	39·5	694·6	31·4	553·3	21·6	130·5	16·8	94·0
1898	41·1	739·3	32·8	600·7	21·8	141·8	16·8	103·0
1899	39·6	755·5	31·9	616·5	22·0	152·4	17·0	110·3
1900	43·5	706·8	35·3	581·4	24·0	153·7	18·7	110·9
1901	44·7	727·9	36·4	602·1	24·1	160·2	19·1	118·2
1902	45·7	721·5	37·5	596·7	33·2	156·9	18·2	115·7
1903	46·6	737·6	38·6	612·1	23·1	140·4	18·4	103·8
1904	47·8	740·3	39·6	615·8	23·5	138·0	18·7	103·3
1905	49·1	724·0	40·8	599·6	23·7	138·3	18·4	103·5
1906	46·3	695·9	38·4	573·7	19·2	114·6	17·9	111·8
1907	48·8	680·6	39·9	557·1	23·5	155·2	18·4	115·7
1908	54·0	683·8	33·0	548·2	25·0	152·3	18·6	115·1
1909	53·4	654·5	31·8	519·9	23·3	130·1	17·4	99·1
1910	52·7	631·9	29·2	496·7	23·8	125·0	16·9	93·8
1911	49·4	635·1	27·2	500·9	23·4	130·8	16·8	96·9
1912	54·2	663·1	29·5	526·0	25·5	135·9	18·5	100·2
1913	50·8	680·3	27·1	542·8	24·7	147·3	17·6	106·9
1914	47·8	626·8	24·9	491·8	24·0	141·8	17·0	102·1
1915	49·5	532·4	24·9	423·4	22·9	119·3	16·2	76·3
1916	53·6	610·2	28·2	512·5	19·6	106·7	13·8	71·6
1917	57·4	445·8	31·0	362·8	21·1	82·7	14·8	51·4
1918	52·5	375·1	28·4	299·6	18·9	60·5	13·5	36·0
1919	45·7	493·0	25·3	397·1	19·2	81·1	14·0	54·4
1920	51·5	611·8	28·1	497·1	20·8	120·7	15·6	83·5
1921	52·4	523·7	28·5	419·3	24·1	89·7	18·7	65·9
1922	49·7	524·7	25·0	421·8	20·5	84·1	14·7	65·4
1923	48·6	546·6	22·6	441·9	19·5	86·4	14·6	67·2
1924	49·5	584·5	21·5	477·5	19·4	91·0	14·7	70·5
1925	49·4	610·8	21·2	499·2	19·8	94·2	14·8	73·6
1926	69·7	602·6	33·3	492·2	28·1	92·8	21·9	73·9
1927	56·3	617·8	25·2	513·2	19·5	99·5	14·6	78·5
1928	54·2	597·6	23·0	493·9	18·7	98·6	13·8	78·4
1929	52·8	585·4	21·9	480·1	18·3	97·2	13·0	77·4
1930	55·7	609·7	22·6	499·2	18·7	89·6	13·4	71·0
1931	58·3	572·0	24·2	462·1	19·1	83·4	13·8	67·0
1932	62·1	540·3	26·1	436·8	20·1	75·3	14·7	61·5
1933	61·3	578·4	24·9	473·3	20·2	74·9	14·7	61·6

(in thousands)

	England & Wales				Scotland			
	Persons Proceeded against for Offences (c)		Persons Found Guilty at Summary Courts (c)		Persons Proceeded against Summarily for		Persons Found Guilty at Summary Courts (c)	
	Indictable	Non-indict-able (d)	Indictable	Non-indict-able (d)	Crimes	Offences (d)	Crimes	Offences (d)
1933	72·2	581·5	54·9	541·0	20·2	74·9	17·9	62·4
1934	75·8	634·2	58·4	592·0	21·0	81·6	18·8	70·9
1935	79·6	733·2	63·0	689·6	21·1	95·3	18·9	83·9
1936	82·5	795·7	65·7	752·2	21·6	106·1	19·5	94·3
1937	87·3	770·4	69·9	727·8	21·5	113·3	19·4	100·4
1938	88·3	751·2	69·9	709·0	21·1	115·4	19·2	102·0
1939	86·6	658·5 (d)	69·6	617·8 (d)	21·2	111·2	19·0	96·7
1940	99·0	764·7 (d)	83·1	713·8 (d)	24·2	123·6 (d)	21·8	101·4 (d)
1941	118·7	760·9 (d)	99·1	695·1 (d)	25·7	121·4 (d)	23·1	95·1 (d)
1942	118·3	641·5 (d)	97·3	581·8 (d)	26·1	101·4 (d)	23·4	79·6 (d)
1943	115·5	508·5 (d)	94·6	464·6 (d)	25·7	87·6 (d)	23·2	69·7 (d)
1944	118·8	435·2 (d)	96·0	393·6 (d)	24·5	80·3 (d)	22·3	66·2 (d)
1945	128·7	388·8 (d)	101·9	351·4 (d)	26·5	64·1 (d)	24·2	53·5 (d)
1946	119·8	467·8 (d)	92·0	434·4 (d)	22·4	75·5 (d)	20·3	64·3 (d)
1947	128·5	554·1 (d)	97·7	517·4 (d)	21·6	82·7 (d)	19·7	71·2 (d)
1948	141·6	589·5	108·7	547·5	24·1	82·3	22·1	71·4
1949	124·4	575·9	96·9	536·1	21·0	83·4	19·2	72·2
1950	125·6	612·6	99·0	572·5	22·0	85·4	20·2	74·7
1951	143·6	632·6	114·8	590·4	24·3	86·9	22·5	76·0
1952	141·3	663·0	111·1	621·9	25·2	91·0	23·3	79·6
1953	124·9	627·4	97·6	588·6	22·6	95·7	21·1	84·0
1954	114·4	657·2	89·7	619·2	21·4	100·0	19·9	88·2
1955	115·2	665·3	91·2	627·8	21·7	105·4	20·3	93·2
1956	124·0	704·7	98·2	668·3	22·9	114·7	21·5	101·3
1957	140·2	771·1	110·2	733·5	22·5	119·3	21·2	106·2
1958	157·1	886·5	121·5	846·7	23·9	129·0	22·5	116·8
1959	163·0	927·9	126·3	887·6	24·6	141·7	23·2	129·8
1960	174·7	912·5	135·7	871·7	25·1	150·0	23·7	138·0
1961	192·7	1,013·6	150·9	970·2	27·9	142·1	26·3	130·2
1962	212·5	1,107·1	174·2	1,062·8	30·4	145·0	28·7	133·4
1963	222·6	1,154·1	189·5	1,107·4	32·7	149·1	30·5	138·2
1964	220·8	1,177·2	184·9	1,122·4	30·8	156·0	28·9	145·5
1965	235·1	1,203·9	196·1	1,149·6	32·5	159·9	30·2	148·6

(a) There is a break here owing to a reorganisation of the statistics. In the 1893 and subsequent volumes of *Judicial Statistics*, however, comparative tables were published which adjusted the 1857–92 figures to the new basis so far as possible. Later still slightly revised figures were published for non-indictable offences back to 1893. The figure for the latter in 1893 shown in the 1893 volume, and supposedly quite closely comparable with earlier figures, was 604·3.

(b) No comparative table was published for convictions, and it is impossible to estimate the size of the break here.

(c) The figures of those proceeded against summarily can be pushed back much earlier than this, and the decision to make the break at this point has been made because it is no longer possible to give exactly comparable figures of convictions after 1933. The figures of persons found guilty at summary courts can also be pushed back much further in the original sources. The English figures for those proceeded against for offences include people tried in superior courts.

(d) Including offences against the Defence Regulations at all times. For the period when these were important, the numbers of such offences and findings of guilty are shown below.

	Persons Proceeded against for Offences against the Defence Regulations		Persons Found Guilty of Offences against the Defence Regulations	
	E. & W.	Scot.	E. & W.	Scot.
1939	61·4	—	59·9	—
1940	340·3	35·6	332·4	34·7
1941	286·4	34·0	278·1	32·9
1942	234·5	27·0	227·4	26·0
1943	194·8	24·5	186·4	23·2
1944	144·1	22·6	137·7	21·5
1945	58·1	7·6	54·0	7·0
1946	22·4	3·2	20·2	3·1
1947	20·9	2·4	18·7	2·3

Miscellaneous Statistics 3. Trials and Convictions in Superior Courts – England & Wales 1805–1965, Scotland 1830–1965

NOTES

[1] SOURCES: 1805–57 – *Returns of Criminal Offenders* and/or *of Committals*, published from time to time in Sessional Papers; after 1857 – *Judicial Statistics* (later called *Criminal Statistics*), published for each year, separately for England & Wales and for Scotland, in Sessional Papers.

[2] In the earlier years a few people tried by lower courts on criminal charges are included in the statistics. This practice ceased after 1892 in England & Wales, but it is not clear when it ceased in Scotland.

[3] The figures of convictions in England & Wales include those of incorrigible rogues sent for sentence to Quarter Sessions.

[4] The figures of convictions in Scotland do not include those outlawed or cases where bail was forfeited for non-appearance.

	Numbers for Trial		Numbers Convicted	
	E. & W.	Scot.	E. & W.	Scot.
1805	4,605	...	2,783	...
1806	4,346	...	2,515	...
1807	4,446	...	2,567	...
1808	4,735	...	2,723	...
1809	5,330	...	3,238	...
1810	5,146	...	3,158	...
1811	5,337	...	3,163	...
1812	6,576	...	3,913	...
1813	7,164	...	4,422	...
1814	6,390	...	4,025	...
1815	7,818	...	4,883	...
1816	9,091	...	5,797	...
1817	13,932	...	9,056	...
1818	13,567	...	8,958	...
1819	14,254	...	...	...
1820	13,710	...	9,318	...
1821	13,115	...	8,788	...
1822	12,241	...	8,209	...
1823	12,263	...	8,204	...
1824	13,698	...	9,425	...
1825	14,437	...	9,964	...
1826	16,164	...	11,107	...
1827	17,924	...	12,567	...
1828	16,564	...	11,723	...
1829	18,675	...	13,261	...
1830	18,107	1,429	12,805	1,274
1831	19,647	...	13,830	...
1832	20,829	1,758	14,947	1,577
1833	20,072	2,038	14,446	1,796
1834	20,168	1,987	14,261	1,790
	——— (a)		——— (a)	
1834	22,451		15,995	
1835	20,731	2,156	14,729	1,902
1836	20,984	2,414	14,771	2,152
1837	23,612	2,594	17,090	2,332
1838	23,094	2,885	16,785	2,623
1839	24,443	2,837	17,832	2,585
1840	27,187	3,213	19,927	2,909
1841	27,760	2,907	20,280	2,667
1842	31,309	3,572	22,733	3,145
1843	29,591	2,937	21,092	2,584
1844	26,542	3,023	18,919	2,719

	Numbers for Trial		Numbers Convicted	
	E. & W.	Scot.	E. & W.	Scot.
1845	24,303	2,973	17,402	2,679
1846	25,107	3,409	18,144	3,092
1847	28,833	3,881	21,542	3,558
1848	30,349	3,975	22,900	3,689
1849	27,816	3,543	21,001	3,274
1850	26,813	3,638	20,537	3,363
1851	27,960	3,328	21,579	3,070
1852	27,510	3,288	21,304	3,018
1853	27,057	3,109	20,756	2,821
1854	29,359	3,994	23,047	2,989
1855	25,972	3,630	19,971	2,689
1856	19,437	3,713	14,734	2,723
1857	20,269	3,840	15,307	2,920
1858	17,855	3,782	13,246	2,850
1859	16,674	3,472	12,470	2,563
1860	15,999	3,287	12,068	2,414
1861	18,326	3,229	13,879	2,418
1862	20,001	3,630	15,312	2,693
1863	20,818	3,404	15,799	2,438
1864	19,506	3,212	14,726	2,359
1865	19,614	3,117	14,740	2,355
1866	18,849	3,003	14,254	2,292
1867	18,971	3,305	14,207	2,510
1868	20,091	3,384	15,033	2,490
1869	19,318	3,510	14,340	2,592
1870	17,578	3,046	12,953	2,400
1871	16,269	2,948	11,946	2,184
1872	14,801	3,044	10,862	2,259
1873	14,893	2,755	11,089	2,110
	----- (b)			
1874	15,111	2,880	11,509	2,231
1875	14,665	2,872	10,954	2,205
1876	16,012	2,716	12,195	2,051
1877	15,809	2,684	11,942	2,009
1878	16,305	2,922	12,473	2,273
1879	16,303	2,700	12,525	2,091
1880	14,711	2,583	11,214	2,046
1881	14,708	2,444	11,353	1,832
1882	15,190	2,469	11,699	1,943
1883	14,572	2,567	11,347	1,916
1884	14,336	2,610	11,134	2,085

See p. 207 for footnotes.

	Numbers for Trial		Numbers Convicted			Numbers for Trial		Numbers Convicted	
	E. & W.	Scot.	E. & W.	Scot.		E. & W.	Scot.	E. & W.	Scot.
1885	13,494	2,535	10,500	1,956	1925	8,139	1,196	6,639	953
1886	13,923	2,437	10,686	1,838	1926	7,924	1,197	6,350	994
1887	13,215	2,357	10,338	1,843	1927	7,136	1,214	5,773	963
1888	13,684	2,352	10,561	1,853	1928	7,282	1,180	6,019	929
1889	12,006	2,250	9,348	1,737	1929	7,072	1,049	5,879	872
1890	11,897	2,312	9,242	1,825	1930	8,384	1,131	6,921	894
1891	11,605	2,354	9,055	1,823	1931	8,667	1,174	7,389	932
1892	12,130	2,252	9,607	1,778	1932	10,410	1,199	8,968	957
			- - - - (c)		1933	9,201	1,307	7,759	1,083
1893	12,296	2,394	9,694	1,903	1934	8,675	1,395	7,297	1,114
1894	12,033	2,371	9,518	1,937					
					1935	8,270	1,303	6,828	1,014
1895	11,516	2,027	6,155	1,652	1936	8,492	1,217	7,079	1,006
1896	11,103	2,120	8,745	1,704	1937	9,083	1,142	7,649	928
1897	11,215	2,203	8,867	1,796	1938	10,003	1,130	8,612	912
1898	11,454	2,290	9,133	1,877	1939	9,751	1,072	8,428	858
1899	10,902	2,153	8,608	1,785					
					1940 (d)	7,829	1,271	6,825	1,072
1900	10,149	2,167	7,975	1,835	1941	10,079	1,931	8,832	1,646
1901	10,797	2,291	8,631	1,872	1942	11,565	1,907	10,176	1,512
1902	11,392	2,477	9,138	2,052	1943	11,944	2,480	10,653	2,007
1903	11,882	2,590	9,642	2,114	1944	12,279	1,656	10,894	1,434
1904	12,158	2,631	9,918	2,208					
					1945	15,903	1,886	14,397	1,612
1905	12,325	2,832	10,118	2,314	1946	17,750	1,843	16,062	1,505
1906	12,757	2,631	10,390	2,157	1947	20,216	1,831	18,138	1,485
1907	12,599	2,456	10,382	2,102	1948	23,018	1,771	20,890	1,434
1908	14,122	2,559	11,628	2,115	1949	19,544	1,638	17,552	1,400
1909	13,749	1,977	11,328	1,618					
					1950	19,935	1,618	17,149	1,357
1910	13,680	1,488	11,337	1,225	1951	19,989	1,823	18,092	1,420
1911	12,951	1,401	10,646	1,121	1952	22,153	1,778	19,971	1,443
1912	13,286	1,533	10,931	1,189	1953	20,263	1,791	18,259	1,471
1913	12,511	1,358	10,165	1,056	1954	18,736	1,646	16,740	1,301
1914	10,800	1,292	8,668	1,012					
					1955	18,091	1,656	16,249	1,384
1915	6,010	1,095	4,677	822	1956	19,572	1,701	17,700	1,378
1916	5,011	1,085	3,878	874	1957	22,935	1,859	20,728	1,517
1917	5,586	997	4,384	826	1958	27,801	2,204	25,305	1,902
1918	5,904	780	4,694	630	1959	29,601	2,289	26,931	1,975
1919	7,883	1,294	6,192	1,018					
					1960	30,591	2,283	27,830	2,032
1920	9,130	1,550	7,225	1,231	1961	34,324	2,526	31,283	2,200
1921	8,934	1,825	7,152	1,386	1962	33,009	2,811	29,570	2,363
1922	8,435	1,774	6,784	1,413	1963	25,594	2,832	22,267	2,376
1923	8,126	1,415	6,541	1,170	1964	24,369	2,687	20,397	2,217
1924	7,845	1,188	6,379	981					
					1965	26,864	2,591	22,355	2,079

(a) Seven categories of offences were included in the figures for the first time in 1834. Figures are given here for that year both including and excluding these categories.

(b) The figures do not subsequently include incorrigible rogues sent for sentence to Quarter Sessions.

(c) See note [2] above.

(d) Subsequently includes offences against the Defence Regulations. For the period when these were of some significance these were as follows:

	Numbers for Trial England & Wales	Numbers Convicted England & Wales
1940	107	84
1941	373	312

	Numbers for Trial England & Wales	Numbers Convicted England & Wales
1942	387	327
1943	464	396
1944	407	348
1945	360	287
1946	253	214
1947	191	156
1948	269	221
1949	182	147
1950	156	140

Miscellaneous Statistics 4. Bankruptcies – Great Britain 1870–1965

NOTES
[1] SOURCE: *Abstract.*
[2] Scottish figures up to 1896 are for years ended 31 October.

Subsequent Scottish figures and all English ones are for calendar years.

	England & Wales						Scotland		
	Numbers Adjudicated Bankrupt	Bankrupts' Liabilities (£000)	Bankrupts' Assets (£000)	Number of Deeds of Arrangement	Liabilities Involved in Deeds (£000)	Assets Involved in Deeds (£000)	Sequestrations Awarded (a)	Bankrupts' Liabilities (£000)	Bankrupts' Assets (£000)
1870	1,351	7,933	1,966				555	1,004	434
1871	1,238	3,975	555				490	1,429	422
1872	933	2,650	622				368	1,002	492
1873	915	4,045	675				391	786	498
1874	930	3,789	485				382	798	353
1875	965	6,981	961				441	743	348
1876	976	3,834	518				482	2,269	1,113
1877	967	2,924	487				543	1,666	725
1878	1,084	9,287	1,951				717	1,614	748
1879	1,156	4,299	571				1,077	1,164	591
1880	995	2,733	337				582	1,243	602
1881	1,005	2,728	320				450	1,610	696
1882	995	3,367	401				452	14,296 (b)	871
1883	1,046	4,321	462				342	1,625	740
1884	2,998	8,590	2,192				406	7,596 (b)	521
1885	3,965	7,497	2,416				362	1,137	934
1886	4,566	6,673	2,101				450	1,337	294
1887	4,681	8,129	2,368				444	1,530	790
1888	4,695	6,584	2,013	3,495	4,803	2,417	442	1,804	721
1889	4,415	5,481	1,627	3,337	4,774	2,719	388	8,956 (b)	1,244
1890	3,924	5,526	1,787	3,097	4,360	2,353	339	7,994 (b)	454
1891	4,150	7,370	2,520	3,008	5,092	3,107	348	8,048 (b)	1,278
1892	4,575	8,531	2,996	3,333	5,957	2,937	346	1,548	543
1893	4,805	7,216	2,707	3,938	7,574	3,441	356	918	544
1894	4,702	6,791	2,296	3,894	6,419	3,162	341	7,504 (b)	560
1895	4,349	6,247	1,937	3,462	4,879	2,542	356	909	398
1896	4,109	5,796	2,275	3,271	4,480	2,339	317	1,475	626
1897	4,032	5,546	2,520	3,208	3,981	1,910	278	1,019	484
1898	4,247	6,686	2,451	3,246	3,847	1,979	282	873	788
1899	4,045	5,784	1,895	2,974	3,372	1,774	297	1,572	391
1900	4,343	6,325	2,555	3,354	4,264	2,487	341	662	322
1901	4,176	6,513	3,111	3,369	4,000	2,255	312	1,008	326
1902	4,145	5,435	2,729	3,305	4,483	2,757	294	1,918	470
1903	4,243	5,255	2,506	3,622	4,354	2,506	302	1,473	611
1904	4,481	6,801	2,757	4,085	5,125	2,967	317	693	310
							--- (a)	---- (c)	--- (c)
1905	4,700	5,785	2,287	3,839	3,759	2,047	259	538	178
1906	4,366	5,542	1,771	3,641	4,364	2,619	259	809	287
1907	4,051	5,440	1,828	3,488	5,215	3,101	257	805	227
1908	4,241	5,275	2,033	3,822	5,858	3,545	284	857	182
1909	3,998	5,600	2,035	3,491	3,911	2,033	278	880	287

See p. 210 for footnotes.

	England & Wales						Scotland		
	Numbers Adjudicated Bankrupt	Bankrupts' Liabilities (£000)	Bankrupts' Assets (£000)	Number of Deeds of Arrangement	Liabilities Involved in Deeds (£000)	Assets Involved in Deeds (£000)	Sequestrations Awarded (a)	Bankrupts' Liabilities (£000)	Bankrupts' Assets (£000)
1910	3,790	7,642	2,742	3,364	3,451	1,937	228	845	202
1911	3,670	6,526	1,923	2,950	4,006	2,084	230	1,010	311
1912	3,497	4,661	1,716	2,770	3,140	1,655	204	584	145
1913	3,275	4,900	1,659	2,411	2,766	1,513	169	410	87
1914	2,791	5,905	2,036	1,776	3,826	1,719	195	397	121
1915	2,285	3,465	1,088	1,652	2,064	996	199	424	102
1916	1,503	2,634	933	1,050	1,465	751	126	255	69
1917	1,045	1,637	1,119	612	1,026	529	109	326	52
1918	592	851	869	198	414	176	65	167	43
1919	709	1,740	615	165	551	320	65	73	18
1920	1,521	4,638	1,920	451	2,150	1,085	77	91	30
1921	3,397	13,359	3,856	1,368	8,067	4,908	209	583	173
1922	4,635	15,967	3,859	1,847	8,604	3,534	259	763	158
1923	4,965	10,515	2,269	1,808	5,249	2,472	291	707	148
1924	4,706	12,224	2,284	1,901	4,329	1,967	247	1,993	199
1925	4,627	9,946	1,907	1,877	4,455	1,974	248	690	148
1926	4,149	9,357	2,724	1,763	4,232	1,959	199	686	88
1927	4,234	8,015	1,737	1,856	4,392	1,967	252	463	151
1928	4,081	7,668	1,638	2,054	4,375	2,132	208	485	135
1929	3,856	8,890	2,637	1,971	5,263	2,496	216	791	99
1930	4,063	9,064	1,721	2,154	5,574	2,555	209	501	137
1931	4,317	10,787	2,154	2,415	5,412	2,685	203	1,213	128
1932	4,547	9,864	1,996	2,676	6,291	3,167	230	660	142
1933	4,030	6,366	1,250	2,102	3,818	1,771	202	417	89
1934	3,544	5,977	1,223	1,861	3,447	1,399	185	389	121
1935	3,449	5,565	1,034	1,635	5,166	1,592	156	233	49
1936	3,170	4,602	1,286	1,598	2,701	1,186	153	352	67
1937	3,034	5,144	1,002	1,630	3,500	1,825	140	261	60
1938	3,024	6,711	1,787	1,663	3,380	1,579	112	517	41
1939	2,590	6,278	1,195	1,417	2,568	1,318	112	179	41
1940	1,552	3,748	1,271	934	1,619	968	71	127	51
1941	575	1,391	489	184	335	233	38	89	13
1942	332	839	200	64	105	56	28	38	24
1943	229	694	177	44	164	83	21	49	57
1944	210	458	198	21	43	23	7	8	2
1945	194	542	203	26	50	29	17	50	25
1946	311	997	403	31	136	98	6	15	6
1947	607	1,618	498	90	198	141	23	70	12
1948	1,114	2,741	917	152	549	388	37	113	42
1949	1,463	4,639	1,168	202	1,123	609	59	176	62

See p. 210 for footnotes.

Miscellaneous Statistics 4. *continued*

	England & Wales						Scotland		
	Numbers Adjudicated Bankrupt	Bankrupts' Liabilities (£000)	Bankrupts' Assets (£000)	Number of Deeds of Arrangement	Liabilities Involved in Deeds (£000)	Assets Involved in Deeds (£000)	Sequestrations Awarded (a)	Bankrupts' Liabilities (£000)	Bankrupts' Assets (£000)
1950	1,797	5,414	1,702	232	866	463	71	362	113
1951	1,789	4,817	1,468	261	1,120	740	80	265	80
1952	1,987	6,374	1,681	301	1,253	700	125	713	158
1953	2,179	6,493	2,433	302	1,099	553	92	594	116
1954	2,142	6,533	2,172	315	1,376	670	90	601	198
1955	2,119	6,893	1,852	301	1,843	792	100	641	177
1956	2,081	6,444	1,994	325	1,399	889	77	543	133
1957	2,030	6,164	2,224	313	1,445	788	99	530	127
1958	2,215	7,656	1,959	276	1,538	910	85	486	160
1959	2,277	7,250	2,182	255	1,418	698	89	565	195
1960	2,767	10,415	2,087	276	1,677	810	82	816	173
1961	3,482	14,503	2,576	299	1,930	903	106	1,440	295
1962	4,112	14,237	3,089	315	3,779	2,349	85	917	184
1963	3,929	12,779	2,605	235	1,353	654	89	888	138
1964	3,333	13,173	3,641	205	1,774	614	78	705	175
1965	3,375	17,097	3,932	198	1,463	669	83	630	184

(*a*) After 1904 the figures are of the net number of sequestrations *concluded* during the year. The number awarded during 1905 was 278.
(*b*) These figures are affected by bankruptcies arising out of the failure of the City of Glasgow Bank.

(*c*) Up to 1904 the figures are of gross liabilities and assets, subsequently they are of net liabilities and assets. Gross figures for 1905 (in £000) were 821 and 407 respectively.

Miscellaneous Statistics 5. General Elections – United Kingdom 1885–1966

NOTES

[1] SOURCES: 1802–1999 electorate and 1931–66 votes – *Abstract*; 1918 votes and contests – *Dod's Parliamentary Companion*; other figures – *Return of Election Expenses* (published in *Sessional Papers* shortly after each general election except that of 1918).

[2] There are considerable doubts about the complete accuracy of some of the arithmetical computations based on the *Returns of Election Expenses*, and those who require a high degree of accuracy are advised to check the arithmetic in this source, and to cross-check individual constituency figures which appear to be suspicious against the appropriate entries in *Dod's Parliamentary Companion*, *Whitaker's Almanack*, and 'The Times', *House of Commons* for each election. No single source is completely free of errors.

According to M. G. Mulhall, *Dictionary of Statistics* (4th ed., London, 1899), the electorate at earlier periods than are shown here was as follows (in thousands):

	England & Wales	Scotland	Ireland
1835	668	73	98
1846	845	93	129
1871	2,066	260	227
1881	2,538	310	229

(electorate and votes recorded in thousands)

	England & Wales				Scotland				Ireland / Northern Ireland			
	Electorate	Votes Recorded	Seats Contested	Unopposed Returns	Electorate	Votes Recorded	Seats Contested	Unopposed Returns	Electorate	Votes Recorded	Seats Contested	Unopposed Returns
1885	4,391	3,735	460	8	561	448	64	4	742	451	79	22
1886	4,391	2,418	331	140	574	358	60	11	742	199	33	69
1892	4,810	3,726	433	39	606	475	69	2	745	404	81	21
1895	4,960	3,191	356	116	636	456	64	7	737	221	41	59
1900	5,287	2,884	311	160	681	486	66	5	764	149	31	70
1906	5,825	4,880	441	30	750	611	70	1	691	154	21	82
1910 Jan.	6,222	5,770	464	7	(785)(a)	677	71	—	699	221	39	63
1910 Dec.	6,222	4,450	335	136	800	578	57	14	699	208	37	65
1918	17,223	8,601	443	71	2,233	1,140	63	8	1,937	1,025	77	26
									Northern Ireland			
1922	18,002	12,624	474	40	2,261	1,568	67	4	611	208	2	8
1923	18,389	12,780	482	33	2,280	1,501	67	4	615	242	4	6
1924	18,807	14,386	490	25	2,312	1,735	69	2	613	519	7	3
1929	25,096	19,870	510	3	2,980	2,268	71	3	775	510	7	3
1931	26,136	19,200	470	44	3,039	2,174	62	9	777	282	3	7
1935	27,396	19,195	484	30	3,169	2,351	70	1	809	451	4	6
1945	28,992	21,950	537	2	3,407	2,423	71	—	841	722	8	2
1950	30,177	25,483	542	—	3,370	2,727	71	—	865	561	10	2
1951	30,626	25,356	542	—	3,421	2,778	71	—	872	463	8	4
1955	30,591	23,570	547	—	3,388	2,543	71	—	873	647	12	—
1959	31,109	24,619	547	—	3,414	2,668	71	—	875	576	12	—
1964	31,610	24,384	547	—	3,393	2,635	71	—	891	638	12	—
1966	31,695	24,116	547	—	3,360	2,553	71	—	902	596	12	—

(a) The December election *Return* gave a revised figure of 800 and this presumably was also applicable to January 1910, though not given in either the *Return* for the latter election or in the *Abstract*.

Miscellaneous Statistics 6. Primary Schools –
England & Wales and Scotland 1850–1966

NOTES

[1] SOURCES: England & Wales: 1850–64 – M. E. Sadler and J. W. Edwards, 'Summary of Statistics, Regulations, etc., of Elementary Education in England and Wales', in *Special Reports on Educational Subjects*, vol. 2 (London, H.M.S.O., 1898); 1854–99 – *Report of the Committee of Council on Education (England and Wales)* (annually in *Sessional Papers*); 1900–54 – *Statistics of Public Education in England and Wales* (annually in *Sessional Papers*); 1955–66 – *Statistics of Education* (published annually from 1962 by the Ministry of Education). Scotland: 1850–74 (except teachers) – *Abstract*; 1875–99 and teachers 1865–74 – *Report of the Committee of Council on Education (Scotland)* (annually in *Sessional Papers*); 1900–66 – *Statistics of Public Education in Scotland* (annually in *Sessional Papers*).

[2] The description primary schools is used in the title of this table though they were not known as such for the whole period, at any rate in England & Wales. The exact coverage is indicated in column headings and the footnotes.

[3] The figures apply to the following annual periods: England & Wales 1850–2 – year ended 31 October; 1854–1914 – year ended 31 August; 1920–38 – year ended 31 March; 1946–66 – at end January. Scotland: 1850–2 – year ended 31 October; 1854–79 – year ended 31 August; 1880–1901 – year ended 30 September; 1902–38 – year ended 31 August; 1946–7 – at 31 July; 1948–66 (except teachers) – at 31 March; 1951–66 (teachers) – at 1 October.

	England & Wales			Scotland		
	Number of Schools or Departments Inspected (a)	Average Number of Children Attending Inspected Day Schools (000s)	Number of Full-time Teachers (b) (000s)	Number of Schools Inspected	Average Number of Children Attending Inspected Day Schools (000s)	Number of Full-time Teachers (b) (000s)
1850	1,943 (c)	...	...	319	28	...
1851	2,093 (c)	250 (c)	...	315	32	...
1852	2,375 (c)	323 (c)	...	533	64	...
(1853 (d)	2,384 (c)	285 (c)	2·0	577	60	...)
1854	3,147 (c)	394 (c)	2·4	678	68	...
1855	3,853 (c)	447 (c)	3·0	974	91	...
1856	4,237 (c)	480 (c)	3·7	942	92	...
1857	4,438 (c)	531 (c)	4·4	960	95	...
1858	5,435 (c)	636 (c)	5·1	1,206	125	...
1859	5,531 (c)	675 (c)	6·0	1,055	127	...
1860	6,012 (c)	751 (c)	6·7	1,260	133	...
1861	6,259 (c)	774 (c)	7·6	1,446	146	...
1862	6,113 (c)	799 (c)	8·0	1,456	151	...
1863	6,188	826	8·8	1,512	162	...
1864	6,428	829	9·7	1,421	148	...
	— (e)	— (e)	— (f)			
1864	8,675	797	9·1			
1865	9,347	848	10·3	1,573	156	1·9
1866	9,984	863	10·9	1,619	162	2·0
1867	10,364	912	11·7	1,739	169	2·2
1868	10,857	979	12·4	1,843	182	2·3
1869	11,404	1,063	13·0	1,745	179	2·2
1870	12,061	1,152	13·7	1,963	198	2·5
1871	12,788	1,231	14·4	1,944	201	2·4
1872	14,101	1,336	16·4	1,962	206	2·6
1873	15,929	1,482	18·8	2,043	213	2·7
1874	17,646	1,679	21·2	2,587	275	3·2
				— (g)	— (g)	— (g)
1875	19,245	1,837	23·7	2,890	312	3·9
1876	20,782	1,985	26·8	2,912	333	4·3
1877	22,033	2,151	30·0	2,931	360	4·9
1878	23,618	2,405	34·5	2,998	377	5·2
1879	24,890	2,595	38·5	3,003	385	5·5
1880	25,601	2,751	41·4	3,056	405	5·8
1881	26,376	2,864	44·6	3,074	410	6·1
1882	26,779	3,015	48·1	3,073	421	6·4

See p. 214 for footnotes.

	England & Wales			Scotland		
	Number of Schools or Departments Inspected (a)	Average Number of Children Attending Inspected Day Schools (000s)	Number of Full-time Teachers (b) (000s)	Number of Schools Inspected	Average Number of Children Attending Inspected Day Schools (000s)	Number of Full-time Teachers (b) (000s)
1883	27,330	3,127	52·7	3,090	433	6·9
1884	27,958	3,273	57·8	3,131	448	7·2
1885	28,356	3,371	61·6	3,081	456	7·4
1886	28,645	3,438	64·3	3,092	477	7·9
1887	28,935	3,527	66·5	3,111	492	8·2
1888	29,056	3,615	68·7	3,105	496	8·5
1889	29,119	3,683	70·8	3,116	503	8·8
1890	29,339	3,718	73·5	3,076	513	9·1
1891	29,533	3,750	77·0	3,105	538	9·6
1892	29,672	3,871	79·3	3,030	539	9·9
1893	29,804	4,100	83·0	3,004	543	10·2
1894	30,003	4,226	87·0	3,054	567	10·7
1895	30,237	4,325	92·6	3,034	575	10·9
1896	30,521	4,423	94·9	3,083	593	11·5
1897	30,847	4,489	100·7	3,086	605	11·9
1898	30,911	4,554	101·7	3,067	606	12·2
1899	31,173	4,637	109·0	3,062	612	12·7
1900	31,234	4,666	114·0	3,104	626	13·3
1901	31,288	4,754	118·9	3,107	633	13·9
1902	31,397	4,923	121·9	3,110	643	14·2
1903	31,626	5,057	127·4	3,113	665	14·8
1904	31,862	5,177	134·2	3,115	672	15·5
1905	31,960	5,258	140·6	3,123	682	16·3
1906	32,029	5,312	148·5	3,125	689	17·0
1907	32,029	5,302	152·6	3,138	693	17·6
	----- (h)					
1908	32,071	5,301	156·3	3,143	692	18·1
1909	32,112	5,355	160·0	3,149	705	19·0
1910	32,185	5,375	162·3	3,156	719	19·7
1911	32,255	5,382	163·7	3,173	732	20·0
1912	32,290	5,367	164·1	3,164	734	20·4
1913	32,380	5,376	164·7	3,177	729	20·6
1914	32,480	5,393	166·0	3,171	728	20·8
1915	...	...	...	3,168	725	21·3
1916	...	...	...	3,168	716	21·9
1917	...	...	...	3,167	715	22·0
1918	...	...	...	3,159	713	22·1
1919	...	...	...	3,163	694	21·7
				—— (i)	—— (i)	—— (i)
1920	32,233	5,199	...	2,917	620	18·3
	—— (j)	—— (j)				
1920	32,145	5,187	165·5			
1921	32,106	5,206	167·2	2,907	627	17·9
1922	31,969	5,181	168·1	2,904	615	17·8
1923	31,538	5,136	163·6	2,901	608	17·8
1924	31,188	5,025	163·2	2,895	588	17·8
1925	31,001	4,934	164·5	2,894	584	18·1
1926	30,872	4,950	165·6	2,896	587	18·4

See p. 214 for footnotes.

	England & Wales			Scotland		
	Number of Schools or Departments Inspected (*a*)	Average Number of Children Attending Inspected Day Schools (000s)	Number of Full-time Teachers (*b*) (000s)	Number of Schools Inspected	Average Number of Children Attending Inspected Day Schools (000s)	Number of Full-time Teachers (*b*) (000s)
1927	30,724	4,967	166·2	2,903	591	18·7
1928	30,591	4,981	(167·9) (*k*)	2,919	587	18·8
1929	30,522	4,909	167·3	2,915	585	19·1
1930	30,429	4,941	168·0	2,923	591	19·5
1931	30,363	4,930	168·9	2,924	595	19·5
1932	30,226	5,006	170·0	2,924	601	19·4
1933	29,959	5,049	170·6	2,920	606	19·4
1934	29,701	5,066	170·9	2,909	607	19·4
1935	29,589	4,907	170·6	2,898	592	19·4
1936	29,478	4,748	169·6	2,900	581	19·5
1937	29,359	4,588	168·0	2,898	567	19·7
1938	29,224	4,527	166·7	2,895	557	19·6
1939–45			not available			
	—— (*l*)	—— (*l*)	—— (*l*)	—— (*l*)	—— (*l*)	—— (*l*)
1946	23,991	3,736	...	2,144	383	...
1947	23,602	3,700	125·2	2,076	361	...
1948	21,396	3,812	126·8	2,042	364	...
1949	23,201	3,874	128·2	2,150	363	...
1950	23,133	3,955	129·6	2,151	367	...
				—— (*m*)	—— (*m*)	
1951	23,106	4,005	133·9	2,939	551	18·9
1952	23,188	4,214	137·6	2,947	566	19·4
1953	23,349	4,436	141·5	2,930	586	19·9
1954	23,501	4,554	144·1	2,937	595	20·0
1955	23,664	4,601	147·9	2,946	603	19·7
1956	23,731	4,592	149·6	2,955	607	19·8
1957	23,765	4,590	150·5	2,973	608	20·2
1958	23,725	4,508	148·5	2,980	610	20·1
1959	23,615	4,308	144·5	2,982	608	20·2
1960	23,488	4,201	142·2	2,976	598	19·7
1961	23,312	4,133	141·2	2,933	589	20·1
1962	23,191	4,130	141·0	2,902	587	19·9
1963	23,083	4,145	139·3	2,845	589	20·2
1964	22,941	4,204	140·8	2,800	595	20·8
1965	22,882	4,273	144·1	2,788	601	20·8
1966	22,822	4,366	147·4	2,773	608	21·4

(*a*) Up to 1864 evening schools are included, but thereafter the figures are of day schools only.

(*b*) Excluding pupil teachers and probationers.

(*c*) Including Roman Catholic schools in Scotland.

(*d*) The figures are for schools inspected during a ten-month period only.

(*e*) Subsequent figures are of the number of departments with separate head teachers.

(*f*) Earlier figures relate to certificated and assistant teachers employed in *all* schools. Subsequently they relate to Annual Grant schools inspected.

(*g*) Previous figures of schools and attendance exclude Roman Catholic schools. The previous figures of teachers relate to a rather smaller number of schools than those shown here. In 1874 they relate to 2,366 schools with an attendance of 264 thousand.

(*h*) The figures for 1908–14 are revised ones obtained from the 1924 *Annual Abstract*, and are 3 or 4 higher than those in the original source.

(*i*) Three was a reorganisation of Scottish schools between 1919 and 1920. Figures for 1913 on a comparable basis to the later series are 2,948 schools, 641 thousand attendance, and 16·9 thousand teachers.

(*j*) Subsequent figures relate to Local Authority maintained schools only. Figures for 1913 on this basis are 32,300 departments, 5,356 thousand attendance, and 162·6 thousand teachers.

(*k*) Including some occasional emergency teachers.

(*l*) Comparability across the years of the Second World War is impossible owing to the reorganisation following the 1944 Education Act. In the second and fifth columns the number of registered pupils is substituted for attendance figures.

(*m*) Primary departments of secondary schools are subsequently included here.

Miscellaneous Statistics 7. Secondary Schools – England & Wales 1905–66, and Scotland 1899–1966

NOTES

[1] SOURCES: *Abstract* and *Statistics of Education* (published annually since 1961).

[2] The definition of a secondary school was changed in Scotland in 1920, and in both England & Wales and Scotland as a result of the 1944 Act.

[3] All figures relate to public and grant-aided schools only.

	England & Wales			Scotland		
	Number of Schools on 31 Jan.	Number of Pupils on 31 Jan.	Number of Full-time Teachers on 31 Jan.	Number of Schools, year ended 30 Sept.	Number of Pupils at end of school year	Number of Full-time Teachers at 11 March
1899				55	18,251	...
1900				55	18,215	...
1901				55	17,687	937
				year ended 31 Aug.		
1902				55	17,856	884
1903				55	17,921	997
1904				55	18,076	983
1905	575	94,698	...	55	18,210	996
1906	689	115,688	...	55	18,086	997
1907	769	125,802	...	55	18,316	983
1908	843	138,106	...	55	18,973	1,126
1909	912	150,794	9,328	57	20,904	1,117
1910	950	156,266	9,540	57	21,008	1,134
1911	971	160,477	9,832	56	20,532	1,147
1912	995	165,572	10,088	56	20,484	1,175
1913	1,010	174,423	10,398	56	19,557	1,197
1914	1,027	187,647	10,824	56	19,780	1,218
1915	1,047	198,884	...	56	19,866	1,196
1916	1,049	208,690	...	56	20,317	1,334
1917	1,049	218,900	12,045	56	21,012	1,481
1918	1,061	238,528	...	56	22,317	1,323
1919	1,081	269,887	14,499	56 —— (a)	23,978 —— (a)	1,398 —— (a)
1920	1,141	308,266	16,037	252	155,141	6,053
1921	1,205	336,836	17,668	252	154,256	5,679
1922	1,249	354,956	18,964	249	155,024	5,694
1923	1,264	354,165	18,485	249	154,813	5,961
1924	1,270	349,141	18,658	249	153,044	6,103
1925	1,284	352,605	19,069	249	148,699	6,053
1926	1,301	360,503	19,640	249	150,490	6,209
1927	1,319	371,493	19,254	251	151,343	6,280
1928	1,329	377,540	20,102	252	152,804	6,424
1929	1,341	386,993	20,514	252	151,356	6,452
1930	1,354	394,105	21,165	250	151,031	6,573
1931	1,367	411,309	21,694	251	154,072	6,571
1932	1,379	432,061	22,293	251	159,732	6,717
1933	1,378	441,883	22,754	251	161,991	6,708
1934	1,381	448,421	23,024	251	159,218	6,714
1935	1,380	456,783	23,425	251	157,460	6,733
1936	1,389	463,906	24,003	251	154,376	6,764
1937	1,393	466,245	24,451	252	151,989	6,802
1938	1,398	470,003	25,039	252	152,781	6,908
1939–45			not available			

See p. 216 for footnotes.

Miscellaneous Statistics 7. continued

| | Maintained Secondary Schools in England and Wales | | | | | | | | | | | | Scotland | | |
| | Modern | | | Grammar | | | Technical | | | Other Maintained Secondary | | | Public and Grant-aided Secondary | | |
	Number of Schools in Jan.	Number of Pupils in Jan. (000s)	Number of Full-time Teachers at 31 March (000s)	Number of Schools in Jan.	Number of Pupils in Jan. (000s)	Number of Full-time Teachers at 31 March (000s)	Number of Schools in Jan.	Number of Pupils in Jan. (000s)	Number of Full-time Teachers at 31 March (000s)	Number of Schools in Jan.	Number of Pupils in Jan. (000s)	Number of Full-time Teachers at 31 March (000s)	Number of Schools at 31 July or 31 March (b)	Number of Pupils at 31 July or 31 March (b)	Number of Full-time Teachers at (d)
1946	...	720	...	...	489	...	...	60	...	...	...	...	983	348,018	...
1947	3,019	764	34.8	1,207	505	25.3	317	66	3.6	...	...	...	1,037	367,083	...
1948	3,063	961	39.7	1,212	512	25.9	319	72	3.8	...	...	...	1,050	402,784	...
1949	3,141	1,058	44.3	1,229	524	27.0	310	72	3.9	...	...	...	927	417,220	...
1950	3,227	1,095	47.1	1,192	503	26.5	301	72	3.9	45	25	1.2	913	418,617	...
1951	3,301	1,127	49.6	1,190	501	27.0	296	73	3.9	60	32	1.6	909	232,897	13,845
1952	3,365	1,138	51.1	1,189	506	27.4	291	74	4.0	69	38	1.9	869	236,242	14,021
1953	3,423	1,136	52.0	1,184	513	27.7	292	79	4.2	77	42	2.2	871	237,219	14,235
1954	3,480	1,167	53.4	1,181	518	28.0	300	85	4.5	93	52	2.7	817	224,768	14,474
1955	3,550	1,234	55.9	1,180	528	28.5	302	87	4.7	112	65	3.3	809	227,077	15,096
1956	3,636	1,341	58.9	1,193	544	29.3	298	91	4.9	135	81	4.1	803	232,112	15,365
1957	3,719	1,424	62.5	1,206	559	30.1	290	95	5.1	165	109	5.6	787	240,148	15,533
1958	3,690	1,435	63.0	1,241	599	31.9	279	95	5.0	340	201	9.6	785	239,454	15,851
1959	3,808	1,596	68.6	1,252	641	33.5	264	99	5.1	391	257	12.2	776	248,876	16,829
1960	3,837	1,638	71.7	1,268	673	35.3	251	102	5.2	445	310	14.8	791	271,847	17,946
1961	3,872	1,698	75.2	1,284	697	36.9	228	97	5.1	463	337	16.2	771	287,657	18,176
1962	3,869	1,676	77.3	1,287	708	37.9	220	97	5.2	484	354	17.3	752	292,170	18,752
1963	3,906	1,609	75.9	1,295	722	38.8	204	93	5.0	486	357	17.5	744	286,441	19,247
1964	3,906	1,641	76.8	1,298	726	39.7	186	89	4.9	504	375	18.7	726	287,685	19,315
1965	3,727	1,555	74.1	1,285	719	39.8	172	85	4.7	679	461	23.4	704	284,585	19,674
1966	3,642	1,524	73.5	1,273	713	40.0	150	74	4.2	733	506	25.9	680	283,592	19,981

(a) Figures for 1913 on the same basis as the 1920 and subsequent figures were as follows: 249 schools, 130,255 pupils, 4,479 teachers.

(b) 31 July for 1946 and 1947, 31 March subsequently.

(c) Primary departments of secondary schools were subsequently transferred to the 'Primary' heading.

(d) This and subsequent figures relate to 1 October.

Miscellaneous Statistics 8. Direct Grant and Independent Schools – England & Wales 1946–66

NOTES

[1] SOURCES: 1947–54 – *Statistics of Public Education in England and Wales* (annually in *Sessional Papers*); 1955–66 and all figures of pupils – *Statistics of Education* (published annually since 1962 by the Ministry of Education).
[2] All figures relate to a date in January.

	Direct Grant Grammar Schools (a)			Independent Schools (except Nursery Schools) Recognised as Efficient		
	Schools or Departments	Pupils (000s)	Full-time Teachers (000s)	Schools or Departments	Pupils (000s)	Full-time Teachers (000s)
1946	...	88	...	...	144	...
1947	194	81	4·2	945	165	12·8
1948	190	83	4·2	985	178	13·5
1949	186	84	4·3	1,035	189	14·2
1950	181	85	4·4	1,105	204	15·0
1951	181	86	4·5	1,191	219	16·0
1952	178	87	4·6	1,271	234	16·9
1953	176	89	4·7	1,313	244	17·3
1954	176	90	4·8	1,315	249	17·5
1955	173	91	4·8	1,348	259	17·9
1956	173	92	4·9	1,363	268	18·3
1957	172	94	5·0	1,408	279	18·9
1958	181	103	5·4	1,436	281	19·1
1959	182	106	5·6	1,467	288	19·5
1960	186	110	5·9	1,479	294	19·9
1961	186	112	6·0	1,498	300	20·4
1962	186	113	6·2	1,493	300	20·4
1963	186	114	6·2	1,509	305	21·0
1964	186	115	6·4	1,541	307	21·4
1965	185	116	6·5	1,530	306	21·4
1966	185	116	6·6	1,529	309	21·5

(a) Includes institutional and technical schools.

Miscellaneous Statistics 9. University Education – Great Britain 1922–65

NOTES
[1] SOURCE: *Abstract.*
[2] All series cover full-time students and staff only, except the figures of total numbers taking courses, which include part-time students.

	New Students Admitted		Numbers Taking Courses		Courses Taken at Universities										Teaching Staff
					Arts (a)		Pure Science		Medicine (b)		Technology (c)		Agriculture		
	Men	Women	Men	Women	Men	Women	Men	Women	Men	Women	Men	Women	Men	Women	
1922/3	8,424	3,878	42,512	16,440	10,232	7,999	5,634	2,129	9,498	2,368	5,489	78	1,091	101	...
1923/4	8,005	3,842	40,831	16,306	10,393	8,588	5,203	2,199	8,866	1,998	4,652	57	758	98	...
1924/5	8,194	3,910	39,671	16,251	10,950	8,941	5,165	2,164	7,896	1,631	4,156	49	746	96	...
1925/6	8,468	3,865	40,156	16,140	11,622	9,138	5,250	2,081	7,288	1,402	3,999	54	676	96	3,023
1926/7	8,826	3,902	40,859	16,282	12,486	9,426	5,180	2,043	7,179	1,236	3,925	45	723	111	3,085
1927/8	8,945	4,002	41,552	16,203	13,367	9,694	5,229	2,003	7,074	1,148	3,877	54	703	113	3,169
1928/9	9,296	3,704	42,596	15,952	14,005	9,620	5,405	1,972	7,279	1,108	4,108	66	705	133	3,259
1929/30	9,877	3,931	43,561	15,913	14,657	9,652	5,596	1,942	7,623	1,136	4,081	71	725	120	3,349
1930/1	10,078	3,967	46,057	16,255	15,091	9,582	5,866	2,002	8,702	1,187	4,197	77	773	110	3,501
1931/2	10,423	3,879	46,820	15,707	15,384	9,284	6,125	2,006	9,107	1,272	4,401	87	734	110	3,590
1932/3	10,977	4,073	48,200	15,915	15,952	9,223	6,328	2,066	9,835	1,412	4,443	91	700	105	3,629
1933/4	11,031	3,830	49,114	15,306	16,129	8,659	6,598	2,159	10,426	1,525	4,344	95	701	101	3,669
1934/5	10,808	3,679	49,061	14,989	15,898	8,245	6,658	2,126	10,854	1,646	4,274	95	722	120	3,735
1935/6	10,687	3,504	49,153	14,467	15,799	7,885	6,583	2,019	11,176	1,747	4,344	88	748	140	3,772
1936/7	10,424	3,344	48,490	14,002	15,461	7,431	6,231	1,871	11,430	1,833	4,410	82	803	137	3,845
1937/8	10,505	3,558	48,228	14,042	15,046	7,304	5,900	1,849	11,428	1,913	4,690	87	826	146	3,907
1938/9	11,220	3,933	49,202	14,218	14,841	7,533	5,815	1,846	11,623	2,013	5,199	89	890	153	3,994
1939/40	10,514	3,551	37,865	11,900	11,023	6,871	4,980	1,705	11,224	2,102	4,484	80	713	138	...
1940/1	8,784	3,500	32,083	11,951	7,205	6,830	3,947	1,685	10,691	2,261	3,894	75	563	133	...
1941/2	9,258	4,047	33,055	13,402	6,010	7,186	4,224	1,798	10,321	2,411	4,445	129	630	170	...

218

1942/3	9,543	4,544	33,541	14,488	4,761	7,691	4,158	1,923	9,793	2,529	4,879	145	664	221	...
1943/4	7,816	5,095	33,270	15,643	3,464	8,111	4,034	2,023	9,251	2,620	4,894	188	806	257	...
1944/5	8,573	5,484	32,873	16,936	3,904	8,770	4,472	2,311	9,219	2,772	5,036	181	904	270	...
1945/6	12,701	6,165	46,042	21,132	10,466	10,815	6,269	3,040	10,262	2,948	6,008	276	1,209	329	...
1946/7	16,791	5,754	63,785	22,551	18,944	11,829	9,263	3,253	11,400	3,004	8,474	293	1,683	309	...
1947/8	17,325	6,182	73,501	23,003	23,022	12,195	11,234	3,310	12,720	3,187	9,857	289	2,232	461	6,536
1948/9	18,857	5,969	79,141	22,729	25,028	12,119	12,843	3,256	13,635	3,382	10,620	264	2,516	403	7,390
1949/50	18,104	6,227	80,514	22,567	25,106	12,137	13,614	3,303	14,234	3,321	10,709	224	2,405	368	7,930
1950/1	16,537	5,686	79,422	22,590	24,509	12,279	13,862	3,306	14,836	3,325	10,384	207	2,240	366	8,603
1951/2	16,733	5,681	77,934	22,582	23,587	12,349	13,749	3,304	14,507	3,329	10,034	181	2,093	325	8,952
1952/3	15,605	5,750	74,861	22,468	22,432	12,484	13,559	3,442	14,020	3,265	9,822	171	1,953	326	9,134
1953/4	15,513	5,640	73,809	22,548	22,065	12,608	13,488	3,483	13,565	3,291	9,891	145	1,784	282	9,514
1954/5	16,487	5,976	74,687	23,164	22,109	12,996	13,656	3,671	13,406	3,354	10,438	148	1,686	241	9,810
1955/6	16,458	5,956	77,323	24,171	22,934	13,713	14,203	3,930	13,694	3,414	11,226	153	1,706	221	10,202
1956/7	18,796	6,769	80,854	25,220	24,293	14,354	15,549	4,350	13,362	3,448	12,329	167	1,677	237	10,485
1957/8	20,646	7,030	85,526	26,402	26,149	14,972	16,985	4,722	13,317	3,455	13,655	204	1,749	234	10,846
1958/9	21,236	7,041	89,080	27,003	27,909	15,223	18,373	5,029	12,995	3,571	14,788	255	1,814	247	11,125
1959/60	20,823	7,194	92,339	27,602	29,119	15,476	19,481	5,267	12,968	3,665	15,606	326	1,863	238	11,789
1960/1	21,464	8,046	96,423	29,107	30,008	16,378	20,735	5,718	12,901	3,712	15,880	345	1,806	216	12,417
1961/2	22,964	9,196	100,330	31,592	30,658	17,959	22,243	6,433	12,889	3,679	16,819	413	1,816	234	13,104
1962/3	23,956	9,721	101,410	34,018	31,580	19,626	24,460	7,347	13,118	3,749	16,663	348	1,833	280	14,132
1963/4	24,666	10,107	106,402	36,571	33,247	21,290	26,187	8,129	13,330	3,742	18,078	415	1,794	233	15,259
1964/5	27,609	11,959	115,460	41,328	36,991	24,905	27,990	8,796	13,738	3,883	19,781	481	1,881	265	17,117

(a) Including theology, fine art, law, music, commerce, economics, and education.
(b) Including dentistry and veterinary science.
(c) Including engineering, applied chemistry, mining, metallurgy, and architecture.

INDEX

INDEX

INDEX